CONTEMPORARY MEXICAN POLITICS

CONTEMPORARY MEXICAN POLITICS

Emily Edmonds-Poli
and
David A. Shirk

ROWMAN & LITTLEFIELD PUBLISHERS, INC.
Lanham • Boulder • New York • Toronto • Plymouth, UK

ROWMAN & LITTLEFIELD PUBLISHERS, INC.

Published in the United States of America
by Rowman & Littlefield Publishers, Inc.
A wholly owned subsidary of The Rowman & Littlefield Publishing Group, Inc.
4501 Forbes Boulevard, Suite 200, Lanham, Maryland 20706
www.rowmanlittlefield.com

Estover Road, Plymouth PL6 7PY, United Kingdom

British Library Cataloguing in Publication Information Available

Library of Congress Cataloging-in-Publication Data

Edmonds, Emily.
  Contemporary Mexican politics / Emily Edmonds-Poli and David A. Shirk.
    p. cm.
  Includes bibliographical references and index.
  ISBN-13: 978-0-7425-4048-4 (cloth : alk. paper)
  ISBN-10: 0-7425-4048-0 (cloth : alk. paper)
  ISBN-13: 978-0-7425-4049-1 (pbk. : alk. paper)
  ISBN-10: 0-7425-4049-9 (pbk. : alk. paper)
  1. Mexico--Politics and government--2000- I. Shirk, David A., 1971- II. Title.
  F1236.7.E36 2009
  320.972--dc22

                        2008031594

Printed in the United States of America

∞™ The paper used in this publication meets the minimum requirements of American
National Standard for Information Sciences—Permanence of Paper for Printed Library
Materials, ANSI/NISO Z39.48-1992.

To Ann Craig and Wayne Cornelius,
our teachers, mentors, and friends

Contents

Illustrations

Figures

Preface

The idea for this book grew out of our excitement about the political changes taking place in Mexico during the short span of our professional careers, as well as our need to rethink the way we teach students about contemporary Mexican politics. Mexican politics have long perplexed outside observers, since the formal rules rarely apply to how the game is played. Despite a series of nominally democratic constitutions promulgated in 1824, 1854, and 1917, autocratic forces—the political strongmen of the nineteenth century and the monopolistic ruling party formed in 1929—prevailed in Mexico until the end of the twentieth century. In this context, students and political observers often had to read between the lines to decipher the workings of Mexican politics. Today, while we can debate whether Mexico is a "true" democracy, there is widespread agreement that Mexican politics have become more democratic, more transparent, and even more interesting. The advent of free and fair elections—while not tantamount to democracy—has dramatically changed the nature and importance of candidate selection, electoral campaigns, governance, and many other aspects of Mexican politics.

These changes require us to update the way we think about and study Mexico's political system. In the past, studying Mexican politics required a greater focus on the personalities and agendas of Mexico's leaders, as well as the norms and power dynamics that influenced political behavior. While these considerations are still important, the realities of contemporary Mexican politics now require observers to pay greater attention to the formal role and functioning of Mexico's political institutions, and the evolving relationship between a democratic state and society. For example, since votes matter more than ever before, observers of Mexican politics must devote greater attention to the factors that affect voter attitudes and behavior, including campaigns, the media, political socialization, and other influences. Likewise, since there is now considerable "institutionalized uncertainty" about electoral and political outcomes, candidates and politicians have begun to interact differently with each other and with voters. Amid all of this, Mexico's new democracy now faces major policy challenges that will greatly affect its longer-term consolidation, including promoting sustainable, equitable economic development and strengthening the rule of law. Hence our goal in writing this book was, quite simply, to produce a text that focuses students on the new structure, function, and policy aspects of contemporary Mexican politics.

Since no other country has as powerful and direct an impact on the United States as Mexico, it is essential for U.S. citizens to understand these changing political dynamics, as well as their bearing on key policy areas that affect the U.S.-Mexican relationship. Moreover, in many ways, contemporary Mexican politics now more closely resemble democratic politics in the United States. Today, Mexican politics exhibit such "American" political characteristics as negative campaigning, political fund-raising, candidate-centered campaigns, legislative logrolling, and carefully orchestrated constituent service appeals. Whether such practices will prove beneficial remains to be seen. But we feel strongly that to understand what is happening in Mexico, and in order to better shape our binational relationship with Mexico, we must change the way we study and evaluate Mexican politics. This book is our small contribution to that end; it is up to the students and teachers who read it to make up the difference.

Like other authors of a work of this nature, we stand on the shoulders of established giants across a wide range of disciplines who have made enormous contributions to the study of Mexican politics. Hence we must recognize those who have shaped and contributed to its development. We wish to begin by thanking those to whom we have dedicated this text, Wayne Cornelius and Ann Craig, who wrote the textbooks we read while learning about Mexico, and cochaired each of our doctoral dissertation committees. Their contributions—not only as great scholars of Mexican politics, but as extraordinary mentors and friends—have greatly shaped our personal and professional development, and inspired us to follow in their footsteps. Their consistent guidance and constructive feedback on our research and scholarship, including this book, is deeply appreciated. Though their works are cited in the endnotes and the text, we especially wish to acknowledge John Bailey, Ambassador Jeffrey Davidow, Federico Estévez, Jim Gerber, Kevin J. Middlebrook, Alejandra Ríos Cázares, and an anonymous reviewer who took the time to give us insightful and invaluable feedback on the entire book manuscript. In addition, numerous colleagues and friends illuminated and inspired us through their own research, assistance with various topics covered in the book, or bits of wisdom about Mexican politics too numerous to detail here. In particular, we are indebted to Manuel Aguilar, Robert Donnelly, David and Teresa Edmonds, Ken Greene, Joy Langston, Eric Magar, Charles Pope, Luis Miguel Rionda, Victoria Rodríguez, Marc Rosenblum, Andrew Selee, Carole and Carrie Shirk, Gabriela Soto-Laveaga, Rose Spalding, Jeffrey Weldon, Steve Wuhs, and all of our departmental colleagues at the University of San Diego. We are also very grateful to Laura McGann and Mark Dreschler for their enthusiastic assistance in preparing the manuscript and index. Additionally, numerous students provided inspired comments, able assistance, and other contributions to our research; in particular we would like to note Nicole Cavino, Judith Dávila, Molly Dishman, Ruth Gómez, Emily Mellott, Stephanie Rubin, and Riley Sutherlin. We would also like to thank Susan McEachern, Jessica Gribble, Jehanne Schweitzer, and Carrie Broadwell-Tkach at Rowman & Littlefield for supporting this project and seeing it through. We appreciate the assistance of Gerardo Caballos and Ulisis Ramírez, who facilitated the photo used on the cover. Naturally, despite all this tremendous support, any errors or omissions are our responsibility. Finally, without the unshakable support of our spouses, Sam Poli and Alexandra Webber, and the inspiration provided by the Poli boys, Sebastian and William, and Tosca, we would be nowhere. Thank you to all.

Abbreviations

AFORES	Administradores de Fondos Para el Retiro
AMLO	Andrés Manuel López Obrador
APPO	Popular Assembly of Oaxacan People
BIP	Border Industrialization Program
CCRI	Comité Clandestino Revolucionario Indígena
CD	Corriente Democrática
CFE	Comisión Federal de Electricidad
CGOCM	Confederación General de Obreros y Campesinos de México
CNC	Confederación Nacional Campesina
CNDP	Comité Nacional de Defensa Proletaria
CNOP	Confederación Nacional de Organizaciones Populares
COCOPA	Comisión de Concordia y Pacificación
CPI	Corruption Perception Index
CRMDT	Confederación Revolucionaria Michoacana del Trabajo
CROM	Confederación Regional Obrera Mexicana
CSTDF	Confederación Sindical de Trabajadores del Distrito Federal
CTM	Confederación de Trabajadores de México
DIF	Desarrollo Integral de la Familia
EPR	Popular Revolutionary Army
ETA	Euskadi Ta Askatasuna
EZLN	Ejercito Zapatista de Liberación Nacional
FDI	foreign direct investment
FMLN	Farabundo Martí Liberation Front
FOBAPROA	Fondo Bancario de Protección al Ahorro

FTAA	Free Trade Agreement of the Americas
FUPDM	Frente Unico Pro Derechos de la Mujer
IFE	Instituto Federal Electoral
IMSS	Instituto Mexicano del Seguro Social
INCD	Instituto Nacional de Combate a las Drogas
INMUN	Instituto Nacional de la Mujer
IPN	Instituto Politécnico Nacional
IRCA	Immigration Reform and Control Act
ISI	import substitution industrialization
ISSSTE	Instituto de Seguridad y Servicios Sociales de los Trabajadores del Estado
ITESM	Monterrey Technological Institute
ITESO	Instituto Tecnológico de Estudios Superiores del Oriente
LCF	Law of Fiscal Coordination
LFOPPE	Ley Federal de Organizaciones Políticas y Procesos Electorales
LNDLR	Liga Nacional de la Defensa de la Libertad Religiosa
MERCOSUR	Mercado Común del Sur
MIR	Movimiento Internacional Revolucionario
MLAT	Mutual Legal Assistance Treaty
NADBANK	North American Development Bank
NIEO	New International Economic Order
PAN	Partido Acción Nacional
PANAL	Partido Nueva Alianza
PARM	Partido Auténtico de la Revolución Mexicana
PASC	Partido Alternativa Socialdemócrata y Campesino
PCM	Partido Comunista Mexicano
PEMEX	Petróleos Mexicanos
PNR	Partido Nacional Revolucionario
PPP	purchasing power parity
PRD	Partido de la Revolución Democrática
PRI	Institutional Revolutionary Party
PRM	Partido de la Revolución Mexicana
PROCUP	Partido Revolucionario Obrero Clandestino-Unión del Pueblo
PRONAF	National Border Program
PRONAFIM	Programa Nacional de Financiamiento al Microempresario
PT	Partido de Trabajo
PVEM	Partido Verde Ecologista Mexicano
SAGARPA	Secretaría de Agricultura, Ganadería, Desarrollo Rural, Pescay Alimentación
SAR	Sistema de Ahorro para el Retiro
SEDESOL	Secretaría de Desarrollo Social

SNPSS	Sistema Nacional de Protección Social en Salud
SNTE	Sindicato Nacional de Trabajadores de la Educación
SSA	Secretaría de Salubridad y Asistencia
STPS	Secretaría del Trabajo y Previsión Social
TRIFE	Tribunal Federal Electoral
UNAM	Universidad Nacional Autónoma de México
VAT	value-added tax

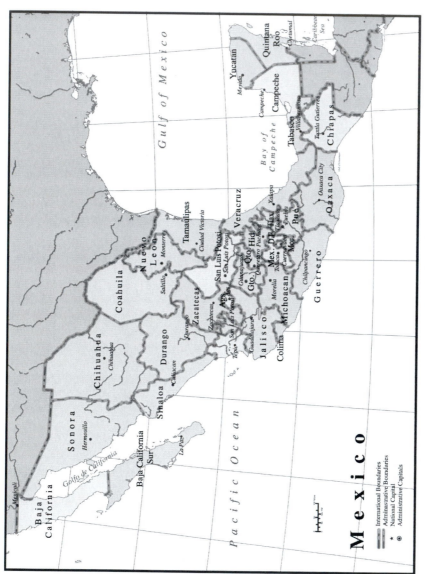

Mexico

International Boundaries
Adminastrative Boundaries
★ National Capital
◉ Administrative Capitals

Produced using Map Resources (www.mapresources.com).

Introduction

What is so interesting about Mexico? Despite the geographic proximity, strong cultural ties, and shared economic interests of the two countries, most people in the United States know very little about their southern neighbor. Most Americans' knowledge of Mexico is informed by a vacation to one of the country's many tourist attractions or is based on cultural stereotypes. And while tropical beaches and corrupt cops rank high among Mexico's claims to fame, it is also a vibrant, complex country full of startling contradictions and incredible achievements. Only by studying Mexico in depth is it possible to fully appreciate its true diversity and many contributions.

Take, for example, Mexico's people. Although the majority of Mexicans are mestizos (of mixed white European and indigenous ancestry), there are a number of other important ethnicities, including indigenous and European, Jewish and Middle Eastern, African and Asian, that make up a small but significant portion of the nation's population. It is therefore not at all uncommon to encounter Mexicans who defy common stereotypes. Furthermore, Mexican culture brings together many different traditions, both foreign and homegrown. From its architecture to its pastimes, from its food to its version of the Spanish language, Mexico is a unique amalgamation of various cultural influences.

Mexico's geography and climate are similarly diverse. Covering approximately 760,000 square miles, it is roughly one-fifth the size of the United States, and the eighth largest country in the world. Home to three major mountain ranges, the Sierra Madre Occidental in the west, the Sierra Madre Oriental in the east, nine major volcanoes in the Cordillera Neovolcanica, and nearly 150 rivers, Mexico has its share of peaks and valleys. Among the most impressive of these are the majestic Pico de Orizaba, the third highest peak in North America, and the stunning Barranca del Cobre, a series of canyons on par with the Grand Canyon of the United States. While the north is character-ized by arid deserts that receive little rainfall, and the central plateau's latitude and altitude bring it rainy summers and mild winters, tropical conditions without a cold season are predominant in the lowlands and rainforests of the southeast.

But it is not just the beauty and diversity of Mexico's people and geography that make it worthy of study. Mexico is a fascinating case study in compara-tive politics because it has a wide array of historical experiences that can be contrasted against similar occurrences in many other countries: religious and military conquest, colonialism, significant class and ethnic divisions, popu-lar revolutionary struggle and civil war, corporatist state-society relations, and dueling political support for economic nationalism and pro-market liberalization. Perhaps the most significant point for comparative analysis in contemporary Mexico is its recent democratization, and ongoing processes of democratic consolidation. For many years, Mexico was known to have the "perfect dictatorship," thus described because one political party, the Institu-tional Revolutionary Party (PRI), ruled single-handedly. This was a "perfect" situation because the PRI enjoyed considerable popular support even though it manipulated the rules to favor itself, rigging elections and maintaining tight control over the media, political participation, and interest representation.

Beginning in the late 1960s, Mexico began a slow and sometimes painful transition away from the single-party dominance of the PRI and toward a more open and competitive political system. For many, the proof that democ-racy had come to stay occurred on July 2, 2000, when opposition candidate Vicente Fox won the presidential election, defeating the PRI in a free and fair contest. Six years later, Fox's party, the National Action Party (PAN), won for a second time when Felipe Calderón Hinojosa narrowly defeated two other challengers. In spite of Calderón's razor-thin margin of victory (0.05 percent) and some irregularities in the vote count, most Mexicans accept the results of the election and feel that Mexico has taken another step toward consolidating its democratic gains.

Without a doubt, Mexico's democracy remains a work in progress. Even so, its achievement is both remarkable and, unfortunately, uncommon. Many countries, especially those also struggling with the challenge of economic development, are unable to permanently cast off the political institutions and legacies of the past that stall their progress in attaining a democratic society. One need only look at the recent history of Latin America to understand how elusive and fleeting democracy has been. During the twentieth century, almost every country in the region experienced a cycle in which it moved from authoritarian rule, often by the military, to a more open political system, only to see authoritarian regimes reappear before democracy could really take hold. So, while virtually all Latin American countries had at least an inchoate form of democracy in the early 1990s, many have struggled to consolidate these gains and others have already begun the slide back to more authoritarian styles of rule.

So how, after seven decades of one-party rule, was Mexico able to peacefully re-create itself as a country with some of the fairest elections in the world? What are the new institutional features and critical challenges in Mexico's new democracy? Will it be able to consolidate its democratic practices so as to avoid returning to the authoritarianism of its past? Our aim in this book is to provide a thorough discussion of Mexico's political development and, in the process, explain the country's democratic transition and evaluate its prospects for survival. Overall we are optimistic about the future of democracy in Mexico. Important transformations in the country's institutions, political culture, and economic stability have created the conditions necessary for consolidation to occur. However, some important challenges in all these areas remain. Accordingly, the chapters that follow will discuss in some detail both recent developments and outstanding issues that need to be addressed if Mexico's democracy is to mature and flourish.

The book is divided into four parts. The first part provides a historical overview of Mexican political development. After a brief discussion of pre-Columbian society, chapter 1 chronicles the transformation of the colony of New Spain into the independent country of Mexico and describes the difficult process of state formation in the latter half of the nineteenth century. Chapter 2 picks up the narrative in the early twentieth century, examining the origin and trajectory of one of Mexico's most defining political events, the Mexican revolution. The chapter highlights the actors and events that led not only to the overthrow of the authoritarian ruler, Porfirio Díaz, and the violence of the revolution, but also to the emergence of the PRI as Mexico's dominant political party. The development of the "classic" PRI system is the subject of chapter 3. Here we explain in detail how the PRI was able to construct institutions and introduce political policies and practices that eliminated all serious sources of competition and facilitated the party's electoral hegemony for over seventy years. Chapter 4 analyzes the reasons for the PRI's decline and explains the confluence of factors that facilitated the emergence of democracy in Mexico.

The second part of the book examines Mexico's political institutions, culture, and society. As a federal republic with thirty-one states, a federal district, and three levels of government, Mexico looks strikingly similar to the United States—at least on paper. The similarities are not surprising given that its postindependence constitutions were significantly influenced by the U.S. constitution. Yet, even though the two governments are structured in much the same way, they operate very differently. Why is this the case? To address this issue, chapters 5–6 examine Mexico's government institutions and processes, and its political parties and electoral system, respectively. These chapters not only provide a detailed look at Mexico's political institutions but further explore their gradual conversion to democracy. Society is the focus of chapters 7–8. Chapter 7 describes Mexican values and beliefs, attitudes and feelings, and norms behaviors in relation to politics, and evaluates the likelihood that a democratic political culture will flourish. Next, chapter 8 examines traditional and contemporary interest representation in Mexico. Together, these four chapters demonstrate how far the Mexican state and society have come since the days of single-party rule.

The future of Mexico's democracy will depend on its ability to address some major policy challenges. The third part focuses on the country's most pressing domestic policy challenges. In chapter 9, the discussion centers on Mexico's political economy and its difficulty in achieving macroeconomic stability and development. Chapter 10 examines one of the consequences of Mexico's recurring economic crises: poverty and income inequality, noting that unless the government addresses these problems, it is unlikely that democracy will deepen. Likewise, providing basic order, reforming the country's legal process, protecting human rights, and generally institutionalizing the rule of law, are imperative if Mexico is to consolidate recent democratic gains. This is the subject of chapter 11.

In the final part, we discuss Mexico's major foreign policy challenges and its role on the world stage. Chapter 12 provides a trajectory of Mexico's foreign relations with the United States and highlights its desire to more fully engage actors such as the European Union and China in order to expand its international trade and investment opportunities. Of course Mexico's greatest international challenges and opportunities arise from its relationship with the United States. Chapter 13 is therefore devoted to assessing the two countries' prospects for cooperation on issues such as migration, trade, and security.

I

MEXICAN POLITICAL DEVELOPMENT

1

Mexico's Historical Foundations

Mexico has a long and fascinating history. To this day, contemporary Mexico is rich with the archeological remnants, languages, and descendants of several advanced indigenous civilizations. The conquest and decimation of those civilizations by Spanish invaders in the early fifteenth century constituted one of the most dramatic and lamentable examples of cultural conflict in world history. For three hundred years after the conquest, Mexico became a colony of the Spanish Crown and fed the development of one of Europe's greatest empires. Eventually, as elsewhere in the Americas, the efforts of the Spanish Crown to gain a stronger hold on its colonial territories—including bureaucratic measures that squeezed producers and merchants and new laws that sharpened class distinctions—inspired insurrection and calls for independence. The bloody struggle to separate from Spain left Mexico to wrestle with the dilemmas of self-governance and the territorial encroachments of the United States. It was not until the late nineteenth century that Mexico achieved some reasonable semblance of order, but only at the cost of the ideals of freedom and equality that inspired some of its greatest patriots and its fight for independence.

This chapter explores Mexico's historical foundations by surveying events leading from its earliest civilizations up to the prerevolutionary period at the start of the twentieth century. No brief account of this sort can do justice to Mexico's rich and captivating history.[1] The purpose here is therefore to provide readers with sufficient background to understand some of the factors that contributed to the formation of Mexico's political development. We first discuss Mexico's ancient indigenous civilizations and some of their political and cultural contributions to modern society. We then turn to the legacy created by three hundred years of Spanish colonialism. In particular, we emphasize the roles of the mercantilist economic model, the hierarchical imperial bureaucracy, extreme social stratification, and tensions between the Catholic Church and the young nation, since all of these significantly shaped the foundations of contemporary Mexican politics.

Pre-Columbian Civilizations

Prior to the arrival of Europeans, several major civilizations made up the region known as Mesoamerica or "Middle America," the area that is today occupied by Mexico and the six countries that now make up Central America. The major civilizations of Mesoamerica developed over the course of several thousand years in four distinct regions of contemporary Mexico: the Gulf Coast (Olmec), the Oaxaca Valley (Zapotec, Mixtec), the Yucatán Peninsula (Maya), and the Central Plateau (Teotihuacán, Toltec, and Aztec) (see table 1.1). Becoming familiar with Mexico's ancient indigenous civilizations is useful because it helps us to understand Mexico's long-standing regional and cultural diversity, and provides background on personalities and events that have become important cultural referents in contemporary Mexico. Doing so also acquaints us with the history and heritage of indigenous people who represent a significant portion of Mexico's population today, and who continue to struggle for justice and equality.[2]

The histories of these ancient civilizations are still somewhat incomplete. Physical evidence and archeological remains are still the subject of scientific

Table 1.1.
Early Mesoamerican Civilization

Dates	Period	Life in Mesoamerica
40000–8000 B.C.	Preagricultural	Nomadic hunter-gatherers arrive in Mesoamerica, finding abundant game.
8000–2000 B.C.	Archaic	After climatic shift, early agricultural domestication allows minor human settlements.
2000 B.C.–A.D. 200	Pre-Classic	The peak of the earliest Mesoamerican civilization (Olmec) was during this period.
A.D. 200–900	Classic	The peaks of several Mesoamerican civilizations (Maya, Zapotec, Mixtec, Toltec, Teotihuacán) occurred during this period.
A.D. 900–1521	Post-Classic	The peak of the last great Mesoamerican civilization (Aztec) occurred during this period.

Source: Adapted from Michael C. Meyer, William L. Sherman, and Susan M. Deeds, *The Course of Mexican History*, 6th ed. (Oxford: Oxford University Press, 1999).

rediscovery and investigation, as researchers try to uncover and explain the clues of the past. Indigenous written histories—of which there were many—were initially indecipherable, or were lost to the ravages of time and conquest. Among the best accounts available are those written by the Spanish, whose cultural interpretations and deliberate revisions were often self-serving and denigrating to their subjects. Hence the material presented here represents our effort to combine multiple and sometimes conflicting sources on the subject.

According to the best available estimates, the story of Mexico's indigenous peoples began approximately 20,000 to 25,000 years ago, when humans first settled in Mesoamerica. Like their nomadic ancestors who crossed the ice-covered Bering Strait from Asia as much as 30,000 years before them, the first people of Mesoamerica engaged in primitive hunting and gathering. Over the next several thousand years, these early Mesoamericans relied on basic tools and technologies—fire, coarsely crafted stone instruments, rope, and woven baskets—and lived lives similar to those of primitive humans around the world.[3]

Mesoamerican settlements increasingly relied on domesticated crops that were unique to the region and eventually became staples, including early varieties of corn (maize), squash, and beans. Corn, in particular, developed and maintains a deep cultural significance in Mexico. Early Mesoamericans also domesticated other plants—chile peppers, cocoa beans (chocolate), avocados, and henequen (sisal)—that we commonly identify with Mexico today. With the advance of agricultural production came larger and more established settlements, and the foundations for Mesoamerica's great civilizations. The people learned to make tools and crafts—knives, millstones, and pottery—and basic structures, and eventually developed advanced technologies (such as astronomy), architecture, and systems of governance that rivaled the early civilizations of Europe, Asia, and Africa.

At their apex, Mesoamerican civilizations developed unique identities and legacies that found representation in great monuments, majestic pyramids, and impressive religious structures (see figure 1.1). To accomplish these feats, most Mesoamerican civilizations relied on hierarchical political systems, which featured specialized economic production that was marked by stratified social divisions between elites (nobles, priests, and military leaders) and commoners (merchants, artisans, farmers, and slaves). While elites typically had a monopoly on the scientific, intellectual, and ritualistic achievements in these ancient societies, they depended on the labor and tribute of their subjects. It is also worth noting that slavery in Mesoamerica could be a temporal category (entered into by persons who became indebted and might one day win their freedom) or a terminal fate (especially for those captured in battle and sacrificed to the gods). To better understand these unique and sophisticated civilizations, we look at each in turn below.

FIGURE 1.1   Representations of Mexico's Major Indigenous Civilizations

The Gulf Coast: The Olmecs

The first major civilization to emerge in Mesoamerica was that of the Olmecs (1500 B.C. to 400 B.C.), during what archeologists call the Pre-Classic Era. Some estimates suggest that there were as many as 350,000 inhabitants of the Olmec civilization, and at its peak the size of some of the largest Olmec settlements—such as San Lorenzo, La Venta, and Zapotes—may have exceeded 1,000 inhabitants, making them the largest conurbations in Mesoamerica up to that point, and most likely the first major civilization in all of the Americas.[4] Indeed, many scholars have described Olmec society as one of only six "pristine" or sui generis civilizations in human history, though it appears that they may have also had interactions with and influences from elsewhere in Mesoamerica (notably the Zapotecs). Still, the Olmec are believed to be the first people in Mesoamerica to have constructed crude pyramids, used advanced mathematical concepts (such as the use of "zero"), and developed sizable settlements with organized methods of planning and design for urban communities.[5]

One of the most distinctive aspects of Olmec civilization was their construction of colossal stone-carved heads with thick, broad facial features, thirteen of which have been discovered in different settlements. Among the most significant subsequent influences of the Olmecs were their spiritual beliefs. Sacred images of jaguars and mixed human-jaguar figures occupied a central place in Olmec sculpture and artwork. Later Mesoamerican cultures combined the Olmecs' reverence for both the jaguar and the eagle as sacred symbols, and adopted similar religious practices. Olmec shamans also produced balls from local rubber trees to conduct ritualistic games involving competition between two opposing teams in specially constructed ball courts. Ball courts and other aspects of Olmec culture were widely adopted in Mesoamerica by later civilizations.

The Oaxaca Valley: The Zapotecs and Mixtecs

The Zapotec people centered in modern-day Oaxaca began to develop their initial settlements around the same time as the Olmecs. By approximately 500 B.C., centuries before the rise of the Maya, the Zapotecs eclipsed the scale of any Mesoamerican civilization to that point. By its peak between A.D. 450 and 700, the Zapotec city of Monte Albán grew to as many as 25,000 inhabitants, traded actively with neighboring residents of Teotihuacán, and held dominance over surrounding settlements in the Oaxaca Valley. The Zapotecs likely originated some of the most important and widely diffused aspects of Mesoamerican culture, including hieroglyphic writing, masonry, and advanced astronomy. Indeed, Zapotec astronomers are credited with inventing the complex but highly accurate 365-day solar calendar (18 months with 20 days, plus a period of 5 additional "unlucky" days), as well as a sacred cyclical calendar (with 260 days drawn from 13 cycles of 20 named days), later used by the Olmecs and throughout Mesoamerica.

The causes of Zapotec decline are unknown, but it is clear that the decline of Monte Albán coincided with—and was likely linked to—the fall of its major trading partner, Teotihuacán. Over time, Monte Albán's influence waned and the Zapotecs were gradually eclipsed by the growing influence and military superiority of the Mixtec civilization. The Mixtecs were a distinct linguistic and ethnic grouping that first grew out of mountainous central areas of the Oaxaca Valley as early as 7000 B.C., and later spread to the northern highlands and coastal areas. By the fall of the Zapotec civilization, the Mixtecs had developed a series of small kingdoms that achieved important accomplishments in writing, artisan work, and construction between A.D. 1000 and 1400. Yet during this period, the Mixtecs also faced the encroachment of militaristic expansion from their neighbors.[6]

The Yucatán Peninsula: The Maya

During the Classic Era (from around A.D. 250 to 900) Mayan civilization grew to become one of the most expansive and enduring in Mesoamerica. At its apex, around A.D. 600, Mayan civilization likely consisted of as many as 2 million people, speaking more than two dozen languages. Tik'al, the largest Mayan city of the time, may have had as many as 60,000 inhabitants, with an additional 30,000 people in surrounding rural areas. Eventually, through a loose agglomeration of city-states or kingdoms, the Maya came to occupy most of the Yucatán Peninsula, southern Mexico, and present-day Guatemala, Belize, El Salvador, and western Honduras.

Early Mayan civilization was likely influenced in important ways by trade, migration, and other interactions with the Olmec and Teotihuacán civilizations. The nature and extent of these influences continue to be debated by experts. For example, the Maya utilized a cyclical calendar that was probably passed on to them by the Olmecs, who likely obtained it from the Zapotecs. Yet the Maya developed a unique and sophisticated iteration of the same calendar with its own merits.[7] Adaptation of various agricultural methods—including fertilization, terracing, hydrology, draining, and crop rotation—allowed the Maya to develop a large, densely populated civilization in a difficult tropical environment.[8] Major Mayan cities also featured uniquely designed and lavishly ornamented pyramids, temples, and other architectural structures, built at steep angles from the white limestone prevalent throughout the Yucatán Peninsula. The Mayans, like the Zapotecs, also developed a written language of elaborate hieroglyphs, leaving important Mayan texts—or codices—that still survive and help to document their experiences.

Mayan civilization fell into decline and disarray beginning in the Late Classic Period probably as the result of the combined influences of drought, overexploitation of the region's natural resources, increased warfare, famine, social dissolution, and (later) invasion and conquest by the Toltecs of central Mexico.[9] Yet even after its decline, the people and remnants of Mayan civilization survived until the arrival of the Europeans in the early sixteenth century and even today.

The Central Mexican Plateau: Teotihuacán, Toltec, and Aztec Civilizations

The Central Plateau of Mexico gave rise to a series of prominent and influential civilizations that arguably dominated much of Mesoamerican history and modern-day fascination with pre-Columbian times. The first major civilization, was based in the city of Teotihuacán, located northeast of present-day Mexico City, rose to prominence between 300 and 100 B.C. and began to decline after A.D. 700. At its peak, Teotihuacán was inhabited by as many as 200,000 people, making it one of the largest cities in the world at that time. By then, the city boasted over 600 pyramids, thousands of dwellings, and hundreds of workshops. The most significant structure, the Pyramid of the

Sun—completed around the time of Christ in the Western calendar—was of great religious significance, and was believed to establish a connection to the underworld through the caves beneath it.[10] Teotihuacanos succeeded in dominating nearby peoples, like the Tlaxcalans, and established trading relationships that extended throughout central and southeast Mexico. Moreover, long after Teotihuacán fell into decline, the city retained a prominent place in Toltec and Aztec civilizations, who called it the City of the Gods.

The Toltecs were the second major civilization to arise in central Mexico, following the decline of Teotihuacán. The Toltec civilization was centered in the city of Tula, in the present-day state of Hidalgo in central Mexico (just north of Mexico City). It came to prominence between A.D. 900 and 1100. By its zenith, the Toltec capital of Tula may have reached as many as 60,000 inhabitants. While less populous than Teotihuacán, Tula nonetheless achieved remarkable influence throughout Mesoamerica. The Toltecs expanded militarily, traded with, and otherwise influenced people of the Gulf Coast, the Yucatán, southwestern Mexico, Central America, and even native peoples in North America. Toltec influences can be seen in the dissemination of religious practices and mythology, including their worship of the feathered serpent god Quetzalcoatl, their continuation of Olmec-style ball court games, and their use of certain religious symbols (such as the reclining figure of the *chacmool*). Above all, the Toltecs are remembered for their militaristic orientation.[11]

Their accomplishments were documented, extolled, and possibly embellished by the Aztecs, who emulated Toltec militarism and ferocity. In actual fact, the Aztecs descended from the Mexica people (from which Mexico's name is derived), who arrived in central Mexico in the aftermath of Toltec decline. These early Aztecs initially served as mercenaries for the people of Colhuacan, but when the Mexica evidently killed a Colhuacan princess in a religious ritual they were banished in A.D. 1325, whereupon they relocated to the marshlands of Lake Texcoco. Aztec legend suggests that this site was foreseen by prophecy, and was revealed by the sighting of an eagle perched on a cactus and consuming a serpent (from which Mexico's national seal is derived today). The Aztecs began to reclaim the marshes of Lake Texcoco by erecting artificial agricultural fields (*chinampas*), constructing canals, and building dikes to separate salt and freshwater systems. The lake's islands, Tenochtitlán and Tlatelolco, were connected to the mainland by three extended causeways and an aqueduct.[12]

Within a century, the Aztecs established themselves as the predominant power in central Mexico, thanks to the establishment of the so-called Triple Alliance between three great kingdoms centered in Tenochtitlán, Texcoco, and Tlacopan. While the three entities ostensibly shared power equally, the great city of Tenochtitlán became the center of this loosely administered political system. Led by a series of fierce and audacious leaders, notably Itzcoatl (1427–1440) and Ahuitzotl (1486–1502), the Aztecs established an expansive sphere of influence—some might say an empire—that stretched from the Gulf Coast to the Pacific. Aztec expansion was achieved through alliances with the willing and the military conquest of the defiant, both of which were required to pay tribute and sometimes became the victims of ritual sacrifices. By its peak in the early sixteenth century, under the reign of Moctezuma II, who led the kingdom from 1502 until the arrival of the Spanish, the Aztec capital of Tenochtitlán numbered as many as 300,000 people.[13]

Spanish Exploration and Conquest in Mexico

In Europe and Africa, half a world away from Mesoamerica, impressive civilizations also rose, fell, and competed for dominance. In the struggle for dominance among civilizations, the year 1492 was an auspicious one for the Spanish: Christian nobles reconquered the last Moorish stronghold and reestablished Spanish sovereignty after 300 years of domination by Muslims from Northern Africa. Spain's attempt to reclaim its identity, particularly with respect to religion, contributed to the strength of the Catholic Church—and the zealousness of the Spanish Inquisition to root out the unfaithful—under the reestablished monarchy.

The Spanish Restoration, which placed King Ferdinand and Isabela "La Católica" on the throne, also marked the beginning of a new age of exploration, conquest, and empire. At the time of the restoration, Spain was a latecomer to the game of exploration and imperialism in which other European powers—especially the Italians and the Portuguese—were already much advanced. The exploration of the New World was in actuality a search for alternative access to lucrative trade with Asia, and therefore represented the efforts of the Spanish Crown to catch up to other parts of Europe. The discovery of a new continent gave Spain an opportunity to plunder new sources of wealth and enabled its ascent as Europe's strongest power by the end of the seventeenth century. Mexico soon became Spain's most important source of wealth in the New World.

The Great Clash of Civilizations

The Spanish conquest (1492–1533) in Mexico began as explorers moved from the Caribbean coast and inward to the mainland empires of the Mayans and the Aztecs. The man we know as Christopher Columbus—an Italian named Cristobal Colón—led the way in the era of Spanish exploration and expansion. He was later followed by Hernán Cortés, the principal actor in the conquest of what became known as New Spain (the area that comprises Mexico and Guatemala today). Cortés set off from Cuba toward Mexico in 1519 with just a few hundred men and sixteen horses with authorization from Diego Velázquez, the governor of Cuba, to explore the coast of the "island" of Yucatán. Once there, it took Cortés just two and a half years to conquer millions of native people. What made Cortés so successful against such overwhelming odds?

Understanding the confrontation between the civilizations of the Old and New World requires careful consideration of the relative advantages favoring the Spanish, as well as the particular circumstances of the Aztecs, the dominant indigenous civilization of the time. The Europeans benefited from technologies—guns, steel armor, and horses—which were not indigenous to the New World. Steel swords and armor were far more durable and lethal than the blunt stone and wooden weapons and the light protection employed by indigenous people of the Americas. Given the premium that the Aztecs and other native people placed on obtaining captives for sacrifice, slavery, or submission, native weapons and battle tactics were often intended mainly to stun or subdue an opponent, rather than to kill. At the same time, as one scholar observes, despite the real and psychological advantages these weapons gave the Spanish, technology did not ensure victory. The sheer number of their opponents would have easily overwhelmed the Spanish if not for other factors.[14]

In particular, the Europeans brought diseases such as smallpox and syphilis, viruses previously unknown in the New World. Such diseases inflicted a devastating plague on the native population because they had not developed the kind of natural immunity found on the more densely populated and urbanized European continent. One of the primary results of the influx of disease in the Americas was the rapid decimation of the indigenous population. Demographers continue to debate the indigenous population of the Americas at the time of European contact; it was certainly no less than 13 million and, more likely, several times that number: some estimates reach above 100 million. Whatever the total, many scholars estimate that depopulation occurred at a horrifying rate, and within 130 years of the arrival of the Europeans, as few as 3 million indigenous people remained. Thus the colonization of the New World resulted in a massive decline in the native population.[15]

Many experts suggest that Cortés and other conquerors also benefited from the political fragmentation of the Aztec empire, which essentially relied on a system of military conquest and mandatory tribute that inspired significant resentment in the groups it dominated. With the help of members of such subjected indigenous groups, Cortés was able to draw on anti-Aztec sentiments to forge alliances, most notably with the Tlaxcalans, to overthrow the Aztecs.[16] Furthermore, the conquest would not likely have been possible without the skills and assistance of an indigenous woman, known today as La Malinche, whom the Spanish called "Marina," and whom some have called "Malintzin." Likely born in the area near modern-day Coatzacoalcos, there is no record of her given name, as she was initially enslaved as a young girl and taken to the Gulf Coast by her captors. Later she became one of twenty female slaves awarded to Cortés's expedition as tribute by a local chieftain (cacique). Initially, Cortés had enlisted the services of a Spaniard named Jerónimo, who lived shipwrecked for several years among the Maya and learned their language. Because Malinche spoke Mayan and Náhuatl, the language of the Aztecs, she was able to work with Jerónimo to provide Cortés with translation. However, Malinche quickly learned Spanish and thus became an indispensable asset, as both a confidante and consort to Cortés. Her place in history is one that many Mexicans equate with betrayal of all indigenous people. Yet, confronted with limited options, Malinche likely made the same strategic choices other indigenous people made during this troubled time. Had it not been this particular indigenous woman who aided Cortés, it is quite possible that another indigenous speaker would have become a similar instrument of Spanish power.[17]

Cortés and his men battled against indigenous tribes for months as they made their way inland from the Yucatán coast. Upon landing at Veracruz, Cortés hastily established a local government in the name of the Crown—La Villa Rica de la Vera Cruz, known today as Veracruz—giving himself some measure of legal autonomy from Governor Velásquez. Cortés then tested his men by offering safe passage to Cuba for those disinclined to continue; his ruse was actually intended to expose the fainthearted and the disloyal. Leaving a small battalion to defend his base along the coast, Cortés burned the ships and marched on to the interior.

As was likely his intent, the news of Cortés's advance toward the Aztec capital preceded him. The messages were not lost upon Moctezuma, the ninth Aztec ruler of the city of Tenochtitlán, and the leader of the Triple Alliance. Moctezuma was the great-grandson of Moctezuma Ilhuicamina, the ruler of the Aztecs from 1440 to 1468, who introduced the universal military training that facilitated Aztec hegemony.[18] According to Spanish accounts, Moctezuma believed that Cortés was, in fact, the Toltec god Quetzalcoatl, and that a series of mysterious events—a comet, silent lightning flashes that caused a fire in a temple, and ghostly apparitions—served as supernatural omens of his second coming.[19] This portrayal of Moctezuma as a naïve and superstitious leader may merely reflect the biases of the Spanish themselves, or convenient interpretations of the ultimate outcome of the conquest through the lens of history. Indeed, it would be wrong to believe that Moctezuma was a complete fool. Like his predecessors, Moctezuma was a warrior king who dramatically expanded Aztec influence, consolidating their reach into Mixtec territory, and receiving tribute from numerous surrounding peoples. With roughly 30 million people, Moctezuma's realm likely held three times the population of Spain (and more than any other European nation). With 1,000 concubines and 3,000 servants, Moctezuma enjoyed every possible luxury for his time. He was also an accomplished scholar, a careful student of history, and widely regarded as a great leader until his ultimate defeat.[20]

Yet, despite multiple opportunities to crush Cortés and avert his own defeat, Moctezuma hesitated to do so. Possibly the Aztec leader miscalculated or misinterpreted the unprecedented situation before him. Wary, and perhaps uncertain as to whether Cortés was indeed a returning god, Moctezuma initially attempted to dissuade the Spanish. Moctezuma sent Cortés warnings of the hardships of the journey to the highlands, and offered gifts of gold to encourage the Spaniards to turn back. It is also possible that Moctezuma's overtures were a strategic delay tactic. Since most able-bodied men were in their fields tending to the harvest, the readiness of the Aztec army may have been limited.[21]

For his part, Cortés sought to intimidate Moctezuma by enlisting the support of thousands of Tlaxcalan warriors and displaying his willingness to use extreme force. When Spanish forces next arrived at Cholula, an Aztec religious center, Cortés butchered an estimated 300 of the town's leaders in a public square, on rumors that they were plotting to kill the Spaniards. Hence, by the time the Spaniards reached Tenochtitlán, Cortés had amassed considerable military strength and a forceful reputation. Moctezuma decided at that point that the best approach was to offer Cortés an audience and evaluate the situation for himself.[22]

As Cortés and his men made their way over the great causeway across the lake and into the Aztec city, Moctezuma greeted him personally with a dramatic procession to the plaza of Tlatelolco. Yet, once within the walls of Moctezuma's palace, Cortés took the emperor hostage and forced him to issue decrees that effectively abdicated power to the Spaniards. This worked for a time, as the Aztecs were reluctant to attack while their leader was held hostage. However, the tide turned after Spaniards evidently misinterpreted an Aztec religious rite as an impending attack, and responded violently. After the ensuing melee, Moctezuma was killed and the Spaniards, together with their Tlaxcalan allies, now fought to make their way out of the seething Aztec capital. Over half of Cortés's men and hundreds of Tlaxcalans died as the rest made a miraculous escape on a turbulent and rainy night on June 30, 1520, labeled by the Spanish as the Sad Night (*La Noche Triste*). According to legend, that night Cortés wept beneath an *ahuehuete* tree—a conifer that is today Mexico's national tree—lamenting the loss of his men, their treasure, and victory.[23]

Though they lost this battle, the Spaniards and their allies ultimately won the war against the Aztecs. After their initial defeat, Cortés and his men plotted for months to retake the Aztec city. Meanwhile, the Aztecs suffered a major outbreak of smallpox, which killed Moctezuma's immediate successor, Cuitlahuac, just three months into his reign and dramatically weakened Aztec forces. Together, the Spaniards and the Tlaxcalans constructed a miniature armada of boats—large enough to transport horses and soldiers—that could be disassembled for transport over land and deployed into Lake Texcoco. With these technological innovations and some new allies, the Spaniards and Tlaxcalans laid siege to Tenochtitlán. After the Spaniards captured Cuauhtémoc, Moctezuma's nephew and the newly designated leader of the Aztecs, they were able to force the final surrender.

Spanish Colonialism

After the surrender of the Aztecs, Cortés rapidly asserted Spanish authority by extracting pledges of allegiance from neighboring native peoples—sometimes by replacing existing chieftains with leaders who vowed their support—and by extending the conquest to the rest of the mainland and into present-day Guatemala. Those Spanish fortune seekers who prevailed during the conquest and continued the exploration of the New World were richly rewarded with land grants (*encomiendas*) and privileges that enabled them to exploit the people and riches of the New World. Spain's colonial holdings in the Americas—of which Mexico was perhaps the greatest asset—made it the dominant power in Europe for most of the next 300 years.

Meanwhile, the indigenous people of the New World had a very different perspective on Spanish colonialism. Most troubling was the decimation of the indigenous population of Mesoamerica, now called New Spain, which was reduced to as few as 3 million people. Although their numbers later rebounded somewhat, the indigenous people (and all nonwhites) of New Spain were effectively marginalized and controlled. The Spanish gradually undermined and usurped the power of even their elite indigenous allies, eventually reducing all indigenous people—including those with whom the Spanish cohabited—to a category of inferior social status.[24]

Numerous important developments unfolded over the course of Spanish colonial history, and the details of life during this time are rich and complex.[25] However, rather than retrace the detailed history or daily life of the Spanish colonial era, we instead focus our analysis on four key features of the time period: the mercantilist economic model, the colonial bureaucracy, the stratification of social classes, and the significant role of the Catholic Church. Each of these phenomena had a direct impact on Mexican political development that lasted after independence in 1821 and into the twentieth century.

Mercantilist Economic Model

The decision by European monarchs to fund expeditions such as those led by Columbus and Cortés was driven above all by the desire to acquire greater wealth and power. Only by extending their reach outside of Europe could rulers like King Ferdinand hope to achieve economic and political dominance on the home continent. Thus, once the task of defeating indigenous armies was complete, the conquerors immediately set about establishing a colonial economy that served the Crown. This economic model, known as mercantilism, held that all economic activity should enhance the wealth and power of the state. In practice it meant that the economy was based on the production of primary goods (e.g., precious metals, textiles, foodstuffs) to be exported to Europe, and on the creation of a market for the sale of Spain's manufactured goods (e.g., clothing, processed foods, luxury items) to the elites now living in New Spain. While the mercantilist model greatly benefited Spain and other European empires, it had at least some detrimental effects on the colonies themselves.[26]

First, because it was based on the extraction of resources for the benefit of Spain, there was almost no attention given to promoting economic diversity in the colonies. The only commodities of value were those sought by the Crown. Second, all economic infrastructure was concentrated in areas that served Spanish economic and political demands. Together, the lack of economic diversity and adequate infrastructure (including roads to administrative institutions to local financial institutions) put Mexico at a severe disadvantage once it secured its independence from Spain. Faced with the task of restarting the economy after independence, the new ruling elite, perhaps quite naturally, chose to replicate many aspects of the mercantilist model, including a dependent trade relationship with Europe. Though the Mexican version of mercantilism had the advantage of bringing wealth and power to Mexico rather than a foreign Crown, it was ill suited to Mexico's long-term economic success because it was based on repressive labor conditions, extreme concentration of resources, and the need for foreign capital investment. As we will see in the coming chapters, throughout the course of Mexican history, these three characteristics have served as a source of social and political instability.

Colonial Bureaucracy

Successful administration of the mercantilist system required an organizational apparatus to monitor and regulate activities in the colonies and protect the interests of the Crown. The development of the administrative bureaucracy was especially necessary to counter the power of *encomendados*—conquistadors who were granted ownership of vast land holdings (*encomiendas*) and their populations (sometimes including entire towns and villages)—who had a great deal of autonomy from the Crown. The Spanish Crown appointed viceroys (*virreyes*) who were supervised by the king's representatives in an appointed body known as the Council of the Indies. There were viceroyalties for New Spain (Mexico), Peru, New Granada (Venezuela, Ecuador), and La Plata (Argentina).

The viceroys helped to oversee the vast administrative bureaucracy created to regulate the customs and duties of the Crown with regard to economic transactions in the colonial economy. In addition, the viceroys commanded the military, the coercive apparatus that served as both an exploratory force for expanding Spain's territorial holdings and as the protector of the Crown's interests in the New World. Gradually, the Crown did away with the *encomienda,* and local mechanisms of colonial administration became institutionalized below the authority of the viceroys. Governors headed the more populated territories and became the basis for the subsequent development of state governments in the nineteenth century. Similarly, hundreds of local government districts, known as *ayuntamientos*, emerged, with power centered in the figures of the mayor (*alcalde*) and city counselors (*corregidores*).[27] Thus, the colonial bureaucracy laid the foundation for subnational administrative and political divisions in Mexico that persisted well after the colony of New Spain won her independence.

Social Stratification

Another important aspect of Spanish colonialism was the extreme social stratification that developed in Mexico over 300 years. The fact that Spanish colonization of the New World initially took the form of a series of military campaigns meant that for the most part the conquistadors did not bring their wives and families to the Americas. Consequently many Spaniards cohabitated and bore children with native women (who often had little choice). Even after the conquest, mixing between the New World's three races—the socially constructed categories of white, black, and Indian—produced a diverse array of class and ethnic identities. Indeed, during this period there developed a hierarchical "pigmentocracy" in which an individual's social status, and perceived value, was determined entirely by his place of birth and racial background.[28]

At the top of the pigmentocracy were "whites": both *peninsulares* (pure-blooded Europeans born on the Iberian Peninsula) and *criollos* (Europeans born in the Americas). Through most of the colonial period, the *peninsulares* were the smallest but most powerful group. By virtue of their European birth, education, and socialization, they dominated virtually all positions of economic and political power. Even their offspring, the *criollos,* were considered inferior in their readiness to govern and hold important economic posts. Therefore *criollos* were relegated to midlevel positions in the bureaucracy (as lawyers, accountants, etc.) and economy (as merchants, import-exporters, bankers, etc.). At the bottom of the social pyramid were the full-blooded indigenous people and the African slaves, imported to many places in the Americas to offset labor shortages after the decimation of local populations. Mixing among these "lower" races produced a colorful social caste system with various shades of mestizos (white-Indian), mulattos (black-white), and zambos (black-Indian) who tended to work as manual laborers, artisans, and domestic servants in colonial society. While mestizos eventually became the vast majority in Mexican society, in the long run, the pigmentocracy introduced with the arrival of the Spaniards created patterns of social and economic interaction that sustained asymmetrical power relations and mitigated against the development of equal political rights in Mexico.

The Catholic Church

The Catholic Church was an important facilitator of the colonization of Mexico and the rest of Latin America. Indeed, Spanish military explorers and the agents of the Church worked together with sword and cross to settle untamed lands through an integrated network of fortresses (*presidios*) and missions (*misiones*). The dissemination of religion was vital to the overall effort of the Spanish conquest, and the success of the Church in disseminating the Catholic faith was enormous: in a few years the Church converted millions of indigenous people to the Catholic faith.[29]

One factor that made this wholesale conversion possible was the fact that religion had long been an agent of cultural diffusion among various indigenous civilizations. Religious icons and practices were commonly disseminated and blended through various cultural interactions, and directly imposed by civilizations that conquered neighboring peoples. In conquering other civilizations, enemy temples were torn down and new temples reconstructed on top of the remains, often using the same stones to rebuild. Hence, while not necessarily immediately embraced by native peoples, the phenomena of cultural conquest and religious blending were hardly unfamiliar when later perpetuated by the Spanish, who similarly constructed new Catholic sanctuaries from the indigenous temples that they destroyed.[30]

Perhaps because of past patterns of cultural conquest, the native people adapted to the new religion with relative ease, and agents of the Church appeared eager to blend Catholic and native religious symbols, a phenomenon known as "syncretism," to win converts to the Church. For example, the existence of a wide array of Catholic saints made it relatively easy to map the religious symbols of Christianity onto the pantheon of indigenous gods.[31] Perhaps the best-known example of syncretism in Mexico is the deeply revered Virgin of Guadalupe—a brown-skinned, Náhuatl-speaking image of the Madonna. See textbox 1.1.

While the Church can be rightly seen as an agent of the Spanish Crown, some members of the clergy made important efforts to promote the rights of indigenous people. Two prominent examples are Juan de Zumárraga, named the first bishop of New Spain and the Protector of the Indigenous, and Father Bartolomé de las Casas, whose revelatory book, *History of the Indies*, and activism in Spain were instrumental in the adoption of the New Laws in 1542 to protect the rights of indigenous peoples. The ministry and activism of such early Catholic priests won important converts. Thus part of the colonial legacy of the Catholic Church is that, even today, an overwhelming number of people in Mexico and the rest of Latin America identify themselves as Catholics. Yet its legacy also sowed the seeds for a bitter conflict between church and state. Like the conquistadors, most representatives of the Catholic Church were closely allied with the Crown. Many committed significant abuses and amassed enormous wealth and large tracts of land, used for agricultural production and vineyards, which gave the Church great political power in the New World. Over time, in a series of contentious church-state conflicts that lasted into the twentieth century, anticlerical elements would work to divest the Church of its holdings and restrict its influence to religious matters.

Independence and Postcolonial Instability

At the beginning of the eighteenth century, the Spanish Crown fell under the control of the Bourbon dynasty of France. The Bourbons allied Spain with France in its conflicts with other European powers, notably England, and imposed a series of new regulations to impose order and extract greater resources from the colonies. These changes, which further heightened the political and economic status of *peninsulares* at the expense of *criollos*, exacerbated existing tensions between the two groups and ultimately contributed to the latter's quest for expanded opportunities via independence from Spain.[32]

Miguel Hidalgo, a priest who had lost his lands and been relegated to a remote parish because of his *criollo* status, developed a loyal following of *criollos*, mestizos, and indigenous people. Resentful of the repression of these groups in the colonial hierarchy, Hidalgo joined other liberally minded *crio-*

Textbox 1.1. The Virgin of Guadalupe

According to Church teachings, the Virgin of Guadalupe appeared to Juan Diego, an early convert to Christianity, three times, beginning on December 9, 1531, on the hill of Tepeyac, close to the destroyed Aztec temple honoring the goddess Tonanzin. Speaking to Juan Diego in his native tongue, the apparition asked him to appeal to the bishop, Juan de Zumárraga, to build a church for her over the ruins of Tonanzin's temple. Despite multiple entreaties, the bishop initially denied Juan Diego's request and demanded proof of his vision. Hence, upon her final apparition, the Virgin provided proof by miraculously directing Juan Diego to a crop of Spanish roses in the dead of winter. When Juan Diego opened his cloak to reveal the roses to the bishop, emblazoned on the material was the image of the Virgin that appears here. Bishop Zumárraga immediately began building the Basilica of Guadalupe in her honor. In 1745 the Vatican officially recognized the appearance of the Virgin of Guadalupe as a miracle. Juan Diego was venerated in 1987, beatified in 1990, and canonized as a saint in 2002.

The Virgin of Guadalupe has acquired such a significant following in Mexico that her image is nearly as popular as the country's flag. She was the symbol behind which Father Miguel Hidalgo rallied his cry for Mexican independence in 1810, and behind which the revolutionary forces of Zapata fought in the 1910 Mexican revolution. Today, the feast day of the Virgin of Guadalupe continues to be celebrated by an estimated 11 million visitors to the Basilica of Guadalupe on December 12.

The Virgin of Guadalupe

llos in plotting for independence. In September 1810, Hidalgo was warned by Ignacio José Allende Unzaga, a fellow *criollo* and co-conspirator, that Spanish officials planned to arrest him. In the first hours of September 16, 1810, Hidalgo rallied his supporters and parishioners by tolling the church bells of the small town of Dolores, Guanajuato, issuing the rallying cry: "Death to the Spaniards, long live the Virgin of Guadalupe" (*¡Mueren los gachupines, Viva la Virgen de Guadalupe!*).[33] So began an independence movement that quickly mobilized over 80,000 people to Hidalgo's cause. Although Hidalgo's forces captured important cities such as Morelia and Puebla, Spanish reinforcements easily defeated the poorly armed and untrained peasants and then executed Hidalgo (whose head was placed on display). Soon after, José María Morelos—a mulatto priest who supported Hidalgo—took up the mantle of independence (along with the zambo military commander, Vicente Guerrero), which greatly expanded the military capability of the insurgent forces.[34]

As it turned out, Mexican independence was stalled by events in Europe. With the defeat of Napoleon's armies in 1812, Ferdinand VII was restored to the Spanish throne and he moved swiftly to deploy Spanish forces to put down the rebellion in the New World. With these reinforcements the Spanish succeeded in capturing Morelos and executed him in 1815, and significantly reduced insurgent forces over the next few years. Yet by this point, life had deteriorated significantly in the colonies, as economic production was severely disrupted, and wealthy Mexican elites found themselves increasingly supporting the royal treasury out of their own pockets.

Ironically, it was these same conservative elites who revived the independence movement in 1820. Concerned by efforts of liberals in Spain to restrict the Crown under the 1812 Constitution of Cadiz, Mexican conservatives believed that a weaker monarch would threaten their privileges in the New World. Rather than risk the spread of liberalism in New Spain, they sought to ensure their privileged position through independence. A conservative general named Agustín de Iturbide led the break from Spain, issuing the Plan de Iguala, a proclamation favoring Mexican independence, the establishment of a constitutional monarchy, and a guarantee that merit, not race or place of birth, would be the sole criterion used to fill economic and political positions. Under these principles, Iturbide secured both liberal and conservative support and with minimal force succeeded in liberating Mexico in 1821, becoming its first independent head of state.

The Dilemmas of Self-Governance

Independence from Spain may have brought political autonomy, but it also brought considerable chaos and strife, and ground the economy to a virtual halt. The war for independence had destroyed much of the country's agricultural output and severely disrupted mining activity. Indeed, the production of gold and silver—which had reached its peak in Mexico by the 1790s and into the early eighteenth century—struggled throughout the fight for independence, and was operating at less than half capacity by the end of the war. In addition, breaking ties with Spain's mercantilist economy severed the newborn country's historical trade relations. Broader Mexican society was plagued by high levels of unemployment, lack of access to land, and miserable living conditions; as a result, peasant and worker revolts were common during this period, often numbering in the thousands. Under these unenviable circumstances, Mexico's new leaders negotiated a series of unfavorable foreign loans and issued bonds that it was later unable to repay.[35]

Meanwhile, independence created a political free-for-all, with no clear leader or group having sufficient power to govern effectively. In place of the old colonial bureaucracy, there emerged a series of caudillos, or strongmen, who took power by force and maintained their position by use of force. The highly personalistic—rather than institutional—nature of power after Mexican independence became an enduring characteristic of politics in Mexico and elsewhere in Latin America. Indeed, even with the emergence of a constitutional republic in the mid-nineteenth century and the reforms later brought about by revolution, power remained concentrated in the figure of the Mexican president and an array of powerful individuals at the regional and local level. Immediately after independence, General Iturbide declared himself emperor of Mexico and pillaged the national treasury—a move that led to his swift removal thanks to the forces of Vicente Guerrero, who advocated the creation of a constitutional republic with a popularly elected president and legislature. Yet, even after the promulgation of the 1824 constitution, political stability remained elusive. Between 1824 and 1857 there were nearly fifty different governments (and more than 25 different heads of state), at least half of which came to power as the result of violent insurrection.[36]

Within this context General Antonio López de Santa Anna emerged as one of Mexico's most famous caudillos, and was both respected and reviled. Santa Anna had proved himself an effective military leader during the wars of independence, and he ruled Mexico (either directly or indirectly) between 1824 and 1855 with a devastating combination of corruption, opportunism, and authoritarianism. In retrospect, Santa Anna's character should have been ominously clear when, after being elected for the first time in May 1833, he unabashedly spent government resources on frivolous affairs of state, posh public works of little use to ordinary Mexicans (e.g., an elegant opera house), and his own luxurious lifestyle. Furthermore, Santa Anna left the actual task of governing to his vice president, Valentín Gómez Farías. When Gómez Farias sought to curtail the power of the Church and the military, Santa Anna staged a coup against him in June 1833, and then, inexplicably, restored Gómez Farias to govern in his place. This pattern repeated itself multiple times over the next several years. Perhaps his most ignominious feat was to lose and sell nearly half of Mexico's territory to the United States, which we discuss below.

The War of the North American Invasion (1845–1848)

Compounding Mexico's problems at this time was its geographic location next door to the United States, an ambitious nation with a fifty-year head start on independence. The origins of the War of North American Invasion (known in the United States as the Mexican-American War) are found in Texas. In the 1820s, the Spanish Crown had encouraged settlement in its northern territories in an effort to dissuade U.S. expansionism. Settlers of any nationality could obtain land for next to nothing in exchange for becoming Mexican citizens and Catholics. A group of Anglos led by Stephen F. Austin settled in the territory of Texas while actively resisting the terms of the agreement, refusing to become Mexican citizens or convert to Catholicism. Initially these Anglos posed little threat to Mexican interests, but by the 1830s, they outnumbered Mexicans five to one. Supported by the United States, leaders like Austin began calling for independence from Mexico, which was increasingly trying to exert its authority on the remote territory. In order to put down the budding insurgency, in 1835 Santa Anna led his troops to Texas and decisively defeated the rebels at the Alamo. The Mexican victory prompted a fierce response by the Texans and the U.S. government, which actively supported retribution, and in 1836 Texas captured Santa Anna and won its independence from Mexico. In order to secure his release, Santa Anna agreed to withdraw his troops south of the Rio Grande—a move that would encourage the United States to greatly exaggerate its actual boundaries and add to Mexico's territorial losses just ten years later.[37]

Had Texas remained independent, Mexico might have eventually relinquished its claim and recognized its sovereignty. However, when the United States made clear in 1846 that it intended to extend its reach far beyond Texas to California, Mexico was outraged and obliged to take action. Announcing its plans to annex Texas and claiming that its western boundary was a line drawn from modern-day El Paso north all the way through modern-day Colorado, the United States took advantage of Santa Anna's agreement to retreat south of the Rio Grande and disregarded the traditional southern and western boundaries of the territory. Not surprisingly, Mexico disputed this claim and sent troops to defend its interests. In May 1846, U.S. forces led by General

Zachary Taylor entered the disputed territory, provoking a hostile response by the Mexican forces that left several dead. Claiming that Mexico had "invaded" U.S. territory, when in fact the opposite had occurred, U.S. President James Polk declared war on Mexico and for a year the two armies battled over the location of their countries' shared border.

The United States steadily advanced into Mexican territory from the north and east through the gulf port of Veracruz. After a bloody battle that left a number of military and civilian casualties, U.S. forces made their way to Mexico City. Santa Anna's poor strategic decisions and inability to command the loyalty of regional leaders or ordinary Mexican citizens allowed the United States to defeat Mexico relatively easy, despite fierce final shows of resistance in Mexico City.[38] In the end, Mexico was forced to surrender and accept the terms of the Treaty of Guadalupe Hidalgo (1848), which ceded approximately one-third of Mexico's northern territory to the United States in exchange for $15 million in war indemnities. In the wake of his humiliating defeat at the hands of the North American armies, Santa Anna was forced into exile and Mexico was at least as bad off as it had been on the eve of independence. Furthermore, to the dismay of Mexicans and at the expense of Mexico, the United States had established itself as the larger and more powerful of the two countries.[39]

La Reforma: The Conservative-Liberal Divide

The nationalism generated by the Mexican-American War intensified the domestic tensions between Mexico's two opposing elite factions, the "liberals" and the "conservatives." Each had a different vision of how Mexico should assert its national identity. The liberals were primarily *criollos* who claimed to stand for the defense of liberal democratic practices, advocated the separation of church and state, and called for the integration of indigenous people into modern society.[40] Conversely, the conservatives traced their roots to the traditional beliefs of *peninsulares* and favored maintaining autocratic forms of governance, preserving the privileged status of the Catholic Church, and upholding strict social divisions.

While the conservatives had the upper hand at the outset of Mexican independence, political backlash against Santa Anna's abuses of power advantaged the liberals, who took power after his exile. They quickly convened a constitutional convention and drew up a new charter that reinforced the liberal commitment to a federalist republic, free elections, clear separation between church and state, and access to public education. In order to bring the constitution of 1857 into force, the liberals also enacted a series of reforms—known as the Reform Laws (La Reforma)—to strip the military and the Catholic

Church of their power. In particular, the Reform Laws eliminated exemptions given to the military and the clergy from being tried in civil courts; forced the Church to sell off all property except for churches and monasteries; and removed birth, death, marriage, and other registries from Church control and gave them to the state. By December 1857, conservatives responded by declaring General Félix Zuloaga president in an attempt to oust the liberals from power. The liberals responded in kind by declaring Benito Juárez, a well-respected Zapotec lawyer and Oaxacan governor, president. What followed was a brutal war between liberals and conservatives, also called the War of Reform, a three-year affair that ended with a liberal victory and the installation of Juárez as Mexico's first indigenous president.

Textbox 1.2. Benito Juárez

Benito Juárez was born March 21, 1806, a Zapotec Indian. He was one of only a few ethnically indigenous Mexicans to serve as president, a position he held for a total of five terms. Trained as a lawyer, he served as governor of Oaxaca, where he focused on public works projects. He was later expelled and went into exile in the United States for opposing the Santa Anna regime. There he helped draft the Plan of Ayutla, a strong foundation of the liberal revolutionary movement that called for the removal of Santa Anna as dictator and the drafting of a Mexican constitution. In 1855 Juárez was appointed minister of justice and public education, a position he utilized to eliminate *fueros,* the special privileges of the military and clergy. In a very short time he also served as minister of the interior and president of the Supreme Court of Justice.

Juárez was first elected president in 1857, and he focused on limiting the power of the Roman Catholic Church and the military, promoting citizen equality, and establishing a federalist constitution. He also reduced the size of the military and introduced educational reform. Juárez was ousted by the invasion of the French in 1863 but returned to power after the defeat of Napoleon's forces and the execution of Emperor Maximilian. Today, Juárez is regarded as a great Mexican hero because of his opposition to Santa Anna's corrupt regime and his dedication to democracy, equality for indigenous populations, and defense of nationalism. His death in 1872 created a political vacuum that allowed Porfirio Díaz to reintroduce autocratic rule and ignore socioeconomic inequality, two important contributors to the Mexican revolution.

In 1861, Benito Juárez declared that Mexico's economic situation would prevent it from paying its sizable foreign debt to countries like France, Britain, and Spain. Unhappy with this pronouncement, the French, under Napoleon III, sent troops to collect the debt, and were invited by bitter conservatives to occupy the country and install a monarch. Initially, the French suffered a decisive defeat at the hands of Mexican forces in the battle of Puebla on May 5, 1862.[41] By the end of the year, the French returned with 24,000 reinforcements and, in collaboration with a council of Mexican conservatives, installed Maximilian von Hapsburg of Austria as emperor of Mexico in 1864.

Maximilian proved to be a sore disappointment to conservatives who believed that monarchical rule was the only way to reestablish the correct order of things. Showing decidedly liberal tendencies, he upheld the Reform Laws, restored communal lands to indigenous villages, and outlawed debt peonage. Yet these acts were not enough to appease the liberals, who continuously mobilized armed attacks on his royal forces. With virtually all Mexicans opposed to his rule, Maximilian sat uncomfortably on what one historian has referred to as a "cactus throne." As Napoleon III's power began to wane in Europe, the unfortunate Maximilian's days were numbered. By 1867, liberal forces had succeeded in recapturing northern Mexico and forced Maximilian's surrender. He was tried, found guilty of violating Mexico's sovereignty, and executed by firing squad.[42]

The restoration of the republic paved the way for Juárez's return, and during his next several years of rule, Mexico experienced more peace and stability than ever before in the independence era. With the conservatives soundly defeated, Juárez enjoyed widespread popular support, in part because of his solid reputation but also because he shrewdly managed to secure the backing of many of society's most powerful groups, whose interests often contradicted one another's. Moreover, true to liberal principles, Juárez actively promoted honest elections and greater access to free public education, and brought Mexico increased economic progress by investing in infrastructure and increasing exports. Relative peace and prosperity notwithstanding, however, a number of domestic tensions were brewing, and not everyone was pleased with Juárez or his decision to seek reelection in 1871. Indeed, one of his most notable detractors was General Porfirio Díaz, a hero who served Juárez in the battle of Puebla and later a member of Congress. Drawing support from conservatives, Díaz argued that the reelection of Juárez actually violated liberal principles and campaigned on the slogan "Effective Suffrage, No Reelection."

While Juárez handily won the 1871 election, his term came to an abrupt end when he died of natural causes in July the following year. Sebastián Lerdo de Tejada, the president of the Mexican Supreme Court, was named as the interim replacement for Juárez. Though he too had run for president in 1871, Lerdo was a close ally of Juárez, and strongly committed to the liberal project. Indeed, the Reform Laws requiring the sale of Church properties were his brainchild, and were also known as the Lerdo Laws. By December 1872, Lerdo was formally appointed by the Mexican Congress to serve as president and reelected in July 1876, presumably placing the liberal agenda back on track. However, this was not to be. Lerdo's aspirations to a third term, as well as the Mexican republic itself, came to an abrupt end when Porfirio Díaz ousted Lerdo de Tejada and seized the presidency in November 1876.

The Porfiriato

General Porfirio Díaz governed Mexico for thirty-four years, finally relinquishing power in 1910. For a brief, four-year period, Díaz ruled from the sidelines when his friend and military comrade Manuel González sat as president. However, throughout the Porfiriato—the period of Díaz's uncontested rule—there was little doubt about who dominated Mexican politics. Ideologically, Díaz successfully positioned himself between liberals and conservatives, with a pragmatic approach to civil and political liberties and religion. In the process, Díaz successfully transformed the model and motto of the Mexican republic from "Liberty and Progress" to "Order and Progress." For Díaz, political stability ("order") was essential for economic modernization and growth ("progress"), and the dictator successfully achieved both to a degree heretofore unprecedented during Mexico's independence. In this sense, one of the most important accomplishments of the Porfiriato was the development of national unity and a sense of nationalism in a long-fragmented country. Still, the inequity and repressiveness of the Díaz regime would lead to its own undoing in the 1910 Mexican revolution.[43]

Order: The Pax Porfiriana

The Porfiriato was characterized by a strong central government headed by Díaz and fortified by his hierarchical, highly personalized style of rule. One of Díaz's first tasks after taking power was to develop a loyal base of support. Díaz achieved this by placing faithful allies and military comrades in key positions in the legislature, courts, government ministries, and state governments. Moreover, he used his military rank and personal connections to blur the civil-military relationship and channel all institutional lines of authority to the executive. The practical result was that the military answered to him and other branches of government lacked the authority or the will to check his actions. Overall, Díaz's efforts to centralize power in his own hands and use force to maintain order effectively rendered moot the constitution of 1857, and made it easy to liken the general to other Latin American caudillos, par excellence.[44]

First, as documented in John K. Turner's 1908 book *Barbarous Mexico*, Díaz did not hesitate to use the military, rural police, secret police (*acordadas*), and even death squads to assert the state's power to impose order.[45] Dissidents and other rebellious or uncooperative elements became the unenviable targets of state-sponsored repression. One tool of repression was the notorious *ley fuga* or escape law, which permitted authorities to execute any prisoner who attempted to flee and led to numerous extrajudicial killings. On a grander scale, Díaz was particularly unmerciful in his repression of a Yaqui rebellion (1876–1910) in the northeastern state of Sonora; thousands of captives were deported to their enslavement and rapid demise in Yucatán and Quintana Roo.[46]

Second, while the use of coercion was an effective way to subdue relatively small, remote, or powerless groups, Díaz had to employ other methods in order to cultivate the support of wealthy local and regional elites who had grown accustomed to using their clout to exact generous concessions from the state. To keep them under his control, he developed a hierarchical elite network that extended to the remotest corners of the republic. Díaz placed himself squarely at the top of the network and selectively bestowed favors and state resources in order to reward the preservation of social order, and to prevent elites from uniting against him. He also assumed the role of a political godfather, brokering solutions for the disputes among elites that he had, in effect, played an important role in creating. To ensure the support of the most prominent local elites, Díaz allowed them considerable autonomy in controlling their strongholds on the condition that they reserve their ultimate loyalty for him and actively support his drive to modernize Mexico's economy and society. Many elites readily embraced the terms of a bargain so favorable to them. Not only did Díaz respect their local authority, he had also earned their loyalty by using state resources to reinforce their positions of power in the face of popular uprisings. For example, in order to put down the indigenous revolts and peasant land invasions that had become common during this era, Díaz created a rural police corps to use force to protect private property. These *rurales*—sometimes called *federales*—acquired a dubious reputation as they helped to bring disgruntled and disobedient peasants and laborers back in line with the demands of their employers and the government. Furthermore, as we explain below, it was not difficult for them to support Díaz's economic model because it greatly benefited them as large landholders, owners of capital, and members of the social elite.

Progress: Economic and Social Modernization

With the benefit of political order, Díaz could implement his plan to modernize Mexico. At the heart of Díaz's modernization project was the European philosophy of "positivism," or the belief that a country's economic and social problems could be solved using rational, scientific, and systematic methods.

Díaz filled his government with *científicos,* trained professionals who es-
poused the positivist view that Mexico had the potential to become a modern,
prosperous state. In economic terms, "progress" meant infusing the Mexican
economy with foreign capital, which would introduce modern and efficient
technologies and production methods to create significant economic growth
and increased prosperity for Mexico. Therefore, the Mexican government created attractive incentives for foreign investors to invest in a variety of different
domestic economic sectors. For example, foreign companies were given tax
and legal exemptions and subsoil rights of ownership. Together these measures created highly favorable terms for making profits. And because political
order was virtually guaranteed under Díaz, Mexico became one of the most
attractive investment opportunities in Latin America.[47]

It is hardly a surprise, then, that foreign investors, mainly from the United
States, Britain, and France, flocked to Mexico and foreign investment increased dramatically. Indeed, by 1910, 90 percent of investments in mining,
electricity, oil, and banking were foreign owned. The United States accounted
for the greatest share of all foreign investment over the course of the Porfiriato, buying the lion's share of Mexican exports (see figure 1.2). The dramatic increase in capital modernized most sectors of the Mexican economy,
especially those most targeted by foreigners: infrastructure, mining, and commercialized agriculture. Perhaps the most notable infrastructure development
of the time was the vast communications and transportation network Díaz
developed throughout the country, drastically reducing transportation costs
for other commodities such as agricultural products and metals and minerals.
When Díaz took power in 1876, there were only 691 kilometers of railroads;
by 1911, there were nearly 25,000 kilometers. Meanwhile, the number of
mines operating in Mexico tripled in the first decade of the twentieth century
alone. Thanks to these developments, Mexico's economy boomed and became
significantly more integrated into the overall world economy, with exports
expanding nearly tenfold and imports increasing by nearly sixfold from the
start of the Porfiriato (see figure 1.3). At the same time, Mexico's dependence
on foreigners and the emerging global economy made it vulnerable to instability in the international economy, and the privileges granted to foreigners in
Mexico would later become a point of serious resentment.[48]

Finally, Díaz and the *científicos* believed that an equally important component of modernization was the incorporation of "superior" social traits that
emanated from Europe and especially France, which was seen as the most
intellectually and culturally sophisticated country in the world. An integral
part of the *científico* philosophy included a firm belief in the tenets of social
Darwinism, which posited that certain races, such as black Africans and indigenous Americans, were physically, intellectually, and morally inferior to white

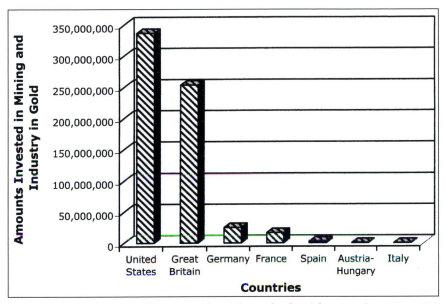

FIGURE 1.2 Foreign Capital Investment in Mining and Industrial Companies, 1886–1907
Source: José F. Godoy, *Porfirio Diaz: President of Mexico, The Master Builder of a Great Commonwealth* (New York, London: Knickerbocker Press, 1910), 128.

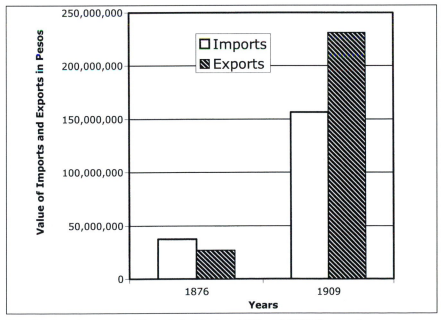

FIGURE 1.3 Imports and Exports in Mexico, 1876 and 1909 (in pesos)
Source: José Godoy, *Porfirio Diaz: President of Mexico, The Master Builder of a Great Commonwealth* (New York, London: Knickerbocker Press, 1910), 188.

Europeans. Therefore, for Mexico to overcome its "Indian problem," it would have to "whiten" itself and thereby successfully achieve modernity. To this end, the regime actively encouraged the immigration of Europeans who, generally speaking, possessed more labor skills, higher levels of education, and especially the kind of work ethic and cultural traits believed to be necessary to move the country forward. Furthermore, the government made an effort to incorporate what were perceived to be superior architectural styles and materials, while the elites emulated everything French, from education to cultural practices and fashions. In sum, during the Porfiriato, government and society likened modernity to a cultural identity that was exclusionary and decidedly inorganic.[49]

Conclusion

Despite its significant shortcomings, the Porfiriato made Mexico into a more politically stable, economically successful, and socially vibrant modern polity. The political and economic instability of the independence and reform eras were distant memories, and at the turn of the twentieth century, Mexico appeared to have a very bright future. Mexico City had become a booming cosmopolitan capital with majestically constructed buildings and monuments, many of which survive even today as a testament to the grandeur of the Porfiriato. However, to focus solely on the great strides Mexico made in state formation and economic stability during the Porfiriato ignores the deep problems wrought during the same era.

Indeed, at almost every level of society, there was visceral resentment against the Díaz regime. Within the elite, domestic owners of capital were frustrated that foreign capital enjoyed so many advantages at their expense. Similarly, industrialists felt that the government's economic policies overwhelmingly favored agricultural exporters. The middle classes were resentful because, although they had benefited from greater economic prosperity, the elite still tightly controlled access to capital and higher education. Further, many in the middle classes objected to being effectively locked out of important political positions in a country that was ostensibly a liberal republic. Artists and intellectuals began to chafe at restrictions on free speech and freedom of expression, and questioned the perceived superiority of European trends and thought. At the bottom, the working classes experienced little of the greater economic prosperity enjoyed by the upper and middle classes, and were instead exploited by labor practices that blatantly favored employers. In their traditional roles as indentured servants on elite-owned haciendas, indigenous people were viewed as inherently inferior, and had no prospects for social mobility or access to land. These resentments, combined with the contractions in the international market on which Mexico had grown highly dependent, ultimately coalesced to produce a unified, if decentralized, effort to bring about meaningful change. The result was the Mexican revolution, which began in 1910 as an effort to oust Porfirio Díaz, and would last roughly a decade until it produced the foundations for Mexico's contemporary political system.

Key Terms

Agustín de Iturbide
Aztecs
científicos
conservatives
Constitution of 1857
Cortés, Hernán
criollos
Díaz, Porfirio
encomendados
Hidalgo, Miguel
Juárez, Benito
La Malinche
La Reforma
liberals

Maya
mercantilism
Mesoamerica
Mixtecs
Olmecs
peninsulares
pigmentocracy
Santa Anna
Teotihuacán
Toltecs
Treaty of Guadalupe Hidalgo
Virgin of Guadalupe
Zapotecs

Recommended Readings

Aguilar, Manuel. *Handbook to Life in the Aztec World*. New York: Facts on File, 2006.
Centro de Estudios Históricos. *Historia General de Mexico*. Mexico City: El Colegio de Mexico, 2000.
Coe, Michael. *Mexico: From the Olmecs to the Aztecs*. New York: Thames & Hudson, 1994.
Knight, Alan. *Mexico: The Colonial Era*. Cambridge: Cambridge University Press, 2002.
Meyer, Michael C., William L. Sherman, and Susan M. Deeds. *The Course of Mexican History*. 6th ed. Oxford: Oxford University Press, 1999.

Notes

1. For a comprehensive history of Mexico, see Enrique Krauze, *Mexico: Biography of Power: A History of Modern Mexico, 1810–1996* (New York: HarperPerennial, 1997);

and Michael C. Meyer, William L. Sherman, and Susan M. Deeds, *The Course of Mexican History* (New York: Oxford University Press, 1999).

2. For a comprehensive historical overview of ancient Mexican civilizations, see Robert M. Carmack, Janine Gasco, and Gary H. Gossen, *The Legacy of Mesoamerica: History and Culture of a Native American Civilization* (Upper Saddle River, N.J.: Prentice Hall, 1996); and Michael D. Coe and Rex Koontz, *Mexico: From the Olmecs to the Aztecs* (New York: Thames & Hudson, 2002).

3. These early inhabitants likely came from Asia. See Coe and Koontz, *Mexico*, 22.

4. Michael D. Coe, *America's First Civilization* (Princeton, N.J.: American Heritage, 1968).

5. Olmec society was also the only "pristine" civilization to develop in a lowland tropical forest. Richard A. Diehl, *The Olmecs: America's First Civilization* (London: Thames & Hudson, 2004), 12.

6. Ronald Spores, *The Mixtecs: In Ancient and Colonial Times* (Norman: University of Oklahoma Press, 1984).

7. Geoffrey E. Braswell, *The Maya and Teotihuacán: Reinterpreting Early Classic Interaction* (Austin: University of Texas Press, 2003); Michael D. Coe, *The Maya* (New York: Praeger, 1970); Coe, *Breaking the Maya Code* (New York: Thames & Hudson, 1992).

8. The Mayans also domesticated an array of nonstaple crops for commercial trade, including cacao, cotton, and henequen. See A. Gómez-Pampa, M. F. Allen, S. L. Fedick, and J. J. Jiménez-Osornio, eds., *The Lowland Maya Area: Three Millennia at the Human-Wildland Interface* (Binghamton, N.Y.: Food Products Press, 2003).

9. For competing explanations of the sudden decline of the Maya, see Arlen Chase and Prudence M. Rice, eds., *The Lowland Maya Postclassic* (Austin: University of Texas Press, 1985); T. Patrick Culbert, ed., *The Classic Maya Collapse* (Albuquerque: University of New Mexico Press, 1991); Richardson B. Gill, *The Great Maya Droughts: Water, Life, and Death* (Albuquerque: University of New Mexico Press, 2000); David Webster, *The Fall of the Ancient Maya* (London: Thames & Hudson, 2002).

10. Some scholars believe those caves were the reason why the Teotihuacanos, as the city's residents have become known, decided to settle there. Manuel Aguilar-Moreno, *Handbook to Life in the Aztec World* (New York: Facts on File, 2006).

11. Richard A. Diehl, *Tula: The Toltec Capital of Ancient Mexico* (London: Thames & Hudson, 1983).

12. Warwick Bray, *Everyday Life of the Aztecs* (New York: Peter Bedrick Books, 1991).

13. Aguilar-Moreno, *Handbook*.

14. Jared Diamond, *Guns, Germs, and Steel: The Fates of Human Societies* (New York: Norton, 1997); Ross Hassig, *Mexico and the Spanish Conquest* (Norman: University of Oklahoma Press, 2006); Miguel León-Portilla, ed., *The Broken Spears: The Aztec Account of the Conquest of Mexico* (Boston: Beacon, 2006).

15. Karl H. Schwerin, "The Indigenous Populations of Latin America," in *Latin America: Its Problems and Its Promise,* ed. Jan Knippers Black (Boulder: Westview, 2005), 42.

16. Jean Gillespie, *Saints and Warriors: Tlaxcalan Perspectives on the Conquest of Tenochtitlán* (New Orleans: University Press of the South, 2004).

17. Camilla Townsend, *Malintzin's Choices: An Indian Woman in the Conquest of Mexico* (Albuquerque: University of New Mexico Press, 2006).

18. Hassig, *Mexico*, 142.

19. Hernán Cortés, *Letters from Mexico* (New York: Grossman, 1971); Bernal Díaz del Castillo, *The Conquest Of New Spain* (Baltimore: Penguin, 1963).

20. Richard F. Townsend, *The Aztecs* (New York: Thames & Hudson, 2000).

21. Ross Hassig, *War and Society in Ancient Mesoamerica* (Berkeley: University of California Press, 1992), 135–64.

22. Hassig, *Mexico*.

23. Carlos Romero Giordano, *Moctezuma II: El misterio de su muerte* (Mexico City: Panorama Editorial, 1986).

24. Centro de Estudios Históricos, ed., *Historia General de Mexico* (Mexico City: El Colegio de Mexico, 2000), 257.

25. Those interested in a more detailed account of the colonial era should see Stephanie Gail, *Transcending Conquest: Nahua Views of Spanish Colonial Mexico* (Norman: University of Oklahoma Press, 2003); and Alan Knight, *Mexico: The Colonial Era* (Cambridge: Cambridge University Press, 2002).

26. Robert B. Ekelund and Robert D. Tollison, *Politicized Economies: Monarchy, Monopoly, and Mercantilism* (College Station: Texas A&M University Press, 1997).

27. Alicia Hernández Chávez, *Mexico: A Brief History* (Berkeley: University of California, 2000), 46–56.

28. Hugo G. Nutini, "Class and Ethnicity in Mexico: Somatic and Racial Considerations," *Ethnology* 36, no. 3 (1997): 227–38.

29. Susan Schroeder and Stafford Poole, eds., *Religion in New Spain* (Albuquerque: University of New Mexico Press, 2007).

30. Gary H. Gossen, ed., *South and Meso-American Native Spirituality: From the Cult of the Feathered Serpent to the Theology of Liberation* (New York: Crossroad, 1993).

31. Martin Austin Nesvig, ed., *Local Religion in Colonial Mexico* (Albuquerque: University of New Mexico, 2006).

32. Richard L. Garner, *Economic Growth and Change in Bourbon Mexico* (Gainesville: University Press of Florida, 1993).

33. Enrique Krauze Magú, *Hidalgo y sus gritos* (Mexico City: Hoja Casa Editorial, 1993).

34. Virginia Guedea, "The Conspiracies of 1811: How the Criollos Learned to Organize in Secret," in *The Birth of Modern Mexico, 1780–1824,* ed. Christon I. Archer (Wilmington, Del.: Scholarly Resources, 2003).

35. Jaime E. Rodríguez O, "Mexico's First Foreign Loans," in *The Independence of Mexico and the Creation of the New Nation* (Los Angeles: UCLA Latin American Center Publications, 1989).

36. José Manuel Villalpando and Alejandro Rosas, *Historia de México: A través de sus gobernantes* (Mexico City: Planeta, 2003).

37. John S. D. Eishenhower, *So Far from God: The U.S. War with Mexico, 1846–1848* (Norman: University of Oklahoma Press, 2000).

38. The losses sustained by U.S. forces are remembered by the Marines to this day, who memorialize the Mexico City campaign in their military anthem ("from the halls

of Montezuma") and wear a red stripe on their dress uniforms. Gabrielle M. Neufeld Santelli, *Marines in the Mexican War* (Washington, D.C.: History and Museums Division, Headquarters, U.S. Marine Corps, 1991).

39. Mexico's loss of the war with the United States did not definitively end Santa Anna's career. He continued to exercise power behind the scenes and then reemerged as president just long enough to arrange the Gadsden Purchase in 1854: an agreement that sold much of what is now southern New Mexico and Arizona to the United States for $10 million.

40. Because the liberals advocated assimilation, rather than respect for indigenous traditions, many indigenous communities resisted liberal legislation, preferring the old viceregal system that, while oppressive, gave them autonomy and respected their traditional practices. However, this did not mean that indigenous communities passively accepted their fate. During the nineteenth century there were a number of indigenous uprisings to demand greater access to land, cultural and personal freedom, and economic opportunities. The largest of these occurred in the Yucatán between 1847 and 1849. Large landowners narrowly escaped defeat in the series of battles known as the Mayan Caste Wars. Nelson A. Reed, *The Caste War of Yucatán* (Stanford, Calif.: Stanford University Press, 2001).

41. Mexicans still celebrate their victory over the French in the battle of Puebla each year on May 5 (Cinco de Mayo). However, the date appears to be even more popular in the United States, where many people wrongly associate the holiday with Mexican Independence Day, which is actually celebrated on September 16.

42. Richard O'Connor, *The Cactus Throne: The Tragedy of Maximilian and Carlotta* (New York: Putnam, 1971).

43. Detailed treatment of the Porfiriato can be found in José F. Godoy, *Porfirio Díaz: President of Mexico, The Master Builder of a Great Commonwealth* (New York: Knickerbocker, 1910); Charles A. Hale, *The Transformation of Liberalism in Late Nineteenth Century Mexico* (Princeton: Princeton University Press, 1990).

44. Other "liberal dictators" who ruled in a similar style included Manuel Rosas of Argentina and Juan Vicente Gómez of Venezuela.

45. Turner was praised by Francisco I. Madero for helping expose the nature of the Díaz regime, thereby contributing to the overthrow of the Porfiriato. John Kenneth Turner, *Barbarous Mexico* (Austin: University of Texas Press, 1969).

46. Most of the Yaqui prisoners died within a year. Michael J. Gonzales, *The Mexican Revolution, 1910–1940* (Albuquerque: University of New Mexico Press, 2002), 32.

47. Fernando Paz Sánchez, *La política económica del Porfiriato* (Mexico City: Instituto Nacional de Estudios Históricos de la Revolución Mexicana, 2000).

48. Godoy, *Porfiro Díaz*, 200.

49. William D. Raat, "Ideas and Society in Don Porfirio's Mexico," *The Americas* 30, no. 1 (1973): 32–53.

2

The Mexican Revolution and Its Legacy

The first major social revolution of the twentieth century began in
northern Mexico in 1910, and spread throughout the country over
most of the next decade.[1] From 1910 to 1917, the revolution mobilized
hundreds of thousands of men, women, and children, resulting in at least
one million deaths (more than one in ten Mexicans), a brief U.S. invasion, the elimination of entire towns, and the extended disruption of the
Mexican economy. Despite the upheaval they create, such massive social
revolutions have long fed the utopian visions of political thinkers and actors who have heralded violent political change as a means for progress
toward greater freedom and equality. Yet ironically, like the other major
social revolutions of the twentieth century—Russia (1917), China (1949),
Cuba (1959)—the Mexican revolution ultimately led instead to the establishment of an authoritarian order that lasted for several decades.[2] Understanding contemporary Mexican politics therefore requires a solid grasp
of the causes and course of the revolution, the major figures involved,
and the long-term consequences for Mexico's postrevolutionary political
system. This chapter examines how the revolution came about and how
its legacy shaped the Mexican political system thereafter. In the process,
we examine the process of Mexican political development over the course
of three key periods: the breakdown and overthrow of the Porfiriato, the
struggle for control in the postrevolutionary period, and the gradual consolidation and institutionalization of power under a new revolutionary
government.

Breakdown and Overthrow of the Porfiriato

Given the appearance of growth and prosperity during the thirty-four years of the Porfiriato, few people expected that Mexico would experience a full-scale social revolution just after the turn of the century. Yet a number of factors contributed to the development of a viable revolutionary scenario. The evident "economic progress" of the Díaz regime disguised some of the underlying problems with the Porfirian growth model. In particular, Mexico's heavy dependence on foreign investment—most banks, mines, railroads, and electric power were under foreign control—made its economy particularly vulnerable to a series of international economic crises and contractions of capital that occurred in 1904 and 1907. As crops were shifted to promote exports like henequen (sisal), everyday Mexicans suffered from the resulting price increases and occasional shortages in staple products like corn (which increasingly had to be imported to meet domestic needs). At the same time, a deep resentment toward foreigners grew from the persistent inequality and mistreatment of Mexicans in their own country. In some foreign companies operating in Mexico, for example, wages paid to foreigners were as much as double those earned by Mexican laborers doing the same work.[3] In short, as one historian describes, in the case of other twentieth-century revolutions in Russia, China, and Iran, Mexico experienced "growing foreign influence and abuses; humiliating subordination to foreign regimes; state collaboration with international financiers while excluding domestic capitalists; and the social, political, cultural, and economic displacement of provincial and local elites, artisans, and peasants."[4]

Meanwhile, the persistence of poverty and severe inequalities in this era of "prosperity" made sustainable and widespread economic progress ultimately unfeasible under the Porfirian model. The everyday lives of Mexicans were compromised by limited economic opportunities, harsh working conditions, high infant mortality rates, rampant disease, and occasional food shortages. By mid-decade, a growing number of food riots and strikes—by tens of thousands of miners, textile workers, and other industrial workers—illustrated the many economic hardships faced by ordinary Mexicans. Meanwhile, over the course of the Porfiriato, small family farmers found themselves increasingly squeezed out by encroachment from wealthy foreigners and hacienda owners. Indeed, by the time of the revolution, over two-thirds of the population was employed in the agricultural sector, but most found themselves working for wealthy land owners on the roughly 800 enormous haciendas that comprised half of Mexico's workable land. Furthermore, despite its abolition in 1814, slavery persisted for hundreds of thousands of indigenous people—sold at prices of $50 a head—in parts of southern Mexico.[5]

In the end, however, it was not the economic inequality or repressiveness of the Díaz regime that sparked the revolution. Rather, it was the frustration and ambition of relatively wealthy elites. Some young elites, especially, felt that their upward political mobility and influence in the regime was circumscribed by the power structure: a network of generals, political bosses, and cronies that was as enduring and impervious as the great dictator himself. By the later part of the Díaz regime, only 8 percent of Mexico's population was over the age of fifty, yet the power structure overwhelmingly represented an older demographic: the average age of ministers of Díaz's government was nearly sixty-eight years old, and few of them appeared likely to retire anytime soon.[6] Thus, among ambitious young elites, opportunities for advancement to the positions of power occupied by Díaz and his fossilized cronies must have seemed very far away. Nevertheless, even as late as 1910, very few people—perhaps Díaz least of all—seemed to even imagine the possibility of a complete revolutionary overthrow in Mexico.

The course of Mexico's revolution began innocently enough with a casual but fateful remark made by Díaz in an English-language interview conducted by reporter James Creelman for *Pearson's Magazine* at Díaz's residence, Chapultepec Palace, in 1908. The interview produced a glowing portrayal of the Díaz regime, describing the great dictator as the "hero of the Americas" and "the greatest man of the continent," and emphasizing Díaz's commitment to "the democratic idea." Indeed, in the interview, Díaz expressed that he welcomed opposition candidates to run against him in the next election, and would gladly step down if defeated. To be sure, since Díaz ran virtually uncontested and still employed blatant fraud in the previous eight elections, the invitation was most likely insincere. Yet his remark drew interest from many in Mexico; most importantly, from a young man named Francisco Ignacio Madero.

As the grandson of one of the five richest men in Mexico, Madero came from a privileged background. He was foreign educated (Paris and University of California, Berkeley) and came from a wealthy northern family from Coahuila with a fortune in cattle and mining. Like many other progressive Mexican intellectuals of his generation, Madero was inspired by the liberal vision of Benito Juárez and the Reform Era, and by the democratic experiences of the United States. Yet as a man of means, Madero's initial intention was not to generate a full-scale social revolution to benefit the masses. Rather, his goal was to find a way to facilitate the transition from Díaz's oligarchic power structure into a liberal democratic system that would incorporate new elites through the application of democratic practices. His plan for this transition—which he outlined in his book *The Presidential Succession of 1910*—was for Díaz to choose someone from Mexico's young, progressive elite to serve as his running mate in the next presidential election. Ideally, that someone could learn from Díaz and pick up the reins of power once he was gone. Yet when Madero approached the president to propose himself as the vice presidential running mate, Díaz cordially but firmly declined.[7]

Frustrated but ambitious, Madero viewed Díaz's interview with Creelman as an open invitation to challenge the dictator in the upcoming election. Madero opted to run for president under the slogan: "Effective suffrage, no reelection" (*Sufragio efectivo, no reelección*): the same slogan Díaz used to run against Benito Juárez decades before. However, when Madero's campaign began to attract popular support, he was arrested by Díaz supporters in Monterrey. After Díaz won the election handily, Madero escaped from prison with the help of his supporters. Madero then issued the *Plan de San Luís Potosí*, a call to arms to overthrow the Díaz regime, and fled to the United States to prepare for the implementation of his plan.

Violent Struggle for Political Control

The Mexican revolution was a violent struggle to replace the existing political order. The impact was enormous and far-reaching, with at least a million people killed over the course of roughly a decade. Yet the start of the violent phase of the revolution was rather unimpressive. On November 20, 1910, Francisco I. Madero returned to Mexico with just ten men and 100 rifles, prepared to launch a revolution. He was supposed to meet with 400 reinforcements but found only ten more men. Rather than attack, Madero returned to the United States and traveled to New Orleans to plan a second invasion. By the time Madero returned a few months later, now with 130 armed men, he was in a better position to challenge the regime, benefiting from critical allies and other armed insurgent groups now working to overthrow the Díaz regime. Along with Madero, several of the key figures who emerged in the Mexican revolution would also go on to represent the ideals of the revolution itself.[8]

One of Madero's most important sources of support came from a man known as Francisco "Pancho" Villa. Villa emerged as a revolutionary representative of the poor and disenfranchised. Villa himself was born to a poor family on a hacienda in the north-central state of Durango, and given the name of Doroteo Arango. The details of his early life are much debated. However, it seems that Arango became a fugitive at the age of sixteen after he murdered Augustín López Negrete—the owner of the hacienda—allegedly in retaliation for his sexual advances toward Arango's sister. Arango turned to illegal activities like rustling cattle and stealing horses, evading the forces of the Díaz regime in the mountainous areas of Chihuahua. During this time Arango changed his name to Villa and acquired a reputation as a bandit and folk hero. By the age of thirty-two, Villa made the switch from bandit to revolutionary when he joined Madero in the struggle against the Díaz regime in 1910.[9] A fine sharpshooter and a superlative horseman—known by some as the Centaur of the North—Villa proved himself a bold military commander and an innovative strategist. Villa quickly became the head of Madero's forces in Chihuahua, eventually forming what became known as the Northern Division (División del Norte). Villa began collaborating with other rebel units under the command of Pascual Orozco, and their forces gradually grew from a few hundred guerrillas to thousands of seasoned troops, with large numbers of women and children in tow (see textbox 2.1).

Textbox 2.1. Mexico's *Soldaderas*: Women in Revolution

The violent upheaval from 1910 to 1917 mobilized not only men but thousands of women. Mixed in with both federal troops and the irregular forces of various revolutionary factions, these women took on versatile roles as wives, mothers, nurses, spies, arms smugglers, and even armed combatants. Many *soldaderas* fought bravely alongside the men, and some even rose to the ranks of officers. However, most women brought onto the battlefield performed less glamorous and more grueling tasks, such as cooking, cleaning, doing laundry, and burying the dead. Nevertheless, the contributions of all *soldaderas* were essential, if less well documented than they should be, in the telling of the story of the Mexican revolution.

Source: Michael C. Meyer, William L. Sherman, and Susan M. Deeds, *The Course of Mexican History* (New York: Oxford University Press, 1999), 535–37.

Also important at this early phase of the revolution were the agrarian forces that arose in southern Mexico to demand land redistribution and property rights. The predominant symbol of these social forces was Emiliano Zapata. Zapata, a small landowner and horse trainer orphaned at age sixteen, came from a small village in Morelos. Dark skinned and contemplative, Zapata spoke both Spanish and Náhuatl fluently. In character and appearance—with his excellent horsemanship, his enormous sombrero, his cigars, and his thick mustache—he conjured visions of the *charro* bandits who roamed his region. Zapata's village had appealed to the Díaz government for many years to defend their land rights from large commercial farmers. When Zapata was selected as the leader of his village in 1909, he began to use force to take back the lands that his village had lost. These land seizures were quickly followed by similar efforts in other towns and soon Zapata commanded a revolutionary army of several thousand rural fighters throughout Morelos. These guerrilla forces often attacked enemy troops and quickly resumed normal agrarian activities to avoid detection. Having an agrarian base was also a serious limitation of the Zapatistas, since they were unable to stray far from their home communities. In the end, Zapata's primary goal in participating in the revolution was to achieve land and freedom for his people.[10]

Confronted with these uprisings, as well as other separate attacks by rebels in northeast Mexico, Díaz began to realize the seriousness of the situation, which was clearly spiraling out of his control. By early 1911, his advisers warned that the strength of rebel forces in Chihuahua alone required that he amass 30,000 troops if he hoped to control the state.[11] Over the course of his administration, Díaz had cut the size of the armed forces by more than half, and now had only about 14,000 men under his command. The prospect of increasing the number of federal troops was unattractive, since arming unwilling conscripts would have simply placed more weapons into the hands of potential rebels who now enjoyed the support of some of the wealthy northern elites.

As the rebels redoubled their efforts and the conflict spread throughout the country, Díaz realized that defeating the rebels would be next to impossible. Consequently he proposed sweeping reforms in April 1911 to regain favor. However, even his purge of high-ranking officials and pledge to redistribute land merely revealed his weakness and served to embolden the rebels, who continued their assault in both the north and the south. In Chihuahua, Madero's forces began to use the regime's own infrastructure against him by seizing control of railroads as a means of deploying troops in attacks on the city of Agua Prieta. Soon after, they captured the city of Casas Grandes and moved on to lay siege to Ciudad Juárez, a critical military stronghold for Díaz. With Zapata's forces also gaining ground in Morelos, Díaz offered a truce and began negotiations with Madero. Madero initially only demanded political representation for his supporters in the government. Both Villa and Orozco, however, pressured Madero to demand Díaz's resignation, a point on which Madero halfheartedly conceded.

When they later seized control of Ciudad Juárez, Villa and Orozco were again at odds with Madero when he granted absolution to General Juan Navarro, the commander of Díaz's forces in Chihuahua, instead of executing him for atrocities committed against their men. The incident illustrated an important rift between Madero's mild, reformist intentions—and his basic acceptance of the Porfirian order, with modifications—compared to the more radical vision of those who sought a more comprehensive change. While Villa remained fiercely loyal to Madero despite this fact, other revolutionary forces would eventually turn against him. Indeed, Orozco and Zapata later disavowed Madero for his general acceptance of the existing order and his failure to press for more radical change.

In the meantime, thanks to the initial support of the insurgent forces, Madero emerged victorious. On May 17, 1911, Díaz reluctantly conceded to the terms of the Treaty of Ciudad Juárez, establishing the terms for an interim presidency and a transfer of power through national elections. On May 25, 1911, Díaz resigned as president and departed from Veracruz on a ship bound for Europe, where he would be lauded till the end of his days. Before he left, however, Díaz made the fateful observation that "Madero has unleashed a tiger, let us see if he can control him." Indeed, getting rid of Díaz was just the beginning of a long contest to achieve political control and consolidate a new regime. Even before he was elected president in a landslide election in October 1911, Madero clashed with Zapata over the issue of land rights and refused to return properties that had been taken from agrarian workers by large landowners. Hoping to assuage the concerns of those landowners whose support he needed to reestablish order, Madero sent a general named Victoriano Huerta to Morelos to disarm the Zapatistas. In response, in November 1911, Zapata issued his Plan de Ayala, demanding "land and liberty" for Mexico's rural sector and declaring Madero a traitor to the revolution.

Zapata's insurgence was soon complemented, in March 1912, by a larger, more serious challenge from Pascual Orozco. In his Plan Orozquista, Orozco called for major labor concessions (such as wage increases, a ten-hour workday, stronger child labor laws), nationalist protections (especially for railroads), local autonomy, and agrarian reform and land redistribution. Strongly in agreement with these objectives, Zapata quickly aligned himself with Orozco, whom he viewed as the rightful leader of Mexico. Together, Orozco and Zapata viewed revolution as a movement to promote greater social equality in Mexico through land, labor, and educational reform. While Villa shared this view, he nonetheless stayed loyal to Madero, whose main objectives were far less progressive. Indeed, for Madero, the real purpose of the revolution was to return to the glorious era of Mexican liberalism: reinvigorating Mexico's liberal democratic republic by strengthening the legislature and courts, fostering democratic contestation, and allowing greater freedom of the press. Madero's efforts to promote social reform—agrarian, labor, and educational reforms in particular—were extremely limited, poorly funded, and clearly not a major priority.

In a sense, Madero's failure to embrace a social reform agenda and his strong commitment to liberal democratic reform became his undoing. While Madero battled against erstwhile supporters, he was perhaps democratic to a fault toward his enemies. Indeed, political deadlock and the proliferation of opposition forces in the legislature plagued and undermined his government. Meanwhile, heckled by a newly liberated media, Madero was badly maligned and ultimately appeared to be a weak and ineffective president. In this context, Madero's apparent weakness invited two coup attempts. But rather than

execute the traitors, Madero ordered their imprisonment, enabling his detractors to conspire for a third, successful coup attempt in February 1913.[12]

In responding to these rebellions, Madero regularly called on General
Victoriano Huerta, his military chief of staff, to help defend his government.
However, during the 1913 coup attempt, Huerta seized the opportunity to
betray Madero and take power for himself. Huerta's takeover was supported
by U.S. Ambassador Henry Lane Wilson, who detested Madero and viewed
him as incompetent. Madero's alliances with forces advocating land redistribution (however limited) and the constraints he was considering on foreign
businesses (especially oil) contributed to antirevolutionary sentiments in the
United States. In Mexico, however, Huerta was seen as a usurper by other
revolutionary forces and only held Mexico City for eighteen months, from
February 1913 to July 1914.[13]

Chief among Huerta's opponents was the governor of Coahuila, Venustiano
Carranza, leader of the "Constitutionalist" forces that sought to restore order.
Carranza was a large landholder in Coahuila and had been a senator during
the Porfiriato. Carranza seems to have seen himself as a modern-day Benito
Juárez bringing justice and order. Carranza's main objective was to return to
the legal framework originally established under the 1857 constitution. With
dutiful respect to procedure, Carranza had obtained legislative approval to
rebel against Madero's usurpers. His Plan of Guadalupe denounced Huerta
and proposed himself as leader of the constitutionalist army.

Thus began roughly two years of violent struggle between opposing forces
in the revolution, in which Villa and Zapata vied for control against Carranza.
For Villa and Zapata, Carranza and his supporters represented the aspirations
of landowners, industrialists, and an ambitious middle class. In 1914, the
armies of Villa and Zapata converged on Mexico City and successfully rousted
Carranza. Villa tried to hold the city while Zapata returned to Morelos for
reinforcements. Carranza called on General Álvaro Obregón and his work-
ing-class supporters to oust Villa. Obregón retook the city in January 1915,
and pursued Villa to the north. Decisive victories by Obregón in 1915 and
1916 drove Villa into hiding. As he began to consolidate his power, Carranza
nominally embraced the Plan de Ayala, while sending General Pablo González
to pursue Zapata in the summer of 1916.

The 1917 Constitution

In 1916, the midst of the battle against Villa and Zapata, Carranza assembled
delegates in the city of Querétaro for the promulgation of a new constitution,
which was ultimately completed and approved on February 5, 1917. In accor-
dance with Carranza's objectives, the 1917 constitution was modeled after the

liberal reform constitution of 1857. Rooted in liberal democratic principles intended to ensure a representative democracy composed of elites, the 1917 constitution also stipulated the protection of basic political liberties, such as free speech (Article 6), a free press (Article 7), freedom of peaceful assembly (Article 9), religious freedom (Article 24), rights of the criminally accused (Article 20), and provisions for the division and balance of political power in government (Article 49 and subsequent articles).

Yet the 1917 constitution, which is still in effect today, also went further to include important socially progressive goals associated with more radical revolutionaries, like Orozco and Zapata. These progressive provisions included universal public education (Article 3), national ownership and redistribution of lands and natural resources like minerals and petroleum (Article 27), local autonomy (Article 115), and recognition of worker rights (Article 123). These revolutionary provisions went against Carranza's own designs and had been forced onto the agenda of the constitutional convention in Querétaro by sympathizers of Villa, Zapata, and Obregón, making it one of the most progressive founding charters ever produced. In the short run, however, the constitution of 1917 was largely symbolic because the government had neither the resources nor the will to enforce many of the new laws. The weak state of the economy made worker protections difficult to sustain. Furthermore, the interests of many elites, including Carranza, were directly opposed to some of the new constitution's main principles like land reform. After 1917, landowners regularly allied with the Church to oppose land redistribution and takeovers. Foreign landowners (who still owned a substantial portion of agricultural lands) also opposed reform.[14]

Thus the interests of those for whom the revolution had been fought—the poor, the peasants, and the workers of Mexico—were overshadowed by those of a new ruling coalition formed under Carranza. This coalition included revolutionary generals, wealthy industrialists, and turncoats from the old landed elite who declared their loyalty to the new post-Díaz regime. Meanwhile, within a few years, Carranza was able to neutralize the two major forces fighting for revolutionary social justice. Zapata was tricked and killed by Carranza's forces in 1919. Villa was driven into hiding and later retired to civilian life by 1920; he was finally murdered three years later (possibly because of a land dispute or his philandering). Over the next eight decades, both the liberal democratic and revolutionary provisions of the 1917 constitution were eroded, as vested interests and political convenience led to its frequent abrogation and amendment.

Still, by the end of his term in 1920, Carranza was unable to fully consolidate his control of the political system. In May of that year, with the evident intention of ruling from behind the scenes in the next administration, Carranza attempted to impose his successor, an obscure fellow Sonoran named Ignacio Bonillas. Obregón, who had supported Carranza against Huerta, felt slighted and issued the Plan de Agua Prieta, a proclamation urging Mexico to rebel against the president. In addition to popular support among workers, Obregón had the overwhelming support of the military, including General Plutarco Elías Calles, who helped Obregón drive Carranza from office. Carranza fled Mexico City to Veracruz, taking with him 50 million pesos from the national treasury. Ultimately Carranza did not escape. Conflicting accounts suggest that he was assassinated by one of his own guards or caught by Obregón's supporters and shot. Whichever the case, Carranza's ouster was the last successful armed uprising in Mexican history and led to a new phase of postrevolutionary consolidation in which subsequent governments maintained a monopoly on coercive force.

Postrevolutionary Consolidation

After Carranza's ouster, an interim president oversaw new elections in 1920 that brought Álvaro Obregón to the presidency (1920–1924). Hailing from Sonora, Obregón continued the Northern Dynasty of prominent strongmen from the north who dominated national politics after Díaz's fall. Because Obregón's political orientation lay somewhere between those of elite interests and those of the more progressive revolutionary forces, he was considered a dangerous conservative by some and a dangerous radical by others. During his term of office, President Obregón spent most of his efforts ensuring international recognition of the new regime and consolidating his power vis-à-vis potential rebels against the government. However, Obregón made relatively little progress in implementing the revolutionary ideals that toppled the Porfiriato. His major contribution to the revolution was his ability to restore political order and initiate the consolidation of the new regime. It was Calles, his close collaborator and successor, who would put the finishing touches on this process of regime consolidation, and lay the institutional foundations to secure the legacy of the revolution.

Álvaro Obregón and the End of Extralegal Succession

Even though Obregón received much of his support from the working classes and the Mexican Worker's Regional Confederation (Confederación Regional Obrera Mexicana, CROM) founded during his administration, his government gave few concessions to workers and even harassed communist and anarchist-led unions.[15] Obregón was also fairly conservative on land distribution; he mostly protected the interests of large landholders and was personally skeptical of the efficiency of redistributing land in small plots. Furthermore, Obregón's administration was friendly toward foreign business interests, particularly those in the United States. Though President Wilson had refused to recognize Obregón's new government after Carranza was murdered, under the administration of President Warren G. Harding (1921–1923), Obregón launched a series of prolonged negotiations that were finalized in 1923 with the Bucareli Agreement.

This pact established that the United States would recognize Obregón's government in exchange for guaranteed protections for U.S.-owned agricultural lands and concessions to foreign oil interests. Many Mexicans perceived this as a breach of revolutionary nationalism and protested loudly. However, after Obregón easily quashed a revolt by one of his generals, he preempted other possible revolts by downsizing the military and its budget by roughly 40 percent. These efforts gradually consolidated Obregón's power and established the authority of the new revolutionary government. As a result, in 1924, Obregón became the first postrevolutionary president to successfully complete a four-year term.

To ensure a peaceful transfer of power, Obregón asserted himself in the selection of his successor, backing fellow Sonoran, General Plutarco Elías Calles, as Mexico's next president. The imposition of Calles provoked an uprising by several military commanders, but with renewed support from the United States, Obregón's government put down the rebellion in a few months. The quelling of this rebellion clearly demonstrated Obregón's monopoly on coercive force and gave his government an upper hand in securing political support for the final ratification of the Bucareli Agreement. Significantly, it also established a tradition of presidential imposition in the succession process that lasted for most of the twentieth century.

Plutarco Elías Calles

For some, President Calles represented a more progressive orientation than his predecessor in that he openly proclaimed his commitment to socialism, provoked foreign oil companies with new reforms, introduced significant agrarian reforms, and invoked anticlerical provisions of the Mexican constitution. Calles also gave increased influence to the CROM, naming its leader Luis N. Morones to the cabinet post of minister of industry, commerce, and labor (a position Calles had himself occupied under Carranza). Under the Agrarian Law of 1925, Calles also implemented a more ambitious program of land redistribution than his predecessor—distributing over 3 million hectares of land, compared to the less than 1 million hectares distributed by Obregón.

In addition, as a former schoolteacher, Calles placed heavy emphasis on educational reform. Yet Calles's evident commitment to progressive revolutionary goals confronted significant opposition and obstacles. Indeed, Calles ultimately removed Morones from his cabinet due to pressure from Obregón's supporters, who still controlled the Congress. Calles also later abandoned his minor efforts at agrarian reform to deal with other pressing challenges.

One such challenge was to smooth relations with the United States, which viewed Calles's self-professed socialism with suspicion. Mexico had recognized the Soviet Union in 1923 and enjoyed very amiable relations with Moscow, thanks to the efforts of envoys such as Alexandra Kollontai (1926–1928), the first female ambassador in the Western Hemisphere. However, at the height of the Red Scare, U.S. politicians and oil interests grew increasingly concerned about Mexico's leftward drift, particularly as the Calles administration sought to restructure laws regulating foreign petroleum companies beginning in 1925. When Calles later actively opposed U.S. foreign policy in Nicaragua, Mexico and the United States actually slid dangerously close to the brink of war. These tensions were eased by an eventual shift in Soviet policy toward Mexico (due to clashes between Stalinist and Trotskyist factions), a juggling of the U.S. diplomatic corps, and a shift in Calles's own policies. For example, in order to take advantage of the booming international economy of the 1920s, Calles began investing in the necessary financial and industrial infrastructure. The establishment of new laws (e.g., income tax, banking, credit) put Mexico on a more solid economic footing and helped assuage the fears of the U.S. government and international investors because they laid the groundwork for capitalist economic expansion.

If Calles's efforts to smooth political and economic relations with the United States were considered antirevolutionary by some, his commitment to the revolutionary goal of separating church and state was unquestionable. With his approval and encouragement, various state governments enacted policies that called for government registration of priests, the prohibition of priestly garments in public, and restrictions on worship services. In response to such harassment, outraged Catholics founded the National League for the Defense of Religious Liberty (Liga Nacional de la Defensa de la Libertad Religiosa, LNDLR) with the implicit sanction of the Church. When the president called for a package of anticlerical policies—dubbed the Calles Laws—that included a suspension of church services, Catholic opposition became increasingly vocal and assertive. Tensions grew when the press reported that Archbishop José Mora y Ríos opposed the 1917 constitution, which provoked the government to close religious schools and deport 200 foreign priests and nuns. The LNDLR collaborated with Church officials to implement a nationwide boycott of businesses and government services. By late summer, however, Catholic activism boiled over into violence. Growing outrage at government restrictions and continued persecution of the clergy led to a series of uprisings in central Mexico known collectively as the Cristero rebellion (see textbox 2.2).

Textbox 2.2. The Cristero Rebellion

The Cristeros consisted mainly of devout Catholics and a few priests who engaged government forces in a violent guerrilla war between 1926 and 1928. Under the battle cry "Viva Cristo Rey" (Long live Christ the King), the Cristeros were primarily concentrated in Jalisco and the Bajío region, an agricultural zone in central Mexico that historically served as the center of mining and industry. At the peak of the Cristero rebellion, also known as the Cristiada, the religious combatants numbered as many as 50,000 irregular troops. Clashes with government forces led to as many as 70,000 deaths (including nearly 100 priests), and over half a million Mexicans were displaced in the conflict. A diaspora of Catholic activists fled to urban centers and the farthest reaches of Mexico—including Baja California and Yucatán—and the United States.

Perhaps the best remembered Cristero is Jose de León Toral, the young seminary student who assassinated Álvaro Obregón. Evidently he feared that the persecution of Catholics would continue unabated if Obregón, a close ally of the hated Calles, returned to the presidency. However, these concerns were likely misplaced. By 1928 a mediated settlement between Church and state was already under way, thanks to the intervention of the U.S. embassy and U.S. Catholics designated by the Vatican to facilitate a peaceful resolution of the conflict. The murder of the president-elect set these negotiations back for over a year and solidified in the minds of many Mexicans the notion that the Catholic Church has no place in the national political arena.

Source: Jean A. Meyer, *La Cristiada*, vol. 1. (México, D.F.: Siglo Veintiuno Editores, 1976).

Meanwhile, in the midst of this great conflict, Obregón and his supporters maneuvered to position the former president as Calles's successor. In 1926, the Obregonistas who dominated the legislature passed constitutional amendments to permit nonconsecutive reelection and increase the presidential term to a full *sexenio*, or six-year term (to become effective during the next term). In 1927, in reaction to these developments, two generals plotted to overthrow Calles and prevent Obregón's return to power. However, over the course of a brief rebellion, both men were captured and executed for treason. Obregón also survived two assassination attempts before winning the election on July 1, 1928. Two weeks later, however, Obregón was fatally shot by a twenty-six-year-old Catholic seminary student posing as a cartoonist.

Obregón's assassination presented a severe political crisis for the new regime, creating a power vacuum that needed to be filled carefully and with renewed deference to the revolutionary maxim of "effective suffrage, no reelection." Initially suspected (though quickly exonerated) of being the architect of Obregón's assassination, President Calles was under significant pressure to step down. In his presidential address on September 1, 1928, Calles called on the Congress to name an interim president for the next term, declaring himself out of the running. Moreover, Calles emphasized his renewed commitment to the principle of no reelection: "never again will an incumbent president of the Mexican Republic return to occupy the presidency." Calles argued earnestly that this was a critical juncture in Mexican history; in his words, it was an "opportunity to direct the country's politics toward a true institutional life."[16]

The *Maximato* and Birth of the Revolutionary Party

Three weeks after President-elect Obregón's assassination, the legislature selected a civilian, Emilio Portes Gil, to serve as interim president. Portes Gil was favored by many because of his commitment to socialist ideology, his public criticism of CROM corruption, and his past efforts to promote land reform in his home state of Tamaulipas. Serving for little more than a year, Portes Gil was primarily charged with the task of holding new elections in 1929. He was the first of three interim or provisional presidents over the next six years, a period that many have since described as the *maximato* because of the ongoing influence of former president Calles, who was referred to as the *jefe máximo*.

Indeed, soon after Obregón's assassination, Calles had set about creating a new political party to assemble what he called the "revolutionary family" of previously unconnected military leaders, regional political bosses (caciques), and other subnational political interests under one national umbrella. It was implicit in Calles's vision, of course, that the *jefe máximo* would be holding that umbrella to ensure Mexico's continued postrevolutionary stability and progress. However, at the time, the destiny of Calles's National Revolutionary Party (Partido Nacional Revolucionario, or PNR) was by no means certain. In the preceding decade, literally hundreds of minor political parties had vied for power at the state and national level. Since 1910, each president had run on a different party's ticket, and legislative coalitions were built more around the personal power of national and regional caudillos than around programmatic or policy agendas.[17]

The PNR was further hindered by concerns about Calles's blatant personal ambition to retain control of the organization. For this reason, the former president avoided taking a formal leadership role in the party and actually abstained from its founding convention, held in March 1929. Still, when another Calles follower, Pascual Ortiz Rubio, received the PNR's nomination for the presidency, renewed opposition and violence followed. Over the course of the next six months, ambitious military generals, Catholic zealots, and traditional liberals mobilized in opposition to the emerging regime. Each in turn failed to prevent the continued influence of Calles and, more important, the institutionalization of the PNR as a political force.[19] Meanwhile, Calles's continued influence was facilitated by the relative weakness of Ortiz Rubio, who was shot in the jaw in an assassination attempt on the day of his inauguration. As a result of this injury, which some attributed to a plot by the *jefe máximo* himself, Ortiz Rubio continued to suffer physical and mental anguish until he finally resigned prematurely in 1932.

More than halfway into the term for which Obregón was elected, it was now constitutionally possible for Congress to appoint a new interim president without holding a special election. From a list of Callista favorites, the PNR selected General Abelardo L. Rodríguez to serve in this capacity. Rodríguez's term, short as it was, laid an important foundation for the future: the no reelection clause was formally and permanently reintroduced to the constitution. This shift prompted the PNR to adopt (at its second national convention to select a presidential candidate) a plan to ensure the continuity of its programs into the next administration. In its first six-year plan, the PNR proclaimed its commitment to the subdivision and redistribution of agricultural lands, improved irrigation and access to water, and modernized agricultural methods, more effective conservation and regulation of forestry, vigorous application of federal labor laws, new protections for domestic industries to help substitute imports from abroad, investments in transportation and communications infrastructure, greater federal resources to promote health care and proper hygiene, greater public investments in education (as well as the promotion of nonreligious, socialist education in public schools), and federal involvement in the development of the country's minerals and energy policy.

This renewed emphasis on key revolutionary and even socialist objectives demonstrated a shift in the political orientation of the ruling coalition, and hinted at the coming downfall of the *jefe máximo*. In the aftermath of the revolution, the interests of agrarian and industrial workers had appeared to fall by the wayside as the Mexican economy recovered over the course of the 1920s. Indeed, by the end of that decade, fewer than four million hectares of agricultural land had been redistributed and numerous industrial and mineral holdings remained in foreign hands. This, combined with the economic downturn wrought by the Great Depression, gave revolutionary, nationalistic, and even socialist slogans fresh appeal, setting the stage for a major shift in national policy.

To be sure, under Calles and throughout the *maximato*, modest labor and land reforms were enacted, and limited attempts were made to check foreign interests in the energy sector. However, over time, Calles grew resistant to radical labor demands and skeptical of the merits of land redistribution as a means of modernizing Mexican agriculture. On the one hand, it is possible that Calles's movement away from his self-professed socialist orientation in later years was due to the growing influence of U.S. interests in Mexico. On the other hand, some historians speculate that Calles was leaning toward the ideological tenets of fascism then waxing in Europe. Whichever the case, progress toward revolutionary goals took a backseat to Calles's primary objective: personal power.[18] In this sense, Calles himself had become the biggest obstacle to what he called for in his outgoing presidential address in 1928: for Mexico to move toward being a "nation of institutions and laws." Ultimately, the influence of the *jefe máximo* would be undone by the growing pressure for progressive social reform, the institutionalization of the PNR, and one of his own followers, General Lázaro Cárdenas.

Cardenismo and Revolutionary Mexican Nationalism

By explicitly adopting the 1910 Mexican revolution in its name, the PNR symbolically embraced the hopes, themes, and heroic struggles of the Mexican revolution. However, well into the 1930s, many of the revolution's socially progressive goals remained largely unrealized. The PNR's selection of Lázaro Cárdenas as its presidential candidate in 1934 reflected three important shifts in Mexico. First, it represented a geographic shift of some significance. Unlike most previous postrevolutionary presidents, Cárdenas did not hail from the Northern Dynasty. Instead, Cárdenas came from the central state of Michoacán, and his presidency marked the beginning of a new era in which virtually all subsequent presidents would similarly come from Central Mexico.

Second, the selection of Cárdenas reflected growing support in the PNR and in Mexico for sweeping progressive reforms. As noted above, several major reforms were introduced during the *maximato* that paved the way for unprecedented agricultural, labor, and educational reforms under Cárdenas. In 1931, under Portes Gil, a new federal labor law established a minimum wage and basic workplace protections. Later, under President Rodríguez, a new agrarian code was introduced in 1934 to break up and redistribute large landed estates in the form of communal lands (*ejidos*). Yet by fully implementing these reforms, President Cárdenas ultimately became the avatar of progressive revolutionary reform and one of the most revered Mexican presidents of all time.

Third, Cárdenas's nomination illustrated the weakening of Calles and his influence in the PNR. Calles's chronic health ailments worked together with the corruption and ineffectiveness of the CROM, increased strikes and activism of independent unions, and a worsening economy to undermine the *jefe máximo's* power.[19] In this context, the PNR selected Cárdenas over two other candidates with closer ties to Calles. Born to an upper-middle-class family in Michoacán but unable to go on to high school after his father died prematurely, Cárdenas joined the revolution at the age of eighteen. He quickly rose through the ranks, making his way from first lieutenant to brigadier general in just seven years. After the revolution, Cárdenas's military career and connections to both Obregón and Calles made him eligible for political office. For most of the 1920s, however, Cárdenas remained active in the military, fighting to put down the rebellion in 1923 and deployed by Calles to protect Mexico's northern oil fields when tensions flared with foreign business interests in 1925.

Later, in 1928, Cárdenas ran as the unopposed candidate for governor of his home state of Michoacán. His gubernatorial experience offered him an opportunity to develop his own programs, political vision, and style of governance. With hindsight, three aspects of Cárdenas's approach in Michoacán stand out as particularly relevant to his future presidential administration: a commitment to agrarian reform, a skillful mobilization of support from organized labor and civic groups, and a significantly greater tolerance for the Church than Calles had.[20] Cárdenas redistributed an enormous amount of land, with many of the new landholdings organized as collective farms or *ejidos*. Michoacán was the site of assertive agrarian demonstrations in the 1920s, led by local icons such as the indigenous leader Primo Tapia, who died in the grassroots struggle for land. As governor, Cárdenas pooled the support of workers, agrarians, and teachers and intellectuals into a single union: the Revolutionary Workers Confederation of Michoacán (Confederación Revolucionaria Michoacana del Trabajo, CRMDT). Formal incorporation of interests under the CRMDT provided Cárdenas with a mass base of support and a model for the future restructuring of the official party of the revolution. As governor of Michoacán during the later years of the Cristero rebellion, Cárdenas also showed considerable tolerance toward and maintained relatively friendly relations with the local Church hierarchy.

Like other populist leaders of the 1930s, Cárdenas successfully promoted a cult of personality that brought massive support from the poor and working classes. Always inclined to travel to remote villages and hear the concerns of the people, Cárdenas eschewed the pretensions of political office and mundane affairs of state. As a result, Cárdenas's persona in Michoacán rose to nearly the same mythic status of another great figure in his home state. Four hundred years earlier, Vasco de Quiroga, a lawyer turned priest, protected local Tarascan indigenous people from the abuses of the Spanish. Quiroga empowered locals with artisan skills that persist even today in the works of craftsmen in Michoacán's Pátzcuaro region. Cárdenas's honesty, benevolent reputation, and compassion for the poor led the people of Michoacán to bestow on him the same honorific once granted to Quiroga: "Tata" (Father).[21]

Cárdenas's ambition to play a role in national politics also became evident during his term as governor, and as the PNR gradually developed more revolutionary and socialist objectives into the 1930s, Cárdenas's progressive record in Michoacán made him seem an ideal candidate for the presidency. In part because of a long, close personal relationship with the young general from Michoacán, but also because he was favored by the revolutionary family, Calles chose Cárdenas to be his successor. Cárdenas embraced his candidacy with unprecedented zeal. Despite the guarantee of victory provided by the PNR nomination, Cárdenas embarked on an ambitious and innovative nationwide campaign, visiting even remote rural areas and using radio to address the nation. Cárdenas's industrious campaign and his more progressive political orientation enabled the PNR to roundly defeat three minor leftist challengers.[22]

On taking office, Cárdenas initially deferred to the *jefe máximo*, incorporating key Callistas into his cabinet. However, as Cárdenas gave license for a significant increase in labor agitation over the first several months of his term, Calles grew visibly displeased and apt to intervene. By June 1935, Calles issued a vituperative public address, criticizing Cárdenas's inability to maintain stable economic conditions and hinting that the new president might suffer the same fate as Ortiz Rubio. Responding with a bold move against the *jefe máximo*, Cárdenas dismissed his entire cabinet (replacing them with loyalists) and sent Calles by presidential plane for a "respite" in the then sleepy western port of Mazatlán. This provided only a temporary solution. Calles returned to Mexico City in December 1935, attempting to counter Cárdenas by rallying the support of workers in the CROM. Over the next few months, minor clashes and acts of violence by Calles supporters hinted at the possibility of a coup. However, backed by thousands of workers and agrarians now mobilized under the banner of the National Committee for Proletarian Defense (Comité Nacional de Defensa Proletaria, CNDP). Cárdenas made his final move against the *jefe máximo*. In April 1936, Calles and his closest supporters were arrested and exiled to the United States.[23]

In effect, by ousting Calles, Cárdenas succeeded in transforming and reasserting the power of the Mexican presidency. The supreme authority of every sitting Mexican president would be unchallenged for the remainder of the twentieth century. However, Cárdenas's experience showed that—in order to move beyond the militant *caudillismo* of the past—effective presidential authority required a strong and coordinated power base. While Calles's PNR provided a framework for unifying regional strongmen, generals, landowners, and elites under the auspices of the revolution, the official party had failed to establish a firm basis for the support of the working class and agrarian sectors. Now unopposed, Cárdenas went to work transforming the PNR into a party that successfully harnessed these interests and more assertively promoted the goals of Mexican revolutionary nationalism.

At the December 1937 PNR convention, the party voted to dissolve and reconstitute itself as the Party of the Mexican Revolution (Partido de la Revolución Mexicana, PRM). This transformation held both emblematic and functional implications. On the one hand, the party's rechristening symbolically embraced the revolutionary and nationalistic agenda of President Cárdenas. On the other hand, the party's reconstitution provided for a specific organizational structure for the representation of key revolutionary interests. Specifically, the party was now formally divided into four sectors: military, labor, agrarian, and middle class.

The first sector comprised the roughly 60,000 members of Mexico's armed forces in a blatant blending of the official party with the coercive apparatus of the federal government. To incorporate labor, Cárdenas lent his full support to Vicente Lombardo Toledano's Mexican Workers Confederation (Confederación de Trabajadores de México, CTM) as the primary representative of labor interests within the ruling party.[24] The CTM was now rewarded with a central role in the PRM's organizational structure. At the same time, the PRM also incorporated the National Agrarian Confederation (Confederación Nacional Campesina, CNC). While Lombardo had formerly worked to unite both urban and rural workers under one union, Cárdenas supported the creation of the CNC in 1935 in part to counterbalance the growing power of the CTM. Finally, in recognition of the influence of the middle classes—particularly teachers and government bureaucrats who supported Cárdenas—the PNR incorporated a popular sector. It was loosely organized during Cárdenas's term but would later be represented by the National Confederation of Popular Organizations (Confederación Nacional de Organizaciones Populares, CNOP), formed in 1942. Ultimately the popular sector held important advantages—higher education levels, greater resources, and more effective organizational skills—relative to the CTM and CNC.

Cárdenas's model of building popular fronts to support the ruling party is an approach to coordinating interest groups in political and decision-making processes that is commonly described as corporatism. Corporatism is a top-down form of interest representation in which the government formally recognizes and incorporates organized groups in society into the policy making process, discussed further in chapter 3. Cárdenas's explicit objective was to provide for the inclusion and representation of the diverse forces that propelled the revolutionary government to power. Indeed, the restructuring of the ruling party provided Cárdenas with the political support to embark on an ambitious restructuring of government policy, living up to the expectations of PNR progressives by implementing the extensive reforms previously contemplated in its six-year plan. Two areas in particular, land reform and the nationalization of oil production, deserve special attention, and we consider them below.

Land Reform

One of Cárdenas's most profound national reforms was the reorganization of land tenure arrangements. Calles had redistributed nearly three times more land than Obregón or Carranza, and slightly more land was redistributed during each of the abbreviated terms of Portes Gil, Ortiz Rubio, and Rodríguez. However, the vast majority of lands redistributed during these postrevolutionary governments were of poor quality, and were relatively small plots intended to provide individual farmers with subsistence production to subsidize their day labor. Over the course of his presidency, Cárdenas subdivided and redistributed over 17 million hectares of land (see figure 2.1).[25]

Still, despite the far-reaching nature of land reform under Cárdenas, the initiative did not result in a long-term improvement of conditions for the rural poor because of problems with implementation and the lack of effort to maintain or improve the program beyond his administration. For example, many *ejidos* not only failed to become major producers but also declined to levels well below self-sufficiency. Hasty implementation of the land redistribution program led to miscalculations in land surveys and in the distribution of water resources for the *ejidos*. Loopholes and special provisions to protect the interests of landowners allowed many to hold on to the most valuable sections of their property, leaving the *ejiditarios* unproductive and fragmented parcels of land. Some large landowners subdivided their lands and sold them to members of their own family to avoid forced redistribution. Faced with competition from large commercial farms, collective farms were relatively inefficient: they could not benefit from scales of economy or lay off their workers.

Collective farms also suffered from a lack of access to credit and machinery, which in many cases was still controlled by the large landowners who previously owned redistributed lands. Furthermore, because *ejiditarios* were restricted by law from using their lands as collateral for private loans, they depended heavily on government support; yet this support became sparse in

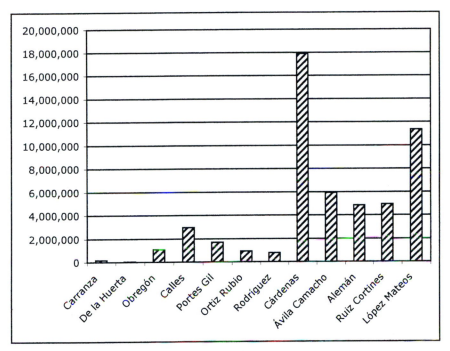

FIGURE 2.1   Land Redistribution in Mexico after 1916
Source: Data from 1916 through 1964 adapted from Figure 2.7 in Roger D. Hansen, *The Politics of Mexican Development* (Baltimore: Johns Hopkins University Press, 1971), p. 33.

the 1940s and 1950s. In contrast, government loans and investments favoring large, private commercial farms during the same period contributed to a boom in Mexican agricultural production. Although land redistribution in Mexico failed to have long-term positive effects, Cárdenas is still revered by many for his efforts to uphold the spirit of the revolution by increasing access to land.

Oil Nationalization

Cárdenas is perhaps most remembered—with admiration by many, and with contempt by others—for his nationalization of foreign-owned oil companies in 1938. Oil production in Mexico began in the 1890s, but it was not until the end of the Porfiriato that the first significant oil wells were tapped and put into operation by foreign investors. These companies had demonstrated their influence in the 1920s—as evident from the pressure on Obregón to negotiate the Bucareli Agreement—and drew significant resentment from many Mexicans. Historians note an alleged incident in which an oil company representative made a crude attempt to bribe Cárdenas when his military unit was protecting Mexico's northern oil fields. Some speculate that this incident may have left the young general with a lingering personal dislike of foreign oil interests. What is certain is that in 1937 foreign oil companies became the target of massive labor strikes protesting low wages and poor working conditions, midway through Cárdenas's term. The dispute went before a federal arbitration committee, the labor court, and eventually the Mexican Supreme Court, which ruled in favor of the workers and required foreign oil companies to abide by government terms for significantly higher wages, hiring of Mexican managers, and improved conditions for workers. The foreign companies' refusal to comply with the Supreme Court decision prompted Cárdenas to claim that they had violated Mexican sovereignty and therefore forfeited the right to operate in Mexico. Drawing on prior congressional authorization to use Article 27 to nationalize private property for public use, Cárdenas expropriated the assets held by mostly U.S. and British foreign oil companies.[26]

Worried international investors reacted sharply to Cárdenas's actions, resulting in an international boycott of Mexican goods and a significant economic downturn. However, some feared that the boycott would threaten to drive Mexico toward a closer relationship with the Axis powers of World War II. Hence, both the U.S. and British governments actively sought to normalize relations with Mexico. The Mexican government went on to establish its own oil operations under the state-owned company called Mexican Oil (Petróleos Mexicanos, PEMEX). To this day, PEMEX remains the sole oil company in Mexico, though it has increasingly become the subject of calls for privatization.

Overall, Cárdenas had a tremendous impact on contemporary Mexican politics. He succeeded in concentrating executive power in the office of the president, rather than in the personality of its occupant or some other figure lurking in the shadows. Cárdenas also gave the official party of the revolution greater legitimacy and staying power by incorporating the revolutionary masses—especially industrial and agrarian workers—within the formal sectors of its organization. Cárdenas helped to realize part of the promise of the Mexican revolution by asserting national control of key economic assets and redistributing massive amounts of land. Finally, unlike Obregón and Calles, Cárdenas withheld any further ambition to wield political power after ceding the presidency to his handpicked successor. This particular decision established a precedent followed by every Mexican president thereafter, which effectively promoted greater loyalty and obedience from future presidential aspirants and their followers. In short, by the end of the Cárdenas administration, Mexican politics had taken on most of the characteristics that predominated throughout the remainder of the twentieth century.

Conclusion: The Legacy of the Mexican Revolution

The 1910 Mexican revolution was an explosion of popular discontent with the political constraints, economic inequality, and innate repressiveness of the Díaz regime. Yet the motivations of Mexico's revolutionaries were not uniformly aligned. The course of the revolution took many turns, had different regional manifestations, and brought together an assortment of interests that were joined only by their repudiation of the ancien régime and a desire for change. While Madero and Carranza saw the revolution as an effort to restore the nineteenth-century liberal principles enshrined in the 1857 constitution, Villa, Orozco, and Zapata were not content with merely restoring the liberal status quo ante, and sought redress for long-standing socioeconomic inequalities. Taking up arms, farmers sought "land and liberty," while urban industrial workers sought basic labor protections and redress for the long-standing injustices of Mexican capitalism. Most who fought for change desired a reduction of the disproportionate privileges that foreigners had accrued in Mexico under Díaz, and some to restore the anticlerical vision of nineteenth-century masons and secular liberal reformers.

Overall, the 1910 revolution provides an important referent for understanding contemporary Mexican politics for two reasons. On the one hand, despite the bloodshed and mayhem that continued well beyond the initial uprising in 1910, the revolution provided the underpinnings for a remarkably stable political system over the remainder of the twentieth century. Perhaps the most significant factor in the consolidation of that regime was the eventual creation of a single, dominant political party that pulled together all elements of the revolutionary family. The birth of a single "revolutionary" party ensured that the methods of military rebellion, reactionary insurgency, and popular uprising never again provided a path to power in Mexico. By the same token, for seventy-one years, it would not be possible for a politician to aspire to the nation's highest political office through any other organization than the ruling party.

On the other hand, the revolution provides an important referent for contemporary Mexican politics as the country engages in a different form of regime change: a relatively peaceful transition from authoritarian to democratic politics. Even as Mexico moves away from single-party hegemony, the heroes and ideals of the revolution are still held dear by most Mexicans. The revolution provides a banner for those who seek to realize its neglected promise of social justice and the protection of national interests in an era of globalization at the beginning of the twenty-first century. In the next chapter we examine the key elements of the political system that emerged in the aftermath of the Mexican revolution. In subsequent chapters, we move on to consider how that system has been transformed in contemporary Mexican politics.

Key Terms

1917 constitution
Bucareli Agreement
Calles, Plutarco Elías
Cárdenas, Lázaro
Carranza, Venustiano
CNC
CNOP
Cristero rebellion
CROM
CTM
División del Norte
ejido
Huerta, Victoriano
land redistribution

Madero, Francisco I.
Plan de Ayala
Plan de San Luis Potosí
Maximato
Obregón, Álvaro
oil nationalization
Orozco, Pascual
PNR
PRM
Soldaderas
Sufragio efectivo, no reelección
Villa, Francisco "Pancho"
Wilson, Henry Lane
Zapata, Emiliano

Recommended Readings

Gonzales, Michael J. *The Mexican Revolution, 1910–1940.* Albuquerque: University of New Mexico Press, 2002.

Knight, Alan. *The Mexican Revolution.* Cambridge: Cambridge University Press, 1986.

Krauze, Enrique. *Mexico: Biography of Power: A History of Modern Mexico, 1810–1996.* New York: HarperPerennial, 1997.

McLynn, Frank. *Villa and Zapata: A Biography of the Mexican Revolution.* London: Jonathan Cape, 2000.

Notes

1. There are many excellent comprehensive treatments of the Mexican revolution available in English and Spanish. See, for example, Héctor Aguilar Camín and Lorenzo Meyer, *In the Shadow of the Mexican Revolution: Contemporary Mexican History, 1910–1989* (Austin: University of Texas Press, 1993); Michael J. Gonzales, *The Mexican Revolution, 1910–1940* (Albuquerque: University of New Mexico Press, 2002); John Mason Hart, *Revolutionary Mexico: The Coming and Process of the Mexican Revolution* (Berkeley: University of California Press, 1987); Alan Knight, *The Mexican Revolution* (Cambridge: Cambridge University Press, 1986).

2. Kevin J. Middlebrook, *The Paradox of Revolution: Labor, the State, and Authoritarianism in Mexico* (Baltimore: Johns Hopkins University Press, 1995).

3. Gonzales, *Mexican Revolution*, 52.

4. Hart, *Revolutionary Mexico*, 188.

5. There were as many as 750,000 slaves during the Porfiriato. Donald Clark Hodges and Daniel Ross Gandy, *Mexico: The End of the Revolution* (Westport, Conn.: Praeger, 2002), 13.

6. Luis González, "El liberalismo triunfante," in *Historía general de México,* ed. El Colegio de México (Mexico City: El Colegio de México, 2000), 696–97.

7. Enrique Krauze, *Mexico: Biography of Power: A History of Modern Mexico, 1810–1996* (New York: HarperPerennial, 1997).

8. Brian Hamnett, *A Concise History of Mexico* (Cambridge: Cambridge University Press, 1999), 178. Krauze, Mexico, 256–257.

9. Historians continue to debate many details of Villa's early life. See Friedrich Katz, *The Life and Times of Pancho Villa* (Stanford, Calif.: Stanford University Press, 1998); Frank McLynn, *Villa and Zapata: A Biography of the Mexican Revolution* (London: Jonathan Cape, 2000).

10. Pablo Moctezuma Barragán, *Vida y lucha de Emiliano Zapata: Vigencia histórica del héroe mexicano* (Mexico City: Grijalbo, 2000); John Womack, *Zapata and the Mexican Revolution* (New York: Knopf, 1969).

11. McLynn, *Villa and Zapata*, 78.

12. Peter V. N. Henderson, *Félix Díaz, the Porfirians, and the Mexican Revolution* (Lincoln: University of Nebraska Press, 1981).

13. Lowell L. Blaisdell, "Henry Lane Wilson and the Overthrow of Madero," *Southwestern Social Science Quarterly* 43 (1962): 126–35.

14. Meyer, Sherman, and Deeds, *Course of Mexican History*, 523–25.

15. José Rubén Romero, *Obregón: Aspectos de su vida* (Mexico City: Editorial Cultura, 1935). Enrique Krauze, Aurelio de los Reyes, and Margarita de Orellana, *El vértigo de la victoria: Alvaro Obregón* (Mexico City: Fondo de Cultura Económica, 1987).

16. Krauze, *Mexico*, 427.

17. Peter Calvert, *Mexico: Nation of the Modern World* (New York: Praeger, 1973).

18. So pervasive was Calles's influence during the *maximato* that although Maximilian's Castle of Chapultepec then served as the presidential residence, Calles's home in a nearby neighborhood was seen as the real seat of power. The saying went, "The president lives in Chapultepec Castle; the man who rules lives in front." Calvert, *Mexico*.

19. Calvert, *Mexico*, 264.

20. Fernando Benítez, *Lázaro Cárdenas y la Revolución Mexicana* (México: Fondo de Cultura Económica, 1977).

21. Meyer, Sherman, and Deeds, *Course of Mexican History*.

22. Cárdenas's challengers were Antonio Villareal (CRPI), Adalberto Tejada (Socialist Party), and Hernán Laborde (Communist Party). Calvert, *Mexico*, 259.

23. Calvert, *Mexico*, 259.

24. Lombardo had established the CTM in 1936 fusing formerly independent unions to challenge the crumbling CROM, with furtive backing from Cárdenas. Lombardo's orchestration of a wave of strikes from 1934 to 1936 had previously provoked the final showdown between Cárdenas and Calles. Calvert, *Mexico*, 259.

25. Figures representing the total amount of land redistributed by Mexican presidents vary depending on the source. Estimates for Cárdenas's term range from 17 million to more than 20 million acres. Calvert, *Mexico*, 259.

26. Terse intercession by the British government in March 1938 led the Cárdenas administration to authorize the wholesale nationalization of oil production in Mexico. While this decision further strained British-Mexican relations, the U.S. government opted for a more tolerant approach as part of its good neighbor policy, basically accepting Mexico's terms and encouraging U.S. oil interests to do likewise.

3

Postrevolutionary Mexican Politics, 1940–1968

From 1940 onward, Mexico held regular elections, boasted high levels of popular participation, featured a wide array of opposing political parties, and observed peaceful transfers of power from one administration to the next. Most important, unlike the Porfiriato, no one person held absolute power. Yet for most of the next several decades, few observers viewed Mexico as a democracy. Indeed, the irony of the Mexican revolution was that it ultimately produced one of the most durable authoritarian regimes of the twentieth century. Contributing to the antidemocratic character of postrevolutionary Mexico was the PRI's utilization of a classic pattern of machine-style politics. While generating genuine support from the party's clientelistic beneficiaries, the machine also restricted competition through exclusion, fraud, and even the coercive use of force. In this chapter, we explore these characteristics of postrevolutionary authoritarianism in Mexico, with special attention to the institutions and practices that held this system in place for more than sixty years. The discussion will illustrate how the PRI's favored institutions and tactics eventually undermined its own legitimacy and set the stage for Mexico's transition to democracy during the latter part of the twentieth century.

Understanding Postrevolutionary Mexican Authoritarianism

Mexico's postrevolutionary political system defied easy classification. It had many of the characteristics of authoritarianism, a political system in which the government derives power through force and coercion. Yet at the same time, Mexican politics also bore the trappings of a democratic political system, in which the government relies on a system of popular participation, political contestation, and representation. As a result, for much of its modern history, political scientists tended to describe Mexico alternately as either a semiauthoritarian regime or a restricted democracy.[1]

Many feel that Peruvian novelist Mario Vargas Llosa said it best when he referred to Mexico's unique political arrangement as the "perfect dictatorship."[2] The postrevolutionary Mexican political system was characterized by severely restricted competition and occasional instances of violent repression. Yet, it was not like other authoritarian regimes. Mexico's revolutionary party held regular elections and relied more on a sophisticated system of cooptation than on the use of coercive force. During a period in which many other Latin American countries fell into military dictatorships—from the 1940s to the 1970s—the Mexican military was notably absent from government and the country's political system appeared relatively stable and even somewhat democratic. Perhaps most important, the regime genuinely enjoyed widespread popular support and achieved important accomplishments in terms of economic performance and the redistribution of wealth. Hence, despite the undemocratic features of the PRI system or "regime," political scientists were reluctant to refer to Mexican politics as authoritarian.[3]

Still, Mexico hardly resembled other democratic political systems and was an enigma for political observers, who viewed it as a democracy with adjectives: an "electoral autocracy," a *democradura,* or (at best) an "emerging democracy."[4] By the 1940s, the ruling party had reorganized itself as the Institutional Revolutionary Party (PRI), which remained the sole party of government for decades to come. Since Mexican elections were anything but "free and fair," PRI candidates for public office almost always won. Not only did they benefit from the partisan support of the media and government resources to buy popular support, but also from fraudulently manipulated election results. Moreover, the PRI's total dominance of all branches and levels of government led to widespread corruption and abuse of power. In the worst cases, when opponents could not be bested or coopted by the system, they were harassed, disappeared, or even killed. While these occurrences were rare, such a system could hardly be labeled as democratic, and—without opportunities for genuine political participation and contestation—appeared to have little prospect of changing. Even as late as 1999, a satirical film about Mexican politics was initially banned because of its critical depictions of the ruling party (see textbox 3.1).

Textbox 3.1. Herod's Law

Written and directed by Luis Estrada, the award-winning film *La Ley de Herodes* (Herod's Law) is a dark political satire set in Mexico in 1949, during the administration of President Miguel Alemán. In the role of Juan Vargas, Mexican actor Damián Alcázar plays an innocent, good-natured junkyard operator who is tapped by his friend Ramírez, a midlevel bureaucrat from the ruling party, to serve as the interim replacement for a corrupt mayor (*presidente municipal*) who was driven out of office. Vargas and his wife Gloria are deeply appreciative of the opportunity and head off to the small indigenous town of San Pedro de los Saguaros. Vargas's initial efforts to play politics on the straight and narrow lead only to disappointment. On the advice of Ramírez's boss, the minister of the interior (Secretario de Gobierno), Vargas gradually comes to understand the crass reality of Mexican politics, which he calls Herod's Law: "screw or be screwed." The film's theatrical release in 1999 was initially prohibited by the Mexican government due to its references to systemic corruption and political assassination. However, filmmakers and the press successfully pressured the government to release the movie, making accusations of political censorship. The film provides a useful, if controversial allegory for thinking about Mexican politics during the classic period of PRI rule.

Remarkably, this political system kept its predominant features over many years. For most of the twentieth century the classic features of Mexico's postrevolutionary system were single-party hegemony, a virtual fusion of party and government, the centralization of power, restricted political opposition, and occasional instances of repression. Moreover, the political system presided over by the PRI appeared so steady and enduring that some observers referred to it as a "living museum."[5] Today, of course, hindsight tells us that the classic PRI political system was not so impervious to change. Indeed, Mexican politics began to undergo a significant transition toward democracy in the latter part of the twentieth century. By the year 2000, the stable, semiauthoritarian political system that grew out of the Mexican revolution was replaced by a system that was significantly more democratic but much less predictable.

To understand Mexico's longer-term transformation over the past few decades, it is essential to have a clear grasp of the dynamics of postrevolutionary authoritarianism in Mexico. One thing that is key to understanding the circumstances of postrevolutionary Mexico is the tremendous challenge of consolidating power after a major violent upheaval. As we saw in chapter 2, reconstructing and establishing control over the state apparatus after 1910 took more than a decade. The massive mobilization of the population required Mexico's leaders to create institutions that would facilitate power sharing and decision making across the diverse sectors and interests mobilized by the revolution. Moreover, like other postrevolutionary societies in the twentieth century, Mexico found unity and long-term stability in the creation of a single, institutionalized political party. We therefore begin our exploration of Mexico's postrevolutionary system with an examination of the role of the Institutional Revolutionary Party.

PRI Hegemony in Elections and Government

As discussed earlier, the National Revolutionary Party (Partido Nacional Revolucionario, PNR) was originally founded in 1929 by Plutarco Elías Calles as a means to harness (and to promote national unity among) the forces unleashed by the revolution. The PNR was dissolved in December 1937 and later reorganized as the Party of the Mexican Revolution (Partido de la Revolución Mexicano, PRM), reflecting the desire of President Lázaro Cárdenas to empower the revolution's neglected labor and agrarian sectors. Cárdenas's successor, Manuel Ávila Camacho (1940–1946), introduced further changes to the ruling party and thereby established the enduring elements of Mexico's postrevolutionary system for the remainder of the twentieth century.

Its symbolic status as the champion of the revolution contributed to the ruling party's genuine popularity among many Mexican voters. The "party of the revolution" bore an intrinsic connection to the founding event and mythology of the Mexican political system, and to revolutionary heroes like Villa and Zapata; as such, the ruling party appealed to many voters' nationalist sentiments.[6] Indeed, the ruling party ultimately took explicit advantage of this connection by adopting the colors of the Mexican flag as its own (sometimes confusing illiterate voters who could be persuaded to simply vote for "Mexico"). Moreover, the fact that the PRI presided over a prolonged period of sustained economic growth during most of the mid-twentieth century provided a substantial degree of "performance legitimacy." Hence, although the PRI's advocacy of revolutionary goals often tended to be merely rhetorical, the widespread support of the PRI should not be underestimated.

However, the ruling party's long-term monopoly on power in Mexico was not just symbolic nor merely the result of a slavish, uneducated electorate. Rather, the dominance of the revolutionary party was the result of a sophisticated system of institutional arrangements and incentives. While several elements of this system were already in place by the beginning of the 1940s, two important changes took place in 1946 that solidified the ruling party and ensured its dominant position in Mexican politics for the remainder of the twentieth century. The first was the creation of the Federal Electoral Law, which established the mechanisms of electoral control that ensured the party's monopoly on power. The second was the reorganization of the ruling party, which completed its evolution as Mexico's dominant political force. Below we examine these major developments, how they contributed to the institutionalization of the ruling party, and the functioning of the PRI's classic postrevolutionary system.

The Institutionalization of the Ruling Party

The long-term hegemony of the ruling party over all other rivals was in part guaranteed by the centralization of control over federal electoral procedures. Specifically, the passage of the Federal Electoral Law of 1946 placed the regulation of elections for the president and all federal legislators under the control of the secretary of the interior (Gobernación). Prior to this reform, state governments were responsible for regulating and tabulating elections, as has been historically the case in the United States. With the 1946 electoral reform, however, Mexico's electoral system now became more centralized, since one of the president's most important cabinet ministries was now the authority responsible for registering political parties, overseeing campaigns, and reporting electoral results. This gave significant advantages to the ruling party, and also greatly affected the structure of power relationships in Mexico, since the sitting president could effectively modify electoral regulations, prohibit the registration of certain political parties, and ultimately control electoral outcomes.[7]

In effect, the Federal Electoral Law enabled the ruling party to establish itself as a nationwide political machine with an automatic or machine-like ability to consistently place its candidates in public office and exercise control over the government. Like political machines elsewhere around the world, including the U.S. political machines of the early- and mid- twentieth century, the power of Mexico's ruling party was derived in large part from its control over the electoral process. Indeed, postrevolutionary governments frequently resorted to fixing electoral contests through a variety of techniques of fraud, such as having voters return to vote multiple times at the same polling place ("carousel" or "merry-go-round" voting), stuffing ballot boxes with folded wads of ballots known as "vote tacos" (*tacos de votos*), adding false names to voter rolls (e.g., Cantinflas or Mickey Mouse), bringing prestuffed or "pregnant" ballot boxes (*urnas embarazadas*) to the polls, or simply manipulating official figures.[8] Because the party's representatives in government controlled the electoral process, there were no legal means to challenge these practices. Hence, the 1946 Federal Electoral Law provided a political instrument to ensure the ruling party's lasting monopoly on power.

The 1946 Federal Electoral Law also had an important impact on the structure of power arrangements within the ruling party. In particular, the centralization of electoral control at the national level significantly empowered federal authorities vis-à-vis state and local officials, who might otherwise have used their control over local elections to build their own, state-level bases of power, as was the case in the United States during the era of machine politics. Instead, in Mexico's postrevolutionary context, machine politics was projected to the national level. Moreover, placing the electoral process under the supervision of the president ensured that political control was not only centralized at the national level, but within the executive branch. Would-be federal legislators and even the president's successor depended on the favor of the sitting president. Indeed, as we discuss below in more detail, the organizational structure of the PRI created a hierarchical chain of relationships and loyalties that helped to ensure a high degree of party loyalty and predictability.

PRI Organizational Structures

In addition to centralizing Mexico's electoral laws, another major development in 1946 occurred when the ruling party underwent a second major reorganization. That year, President Manuel Ávila Camacho was preparing to transfer power to his handpicked successor, then–interior secretary Miguel Alemán Valdés. The ruling party's rebirth as the Institutionalized Revolutionary Party (Partido Revolucionario Institucional, PRI) constituted an emblematic and lasting transformation. The ruling party's new moniker neatly encapsulated both its role as the champion of the revolution and the paradoxical consolidation of a permanent revolution. Moreover, so institutionalized was the ruling party that it would maintain its lock on power and its basic organizational structure for the next half century. On paper, the PRI had a national, state, and local committee structure, formally elected party leaders and appointed officers, as well as established internal democratic procedures for determining its candidates and platforms. In practice, the PRI was a political machine with highly centralized and autocratic features whose survival depended on its symbiotic relationship with the government.

Ávila Camacho's reorganization of the party also had the important effect of demilitarizing the ruling party, which highlighted some of the tensions that had developed in his own election in 1940. Ávila Camacho, Mexico's last president with military experience, had seen very little combat in the revolution, and therefore lacked the military cast of the presidents immediately preceding his candidacy.[9] In the 1940 election, he faced conservative General Juan Andreu Almazán, who broke from the ruling party out of objection to the policies of Lázaro Cárdenas and what he perceived to be a lack of adequate representation of military interests within the ruling party. Though the election was heavily contested and exhibited indications of fraud, Ávila Camacho was named the victor. In the aftermath, Ávila Camacho worked deliberately to diminish the influence of the military and make way for a new breed of civilian political leadership.[10]

In place of the military sector, a new "popular sector" was formed to represent Mexico's middle class, professionals, and government bureaucrats. While Cárdenas had informally integrated such sectors beginning in 1938, in 1943 they were formally incorporated into the PRI's structure through the creation of the National Confederation of Popular Organizations (Confederación Nacional de Organizaciones Populares, CNOP). (See textbox 3.2.) Hence, with the reorganization of 1946, the ruling party now consisted of three formally recognized sectors: a labor sector most prominently represented by the CTM, an agrarian sector represented by the CNC, and a popular sector represented by the CNOP. The relative size of these three sectors could be estimated by their representation among the PRI's federal deputies, with the agrarian sector holding the largest share of seats until the 1960s. The labor and agrarian sectors were well rewarded for their organizational muscle—their capacity to mobilize large groups to support the ruling party at campaign rallies and on election day. Gradually, however, the popular sector proved an especially important source of leadership and political mobilization for the PRI, supplanting the agrarian sector and serving as the brains of the ruling party.[11]

Textbox 3.2. Corporatism

Corporatism is a system in which there is formal and structured incorporation of key interest groups into government decision-making processes. The term "corporatism" comes from the Latin word for "the body," or *corpus*, and refers to the incorporation of separate units as part of an integrated system. The concept of corporatism was first developed within the Catholic Church as a way of coordinating civic groups and unions that were not formally part of the ecclesiastical body of the Church. Corporatist practices were later applied to politics in Europe and Latin America in the mid-twentieth century, when many governments incorporated highly mobilized popular sectors in Italy (Fascism), Germany (Nazism), and Argentina (Peronism). While these earlier forms of corporatism had authoritarian tendencies, contemporary corporatist arrangements or "neocorporatism"—as in Sweden, Norway, and the Netherlands—provide for formal and structured negotiations between democratic governments and key interest groups as a means of facilitating consensus in political decision-making.

In most corporatist arrangements, the government often plays a significant role in the formation of associations and interest groups that are formally "incorporated" within the system. In effect, the government therefore determines which interest groups will have a "seat at the table." Thus, in a corporatist system, interests not formally incorporated or officially recognized may be ignored and may even face harassment or discrimination because they compete with "official" interest groups. In contrast, "pluralism" is an alternative model in which autonomously formed and sometimes inchoate interests (e.g., the National Rifle Association in the United States, Sierra Club, chambers of commerce, etc.) vie for influence on governmental decisions, often with varying degrees of success. That is, in a pluralist system, a group's influence on government tends to be determined by its financial clout or other factors, such as the effectiveness of its lobbying efforts.

In addition to its corporatist features, the PRI's organization relied on a complex structure of hierarchical relationships of political exchange among individuals, frequently described as clientelism. Clientelism refers to an arrangement in which individuals with access to power serve as the patrons—or providers of material benefits and services—to a certain set of constituents, or clients, in exchange for their allegiance and support (see textbox 3.3). In effect, the PRI consisted of a clientelistic power structure of personal relationships that extended through the federal, state, and local levels, from the highest levels of the political arena to everyday citizens. Within that system, a politician's prospects for advancing his own career depended on his connections to and ability to win the favor of higher-ranking politicians. That politician used his access to power to bestow political favors to his most loyal and trusted subordinates, who in turn worked to help that politician advance his goals and mobilize political support, often by drawing on their own network of clients.[12]

A politician's networks with his supporters therefore often reflected long-standing personal relationships accumulated over years of loyalty, trust, and close interaction. Thus transferring political loyalties from one faction to another was rare, and likely to be viewed with suspicion. The networks of personal influence that developed around individual personalities were referred to as *camarillas*, and the more elevated a politician's position became in the PRI hierarchy, the greater the benefits and the support that he could generate for his own *camarilla*.[13] Meanwhile, at lower levels, individuals who failed to advance through the ranks did their best to make lateral moves, sometimes recycling and alternating their positions.[14]

At the bottom of this chain of influence, of course, were individual voters (especially poor urban and rural voters in dire need of assistance) to whom the meager benefits of preferential access might include a sandwich *(torta)* or a T-shirt for showing up to vote, or a chance to resolve an administrative matter through their connections in the ruling party. Yet even such ordinary citizens demonstrated remarkable loyalty and support for the PRI. Given the PRI's proclivity to electoral fraud and given that voter support was often contingent on a system of tangible rewards and punishments, it is of course difficult to determine whether political support for the PRI was legitimate. What is clear is that, for the better part of the twentieth century, large numbers of Mexicans regularly backed the PRI at the ballot box, in opinion polls, and in other public demonstrations of support.[15]

Textbox 3.3. Clientelism

Clientelism is a system in which certain types of goods or favors are exchanged between an individual with access to power and his supporters. The types of benefits bestowed by a "patron" to his "clients" may include tangible material benefits (such as a job, supplies, food, or small gifts) or simply preferential access to certain types of services (such as issuance of public permits, the resolution of fines, or even basic sanitation). The types of support offered by a client may include public demonstrations of support (such as attending a campaign event) or simply showing up to vote for one's patron on election day. Finally, because clientelist systems often depend heavily on long-term, personal relationships and norms of deference, some of the benefits exchanged can be purely symbolic, such as a visit by the patron or the client to the wedding of a family member. Naturally, the more valuable the support rendered by the client, the greater the potential rewards a patron may offer. The concept of clientelism need not be restricted to the political arena, since patron-client relationships are often observed within social organizations, organized crime syndicates, and even in certain professions (not academia, of course). Indeed, the opening scene of *The Godfather* portrays a classic example of clientelism as Vito Corleone offers a favor to Amerigo Bonasera, a humble mortician who asks for his intervention to solve a delicate problem. The Godfather agrees, but notes that "someday, and that day may never come, I may call on you to return the favor." Such patron-client relationships are often employed to determine "who gets what, and how" in politics. However, in the political arena, clientelism has a negative connotation because it frequently results in the unequal distribution of public goods—resources or services that are relatively equally accessible to all members of society, such as access to clean air, public education, and national security. In contrast, a patron-client system provides some individuals with preferential access to government jobs, services, and other benefits. Individuals who do not support the patron can be deprived of these benefits; hence they are no longer "public goods." Some political observers have noted that a system of preferential access can have certain benefits, particularly for otherwise excludable minorities. For example, in the United States, the clientelistic political machines of New York and Chicago provided Irish and other minorities with access to government jobs and resources. However, modern democracies strive toward a system that does not privilege one group over another, but instead reserves public goods for the overall benefit of society.

Party Discipline, Power Sharing, and Ideological Flexibility

Given Mexico's particular institutional context and the prevalence of clientelistic relationships, it is not surprising that there was a very high degree of party discipline within the PRI. The pressure to demonstrate one's loyalty to the party—for example, by supporting the PRI's candidates, official decisions, and legislation—was especially acute because of Mexico's constitutional prohibitions on immediate reelection. Mexico's virtually sacred commitment to the principle of no reelection ensured a high degree of turnover (and a low degree of continuity) in public administration. That is, from one administration to the next, incoming presidents, governors, and mayors would redistribute the spoils of public office—political appointments, bureaucratic positions, and government staff jobs—to their own networks of clientelistic supporters. Thus, at the end of one's term in office, the only hope for career advancement in the next administration was to have the favor of other politicians at higher levels in the party hierarchy. A powerful patron could guarantee an appointment to a new, higher-ranking post, or could influence the party officials with the formal authority over nominations for elected office. Hence in many cases, a politician's merit and ability mattered less for his career advancement than his personal connections and fealty to the system.[16]

One natural result of the consistent maneuvering by PRI politicians vying for power was a significant degree of factionalism and internal competition within the ruling party. Indeed, as in other systems where a single party dominated the political system, different *camarillas* within the PRI necessarily competed for influence within a given administration, or from one administration to the next.[17] Hence the PRI's longevity as a political party depended in part on its ability to minimize the volatility of this competition, and to ensure a certain degree of power sharing within and across different government administrations.

Meanwhile, although PRI factions were highly personalistic, they also frequently represented a wide array of ideological currents. A certain degree of ideological tolerance within the PRI facilitated the expression of these diverse perspectives, and frequently muddled the differences between left and right in Mexico. At the same time, the PRI's broadly inclusive organization and its ability to facilitate power sharing among divergent factions gave the party important advantages vis-à-vis potential competitors by incorporating diverse sectors of society and therefore leaving little ideological space for the opposition to organize around. When outside opposition did arise, the PRI's wide range of political currents also enabled it to shift political positions in order to draw support away from potential opponents. In fact, some observers have noted that, as different factions within the PRI alternated power across different administrations, they tended to move gradually from one end of the political spectrum to another, creating a pendulum that oscillated between left and right. While the PRI began as fundamentally leftist under Lázaro Cárdenas, the party swung to the right under his successor, Manuel Ávila Camacho, who then moved the pendulum toward the center by taking a more favorable position toward the United States than Cárdenas, and greatly appeasing business interests alienated by his predecessor. His successor, Miguel Alemán (1946–1952), implemented right-wing policies that were even more favorable to private capital and industry, strongly opposed to communism, and severely repressive toward labor activists.[18] Partly in response to the reactionary nature of Alemán's government, the PRI shifted moderately to the left during the 1950s and early 1960s, under Presidents Adolfo Ruiz Cortines (1952–1958) and Adolfo López Mateos (1958–1964).[19]

It may be too simple to suggest that there was a conscious PRI political strategy to keep power by continually shifting its ideological orientation. However, in hindsight it is clear that whatever the PRI's symbolic references to revolutionary rhetoric, the party's ideology was quite flexible. Mexican presidents were free to adopt their own ideological positions, and as we shall see in the next chapter, the actions of outgoing presidents very often made it necessary for incoming presidents to adopt positions that directly contradicted those of their predecessors.

In short, by the 1940s, Mexico's ruling party acquired the basic organizational characteristics and political advantages that ensured its hegemonic position in the Mexican political system for the remainder of the twentieth century. As the official party of the revolution, the explicit connection between the party and the postrevolutionary government, which some scholars have described as a kind of "PRI-government symbiosis," provided the ruling party with tremendous political advantages.[20] Through a sophisticated system of favors and influence, government officials maintained close connections with and depended on the support of the PRI's organizational apparatus, which in turn relied heavily on government resources to help sustain the party's clientelistic networks. Its success as a political machine was derived from its effective control over the electoral process, a highly centralized and disciplined political hierarchy, the formal incorporation of key sectors of society, and a degree of ideological flexibility that gave the party the ability to adapt to changing political circumstances. Access to government resources and services provided a means of obtaining political support from the public, and PRI government officials were able to offer their endorsement and resources to the party's candidates for public office. Thus, rather than serving as an agent of political interests in society (as in many democratic countries), in its relationship with society the PRI served primarily as a mechanism for generating political support for the government.

Centralization of Power

Mexico's postrevolutionary political system today comprises thirty-one state governments, a federal district, and over 2,400 municipal governments. At the federal, state, and municipal level, power is divided among the executive, legislative, and judicial branches of government. Yet despite all of these structural characteristics, political authority in Mexico has traditionally been highly centralized (see textbox 3.4). Indeed, for most of its history, all roads led metaphorically to Mexico City, where political decisions were made, governmental resources were concentrated, and from whence the better part of Mexico's ruling elite emanated. As elsewhere in Latin America, most Mexican presidents dominated the legislature and judiciary to such an extent that there were few real checks and balances across branches of government. Moreover, Mexican presidents had the de facto ability to influence the selection of gubernatorial candidates (and replace sitting governors practically at will), giving presidents considerable influence over subnational affairs as well.[21]

Textbox 3.4. Centralization and Decentralization

Organizational systems are often described as "centralized" or "decentralized." What do these terms mean? In a centralized system decision making and policy implementation are concentrated in an entity at high levels within the system or concentrated in one particular entity or division of the system. By contrast, in a decentralized system greater decision making and authority are granted at lower levels of administration or shared more equally across different branches of an organization. Within systems of governance there is often horizontal power sharing across different branches of government, or vertical distribution of resources and authority among the national, state or regional, and local governments.

While partly a continuation of Mexico's "centralist tradition" stretching back to the colonial era, the concentration of power in the postrevolutionary system exhibited particular features. Indeed, political centralization under the PRI was far more institutionalized than during the Porfiriato. As noted in chapter 1, Porfirio Díaz had relied on an extensive personal network of his own cronies to administer other branches and levels of government. While personal ties were still important under the PRI, its corporatist structures provided an institutional context for sustaining relationships and systems of clientelistic exchange that extended beyond and outlived most individual personalities. The key point of difference in the postrevolutionary system had to do with identifiable institutional factors—more than personal ties—that contributed to the power of the Mexican presidency. Specifically, the prohibition of reelection, combined with the total hegemony of the ruling party, concentrated authority in the *office* of the presidency—rather than in the personality in office—and ensured a relatively high degree of elite circulation.[22] Because no one individual or group could easily monopolize power beyond a single six-year term, control of the presidency offered that person a one-shot grab at the privileges and spoils of office for his supporters (and a lifetime of luxury for himself). At the same time, the no reelection rule contributed to a high degree of centralization because ineligibility of governors and legislators for reelection made them heavily dependent on the sitting president and ranking party leaders for future political mobility.[23]

Indeed, in a context without reelection, executive control of the electoral process was critical in enhancing the president's powers, since it gave him complete control over the selection of his party's candidate. In effect, the president handpicked his own successor in a ritual known as the *dedazo* or "finger tap." The *dedazo* was the president's most important means of assuring party loyalty within the party, and therefore his vast power during his six-year term or *sexenio*. Until a successor was named, high-ranking PRI politicians attempted to maintain the favor of the president in the hope that they or the head of their *camarilla* or faction would benefit from the ultimate prize: the presidency itself. Once a successor was identified—through the *destape* or unveiling of the president's preferred candidate—political loyalties naturally gravitated to the man who would become the ultimate authority in the PRI system for the next six years.[24]

Thus, during most of his term, the influence of the sitting president was paramount, extended downward throughout the political system, and was reinforced by the centralization of administrative controls and fiscal revenues in Mexico. The Mexican president had extraordinary control over the federal bureaucracy, including key coercive agencies of the government, such as the military and the intelligence service. The latter agencies answered directly or indirectly to the secretary of the interior, often seen as the president's enforcer and a likely candidate for presidential succession. Indeed, of the thirteen presidents elected from the ruling party from 1928 to 2000, eight were former interior secretaries and only one, Francisco Labastida in 2000, failed in his attempt to be elected. Because they enjoyed the president's trust and because they were likely to succeed him, Mexico's interior secretaries traditionally exercised significant power and few were willing to defy them.

In effect, as we discuss further in chapter 5, Mexico's postrevolutionary political arrangements—and the dominance of a single, hierarchical dominant party—meant that the president's authority was virtually absolute and that the institutional separation of powers that theoretically permits the checks and balances of a federal system to function was practically nonexistent in Mexico.[25] The president's ability to command the allegiance of other politicians and to exercise absolute control over the federal bureaucracy made the executive branch dominant over both the Mexican Congress and the federal judiciary. In effect, the PRI's virtual monopoly in the Congress made legislators a mere rubber stamp for executive legislation, budgetary approval, and even constitutional amendments. Indeed, from 1917 to the fall of the PRI in 2000, the Mexican constitution was amended over 400 times. Meanwhile, the federal judiciary comprised PRI appointees who had little inclination to challenge the president or the Congress. Under the PRI, the federal judiciary lacked a significant budget, and the judiciary's ability to apply judicial review to government actions or legislation was essentially limited to use of the *amparo* (an injunction or waiver from government actions or statutes that adversely affect an individual's constitutional rights). In short, neither the legislative nor the judicial branches of government provided any real check on executive power.[26] The exaggerated powers of postrevolutionary Mexican presidents have been described by Garrido (1989) as meta-constitutional and even anticonstitutional because they greatly exceeded those formally ascribed by the constitution.[27]

Opposition, Cooptation, and Repression

As noted above, the PRI was one of the world's strongest, most extensive political machines and held power longer than any other political party during the twentieth century. One secret of the PRI's success was the fact that—despite its undemocratic tendencies and significant abuses of power—the party enjoyed a remarkable degree of public support, thanks to its strategies for popular incorporation, its use of power sharing among divergent interests, and its appeal to revolutionary themes. For decades the PRI was the choice of millions of Mexicans, who appreciated the stability it provided and believed in the promise that it offered for a better future.[28] Still, as noted above, the reality of the PRI system was that its ability to rely on fraud and repression to maintain its political monopoly diminished the overall legitimacy of the system. Moreover, there were significant sources of opposition to the PRI throughout most of its existence, both in the electorate and in society.

The PRI's approach to managing the political opposition relied on both cooptation and coercion: carrots and sticks. Indeed, many believe that the cornerstone of the PRI's dominance was its ability to achieve a careful balance between persuasive and repressive tactics. Examining the PRI's approach to managing political opposition therefore provides insights into its long-term survival. However, as we discuss below, over the years the cumulative effect of PRI coercion—including a number of particularly severe instances of violent repression—contributed to the unraveling of Mexico's perfect dictatorship. Below, we discuss the sources of political opposition in the PRI regime, as well as the strategies the ruling party alternately employed to coopt or coerce its opponents. During the classic period of PRI dominance, these organizations' relatively small followings, meager resources, and lack of experience meant that they were unlikely to wrest power away from the behemoth. Moreover, they were prevented from gaining a meaningful foothold in the political arena by the patently unfair system of rules set up by the ruling party. This discussion gives us further insights into the sources of PRI power and Mexico's gradual transition to democracy.

Political Opposition

There were effectively three main sources of opposition in the classic Mexican political system. First was the National Action Party (Partido Acción Nacional, PAN). The PAN was founded in 1939, exactly ten years after the birth of the ruling party. The founders of the PAN came from different elements of conservative opposition to the new regime. First, the PAN attracted educated upper-middle-class professionals who, like the U.S. progressive reformers of the early nineteenth century, were averse to the corruption and ineffective government service produced by machine politics. Second, the PAN attracted Catholics who initially reacted negatively to the anticlericism of Calles, and later to the socialist tendencies of Lázaro Cárdenas. Social and religious conservatives were especially incensed by Cárdenas's claims that he would socialize education in Mexico. Last but not least, the PAN initially attracted wealthy business interests that were alarmed and angered by the expropriation of properties and the loss of foreign capital during the Cárdenas administration. The PAN was by far the strongest opposition party in Mexico; however, it never came close to challenging the PRI's electoral dominance until the end of the century.[29]

A second source of opposition was the seemingly endless array of minor parties. Beginning in the 1960s, electoral rules allowed for a limited form of proportional representation and led to the creation of minor parties, also known as "third parties." This helped to create an appearance of democratic competition. Yet because these parties had no real chance of winning, their existence simply fractionalized the Mexican party system. In some cases, they were described as parastatal parties because they were actually created or supported by the PRI in order to mollify or supplant real opposition groups. One classic example was the Authentic Party of the Mexican Revolution (Partido Auténtico de la Revolución Mexicana, PARM), which was created in the 1950s by disgruntled PRI members who split from the ruling party. While the PARM ran its own candidates for legislative and lower offices, it consistently supported the PRI's presidential candidates from its founding until the late 1980s. The PARM also served as an unwavering legislative ally of the ruling party, and may have even received direct financial assistance from the PRI. In general, parastatal parties and other third parties illustrated the way the PRI was able to neutralize opposition at the height of its power either by marginalizing or buying off its political opponents.

Finally, there were a number of unrecognized or even illegal sources of opposition. These were parties or groups that were excluded from power and considered illegal by the PRI government. The most notable illegal source of opposition was the Mexican Communist Party (Partido Comunista Mexicano, PCM), which was outlawed by the PRI's conservative governments of the 1940s and 1950s. However, there were a number of other important social movements and insurgent groups—including splinter movements from the ruling party—that formed in opposition to the political system. Long before Mexico's most famous insurgent group, the National Zapatista Liberation Front (Ejercito Zapatista de Liberación Nacional, EZLN) came into public view in 1994, small groups of irregular armies and guerrilla insurgents engaged in military campaigns against the government. In the 1960s and 1970s, homegrown, armed leftist movements like the student-run September 23 movement, the Clandestine Revolutionary Workers Party-Union of the People (Partido Revolucionario Obrero Clandestino-Unión del Pueblo, PROCUP), and the Popular Revolutionary Army (Ejercito Popular Revolucinario, EPR) fought to provoke what they viewed as true revolutionary change in Mexico.[30] However, while such organizations occasionally caused significant damage and loss of life through organized attacks and bombings against businesses and government facilities, Mexican insurgent groups were generally ephemeral, largely unsuccessful, and therefore of little threat to the overall political order during PRI rule.[31]

Political Cooptation

One of the major reasons why the PRI was so successful at retaining power was its ability to use cooptation to manipulate or reduce opposition to and within the PRI regime. Cooptation involves the use of persuasion or concessions to win over potential adversaries. Groups or individuals are often said to have been coopted when they receive tangible benefits in exchange for some form of tacit or explicit concession on their part. In Mexico, cooptation took a variety of forms during the PRI's hegemony. For example, party leaders often awarded political opponents within the PRI with important political and bureaucratic posts; in exchange the internal opposition might offer its support or simply refrain from an outward challenge against the party. It was also common for the government to grant concessions to critics outside the regime. In such instances, the demands of the interest group, political party, or neighborhood might be partially met (e.g., with a subsidy or government contract, greater revenue or representation, or a public works project, respectively), with the understanding that this was as far as the government was willing to go.

On the whole, cooptation worked well for the PRI, and there is little doubt that its ability to coopt would-be critics and opponents contributed to single-party dominance, since it allowed the PRI to neutralize almost all but its most ardent detractors. Yet as opportunistic and undemocratic as it was to essentially buy off opponents, the PRI's widespread use of cooptation contributed in some measure to the party's inclusiveness. Indeed, it can be argued that this was another way of making the PRI more inclusive and forcing political interests to compete for access within the confines of the party rather than by challenging the system itself. Once incorporated into the party, groups and individuals were far more likely to have their concerns addressed than had they remained outside the revolutionary family.

This is not to say that cooptation yielded positive results for Mexico; rather, it is simply a point of fact that those who could be convinced to play by the PRI's rules tended to fare better than those who rejected the system outright. Of course the line between cooptation and coercion is often very thin, and the PRI was not above using threats, intimidation, and even force when its efforts to coopt would-be opponents failed. While its use of coercion was generally only employed as a last resort, these tactics represented real and tangible danger that effectively prevented the expression of alternative viewpoints, political protest, and freedom of choice. That the PRI used coercive force with such relative infrequency was a testament to its ability to generate genuine support or, at a minimum, to persuade its opponents through cooptation. However, when these tactics failed, the PRI occasionally resorted to the use of repression. When such instances occurred, they illustrated the limits of PRI power, and seriously compromised its claims of legitimacy. In fact, many political scientists consider the use of coercion or force to be a show of weakness, since it demonstrates an inability to influence people by persuasion or mere threats. Moreover, once the PRI resorted to coercive tactics, it often eliminated any possibility to coopt those elements that suffered from repression. In other words, once subjected to its violent side, victims were not so easily won back by the PRI's charms. Below we discuss the coercive use of power by the PRI, with particular attention to a major incident of political repression that occurred during the 1960s.

Coercion and Political Repression

In the era of PRI hegemony, the ruling party's use of coercion was relatively infrequent, thereby attesting to the effectiveness of its other tactics for retaining power. However, when applied, the PRI's use of coercion ran the gamut from threats of violence against individuals to the organized repression of groups by government forces. Government critics (e.g., journalists, artists, opposition candidates, social movements, independent labor unions) were characteristically harassed or otherwise intimidated by threats against them and their families. More subtly, just as those who obeyed the system had opportunities to advance their careers in both the public and private sectors, those same doors were closed to others who were critical of the government. Moreover, the government made significant efforts to identify and monitor its opponents, placing wiretaps on potential sources of opposition (including opposition parties and officials) and infiltrating social movements and popular organizations. While such tactics have been used in the United States—as in the case of intelligence efforts to monitor communist organizations, civil rights activists, and even political campaigns—in Mexico there was little legal recourse for the protection of civil liberties.

Meanwhile, outright repression—while relatively rare—could be severe. The use of police and military units to suppress labor protests was instrumental in establishing the hegemony of the PRI's official unions in the 1930s and 1940s. Over subsequent decades, as Mexico experienced stronger economic growth, there was a corresponding period of labor mobilization and organization. Mexican workers—particularly in the oil and railroad industries—organized numerous labor strikes in different parts of the country. The PRI government viewed these labor strikes as subversive and damaging to the economic interests of the country. The government responded to the unions, and other dissenting voices, with severe repression. In 1958 and 1959, a railway workers' dispute caused the PRI government not only to break the strike but also to imprison numerous railroad workers and supporters from other unions. In the end, strike organizers Demetrio Vallejo and Valentín Campa were sentenced to sixteen years in prison, effectively decapitating the movement. Among the notable personalities who protested the government's harsh repression was the renowned muralist David Alfaro Siqueiros.[32]

Similarly, when Mexican opposition parties attempted to defend apparent victories by their candidates in state and local races, such postelectoral conflicts were likely to expose the PRI's authoritarian side. Such was the case when the government used violence to crack down on opposition protesters in places like León, Guanajuato, in 1945; Mérida, Yucatán in 1967; and Tijuana, Baja California, in 1959 and 1968.[33] Yet by far the single instance of PRI repression that stands out the most was the 1968 massacre of student protesters in Tlatelolco, a middle-class neighborhood on the north side of Mexico City.

1968 Massacre at Tlatelolco

By the late 1960s, Mexico was, to many outside observers, a model Latin American country. While few believed that it was a democracy, it had nevertheless successfully avoided the military coups d'état, large-scale leftist guerrilla movements, and economic crises that plagued most countries in the region during the same time period. Yet Mexicans and insiders knew that for all of Mexico's success, not all was well—especially among the middle and working classes who had not benefited as much as expected from the country's remarkable economic growth between 1940 and 1960. Indeed, while postwar prosperity had led to declines in the overall levels of poverty and inequality, the opportunities created for the middle sectors did not match their expectations and instead created a large population of upwardly mobile young people, whose dreams and aspirations appeared to be growing even faster than Mexico's economy.

At the same time, Mexico's younger generation was being inspired by the cultural dissemination of ideas (through music, art, and literature) that challenged the status quo and sought to address what they saw as the world's injustices. During the late 1950s and 1960s, Mexican students—like many of their counterparts in other countries—were drawn to progressive, even radical political positions by world events like the Cuban revolution and the Vietnam War. On the university campuses of Mexico, students sought ways to get involved in addressing these issues by holding meetings and rallies to voice their discontent. This kind of activism was viewed with significant concern by Mexican authorities. Students who organized marches and became involved in left-wing organizations were studiously monitored. Their events were occasionally dispersed with tear gas and the butt of a rifle, as in 1961 when students marched in Mexico City to celebrate the newly installed Castro government in Cuba. Major leaders in these kinds of activities were sometimes arrested as political prisoners, but nonetheless a growing atmosphere of student activism developed over the course of the 1960s. By 1968, the ten-year anniversary of the Cuban revolution, student activism reached new heights and levels of sophistication that created extreme distress for the PRI government.[34]

The year 1968 was also a particularly sensitive moment for Mexico because the Olympic Games were to be hosted in Mexico City beginning in October. Mexican authorities viewed this as an opportunity to demonstrate the successes of the PRI government to the world. Indeed, the ruling party had reason to boast. After three decades of remarkable economic progress and political stability, Mexico had reestablished itself among the world's most prominent developing nations and was the shining star of Latin America. Anticipating hundreds of international dignitaries and media representatives, President

Díaz Ordáz spent an estimated $240 million on preparations for the twelve-day sporting event.[35]

Despite these efforts to host a magnificent event, trouble began brewing in the months before the Olympics, as the summer brought heightened tensions between Mexican student activists and police. On June 23, 1968, a fight between two groups who appeared to be from rival high schools provoked a severe crackdown by Mexico City police. A legion of 300 police then swarmed and violently subdued those involved in the skirmish. While it appears that the instigators of the fight were not even students, police continued their rampage by storming into an unrelated but nearby vocational school and harassing its students and faculty members. The schools in question were associated with two prominent Mexico City public universities, the National Polytechnic Institute (Instituto Nacional Politécnico, IPN) and the much larger National Autonomous University of Mexico (Universidad Nacional Autónoma de México, UNAM). In response to such an exaggerated show of force, outraged students from these two rival universities banded together in a rare demonstration of unity to protest the recent police brutality and the PRI government in general. With 250,000 students at the time, UNAM was the largest university in the hemisphere, and had been a hotbed of student activism over the course of the 1960s.

Over the next several weeks, students organized strikes and marches throughout the capital. Using their university campuses as a base of operations, they took over classrooms and hallways to produce flyers, rally support, and make public speeches. Off campus, students painted protest signs denouncing the PRI government and calling for the resignation of the Mexico City police chief. In addition to tacit (and sometimes overt) support from university administrators and faculty, what made this movement particularly successful was the fact that students were extremely careful about the structure and organization of their movement. To prevent the government from coopting or intimidating its organizers, the students developed an elaborate system of rotating leadership and decentralized operations.

The most important innovation was the rotating National Strike Council—comprising 250 representatives from over one hundred schools—and a complex system of committees and brigades that prevented the easy identification, cooptation, or coercion of its members. No single student or group could be identified as leaders of the movement, since directions were issued by different students from week to week. This enabled the student organizers to create a movement based on generally accepted ideas and strategies, rather than on individuals or personalities. Also, rather than acting through a single, easily identifiable organizational structure, the movement's separate cells and brigades could act with a high degree of autonomy. The final straw came with the violation of UNAM's hard-fought tradition of autonomy from the government, when the military sent 10,000 troops onto the UNAM campus on September 18. This set off an intense wave of protests and marches that grew increasingly strident in their criticisms against the PRI regime itself.[36]

The Mexican government responded with great concern and frustration, particularly in light of the impending Olympic Games, scheduled to begin on October 12. The government was anxious for an opportunity to show the world how much progress had been made in Mexico under the PRI. Yet the prospect of student demonstrations threatened to embarrass the PRI and project exactly the opposite image that the Mexican government wanted. Most important, the PRI was frustrated by its inability to utilize its usual tactics to undermine political opposition. There was little the government could do to coopt the student movement according to its standard playbook for handling electoral challengers, union organizers, or armed rebels. On the one hand, the government could not readily appeal to particular leaders to buy off their support, and on the other hand it could not legitimately resort to full-scale violence against students and the ordinary citizens who supported them. In short, the PRI government found that cooptation was not an option, and at the same time knew that repression would carry a high political cost.[37]

With each demonstration, the government's response was to call in more fully armed police and even the military in a massive demonstration of the state's coercive capacity. As the movement gathered pace into September, the PRI government began interrupting marches and sending police onto high school and university campuses to try to restore order and identify dissidents. During these increasingly intense clashes, dozens of students were killed and hundreds were injured in the resulting violent conflicts with police. Tens of thousands of people rallied to the cause. Growing sympathy and support from the public soon swelled the movement as it was embraced by ordinary citizens and workers' unions, who participated in marches that now brought together tens of thousands of protesters demanding not only justice for police abuses and the release of political prisoners, but also broader calls for democratic reform in Mexico. As the movement increased in size and support, the government's frustration grew.

This continuing escalation came to a dreadful climax on October 2. Starting around 5:00 p.m., a group of 6,000 protesters gathered for a march that was to begin in a residential area surrounding the Plaza of Tlatelolco—the famed site where Cortés allegedly battled the Aztecs and forged a nation of mestizos—with plans to continue over to the IPN campus. Within an hour, these students were surrounded by a massive contingent of 10,000 soldiers armed with machine guns and bayonets. Rather than risk undertaking the planned march, the protesters instead began speaking in the plaza, in the view and protection of the surrounding apartment buildings of this middle- and work-ing-class neighborhood. As they spoke, helicopters and armored cars began to arrive, as soldiers moved into fortified positions in and above apartment complexes and buildings surrounding the plaza. Some students also noticed the arrival of plainclothes men bearing a single white glove and haircuts that seemed to indicate some sort of military affiliation.

Soon after surrounding the plaza, the soldiers opened fire on the stage and the front of the crowd. Soldiers aimed first at the speakers and then at the pan-icked crowd. Soon soldiers flooded the plaza and began beating and arrest-ing the demonstrators. Those believed to be members of the National Strike Council were lined up along walls and forced to strip to their underwear. Stu-dents, ordinary citizens, and journalists alike were assaulted, abused, and oth-erwise terrorized in the police rampage. One terrified witness in the plaza was a young future politician by the name of Ernesto Zedillo, who would become Mexico's president a quarter of a century later. In the end, official government figures claimed that only a few dozen protestors were killed, and asserted that these individuals had provoked and fired on police. Yet independent, inter-national media sources and activists believed the toll to be much higher, not least because dozens of protesters and student leaders simply disappeared in the wake of the incident.

Whatever the number of people who were killed or injured in the assault, the incident came to be aptly described as the 1968 student massacre. What was especially disturbing is that the massacre appeared to be part of a well-orchestrated and premeditated plan that could only have been organized and authorized at the highest levels of the Mexican government. Indeed, in addition to participation by the military, the white-gloved agents who took part in the massacre turned out to be members of a branch of the Mexican secret police known as the Olympia Battalion. Many critics now believe that the massacre was ordered directly by the Office of the Presi-dent, though it remains unclear who specifically issued the order. While President Gustavo Díaz Ordaz was much criticized for his administration's actions, human rights activists have focused primary responsibility on then interior secretary Luis Echeverría Álvarez for planning and order-ing this and subsequent acts of government repression. Over the past few years, Mexico's new democratic government and civil rights activists have worked together to sort out the details through the Mexican court system. Still, it will take many years until allegations against high-ranking officials are resolved, if ever.

Part of the problem of assigning responsibility is that the incident was effectively covered up by the PRI. Most domestic and international media sources were effectively dissuaded or diverted from covering the story, as the government successfully focused greater attention on the 1968 Olympic Games. To the dismay of Mexican journalist Elena Poniatowski, one of the few who reported extensively on the story, the incident was effectively buried in the media within hours. To the extent that it was covered in the media, official explanations blamed the students and even foreign terrorists for the "incident."[38] Over the next ten days, the blood and protest signs were wiped away and Mexico City made itself up to shine before the international community. Indeed, the Olympics went on as scheduled. In the immediate aftermath of the games, the most notable memory of Mexico's Olympic games for most of the world was a tribute to black power and human rights issued jointly by African American U.S. gold and bronze medalists Tommy Smith (who had just set a new world record for the 200 meter dash) and John Carlos, with support from Australian silver medalist Peter Norman.

In short, the PRI minimized immediate scrutiny and diverted the negative impact of the massacre. Yet in retrospect this repressive incident appears to have had long-term negative effects for the PRI regime. First, for a large number of Mexicans who were directly involved or subsequently learned about the massacre, the incident dramatically reduced the legitimacy of the PRI regime. Second, this major instance of repression created a new generation of opposition activists fiercely committed to undermining the PRI regime. And third, over the course of the 1970s, it led the Mexican government to make further crackdowns and somewhat imprudent (and largely ineffective) overtures to bolster its political support. In this sense, the repression of the 1968 student movement was for some observers of Mexican politics an incident that ultimately contributed to the downfall of the PRI regime.[39]

Conclusion

During most of the twentieth century, Mexico was at best a democracy with adjectives—a "limited" or "restricted" democracy; at worst Mexico was an authoritarian regime with only the trappings of democracy and none of its substance. Yet, from the revolution until the late 1960s, Mexico was characterized by institutions of political control that generated political stability and economic prosperity during a period of unprecedented growth and development. Widespread cultural acceptance and a revolutionary mythology helped build support for the PRI. Also, the regime's ability to incorporate a wide array of societal groups and coopt would-be detractors provided an essential source of support and political stability.

However, in 1968, the PRI regime showed signs of weakness and failed to effectively respond to key challenges. In the face of the 1968 student protests, the PRI's ability to use cooptation failed, and it was forced to use violence. In the eyes of many, it was the first major illustration of the limits of PRI power. In the aftermath, the PRI would spend decades trying to restore its credibility and control. Over the next three decades, the PRI's power would gradually erode and give way to a more open and democratic political system. In the next chapter we discuss this prolonged transition.

Key Terms

1946 Federal Electoral Law
1968 student massacre
Alemán, Miguel
Ávila Camacho, Manuel
camarillas
centralization of power
clientelism
CNOP
cooptation
corporatism
dedazo
democracy with adjectives
destape
Mexican Revolutionary Party
  (PRM)

Ministry of the Interior
National Revolutionary Party
  (PNR)
National Strike Council
PAN
parastatal parties
party discipline
PCM
personalism
Plaza of Tlatelolco
political machine
PRI
sexenio
vote tacos (*tacos de votos*)

Recommended Readings

Magaloni, Beatriz. *Voting for Autocracy: Hegemonic Party Survival and Its Demise in Mexico.* Cambridge: Cambridge University Press, 2007.
Middlebrook, Kevin J. *The Paradox of Revolution: Labor, the State, and Authoritarianism in Mexico.* Baltimore: Johns Hopkins University Press, 1995.
Molinar, Juan. *El tiempo de la legitimidad: Elecciones, autoritarismo, y democracia en México.* Mexico City: Cal y Arena, 1991.

Notes

1. Robert R. Kaufman, "Mexico and Latin American Authoritarianism," in *Authoritarianism in Mexico,* ed. José Luis Reyna and Richard S. Weinert (Philadelphia: Institute for the Study of Human Issues, 1977).

2. Dan A. Cothran, *Political Stability and Democracy in Mexico: The "Perfect Dictatorship"?* (Westport, Conn.: Praeger, 1994).

3. Magaloni describes Mexico's classical political system as electoral authoritarianism. Beatriz Magaloni, *Voting for Autocracy: Hegemonic Party Survival and Its Demise in Mexico* (New York: Cambridge University Press, 2006), 7.

4. David Collier and Steven Levitsky, "Democracy with Adjectives: Conceptual Innovation in Comparative Research," *World Politics* 49, no. 3 (1997): 430–51.

5. Wayne A. Cornelius, Judith Gentleman, and Peter H. Smith, *Mexico's Alternative Political Futures* (La Jolla: University of California–San Diego, Center for U.S.-Mexican Studies, 1989).

6. Ilene V. O'Malley, *The Myth of the Revolution: Hero Cults and the Institutionalization of the Mexican State, 1920–1940* (New York: Greenwood, 1986).

7. Juan Molinar Horcasitas, *El tiempo de la legitimidad: Elecciones, autoritarismo, y democracia en México* (Mexico City: Cal y Arena, 1991).

8. Pablo Arredondo Ramírez, Gilberto Fregoso Peralta, and Raúl Trejo Delarbre, *Así se calló el sistema: Comunicación y elecciones en 1988* (Guadalajara: University of Guadalajara, 1991); Todd A. Eisenstadt, *Courting Democracy in Mexico: Party Strategies and Electoral Institutions* (Cambridge: Cambridge University Press, 2004); Mónica Serrano, *Governing Mexico: Political Parties and Elections* (London: University of London; Institute of Latin American Studies, 1998).

9. Joy Langston, "Breaking Out Is Hard to Do: Exit, Voice, and Loyalty in Mexico's One-Party Hegemonic Regime," *Latin American Politics and Society* 44, no. 3 (2002): 61–88.

10. Diane E. Davis, "Uncommon Democracy in Mexico: Middle Classes and the Military in the Consolidation of One-Party Rule, 1936–1946," in *The Social Construction of Democracy, 1880–1990,* ed. Herrick Chapman and George Reid Andrews (London: Macmillan, 1995).

11. Octavio Rodríguez Araujo, "Partidos Políticos y Elecciones en México, 1964 a 1985," *Revista Mexicana de Sociología,* Vol. 47, No. 1, Número conmemorativo del XX aniversario de la publicación de "La democracia en México." (Jan.-Mar., 1985), 41–104.

12. S. N. Eisenstadt and René Lemarchand, *Political Clientelism, Patronage, and Development* (Beverly Hills: Sage, 1981); Luigi Graziano, *A Conceptual Framework for the Study of Clientelism* (Ithaca, N.Y.: Western Societies Program Center for International Studies, Cornell University, 1975); Keith R. Legg, *Patrons, Clients, and Politicians: New Perspectives on Political Clientelism* (Berkeley: University of California, Institute of International Studies, 1975); Luis Roniger and Ayşe Güneş-Ayata, *Democracy, Clientelism, and Civil Society* (Boulder: Lynne Rienner, 1994).

13. Wayne A. Cornelius and Ann L. Craig, *Politics in Mexico: An Introduction and Overview* (San Diego: University of California, Center for U.S.-Mexican Studies, 1988).

14. *Camarillas* were commonly "reshuffled" following the *destape,* or unveiling of a president's successor. Once the chosen candidate was publicly identified, *camarilla* members of the losing contenders faced the difficult task of positioning themselves well for the incoming administration.

15. Kenneth F. Greene, *Why Dominant Parties Lose: Mexico's Democratization in Comparative Perspective* (Cambridge: Cambridge University Press, 2007); Magaloni, *Voting for Autocracy.*

16. Jeffrey A. Weldon, "Changing Patterns of Executive-Legislative Relations in Mexico," in *Dilemmas of Change in Mexican Politics*, ed. Kevin J. Middlebrook (London: Institute of Latin American Studies, 2003).

17. Similar factional divisions emerged in other single-party dominated systems, like South Korea and Taiwan. Dorothy J. Solinger, "Ending One-Party Dominance: Korea, Taiwan, Mexico," *Journal of Democracy* 12, no. 1 (2001): 30–42.

18. Enrique Krauze, *Mexico: Biography of Power: A History of Modern Mexico, 1810–1996* (New York: HarperPerennial, 1997).

19. The PRI swung back to the right during the late 1960s, and left again in the early 1970s, until the pendulum settled at the right of the political spectrum in the 1980s. Wayne Cornelius and Ann Craig, *The Mexican Political System in Transition* (La Jolla: University of California, Center for U.S.-Mexican Studies, 1991), 39–40.

20. Victoria E. Rodriguez and Peter M. Ward, "Disentangling the PRI from the Government in Mexico," *Mexican Studies-Estudios Mexicanos* 10, no. 1 (Winter, 1994).

21. Victoria Elizabeth Rodríguez, *Decentralization in Mexico: From Reforma Municipal to Solidaridad to Nuevo Federalismo* (Boulder, Colo.: Westview, 1997); Blanca Torres Ramírez, *Decentralización y democracia en México* (México, D.F.: El Colegio de México, 1986).

22. As noted in chapter 2, the principle of no reelection was abrogated somewhat by Obregón's reelection, but reinstated (along with a shift from four- to six-year terms) shortly after he was assassinated.

23. Michael C. Taylor, "Constitutional Crisis: How Reforms to the Legislature Have Doomed Mexico," *Mexican Studies/Estudios Mexicanos* 13, no. 2 (1997): 299–324; Weldon, "Changing Patterns."

24. Jorge Castañeda, *Perpetuating Power: How Mexican Presidents Were Chosen* (New York: New Press, 2000).

25. The same applied to governors and mayors to a lesser extent within their own jurisdictions, since they too were assured of PRI dominance and cooperation (unless their superior decided otherwise).

26. Javier Hurtado, *El sistema presidencial mexicano: Evolución y perspectivas* (Guadalajara: University of Guadalajara, 2001).

27. Luis Javier Garrido, "The Crisis of *Presidencialismo*," in *Mexico's Alternative Political Futures*, ed. Wayne A. Cornelius, Judith Gentleman, and Peter H. Smith (La Jolla: Center for U.S.-Mexican Studies, 1989).

28. Magaloni, *Voting for Autocracy*.

29. Soledad Loaeza, *El Partido Acción Nacional, la larga marcha, 1939–1994: Oposición leal y partido de protesta* (México: Fondo de Cultura Económica, 1999); Donald J. Mabry, *Mexico's Accion Nacional: A Catholic Alternative to Revolution* (Syracuse, N.Y.: Syracuse University Press, 1973); Kevin J. Middlebrook, *Party Politics and the Struggle for Democracy in Mexico: National and State-Level Analyses of the Partido Acción Nacional* (San Diego: University of California, Center for U.S.-Mexican Studies, 2001); Yemile Mizrahi, *From Martyrdom to Power: The Partido Acción Nacional in Mexico* (Notre Dame, Ind.: University of Notre Dame Press, 2003); Pablo Moctezuma Barragán, *Los orígenes del PAN* (México: Ehecatl Ediciones, 1997); David A. Shirk,

Mexico's New Politics: The PAN and Democratic Change (Boulder: Lynne Rienner, 2005); Franz A. Von Sauer, *The Alienated "Loyal" Opposition: Mexico's Partido Acción Nacional* (Albuquerque: University of New Mexico Press, 1974).

30. Even foreign insurgent and terrorist organizations, like the Chilean International Revolutionary Movement (Movimiento Internacional Revolucionario, MIR) and the terrorist organization now known as Basque Homeland and Liberty (Euskadi Ta Askatasuna, ETA), developed operations in Mexico over the latter part of the twentieth century.

31. Ramón Miró, *Organized Crime and Terrorist Activity in Mexico, 1999–2002* (Washington, D.C.: Library of Congress, 2003).

32. Howard Handelman, "The Politics of Labor Protest in Mexico: Two Case Studies," *Journal of Interamerican Studies and World Affairs* 18, no. 3 (1976): 267–94; Raquel Tibol, *Siqueiros, vida y obra* (Mexico City: Departamento del Distrito Federal Secretaría de Obras y Servicios, 1974).

33. Shirk, *Mexico's New Politics.*

34. There is an ample body of literature on the 1968 student movement and government repression. See Mariano Herrera Motte, *1968, lo peor y lo mejor de México* (México: Federación Editorial Mexicana, 1975); Donald J. Mabry, *The Mexican University and the State: Student Conflicts, 1910–1971* (College Station: Texas A&M University Press, 1982); Salvador Martínez Della Rocca, *Estado y universidad en México, 1920–1968: Historia de los movimientos estudiantiles en la UNAM* (México: J. Boldó i Climent, 1986); Manuel Moreno-Sánchez, *México, 1968–1972, crisis y perspectiva* (Austin: Institute of Latin American Studies, University of Texas–Austin, 1973); Tarsicio Ocampo V, *México: Conflicto estudiantil, 1968* (Cuernavaca: Centro Intercultural de Documentación, 1969).

35. Christopher Brasher, *Mexico 1968: A Diary of the XIXth Olympiad* (London: S. Paul, 1968); Oferta Olímpica Mexico, *La Olimpiada en México, 1968* (México, 1968).

36. Judith Adler Hellman, *Mexico in Crisis* (New York: Holmes & Meier, 1988).

37. Hellman, *Mexico in Crisis.*

38. Unfortunately many media sources at that time were coopted through their dependence on lucrative government advertising contracts, subsidies, and even direct payoffs to reporters to favor the PRI government. Hence with the help of the "official" media, the 1968 student massacre was easily swept under the rug.

39. Vivienne Bennett, "The Evolution of Urban Popular Movements in Mexico between 1968 and 1988," in *The Making of Social Movements in Latin America* (Boulder: Westview, 1992); Gerardo Estrada Rodríguez, *1968, Estado y universidad: orígenes de la transición política en México* (México, D.F.: Plaza Janés, 2004); Jorge Moreno Barrera, *La guerra sucia en México: El toro y el lagarto 1968–1980* (México, D.F.: Libros para Todos, 2002); José Luis Tejeda, *El proceso de democratización en México, 1968–1982* (Alvaro Obregón, D.F.: Praxis, 1991).

4

Mexican Democratization, 1968 to the Present

Democratization in Mexico

In some respects the Tlatelolco massacre was the culmination of social unrest that started brewing in the 1950s. The events of 1968 were also the beginning of a slow transition away from single-party dominance and toward more open democracy that would emerge in the late 1980s and coalesce in 2000 with the election of the first opposition candidate to the presidency. Yet the changes to the Mexican political system that occurred between 1968 and 2000 happened so gradually that only in retrospect do they appear to constitute a linear transition away from authoritarianism and toward democracy. In fact, during the decades that the political opening took place, there were many points at which Mexicans and outsiders alike wondered whether the PRI would manage to salvage and further consolidate its hegemony so that democracy would elude Mexico indefinitely. We know now that this did not happen: in 1988 the PRI nearly lost the presidential election and in 1997, the PRI's influence had waned so much that for the first time, the party lost its legislative majority. By 2000 it lost the presidency to the PAN, and in 2006, it ran a distant third in a three-way presidential race.

How did this happen? How did a firmly entrenched party that was accustomed to winning elections with over 60 percent of the vote for more than half a century lose so much support and power? The purpose of this chapter is to explore that question. We suggest that the PRI's fall from grace and the subsequent emergence of greater political competition occurred as the result of three interrelated factors: the inability of the government to effectively promote economic redistribution and stability, the PRI's loss of cohesion and legitimacy, and the institutional changes that created openings for the opposition parties to gain footholds that eventually allowed them to challenge the PRI head on and boost themselves into power. Each of these factors is outlined briefly below as a prelude to a longer discussion of how they combined to erode the PRI's dominance between 1970 and 2000.

Declining PRI Legitimacy

As discussed earlier, the PRI's hegemony was undeniably rooted in its ability to incorporate and coopt a wide range of otherwise disparate interests, and in its electoral dominance. However, another critical factor in the party's success was the strong performance of the national economy between 1940 and 1970. The Mexican Miracle was impressive by any standards: for thirty years, the economy grew at an annual rate of more than 6 percent. (See chapter 9.) The political benefits of such healthy and sustained growth are almost immeasurable. Plentiful resources allowed the government to use material benefits to reward loyalty, elicit support, and build public works that would enhance the party's legitimacy and reinforce its self-created image as the "official" party with such a strong following that it ruled virtually uncontested. As the national economic model began to visibly falter in the 1970s, it became increasingly difficult for the government to use material goods and economic gains to facilitate the smooth operation of corporatist arrangements and clientelistic networks that were pivotal for the party's dominance and legitimacy.[1] Many began to question the benefit of demonstrating allegiance to the PRI—especially when it had shown itself to be a corrupt organization that undergirded a corrupt system. But it was not just the exhaustion of Mexico's economic miracle that undermined the PRI's position; it was also that the national economic gains produced between 1940 and 1970 were not evenly distributed within society. While the private and industrial sectors did very well, most Mexicans suffered from the side effects of growing inflation, stagnant wages, high unemployment, and inadequate public services.[2] Moreover, between the mid-1970s and the mid-1990s, the country experienced a cycle of economic booms and devastating busts that created great uncertainty for ordinary Mexicans and eroded public confidence in the political system. By itself, economic instability was not sufficient to produce political change because support for the PRI was rooted in more than a simple exchange of material goods for votes. But the government's inability to deliver economic stability greatly undermined its practice of using patronage to ensure popular support and contributed to the second source of the PRI's decline—its loss of legitimacy.

From the time of its creation and subsequent institutionalization in the first half of the twentieth century, the PRI claimed to embody the principles the revolutionaries fought for. These principles, while sometimes vague, consistently called for inclusion, redistribution, and stability. Mexicans supported the PRI because it made an effort to create and sustain the revolutionary family. Yet the events of 1968 had made undeniably clear that the regime would use force against outsiders who were too critical or who sought too much independence. To be sure, 1968 was not the first time this truth was apparent. The use of force against independent labor organizers in the 1950s had demonstrated the same point. Yet the government's subsequent use of force against its detractors in the 1970s, in the aftermath of the 1968 massacre, made it undeniable that the government was not above using repression. This fact, combined with the pervasive and unabashed use of graft, patronage, and abuse of power by government officials at every level, created for many Mexicans a deep distrust of the government, and by extension, of the PRI. Thus, when faced with the specter of a corrupt government unable to meet the basic needs of or create meaningful economic opportunities for most of its citizens, Mexicans became increasingly skeptical and less likely to support the party as time went on. The PRI's loss of legitimacy in the eyes of voters also took its toll on the organization. While the party had always been internally divided, competition among its various factions for control of the organization became more fierce as the strain of losing popular support set in. Disputes among factions led to the public airing of differences, accusations, and dirty laundry, and this only exacerbated the party's already tarnished image.

Hoping to restore some legitimacy to the PRI system, the legislature enacted a series of institutional reforms that appeared to open the political system, while still preserving enormous advantages for the ruling party. Specifically, from the 1970s through the 1990s, PRI leaders offered three major types of reforms as concessions to members of the opposition: first, increasing the size of the legislature in 1977; second, decentralizing power to state and local governments in the 1980s; and third, creating an independent electoral authority in the early 1990s. Each of these concessions was instrumental in promoting democratization in Mexico. The first provided opposition parties with expanded opportunities for representation, which while initially more symbolic than real, did contribute significantly to the experience and political training necessary to govern effectively in the future. Fielding candidates for national elections also gave opposition parties electoral experience that would pay off in the 1980s when the regime was more reluctant to overturn opposition victories. Increasing the power of states and municipalities was also important in the democratization process because it meant that when the opposition won subnational elections, they had greater autonomy and sometimes more resources with which to govern. This helped them establish a track record that they could refer to when their candidates went on to run for national office. Finally, perhaps the most important step in leveling the electoral playing field for the opposition was the creation and subsequent strengthening of an independent electoral authority in the early 1990s. Before the creation of the Federal Electoral Institute (Instituto Federal Electoral, IFE), it was the minister of the interior, the right-hand man of the president, who oversaw all elections and decided all electoral disputes. Without independent oversight of elections, the opposition never stood a chance of making meaningful electoral gains. But with a set of independent institutions widely acknowledged to be impartial, Mexico's inchoate democracy made significant strides. The opposition was no longer forced to hope for government goodwill in order to win an election. Instead, parties could focus on the challenges of getting elected and know that victories were almost certain to stand.

Over the course of the 1980s and 1990s, these reforms paved the way for the political opposition to gain expanded representation and power in government, gradually reducing the hegemony of the PRI. Hence, our discussion thus far suggests that the PRI's demise was, in large part, its own doing; without the government's blunders and unilateral decisions to reform the system, it might have held on to power indefinitely. Still, this captures only part of the reality. Although the process of political change in Mexico was in many ways a top-down phenomenon orchestrated by the PRI, democratization in Mexico occurred not just because the regime made the decision to allow a political opening. Rather, the government's view that reform was necessary was strongly influenced by the pressure exerted by opposition parties, independent social movements, and other critics of the status quo who were increasingly vocal and willing to take action to voice their dissent. In other words, society played an equally important role in creating Mexico's democracy by forcing the government's hand when it otherwise would have preferred to maintain the status quo. Furthermore, democracy was almost never the goal or desire of most within the PRI. As we will see below and in subsequent chapters, many of the reforms that we now credit with bringing about a more open and competitive political system were actually designed to consolidate PRI hegemony while merely giving the appearance of greater political competition and representation. These and other issues become clearer with a more detailed account of Mexico's transition to democracy between 1970 and 2000. It is to this subject that we now turn.

Early Political Opening (1970–1988)

With the election of Luis Echeverría to the presidency in 1970 most everyone expected that his administration would try to recapture public support using the PRI's traditional methods of incorporation, cooptation, and coercion.[3] Indeed, as the minister of the interior under the Díaz Ordáz government, Echeverría played a determining role in the decision to use force against the demonstrators, and many believed that he, rather than Díaz Ordaz, had orchestrated the government's repressive response to the demonstrations. Yet upon being selected the party's presidential candidate, Echeverría made a concerted effort to brand himself as a different kind of PRIista, one who was willing to speak publicly about the failures of past administrations and the shortcomings of the revolution, one who was genuinely concerned about making life better for the poor. Echeverría was also quick to state that the economic advances of the previous thirty years had come at the expense of the peasantry and working classes. Upon taking office he announced his intention to address the regime's failings and his country's most pressing needs thereby redeeming his party in the eyes of Mexico and the world. To that end, he introduced a broad set of reforms that ranged from reforming the legislature to promoting the redistribution of wealth.

The legislative reform was ostensibly designed to make it easier for opposition parties to win seats in the Chamber of Deputies by lowering the minimum threshold for obtaining a party seat from 2.5 to 1.5 percent of the national vote. The benefit of this was that the opposition would have a better chance at representation in the national legislature and the Mexican government could reasonably claim to be promoting greater pluralism. Therefore, while the reform did create new spaces for the opposition, it was something of a double-edged sword because it created incentives for more parties to participate in elections, but it also had the (not-unintended) effect of dispersing the opposition, thereby reducing the likelihood that opposition groups would join forces to mount a more serious challenge for the PRI.

Echeverría's other reforms included clamping down on corruption in the government and private sector, significant increases in government spending for education, housing, and other public services, and greater resources for rural development (e.g., expanded credit, subsidized fertilizers, seeds, and irrigation infrastructure). At the same time, he stated in no uncertain terms that the time had come for the wealthy elite to give back to the country. He introduced tax hikes that required the wealthy to pay more in income taxes than they had in the past, and set about reducing the availability of tax breaks and government subsidies that significantly lowered the costs of production for industrialists and large agribusinesses. Further, the government tightened restrictions on foreign capital and investment and redistributed more land to agrarian workers. Despite the apparent comprehensiveness of Echeverría's reforms, they produced little real change, in part because many of the reforms did not go deep enough to alter existing power structures or address pervasive administrative shortcomings, and also because the elites undermined the president's reforms by removing their capital from the national economy.

Reduced public investment and capital flight severely hampered Echeverría's reform efforts because they deprived the government of the capital needed to fund expanded government programs and, equally important, they were as sincere a signal as the elite could send about their unhappiness with the president's policies. Combined with a global economic downturn and an overvalued currency, capital flight and the lack of elite support had a devastating effect on Echeverría's reform project. Halfway through his *sexenio* he was forced to curtail many of his programs and to court the favor of the private sector and others in the ruling class, but by then the damage was far too great to be undone.[4] Mexicans openly discussed the weakness of the president and speculated whether he would be allowed to finish his term of office.[5] By the time Echeverría left office in 1976, Mexico was facing its most serious economic crisis ever with a mushrooming public deficit, a currency devaluation that resulted in the peso's loss of half its value, rising inflation, and stagnant real wages.

In the end, Echeverría had failed to recapture public support for the PRI and Mexico was no better off in 1976 than it had been six years earlier. The vast majority of Mexicans had seen no improvement in their standard of living or any real reform of the political system, and the selection of Jose López Portillo as Echeverría's successor suggested no radical departure from the past. If anything, the future promised to be more difficult because the new president inherited an economic disaster. Moreover, the PRI faced a serious blow to its legitimacy when López Portillo ran unopposed in the 1976 presidential election. After he "won" with nearly 100 percent of the vote, Mexico could hardly claim to be a plural polity. Nevertheless, López Portillo immediately set out to address both the economic and political weaknesses of the system. He began by selecting a fiscally conservative cabinet and pledging to drastically reduce government spending on public services, development projects, and wage increases, while at the same time limiting the foreign debt and tightening the money supply to control inflation and avoid overvaluing the peso—in other words, he set out to dismantle much of what Echeverría had put in place. These moves met with the instant approval of many in the private sector, including international investors and lenders such as private banks and the International Monetary Fund.

López Portillo was lauded at home and abroad for his pragmatism and approach to bringing about economic stability, but few had forgotten the embarrassing circumstances under which López Portillo had assumed the presidency. During the Echeverría administration, the government had managed to keep the opposition subdued and in disarray with the use of authoritarian institutions, corruption, cooptation, and intimidation, but it certainly had not eliminated the regime's critics. Ironically, the failure of the most coherently organized opposition party, the PAN, to run a presidential candidate in the 1976 election probably forced the regime to introduce the next political opening. In all presidential elections between 1952 and 1970 the PAN had fielded a candidate, sometimes the PRI's only challenger, in the hopes of providing a meaningful alternative for critics of the system. In 1976 the party was so internally divided over the selection of its presidential candidate that it put forth none. While this turn of events demonstrated the seriousness of the PAN's internal problems, it had the effect of making a mockery of the PRI.

In an effort to demonstrate the PRI's desire to promote political competition, the López Portillo administration introduced the Federal Law of Political Organizations and Electoral Processes (Ley Federal de Organizaciones Políticas y Procesos Electorales, LFOPPE) in 1977. Like the legislative reform of 1972, the LFOPPE was designed to increase the access of smaller opposition parties by making it easier for them to participate in and win elections. The new law allowed organizations to obtain official registration as they had in the past, by receiving 1.5 percent of the national vote, or by providing a copy of party statutes and evidence of 65,000 nationally distributed members. Furthermore, the new law added 100 seats to the chamber for parties that obtained at least 1.5 percent of the national vote and won fewer than sixty of the 300 single-member district seats. Again, much like the 1972 reform, the LFOPPE did allow for increased participation and representation of the opposition; indeed, in the next few years five new parties obtained official registration. But the reforms also encouraged the formation of many small parties, rather than a unified opposition, and therefore made it highly unlikely that the PRI would ever be seriously threatened. Thus its overall effect was to revive the legitimacy of the Mexican political system, and therefore the PRI, by making it look like the regime was promoting true electoral competition when in fact it was undermining the opposition.

Despite the largely symbolic nature of the LFOPPE, it placated many in the opposition and redeemed the PRI because it coincided with an impressive economic boom brought about by the discovery of sizable oil deposits in the Gulf of Mexico. This event, more than any political maneuvers by the government, was responsible for Mexico's political stability in the late 1970s and early 1980s. López Portillo's economic approach to bring about economic stability involved a huge reduction in government spending, which meant that the government dramatically scaled back public services, food subsidies, wage increases (even to keep them on par with the rate of inflation), and job creation. For ordinary Mexicans, life became significantly more difficult. The deposits made Mexico the world's fourth largest oil producer, with an average annual rate of economic growth of more than 8 percent, and the government once again had resources to spare. However, even an economic boom of this magnitude was not enough to put Mexico on solid economic ground or to definitively rescue the PRI. Despite López Portillo's efforts to avoid the negative effects of a dramatic and rapid economic growth—runaway inflation, an overvalued currency and, in this case, overreliance on oil as a source of revenue—Mexico quickly suffered from all of the above and, for all practical purposes, squandered its incredible good fortune. Although revenue increased significantly once the production and export of oil was ramped up, so too did government spending. The government invested heavily in the petroleum industry and other high-priced industrial development projects, and spent millions on basic food imports. Amazingly enough, oil revenue, which reached $6 billion in 1980—up from $500 million in 1976—was insufficient to cover the government's spending and López Portillo began to expand the money supply and borrow from abroad to pay debts. Mexico had already shown this strategy to be dangerous because of its tendency to lead to inflation and an overvalued currency, but López Portillo believed that this time the country would avoid this fate because it had oil deposits to use as collateral. Nevertheless, by early 1982 internal and external pressures for devaluation were strong enough to force the government's hand and the peso lost 30 percent of its value. This meant not only that Mexicans' purchasing power declined substantially—the rate of inflation had increased to a whopping 100 percent—but also that Mexico's foreign debt nearly doubled, to $80 billion. As if this were not enough, in April, the world price of oil dropped and earnings from the commodity immediately fell off, bringing in less than half the amount of government revenue originally predicted for that year. This confluence of events created an untenable situation and by the end of the summer Mexico declared that it would be unable to meet its foreign debt obligation: it was, in essence, bankrupt. Economic growth, an enviable 8 percent in 1981, had fallen to zero by 1982. In order to prevent mass capital flight and further destabilization, the López Portillo administration nationalized all domestically owned banks—a move that went over well with the poor and working classes but sent shockwaves through the private sector.

Thus the end of the López Portillo *sexenio* looked remarkably like the end of that of his predecessor: the country was on the verge of economic collapse. The PRI had been further discredited by rampant and unabashed corruption and its dismal failure to manage a plentiful endowment of the most valuable resource a country could hope to possess. Ironically, the positive effects of the LFOPPE turned out to be more lasting than Mexico's economic boom of the late 1970s. The introduction of lower thresholds for participating in elections and guaranteed representation, while designed to perpetuate the hegemonic party system, did allow the stronger opposition parties to gain indispensable political experience and public exposure that would begin to bear fruit for some, like the PAN less than ten years later.

Amid the economic chaos of 1982, Miguel de la Madrid was elected president. His first move was to address the country's debt crisis and impending financial collapse by introducing a number of free market measures designed to bring about economic solvency and stability. De la Madrid had served as López Portillo's minister of budget and planning and was strongly committed to attacking Mexico's economic ills with economic policies designed to stabilize and change the orientation of the economy from one with a high level of state involvement and focused on production for domestic consumption to one that was largely regulated by the market and focused on promoting growth through exports. Only if Mexico met these standards would international lenders be willing to renegotiate the terms of its outstanding $80 billion. Therefore he filled his cabinet with technocrats, young professionals with training in liberal economic theory from U.S. institutions, and together they implemented their neoliberal approach to economic recovery.

These policies focused on stabilization and structural reorientation of the economy. Economic restructuring included the dismantling of trade protectionism for domestic production, and an opening to international trade through Mexico's entry into the General Agreement on Tariffs and Trade (GATT) in 1986. At the same time, the government made drastic reductions in public expenditures in all areas, from public works to education and government subsidies for domestic industries to price controls on essential food items. It also had to increase its revenue by raising existing taxes and introducing a 15 percent value-added tax (VAT) on the sale of most items, as well as price hikes on utilities and public transportation. At the same time, the government had tightened the money supply to rein in inflation and increase and diversify exports in order to promote economic growth. De la Madrid initially stated that it would take at least three years of this fiscal austerity to put Mexico back on track. The reality was far worse. The government could not get a firm handle on inflation or produce meaningful economic growth until the end of the decade, with the help of the Economic Solidarity Pact. The pact bound its signatories, labor, agricultural producers, and the business sectors, to respect even tighter monetary policy, trade liberalization, and fixed wages and prices—a clear precursor to the economic approach that would be institutionalized in the next administration.

De la Madrid's economic reforms were accompanied by a three-pronged approach to bring about political change, or at least the appearance of change.

The first aspect of this approach was to call for the "moral renovation" and promise to maintain a zero-tolerance policy toward corruption at all levels of government. This move served an important political purpose but did nothing to clean up the system. In the words of Judith Adler Hellman,

> Responding in this way to the public mood of frustration at the economic humiliation Mexico was suffering, de la Madrid concentrated on the malfeasance of the previous administration as a means to personalize and focus the anger of Mexicans on a relatively limited target. . . . But no systematic investigations of "unexplained wealth" were actually undertaken. To no one's great surprise, even the most highly visible offenders from the López Portillo regime went free. However, the campaign served a short-term purpose of deflecting attention from the more profound questions that needed to be publicly addressed in this period of crisis.[6]

De la Madrid also tried to alleviate the political pressures brought about by the economic crisis by promoting decentralization, or greater power sharing among the federal, state, and local (municipal) levels of government. While the main thrust of this amendment aimed to clarify the responsibilities of the three levels, and somewhat ironically, made life more difficult for local governments, it also introduced proportional representation to municipal elections.[7] As a result, it paved the way for the opposition to gain entry into, and hence valuable hands-on experience from, governing at the local level.

The third part of de la Madrid's effort to promote political change was a constitutional amendment in 1986 that once again increased the size of the Chamber of Deputies by 100 proportional representation seats. On the surface, the addition of the new seats was supposed to create more space for the opposition. This was a particularly welcome development for the PAN, which had made important electoral gains at the state and municipal level, but had run into formidable barriers to winning offices at the national level.[8] However, in reality the reform protected the PRI from the gains made by the opposition since the last round of reforms. Changes to the seat allocation formula gave the PRI access to the proportional representation seats for the first time, and another law guaranteed the party with the highest vote a majority in the Chamber, even if it won less than 51 percent of the national vote.[9] The latter law, commonly known as the "governability clause," meant that the PRI need only obtain a plurality in order to control the lower house of the legislature—a change that would come in handy for the PRI just two years later.

Unlike the reforms of 1977, the 1986 reforms came under close scrutiny by the opposition. Many welcomed the addition of new seats to the national legislature, but they took issue with the governability clause since it virtually guaranteed that the PRI would have a legislative majority for the foreseeable future. Their complaints were rooted in more than just principle since opposition victories at the national level had increased notably since the early 1980s. As if to placate the opposition, de la Madrid also began to recognize more opposition victories in important municipalities. At the time, this seemed like a relatively low-cost concession to make to quiet dissenters, though as mentioned earlier, it was the opposition's success at the local level that formed the basis for its eventual success at the national level.

Although the political reforms enacted by the de la Madrid administration were more far reaching than any that had come before, they were not enough to reverse the PRI's loss of legitimacy. The impact of the economic crisis was simply too great. People in all sectors of society felt the impact of persistent inflation, stagnant wages, high rates of unemployment, and the general difficulties of making ends meet. Unfortunately this scenario was nothing new. But the crisis of the 1980s was deeper and more lasting than any experienced in the past and took a higher toll on society. Although de la Madrid's neoliberal economic program may have met with the approval of the private sector and the international financial community, it imposed great costs on ordinary Mexicans. This, together with the government's incompetent response to the massive earthquakes that hit Mexico City in September 1985 (see textbox 4.1), led an increased number of Mexicans to organize groups that openly expressed their dissatisfaction with the ruling party. What was different this time around was that in the next presidential election, voters for the first time had a meaningful choice to make: should they vote for the PRI and invite more of the same, or support Cuauhtémoc Cárdenas, son of the most revered postrevolutionary hero, in his quest to destroy the monolith? Not surprisingly, many opted for the latter and the 1988 presidential election posed the most serious threat to the PRI's dominance that it had faced to date.

Textbox 4.1. 1985 Earthquake

On the morning of September 19, 1985, a massive earthquake measuring 8.1 on the Richter scale shook Mexico City. The next day, just as the dust was settling, a second temblor, this one measuring 7.5, struck in virtually the same location. Together, these earthquakes destroyed or damaged thousands of buildings, killed or injured hundreds of thousands of citizens, and caused several billion dollars' worth of damage to a country that was already in the throes of economic crisis. There is little doubt that the Mexico City earthquakes exacerbated Mexico's already desperate economic circumstances. Less predictable was the political fallout that occurred as a result of the natural disaster.

Much like the criticisms leveled against the U.S. government for its lackluster response to Hurricane Katrina in 2005, Mexican and international observers alike were horrified at the inadequacy of the city's infrastructure and at the national government's mishandling of the tragedy. Many of those trained and employed by the government to respond in such disasters, such as the police and army, stood by and watched as ordinary citizens set about digging survivors out of the rubble. Rather than provide effective leadership, President de la Madrid appeared aloof and inexplicably rejected all offers of foreign assistance. Public outcry against this attempt at nationalism led de la Madrid to eventually admit international rescue teams, aid, and equipment. But once it arrived much of this help was undermined by the Mexican government's insistence on control over all rescue efforts and by its looking the other way when police and army personnel began to sell donated supplies on the black market rather than distributing them to people in need.

For all of the hardship that the earthquakes brought the inhabitants of Mexico City, the disaster had a silver lining. The government's ineptness forced ordinary citizens to take matters into their own hands and coordinate their own rescue efforts. The success of these efforts became the foundation for further collective action to demand health care, housing, and other basic needs for survivors. Thus the earthquake served as a catalyst for organized popular mobilization that pressured the government to address public demands for services and accountability. These grassroots social movements were one of the many factors that gradually led to greater support of opposition political parties and the demise of the PRI.

Source: Judith Adler Hellman, *Mexico in Crisis* (New York: Holmes & Meier, 1988).

Salinas and the Rise of the Opposition (1988–1994)

Perhaps the greatest irony of the PRI's loss of legitimacy in the late 1980s was that it came from within the party itself. The addition of technocrats to the party in the late 1970s and early 1980s fundamentally altered the ideological orientation and leadership of the PRI. These young, U.S.-trained economists brought with them a belief that free market policies were the key to stabilizing and restructuring the economy in order to produce sustained growth. Given the economic crises of the times and pressure by international governments and lending institutions to use this approach, the technocrats were considered perfectly suited for cabinet level and bureaucratic positions within the López Portillo and de la Madrid governments.[10] Once in positions of power, the technocrats sought to remake the party in their own image, pushing aside members who had long since proven their loyalty, but who held more traditional views about the ideological orientation of the PRI. The subsequent rift between the *técnicos* and *políticos* proved to be extremely bitter and damaging to the party.

When de la Madrid began the process of selecting his successor, it quickly became clear that no old-style *político* stood a chance of being chosen. Indeed, the final choice of Carlos Salinas de Gortari, a tried-and-true technocrat, made it undeniable that the party would continue to pursue a market-oriented approach. This prompted several high-ranking members of the PRI who were ideologically committed to the principles of redistributive justice and other revolutionary myths, to break with the party and launch a bid for the presidency. Cuauhtémoc Cárdenas evoked memories of his father, Lázaro Cárdenas, whose policies are perhaps the best example of the PRI's commitment to upholding and implementing the principles of the revolution. Once he announced his intention to run for president he was eagerly supported by a number of small leftist parties who formed a coalition, the National Democratic Front (Frente Democrático Nacional, FDN), and together nominated him as their presidential candidate.[11] Cárdenas's candidacy tapped into a wellspring of popular discontent with the PRI. One of the most important sources of electoral support came from the myriad civic organizations that had sprung up in the 1980s, especially in the aftermath of the earthquakes, and from people who simply wanted to punish the PRI. With such widespread popular support, the PRI's leadership evidently decided that it could not leave the outcome of the election to fate. On election night, the computerized vote tabulation system mysteriously crashed when Cárdenas appeared to have a 2 to 1 lead in voting. When the system came back on line the PRI's Salinas de Gortari had mysteriously captured the lead. The official results of the election showed that Salinas won with 51 percent of the vote, a decisive victory, but a far cry from the 60-plus percent of the vote obtained by all of his predecessors. Both opposition candidates participating in the election, Cárdenas for the FDN and Manuel Clouthier for the PAN, claimed that the PRI had used electoral fraud to win. Their claims appeared to be substantiated by the fact that there were over 1,700 precincts that reported Salinas receiving 100 percent of the vote—a highly unlikely outcome.

Despite a widespread belief that the election had been stolen, the opposition had few avenues to contest the official outcome because the federal government had close ties to the Federal Electoral Commission, and because Congress voted to certify the results of the election.[12] Therefore Carlos Salinas was able to take office but had to contend with the popular perception that he was an "illegitimate" president. He also had to work quickly to mollify detractors within his own party. To mend fences and protect the PRI's hold on power, he offered members of rival factions minor but powerful cabinet positions and bureaucratic posts. To redeem himself and his party in the eyes of Mexico and the world, Salinas also introduced an ambitious set of economic and political reforms. In the late 1980s this project appeared to have few chances for success. However, Salinas's charisma and political acumen allowed him to implement reforms that would have a huge impact on Mexico and earn for himself and his country, if not his party, national, and international prestige.

In the economic realm, Salinas continued and deepened the country's fiscal discipline and neoliberal reform project. To that end he continued to keep a tight control on government spending, and at the same time sought to encourage greater investment and reduce capital flight by reprivatizing the banks and a number of other industries, renegotiating the foreign debt, and permanently reducing barriers to trade with its most important trading partner, the United States, with a North American Free Trade Agreement (NAFTA). Salinas promised that implementing this set of reforms would gain Mexico entry into the illustrious first world of countries with robust and diverse market-driven economies and high standards of living. At the same time, the president acknowledged that such reforms would disproportionately harm the poor, particularly in the countryside, who were least prepared but most likely to be displaced by structural changes in the economy. In order to soften the transition for the poorest and most marginalized communities, Salinas also introduced the National Solidarity Program (Programa Nacional de Solidaridad, PRONASOL), a government-funded program designed to help communities find ways to meet their most pressing public service and infrastructure needs.[13] The Solidarity program met the needs of some of the neediest people in Mexican society, but it never went far enough or reached all of those in need. It nevertheless did do something to promote economic well-being and it served the very important political purpose of demonstrating the commitment of the government, and therefore the PRI, to addressing poverty.[14]

Recognizing that the opposition and the Mexican people were unlikely to tolerate a repeat of the 1988 election in the future, Salinas also introduced some significant reforms to the political system designed to level the playing field and preserve the PRI's dominance. In 1990, the Federal Code of Electoral Institutions and Procedures (Código Federal de Instituciones y Procesos Electorales, COFIPE) was implemented and created a new voter registry with tamper-proof identification cards, and two new and independent electoral institutions. The Federal Electoral Institute (IFE) replaced the Federal Electoral Commission and was charged with organizing and overseeing elections, while the Federal Electoral Tribunal (Tribunal Federal Electoral, TRIFE) had the authority to adjudicate electoral disputes. These institutions were designed to remove the electoral process from the purview of the federal executive and make the electoral process more objective and transparent. Also included in the COFIPE was a revision of the governability clause introduced in 1986. Under the COFIPE, the revised governability clause guaranteed that the party with the most votes in single member districts for the Chamber of Deputies, as long as it was above 35 percent, was automatically awarded a majority of seats in the legislature.

While the opposition was widely in favor of the creation of the independent electoral bodies, it saw the governability clause for what it was: a clear attempt to preserve the position of the PRI, since no other party could, at the time, hope to win more single-member districts. Therefore many within the opposition refused to support the COFIPE, particularly those affiliated with the newly created Party of the Democratic Revolution (Partido de la Revolución Democrática, PRD) that grew out of the FDN in 1989.[15] Yet the reforms were approved by the legislature, not because the PRI unilaterally amended the constitution as it had in the past; it did not have the necessary two-thirds majority to do this. Rather, Salinas was forced to find outside support for his reforms. Somewhat surprisingly, he found a willing partner in the PAN. Despite its long-standing criticism of and antipathy toward the PRI, many believe that the PAN entered into a *concertación* or surreptitious pact with the PRI during the early 1990s. This pact may have benefited the PAN with key concessions, such as electoral reforms and recognition of its electoral victories, though PAN leaders vigorously denied that there was any collaborative agreement with the PRI. In the final analysis, the PAN was largely in favor of Salinas's neoliberal economic reforms, was leery of Mexico's new opposition on the left, and felt that even with the governability clause, the creation of the IFE was a meaningful step in the right direction. Pact or not, the PAN had many reasons to support the PRI's agenda, and did so.

Meanwhile, under pressure by the increased occurrence of postelectoral disputes, Salinas introduced a second round of reforms in 1993 to expand representation and lessen the PRI's institutional advantages.[16] These reforms had several elements: First, the size of the Senate was doubled, to 128 seats. Each state had four seats, the first three were awarded to the party with the greatest share of the votes, and the last was reserved for the second-place party. This allowed the opposition to have a minimum of 25 percent of Senate seats, but obviously would not threaten a two-thirds majority of the PRI. Second, the contentious governability clause was amended so that no party could hold more than 60 percent of the seats in the Chamber of Deputies. This meant that no party, including the PRI, could have the two-thirds majority needed to unilaterally amend the constitution. Third, the IFE was given the role of certifying legislative electoral results. This greatly enhanced the transparency of a practice that in the past had fallen to the legislature itself.[17]

By late 1993 it appeared that Carlos Salinas had done the impossible: he had placed Mexico on solid economic ground and on the verge of beginning a new era of free trade with the United States and Canada, while at the same time doing something to address the dire need of his country's most disadvantaged citizens; he had mended fences with detractors within his party and reestablished the PRI's hegemony, and he had worked with the opposition to implement some significant political reforms. In fact, Salinas's successes were so impressive that Mexicans openly speculated about the possibility of amending the constitution to allow him to serve a second term of office, and many in the international community had taken to calling Mexico a model for other developing countries to emulate. However, as quickly as Salinas had won the hearts of Mexicans and foreign observers alike, beginning on January 1, 1994, he began a precipitous slide that eleven months later left him one of the most reviled politicians in Mexican history.

Salinas's declining popularity began with an uprising instigated by the Zapatista National Liberation Army (Ejercito Zapatista de Liberación Nacional, EZLN) on New Year's Day. This uprising, which we discuss in more detail in chapter 8, was planned to coincide with the first day that NAFTA went into effect in order to demonstrate to the government and the world that Salinas's reforms had done nothing to meaningfully address the plight of Mexico's most downtrodden, the indigenous communities, nor to convincingly demonstrate that it was committed to constructing an inclusive democracy. While the government struggled to find the right response to the Zapatistas, its image was further tarnished by the assassination of two high-ranking members of the PRI, one of which was Salinas's chosen successor, Luis Donaldo Colosio.[18]

Colosio's assassination put Salinas in the uncomfortable position of naming a second choice from the tiny pool of eligible candidates.[19] His choice was Ernesto Zedillo, the former minister of education, who while a Yale-educated technocrat, had the appearance of a stiff, unimaginative bureaucrat poorly suited to excel in public office, much less the presidency.[20] The final blow came in December, when only eighteen days after his inauguration Ernesto Zedillo was forced to devalue the peso in order to avoid economic collapse. As a result Mexicans who held their savings in the national currency lost nearly half of their savings at the same time that they saw their outstanding debt increase exponentially. While this turn of events was devastating, for many Mexicans it was somehow not as bad as finding out that the Salinas administration had fully understood the nature and consequences of the impending economic crisis, but allowed it to worsen rather than assuming responsibility for the inflated currency and implementing the devaluation.

From Hegemony to Power Sharing (1994–2000)

Like Salinas, Ernesto Zedillo was expected to be a weak, ineffective leader. And while it took some time to dispel rumors that he would not finish his term of office, over his term Zedillo managed to salvage his personal image by shepherding meaningful political reform and deepening the country's economic stability. Thanks largely to the creation of the IFE, the 1994 elections were widely regarded as free and fair, and without a doubt the cleanest in Mexico's history. Seeking to build on this foundation, and to the dismay of many within his party, Zedillo set out to deepen Mexico's transition away from single-party dominance and toward democracy. Building on the reforms of the Salinas administration, in 1996 he introduced legislation that prevented a party from enjoying extreme overrepresentation in the Chamber of Deputies and ensured that half of the Senate seats would go to the second-place party in each contest. Furthermore, under Zedillo the IFE became a truly independent body, governed by nonpartisan citizen councilors rather than the minister of the interior, and with sole authority over electoral matters. Political parties were guaranteed by law more equal access to public funds and media exposure, and at the same time were increasingly required to account for the amounts and sources of their campaign contributions as well as their campaign spending. The cumulative effect of the political reforms implemented between 1990 and 1996 was to gradually erode the PRI's electoral dominance.

The PRI's decline became painfully and undeniably clear in the aftermath of the 1997 midterm elections when it lost its majority in the Chamber of Deputies for the first time in its existence. This development, while profoundly bruising to the PRI, proved to be instrumental in promoting Mexico's transition toward democracy because it introduced, for the first time, a system of checks and balances and forced the executive to negotiate with the legislature even for relatively minor concessions. Of similar importance were Zedillo's efforts to strengthen the judiciary. Reforms in 1994 enhanced power sharing at the federal level by increasing the power and independence of the judiciary and giving it new powers of judicial review.

For all of the reforms that Ernesto Zedillo deepened or introduced, for the PRI, perhaps the most significant of these was his apparent refusal to designate his successor. Under enormous pressure by many in the party to continue the tradition of handpicking the man to carry on the legacy of the party, Zedillo instead chose to downplay his influence, and in so doing, forced the party to adopt new internal rules for candidate selection. The importance of this move should not be underestimated because it weakened the traditional power of the president and brought greater internal democratization to the PRI—an element sorely lacking before the late 1990s. The president's ability to choose his successor has been identified as one of the most important elements of presidential power in Mexico because it guaranteed that he could single-handedly award the highest prize for party and personal loyalty. Zedillo's decision to break with this practice may have stemmed from the fact that he represented no particular faction of the party—all had equally disdained and even challenged him during his *sexenio*—and he therefore did not feel so compelled to remain true to the party's traditional practices. Moreover, given his weakness within his own party, it is possible that his selection would have faced open challenges by the losing factions with potentially devastating consequences for the party.[21]

Whatever the reasons for Zedillo's final decision, in the end it benefited the PRI by forcing it to adopt an internal primary process that modernized the party and probably made it more competitive.[22] Nevertheless, in the short term, the PRI's primary produced a bitter and damaging internal brawl as each of the four main aspirants sought to win the party's nomination. In their attempt to curry popular favor, the contenders slung mud and threw punches, accusing one another of everything from violating internal party rules to participating in the party's use of electoral fraud and corruption. In the end, Francisco Labastida, a technocrat said to be Zedillo's unstated choice, won a decisive victory, but at the personal expense of his challengers, and perhaps more importantly, at the cost of the PRI's credibility and legitimacy.[23] There is little doubt that the bruising primary campaign contributed to the PRI's loss of the presidency in 2000, for once selected, Labastida emerged as a relatively strong candidate who was probably the best (of the four precandidates) the party had to offer. Yet despite this and the fact that the Zedillo administration had managed to right Mexico's economic ship—no small feat given the disastrous consequences of the 1994 devaluation and his predecessors' legacy of passing on an economy on the brink of collapse—Labastida and the PRI were unable to perpetuate the party's seven-decade hold on executive power. The PRI's defeat in 2000 culminated a long and gradual electoral decline for the ruling party (see figure 4.1).

Equally important in the PRI's defeat in 2000 was the growing strength of the opposition, and in particular the PAN. While the PRD and its third-time presidential candidate, Cuauhtémoc Cárdenas, still had significant popular support in the capital, the organization's internal dynamics and infighting had prevented it from becoming a well-consolidated, disciplined political party. Although he was undisputedly among the party's most important leaders, Cárdenas was a controversial candidate in 2000 within the PRD. Many felt that after his poor showing in 1994, winning just 17 percent of the vote, and his mediocre performance as the mayor of Mexico City, the party needed a more dynamic candidate to appeal to voters. Moreover, the party's internal squabbles, public airing of dirty laundry, and perceived ambivalence toward democracy alienated voters who were otherwise sympathetic to its left-of-center ideology. In retrospect, a stronger candidate with more popular appeal and a more coherent party organization with a proven track record were absolutely necessary to counter the challenge put forth by, one the one hand, the incumbent party with a long, if tainted, legacy and copious resources, and

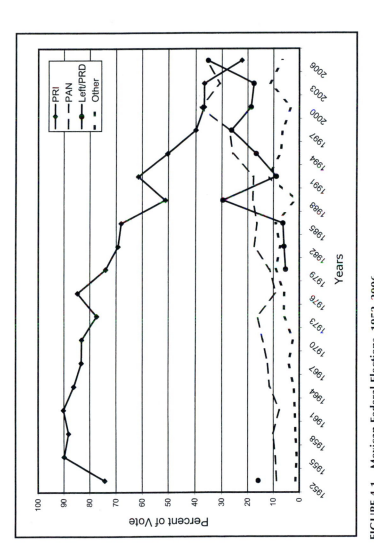

FIGURE 4.1 Mexican Federal Elections, 1952–2006

Sources: 1961 and 1988 figures: Silvia Gómez Tagle, *La Frágil Democracia Mexicana: Partidos Políticos y Elecciones* (Mexico City: García y Valadés Editores, 1993). 1964–1985 figures: Juan Molinar Horcasitas, "The 1985 Federal Elections in Mexico: The Product of a System," in Arturo Alvarado (ed.). *Electoral Patterns and Perspectives in Mexico.* Monograph Series, 20. (La Jolla: Center for U.S.-Mexican Studies, 1987). Figures from 1991–1997 derived from Carlos Sirvent, "Las Elecciones de 1997: El Voto Por La Alternancia," in *Estudios Políticos. Cuarta Época.* No. 16. (September–December 1997), pp. 67–89. 2003 and 2006 data obtained from IFE.

on the other, the PAN, with its upstart candidate, reputation for honesty and transparency, and vast campaign war chest.

To many observers of Mexico, Vicente Fox and the PAN seemed to come out of nowhere to win the presidency in 2000, when in fact Fox's victory represented the culmination of the PAN's growing electoral success throughout the 1990s. Its success in 2000 was determined by several factors, including the party's ability to capitalize on its many subnational electoral victories and solid reputation and parlay these into greater national support.[24] Yet equally important was their choice of candidate. In some senses, the choice of Vicente Fox as the party's presidential candidate was unexpected because although he had a proven track record as a federal deputy and governor of the state of Guanajuato, he was not a member of the party leadership. Indeed, he was thought by many within the PAN to be too pragmatic and not fully committed to the party's principles or statutes. Nevertheless, thanks to his image as a no-nonsense leader who was not afraid to call a spade a spade, and a well-organized political action committee that amassed a small fortune in campaign contributions and began a groundswell of popular support, Fox emerged as the PAN's best chance for defeating the PRI, and even skeptics in the party became obliged to support his candidacy. Although most predictions favored the PRI, Fox's sophisticated campaign convinced voters that Labastida was no different from the party he represented—authoritarian, corrupt, and retrograde. At the same time, Fox also presented himself as the best option for meaningful change by discrediting Labastida's claims of representing a "new" PRI and overshadowing Cárdenas's attempts to present himself as the champion of Mexican nationalism and a credible source of change. In the end, 42 percent of voters felt that Fox was their best hope for defeating the PRI and moving the country forward, and Mexico entered the twenty-first century with its first opposition president in more than seven decades.

Mexico's Democracy in the Twenty-First Century

During his campaign, Fox promised change for Mexico through wide-ranging reforms that included an overhaul of the tax system, modernizing and privatizing the energy sector, and labor reform. Fox also promised to create a million jobs a year, produce 7 percent annual GDP growth, resolve the lingering conflict in Chiapas, reduce crime and corruption, and deliver an immigration accord with the United States. However, skeptics openly questioned whether the first non-PRI president would be able to achieve the kind of policies and reforms necessary to achieve his goals. Indeed, over the course of his term, Mexico's economy muddled through with an average of about 3 percent growth, and key sectors (such as footwear and *maquiladora* production) suffered major hits from overseas competition. Despite Fox's leadership on new legislation for indigenous rights, the Zapatista rebels in Chiapas refused to lay down their arms. Ongoing problems of crime and violence, including a wave of high-profile killings in major drug-trafficking regions, left many Mexicans feeling even less safe than at the start of his administration. Meanwhile, Fox's efforts to negotiate an immigration accord with the United States faltered in the face of newfound concerns about illegal immigration and terrorism following the September 11 terrorist attacks.

In retrospect it is clear that skepticism of Fox's campaign pledges was warranted. Despite the evident sincerity of his ambitions, Fox ultimately faced significant challenges resulting from his governing style, divisions within his own party, and a divided Congress. Critics charged that, while he may have been an excellent candidate to win the presidency, once in office Fox lacked the political skills to overcome these difficulties. Indeed, early in his administration, Fox angered many within the PAN by giving important government posts to members of the opposition and personal allies who lacked strong ties to the party. This was in keeping with Fox's vision of his administration as a "government of transition." It also provided an important break from the PRI's old practices of using cabinet positions mainly to reward loyalty, rather seeking the most qualified candidate for the office. However, not surprisingly, the PAN felt alienated and it reacted by openly questioning what place its agenda had in the new government.

Throughout his *sexenio*, Fox made an effort to mend fences by gradually increasing PAN representation in his government and reaching out to party leaders, but he was nonetheless unable to gain party support for some of his major policy priorities, most notably, his tax reform package. Fox's first tax reform initiative, introduced early in his term, sought to substantially increase tax revenue by extending the national value-added tax (VAT), in effect a 15 percent sales tax, to include previously exempt items such as food, medicine, school tuition, and public transportation. The initiative quickly went down in flames, not just because the opposition fiercely criticized it, but also because Fox never bothered to vet his proposal with members of his own party before presenting to Congress. As a result, though many in the PAN may have supported it, PAN legislators found themselves in the awkward position of advocating a tax increase widely perceived as disproportionately affecting the poor.[25] By the time Fox got his party onboard and proposed a second version of the legislation two years later, the issue had polarized the opposition and elicited organized public condemnation.[26]

Indeed, the highly polarized political climate that prevailed during Fox's term was by far the greatest obstacle to his policy agenda. Fox faced a divided legislature controlled by two opposition parties—the PRI and the PRD—that were in a very strong position to recapture the presidency at the end of his term. In this context, members of the opposition were unlikely to give Fox much quarter, since voter dissatisfaction with his government could translate into support for their parties. Indeed, despite the PAN's slogan during the 2003 midterm elections—"Take the brakes off change"—voters increased their support for the opposition, especially the PRD (which nearly doubled its seats in the Chamber of Deputies from fifty in 2000 to ninety-seven in 2003). Hence the 2003 midterm elections secured Fox's status as a lame duck president, and ensured that major changes would not be forthcoming over the remainder of his administration.

That said, Fox's six years in office were hardly a complete failure. Indeed, his administration can claim credit for some important successes, chief among them economic stability. While the Mexican economy did not grow at nearly the rate promised by Fox, it did grow, and equally important, strict fiscal discipline led to a balanced budget and a significant decrease in inflation, from over 16 percent in 1999 to roughly 4 percent in 2006. These accomplishments are remarkable given the depth of the 1994 peso crisis and the historical tendency of the Mexican economy to fluctuate widely between inflationary booms and devastating recessions. Building on the efforts of the Zedillo administration, Fox's economic team gave Mexico a presidential term without a major financial crisis for the first time in decades.

The Fox administration had other notable successes as well. Among the most important was the introduction of a law akin to the Freedom of Information Act in the United States. The Federal Law for Transparency and Access to Public Government Information allowed citizens to have access for the first time to a wide array of government documents and greatly promoted transparency and accountability at the national level.[27] Also important was the Federal Law to Prevent and Eliminate Discrimination, a law that strengthened existing legislation and made it illegal to discriminate on the basis of "ethnic or national origin, sex, age, disability, social or economic condition, health, pregnancy, language, religion, opinions, sexual preference, or marital status." These are but two examples of several laws that the Fox administration was able to enact by eliciting the support of the opposition.[28] That the Fox administration achieved support for these and other important laws belies the suggestion that partisan competition and legislative deadlock prevented any meaningful progress during Fox's *sexenio*. In fact, it is rather the case that all three of the major parties were able to claim some victories thanks to shifting coalitions: each had the opportunity to ally itself with one of the others and thereby obtain the majority needed to pass legislation. As a result, under Fox, the Mexican Congress actually passed more legislation during his term than under any other president in recent decades.

The Controversial 2006 Elections

The PAN's poor showing in the 2003 midterm elections and Fox's failure to make good his major campaign promises, suggested that the PRI and the PRD had an opportunity to seize the presidency in 2006. As discussed in greater detail in chapter 6, the 2006 presidential election proved extremely controversial, since the result was a virtual tie between PAN candidate Felipe Calderón and PRD candidate Andrés Manuel López Obrador. Ultimately, Calderón was declared the winner by the slimmest of margins, 0.5 percent of the vote, or roughly a quarter of a million votes, and was heavily criticized by López Obrador and his supporters, who alleged electoral fraud and bias in the post-electoral legal decisions.

The 2006 election revealed that Mexico was divided between those in the north and central western parts of the country, who had largely supported Calderón, and those in the south and central east, who had supported López Obrador. Furthermore, the country was almost evenly split between those who favored the existing economic model that called for promoting free market reforms, and those who favored a model that allowed the government to play a more active role in the distribution of resources. These divisions, together with Calderón's tiny margin of victory and the postelectoral disputes, suggested that Mexico was in for a tough six years—a notion that was only reinforced by López Obrador's refusal to accept defeat and walk away.

Instead, between July and September, when the electoral authorities were deliberating whether or not to allow a recount, he rallied his supporters and organized a series of public demonstrations and sit-ins that blocked off significant parts of Mexico City. These manifestations made it clear that López Obrador had a strong following and would not back down. But at the same time, they virtually shut down the center of Mexico City, causing ire and frustration among citizens unable to report for work and school. Furthermore, when Calderón was finally declared the winner of the election, López Obrador claimed that the election had been stolen and that, much like Cuauhtémoc Cárdenas in 1988, he was the "legitimate president." Together with the National Democratic Convention (CND), a "parallel government" that would monitor the actions of the "spurious government" and orchestrate meaningful reforms, López Obrador sought to stay in the public eye and eventually displace Felipe Calderón, who was nothing more than a "usurper." He continually refused to meet with Calderón, stating in characteristically aggressive language: "If we negotiate, if we allow ourselves to be coopted, if we sell ourselves out, we would be dealing a huge blow to the national democratic movement and therefore the minority, and a neofascist oligarchy would always decide Mexico's destiny."[29]

Casting another shadow over the postelectoral dispute was an increasingly violent occupation of the central town square in the capital city of Oaxaca state by members and sympathizers of the teachers' union. The demonstration began as a strike and series of sit-ins and takeovers of government property in an effort to win raises for the severely underpaid teachers and to call for the resignation of the state governor, a PRI dinosaur believed to have used fraud to win the election and accused of using force to silence detractors. At the same time, Mexico was experiencing unprecedented levels of violent crime, including approximately 2,200 homicides related to drug cartel activity in 2006. The result of the 2006 election, along with the unrest in Oaxaca, and unprecedented levels of insecurity, seemed to confirm that many Mexicans have yet to see the kind of change they called for six years before. Calderón thus took office with serious questions about his legitimacy and severe social unrest. While Calderón has made some progress in addressing these issues during his first years in office, it remains far too early to know what his legacy will be in the years to come.

Conclusion

Clearly Mexico's transition away from the single-party dominance of the PRI happened gradually over several decades. New students of Mexican politics are sure to ask why, given the PRI's loss of legitimacy in almost every area, the transition did not happen faster or earlier. With the help of hindsight, it is possible to say that the pace and even the character of Mexico's transition were determined largely by timing and sequence of events. That is, had all of the contributing factors, economic crisis, loss of legitimacy, and institutional openings happened all at once, we might have expected the PRI to lose power more quickly and definitively. But obviously this could not have happened because each event was a consequence of another: the PRI's loss of legitimacy stemmed in no small part from its failure as an economic manager and agent of redistribution, as well as its exclusionary and corrupt tendencies. The loss of legitimacy in turn made it increasingly difficult for the PRI to use its traditional practices (e.g., cooptation, electoral fraud) to perpetuate its power, and forced the administrations of the 1970s, 1980s, and 1990s to create the openings that gradually leveled the playing field and made it possible for the opposition to gain entry into the political system. Meanwhile, the pace of the transition was determined by the regime's periodic runs of good luck (the discovery of vast oil deposits in the mid-1970s) and its understandable reluctance to dismantle the authoritarian institutions that preserved its dominance. Only when faced with serious challenges to its power did it enact the reforms that cumulatively brought greater democracy to Mexico. In some ways the erratic and moderate pace of the transition may have benefited the opposition by providing it time to gain the electoral and governing experience that was essential to its successes in the mid-1990s.

The question we are left with is whether Mexico's transition has proceeded far enough and penetrated deeply enough to establish the country as a definitive democracy. As subsequent chapters will demonstrate, the country has the foundation for a solid democracy: for example, it has some of the strongest electoral institutions in the world, the separation and balance of powers has been considerably strengthened in the past fifteen years, and Mexican voters believe they have a meaningful role to play in the electoral and political processes. However, there also remain vestiges of the past and formidable obstacles that suggest that Mexico's transition is not complete: the lines of representation and accountability between legislators and their constituents are something between fuzzy and nonexistent, the rule of law remains weak, and vast socioeconomic disparities undermine the equality purportedly offered by the Mexican constitution. These and other hurdles notwithstanding, we are optimistic that the maturation of Mexico's democracy will continue. That said, if history is a reliable guide, we should expect future change to occur gradually, in fits and starts, and often as the unintended consequence of another set of events, rather than as a linear or uninterrupted series of improvements.

Key Terms

1985 Mexico City earthquake
Calderón, Felipe
Cárdenas, Cuauhtémoc
Clouthier, Manuel
COFIPE
Colosio, Luis Donaldo
debt crisis
Echeverría, Luis
Federal Electoral Institute (IFE)
Fox, Vicente
governability clause
Labastida, Francisco

López Obrador, Andrés Manuel
López Portillo, José
Madrid, Miguel de la
National Democratic Front (FDN)
neoliberalism
Party of the Democratic Revolution (PRD)
Salinas, Carlos
technocrats
Zapatista National Liberation Army (EZLN)
Zedillo, Ernesto

Recommended Readings

Cornelius, Wayne A., Judith Gentleman, and Peter H. Smith, eds. *Mexico's Alternative Political Futures.* La Jolla: Center for U.S-Mexican Studies, University of California-San Diego, 1989.

Greene, Ken. *Why Dominant Parties Lose: Mexico's Democratization in Comparative Perspective.* Cambridge: Cambridge University Press, 2007.

Levy, Daniel C., and Kathleen Bruhn. *Mexico: The Struggle for Democratic Development.* Berkeley: University of California Press, 2006.

Preston, Julia, and Samuel Dillon. *Opening Mexico: The Making of a Democracy.* New York: Farrar, Straus & Giroux, 2004.

Notes

1. Kenneth Greene, *Why Dominant Parties Lose: Mexico's Democratization in Comparative Perspective* (Cambridge: Cambridge University Press, 2007).

2. The Mexican Miracle is discussed in chapter 9. See also Roger Hansen, *The Politics of Mexican Political Development* (Baltimore: Johns Hopkins University Press, 1971), 11–96; and Judith Adler Hellman, *Mexico in Crisis*, 2nd ed. (New York: Holmes & Meier, 1988), 59–124.

3. This discussion draws on Adler Hellman's thorough discussion of the 1970s and 1980s in *Mexico*, 187–216.

4. Part of this effort included clamping down on journalists known for their independence and promoting older politicos rather than younger, more progressive members as he had in the early part of his term. See Adler Hellman, *Mexico*, 205–206.

5. Much of this speculation included discussion of whether a military coup was possible in Mexico. While the Mexican military had not played an active role in politics since the 1920s, recent military coups in places like Chile, Uruguay, and later Argentina had a profound effect on the region. See Adler Hellman, *Mexico*, 201–15.

6. Adler Hellman, *Mexico*, 229.

7. Although the amendment to Article 115 of the Mexican constitution was supposed to empower local governments, it had the effect of requiring them to assume financial and administrative responsibility for public services they had neither the resources nor training to provide. See R. Andrew Nickson, *Local Government in Latin America* (Boulder: Lynne Rienner, 1995); Victoria Rodriguez, *Decentralization in Mexico: From Reforma Municipal to Solidaridad to Nuevo Federalismo* (Boulder: Westview, 1997).

8. By 1985 PAN members had become increasingly vocal about being singled out for intimidation, forceful repression, and electoral fraud in both subnational and national elections. See David Shirk, *Mexico's New Politics: The PAN and Democratic Change* (Boulder: Lynne Rienner, 2005), 97–132.

9. The 1986 reforms also gave the federal executive the power to name the presidents of all electoral authorities from the Federal Electoral Commission down to the polling places. Clearly this did nothing to increase the transparency or equity of the electoral process.

10. On the rise of the technocrats in the PRI, see Miguel Angel Centeno, *Democracy within Reason: Technocratic Revolution in Mexico* (University Park: Pennsylvania State University Press, 2004).

11. The small parties had a variety of reasons for supporting Cárdenas. Some were still angry about the 1986 reforms and the clear advantage they preserved for the PRI,

and others felt that Cárdenas would be more faithful to their leftist ideological beliefs. On the formation and subsequent performance of the PRD, see Kathleen Bruhn, *Taking on Goliath: The Emergence of a New Left Party and the Struggle for Democracy in Mexico* (University Park: Pennsylvania State University Press, 2004).

12. In 1988 Congress was still dominated by the PRI, but even members of the opposition supported Salinas's victory, either because they did not want to cast doubt on the validity of the same election that brought them to power, or because they did not support a Cárdenas victory.

13. Wayne A. Cornelius, Ann L. Craig, and Jonathan Fox, eds., *Transforming State-Society Relations in Mexico: The National Solidarity Strategy* (La Jolla: Center for U.S.-Mexican Studies, 1994).

14. Solidarity was also an invaluable electoral tool. Juan Molinar Horcasitas and Jeffrey Weldon demonstrated that municipalities and communities that had supported Cuauhtémoc Cárdenas in the 1988 election received a disproportionate amount of the program's resources, seemingly to ensure that they would support the PRI in future elections. "Electoral Determinants and Consequences of National Solidarity," in Wayne Cornelius, Craig, and Fox, eds., *Transforming State-Society Relations*, 123–42.

15. The PRD's opposition to the reforms also stemmed from the party's antipathy toward Salinas himself, who had made life very difficult for the PRD during his short time in office. Indeed, during his entire *sexenio* the PRD was treated as a hostile enemy. There were a number of reasons for this. First, for many within the PRI, Cárdenas had committed an unforgivable act in leaving and then challenging the party in the 1988 election. Second, ideologically, the PRD was highly critical of Salinas's neoliberal economic agenda and used this as the basis for disagreeing with the administration at almost every turn. Finally, given Cárdenas's strong showing in 1988, the PRI perceived that the PRD posed the strongest challenge to its dominance and therefore made a concerted effort to undermine it. The most compelling evidence for the PRI's persecution of the PRD is that more than 300 members of the party were killed or "disappeared" between 1989 and 1994 when Salinas left office. See Bruhn, *Taking on Goliath*.

16. The impetus for this round of reforms came from the fact that after 1988, it was impossible for the PRI to win an election without the opposition crying foul. Salinas was concerned that the 1994 presidential election would be marred by such claims. Furthermore, Salinas was eager to demonstrate to the U.S. Congress, which at the time was debating whether to ratify NAFTA, that Mexico had a strong commitment to democratizing its political system.

17. The 1993 reforms also included the repeal of a law preventing Mexican-born children of foreign parents from running for president. This move was seen as a concession to the PAN and Vicente Fox, who under the previous law was ineligible. The reforms further allowed election observers to be present at the polls and make comments on election day events, and required parties to submit financial reports to the IFE to prove that they had not exceeded newly established campaign spending limits.

18. The other assassination was that of José Francisco Ruiz Massieu, the brother-in-law of Carlos Salinas and secretary-general of the PRI.

19. Mexican electoral laws state that candidates must resign their government posts six months prior to an election. Therefore Salinas's closest allies and cabinet

members were ineligible to run for president. Ernesto Zedillo was eligible because he had stepped down from his post as education minister to run Colosio's presidential campaign.

20. For some, the biggest surprise of 1994 was that, amid all the political unrest that was so clearly directed at or emanating from the PRI, Zedillo was able to win the election, especially given the fact that he was running against Cuauhtémoc Cárdenas on the left and Diego Fernando de Cevallos, a strong candidate on the right. Yet he did win, largely because his campaign succeeded in branding its strongest challenger, Cárdenas, as an unknown and potentially dangerous option. Interestingly, the PRI managed to capitalize on rampant feelings of public insecurity in the aftermath of the Chiapas uprising and political assassinations by posing voters with a choice: stick with the PRI, which may not be perfect but has a proven record of maintaining political stability, or go with an unknown who has close ties to "radical" organizations eager to use violence and civic unrest. Many of the PRI's television ads allowed voters to draw their own conclusions but openly juxtaposed PRD symbols (the sun, the party colors) with video coverage of violent demonstrations.

21. This is not to say that Zedillo was completely removed from the candidate selection process. Indeed, it was clear relatively early on that Francisco Labastida was Zedillo's choice to succeed him.

22. One of the reasons that the opposition was so successful at winning subnational elections in the 1990s was that its internal primaries generated strong candidates with popular appeal.

23. On the events leading up to the 2000 elections, see Shirk, *Mexico's New Politics*, chapter 5.

24. Evidence of this is found in the PAN's incremental but consistent improvement in electoral contests between 1988 and 2000. The three presidential candidates received, respectively, 17, 27, and 42.5 percent of the vote. During the same time period, the party's share of the vote in the Chamber of Deputies also increased substantially.

25. The initial proposal included a monthly stipend to offset the tax increase for the poorest Mexicans, but this provision would have fallen far short of ameliorating the effects of the reform on members of the population who were not among the poorest but still struggled to obtain the basis necessities of life.

26. In late 2003 it appeared that Fox's proposal might receive enough support from the PRI to pass, until the prospect of cooperating with the PAN and supporting a regressive tax led to a bitter public feud within the PRI and dashed the administration's hopes for the reform. See Edmonds-Poli, "Decentralization under Fox: Progress or Stagnation?" *Mexican Studies/Estudios Mexicanos* 22, no. 2 (Summer 2006): 387–416.

27. This law has been used to great effect to uncover the truth about the nature of the government's actions in the 1968 Tlatelolco massacre.

28. Other laws included reforms to the federal tax code, amendments to the federal criminal code, the Law of Promotions and Commendations of the Mexican Army and Air Force, and the science and technology law, designed to increase the coordination of information among government agencies and improve the transparency of government grant-making. Shirk, *Mexico's New Politics*, 198.

29. "Rechaza AMLO dialogo con gobierno," *Reforma*, December 12, 2006.

II

POLITICAL INSTITUTIONS, CULTURE, AND SOCIETY

5

Government Structure and Processes

Mexican Government

Reading Mexico's 1917 constitution might lead one to believe that its political system is very similar to—if not more advanced than—the U.S. constitution, authored nearly 150 years earlier. Comprising 9 title sections and 136 separate articles, Mexico's constitution provides for a presidential executive, a bicameral legislature, an independent judiciary, a federal system of states with constitutionally granted autonomy, and direct popular elections for the selection of political leaders (without a U.S.-style electoral college). Compared to the U.S. constitution, the Mexican constitution is far more progressive, since it provides special protections for indigenous minorities and grants all citizens a right to basic education, labor protections, and other social welfare provisions.

In practice, however, Mexican politics have always been quite different from those of its northern neighbor, and political practices have often deviated very significantly from constitutionally prescribed procedures and rights. As we have seen, for most of the twentieth century, Mexico functioned more like a highly centralized authoritarian regime than a competitive democratic system, since the PRI controlled nearly all aspects of the political process. Single-party domination compromised the spirit of many formal institutions (e.g., legislative and judicial independence), and virtually eliminated the possibility of power sharing. Additionally, the PRI's hegemony made it almost impossible for the opposition to gather enough momentum to pose a serious challenge to the status quo. Yet by the mid-1980s the PRI's power began to decline as Mexicans increasingly questioned its effectiveness and legitimacy as the institutionalized legacy of the revolution. Over the course of the next two decades, the Mexican political system experienced significant changes that signaled the end of single-party authoritarianism and the beginning of Mexican democracy. This chapter discusses Mexico's main governmental structures and describes how they have changed during the country's transition to democracy.

Executive Branch

During most of the period of PRI hegemony, Mexico's president enjoyed the authority and legitimacy of an autocrat. This power was not granted by the constitution, which outlines fewer powers for the Mexican executive than for many of his counterparts in Latin America.[1] Yet during the rule of the PRI, the power of the Mexican president typically exceeded the de jure or legal responsibilities of the office (see textbox 5.1). According to political scientist Jeffrey Weldon, the Mexican president's historically exaggerated powers—described as hyperpresidentialism or *presidencialismo*—stemmed from the coincidence of three conditions that predominated during PRI rule: unified government, a high level of party discipline, and presidential leadership of his political party. Together these three elements created a situation that allowed the president to exercise an inordinate amount of influence in the Mexican political system.[2] Today, the Mexican presidential power is much more limited and the executive must work to forge political consensus with other branches and levels of government.

Hyperpresidentialism in Mexico

Unified government refers to the fact that a single party, the PRI, held a majority in both houses of Congress from the 1930s until 1997, and its electoral dominance virtually guaranteed that the president would enjoy legislative support for all of his proposals. But unified government by itself was not enough to produce *presidencialismo*. Another essential condition was strong party discipline within the ruling party. Unless PRI legislators consistently toed the party line, unified government would not have benefited the president. Party discipline within the PRI was traditionally strong thanks to the ban on consecutive reelection. A ban on reelection gives politicians little motivation to pay attention to constituents in their districts, but provides a strong incentive to demonstrate loyalty to party leaders who can help advance their career aspirations.

Loyalty to the PRI was especially important because candidates for office were almost always selected by the party leadership rather than through a primary system. Party discipline and *presidencialismo* were also a consequence of the president's dual role as the head of government and the formal head of his

Textbox 5.1. De Jure Powers of the Mexican President

The specific authority and responsibilities of the president are outlined in Article 89 of the Mexican Constitution, which empowers him as follows:

- To introduce legislation and execute laws generated by the Congress
- To appoint and remove cabinet-level officials and other federal employees
- To appoint, with Senate approval, the Mexican attorney general, high-level diplomatic personnel (such as ambassadors and consular officials), and top military commanders in Mexico's army, navy, and air force
- To appoint other military personnel without Senate approval
- To serve as commander in chief of Mexico's military forces and national guard to preserve Mexico's national security, and to declare war if passed by law through the Mexican Congress
- To direct Mexican foreign policy—and, with Senate approval, the promulgation of international treaties—toward the goal of respecting the principles of self-determination, nonintervention, peaceful resolution of controversies, minimization of the use of force, the legal equality of nations, international cooperation, and the preservation of international peace and security
- To convoke extraordinary sessions of the legislature with approval by its Permanent Commission
- To assist the judiciary as needed to expedite its functions, and to nominate members of the Supreme Court, with approval by the Senate
- To establish and control all ports, customs, and border installations
- To grant pardons to criminals sentenced by federal tribunals or by the Federal District
- To concede temporary privileges to promote invention, discovery, and industrial innovation
- To make high-level appointments (not including the Supreme Court) with approval by the Permanent Commission when the Senate is not in session

party. As head of the party, the president had the de facto power to nominate nearly all PRI candidates, including his successor. Therefore, members of the party were not simply expressing loyalty to their party, they were also demonstrating loyalty to the president in the hopes that they might be tapped for a higher elected or appointed office. The *dedazo*—the term used to describe the ability of sitting executives to handpick their successor——epitomized the excesses of *presidencialismo*.

Together, these three conditions created and reinforced the power of the presidency in Mexico and endowed the office with what have often been called extra-constitutional powers—political power that goes beyond constitutional authority but stays within the bounds of the law.[3] In practice, the chief executive's extra-constitutional authority was used for a variety of purposes.

Most commonly, Mexican presidents used them to amend the constitution, to assume the role of chief legislator, to influence the judiciary in legal matters, to nominate party candidates for offices at all levels of government, and to overrule or even remove state governors and other elected officials. Today, as a result of Mexico's gradual democratization, there are significant constraints on executive power that must be explored in greater detail.

The Era of Divided Government

When the PRI lost its majority in the Chamber of Deputies in 1997, the conditions that created *presidencialismo* were altered and the Mexican executive no longer enjoyed the same amount of power as his predecessors. While party discipline remained high, and the president was still head of the PRI, without unified government, President Zedillo and the PRI had no choice but to recognize that the halcyon days of *presidencialismo* were over. One of the first reality checks came in 1998, when Congress rejected a presidential proposal to establish the Bank Savings Protection Fund (Fondo Bancario de Protección al Ahorro, FOBAPROA), and instead voted to approve a different version of the bill introduced by the PAN. Yet this is not to say that the president suddenly became a weak political player or that the PRI ceased to be the most dominant political power in Mexico. Indeed, the president continued to be the most powerful political actor in the country and the party still enjoyed substantial support at all levels of government. Yet ironically, it was President Zedillo himself who further diminished the power of the presidency by refusing to exercise the office's remaining extra-constitutional powers or to name his successor, instead proclaiming that he would maintain a healthy distance (*sana distancia*) between himself and his party.

Given that Mexican presidents essentially ruled single-handedly for much of the twentieth century, it is not surprising that other aspects of the executive branch were overshadowed. But like other presidential systems, the executive branch in Mexico also comprises the president's cabinet of twenty ministries (see table 5.1) and other key advisers. The president appoints all members of the cabinet and only the Mexican attorney general (Procurador General de la República) must be approved by the Senate. Like their counterparts in other countries, cabinet officials serve as the core of the administration, providing advice and formulating the policies that become the hallmark of a particular *sexenio*. All cabinet-level officials—such as the ministers of foreign relations, treasury, and public security—specialize in specific areas, make recommendations, and oversee the bureaucratic entities that implement the president's policy initiatives. Historically, the most important cabinet official has been the minister of the interior (Secretario de Gobernación), who oversees Mexico's

Table 5.1.
Executive Cabinet Ministries

Government	Social Development
Foreign Relations	Labor and Social Welfare
Attorney General	Transportation
Public Security and Justice	Environment and Natural Resources
National Defense	Energy
Armed Forces	Agriculture and Rural Development
Navy	Agrarian Reform
Treasury	Education
Economy	Health
Governmental Transparency	Tourism

internal affairs. In addition to playing a pivotal role in policy formation and the preservation of public order, serving as interior minister has traditionally provided a stepping-stone to the presidency.[4]

Advisory posts within the presidential staff tend to vary in number and importance from one administration to the next, depending on a president's priorities. Two important positions are the president's personal secretary (Secretario Particular) and his chief adviser (Jefe de Asesores), who serve as his closest advisers and determine who has access to the president. Equally important is the president's legal adviser, without whom the president cannot effectively interact with legislative and judicial branches of government. The office of the president also typically relies on two offices—public opinion and communications—to gather feedback on the administration's performance and publicize its accomplishments. Other advisory positions generally report directly to the president and work alongside specialized agencies to raise the profile of particular policy areas (e.g., national security and foreign relations, public housing, indigenous affairs). President Fox, for example, appointed his close associate Ramón Muñoz to oversee a much-vaunted program on government innovation, and President Calderón has made public security a major priority by appointing experts in this area to his advisory group.

The Mexican executive and his cabinet also oversee a number of bureaucratic agencies and parastatal (state-owned) enterprises. For example, the minister of energy oversees the bureaucratic organization that manages Mexico's energy policy, including the parastatal organization known as Mexican Petroleum (Petróleos de México), better known by the acronym PEMEX, and the Federal Electric Commission (Comisión Federal de Electricidad, CFE), which respectively control the production and distribution of oil and electricity. There are also a number of state-owned banks (e.g., BANOBRAS, NAFIN, BANCOMEXT) that work to promote development and trade. Many of these agencies and parastatal enterprises—particularly PEMEX—are a holdover from the days of state-led economic development (1940s to 1970s), and for many Mexicans, they are the last bastions of national economic pride.

Still, the Mexican presidency is no longer what it once was. Economic restructuring to liberalize trade and domestic production has fundamentally transformed the role of the Mexican state, and therefore the role of the executive branch. Moreover, because of Mexico's political liberalization, the executive branch has been forced to adjust to a more democratic context where power is shared across all three major branches of government. Since 1997, when President Zedillo headed the country's first divided government—where the party that controls the executive branch faces an opposition majority in the legislature—Mexico's presidential system began to function much more like its counterparts in the region. Under these circumstances, the Mexican president and legislature must now negotiate to approve legislation and budgets, or they may be unable to move forward on key policy initiatives. Indeed, divided government during the Fox administration resulted in significant disagreements between the executive and legislative branches, resulting in a total of nine presidential vetoes of congressional legislation (including one budget). Fox's use of presidential veto power for the first time in decades illustrates that the Mexican Congress is no longer a lackey slavishly advancing the policy agenda of the executive. At the same time, the president is also now subject to the kind of legislative oversight and judicial authority found in other presidential democracies. For this reason, we now turn to the other branches that provide "checks and balances" against the Mexican executive.

The Legislature

The duties and functions of the Mexican Congress are outlined in Article 73 of the Mexican constitution. Like the United States, Mexico has a bicameral legislature, with an upper house (the Senate) and a lower house (the Chamber of Deputies). The Mexican Congress meets in two legislative sessions per year, both a Fall term (September through mid-December) and a spring term (mid-March through late April).

As discussed earlier, the Mexican legislature has been historically limited in its role as a check against the executive, primarily because a single, highly disciplined political party controlled both branches of government. As opposition parties gained strength in—and ultimately came to dominate—the legislature, this branch has become a much more powerful counterweight to the executive. Still, Mexican legislators continue to face important challenges and limitations. Due to prohibitions on immediate reelection in Mexico, legislators cannot serve consecutive terms. While they can be reelected after one term has passed, most Mexican legislators have historically served only one term before moving on to some other area or level of government or running for a different public office. As we discuss below, the prohibition on reelection creates a disincentive to develop strong relationships with their constituents, and makes it difficult for them to develop legislative expertise. Below we describe the structure and function of both houses of the legislature, and then discuss the evolving role of the legislature in contemporary Mexican politics.

The Senate

The Mexican Senate comprises 128 members, who are elected concurrently with the president in one of two different ways. Each of Mexico's thirty-one states and the Federal District elects two senators under the plurality rule, and one senator based on the principle of first minority. In any given senatorial election, the party that receives the highest vote, even if it is less than half, wins two seats and the second place (or first minority) party is awarded one seat. The remaining thirty-two Senate seats are allocated according to proportional representation (PR), that is, in proportion to their share of the total national vote.[5]

This complex method of selection for Mexican senators was intended to provide a degree of access to the Senate for minority parties. However, in practice parties are not necessarily represented in proportion to their actual electoral strength. For example, with only a plurality of the vote, a single party could win two-thirds of the seats in each state and any number of PR seats and be significantly overrepresented in the Senate. Indeed, in the 2006 election, the PAN won 33 percent of the national vote but was awarded a total of fifty-two senatorial seats, and therefore comprises 40 percent of the Senate. The PRD, on the other hand, won just under 30 percent of the national vote, but its members make up just 24 percent of the Senate.[6]

The Executive Committee (Mesa Directiva) heads the Mexican Senate. Its president is similar to the Senate Majority Leader in the United States and presides over Senate debates and plenary votes. The Executive Committee comprises three vice presidents and four secretaries, all of whom must be elected by an absolute majority of the Senate. Each serves a one-year term, with the possibility of reelection. Within the Senate, each political party has a Parliamentary Group (Grupo Parlamentario) for the purpose of facilitating the legislative process by serving as party whips and doing their best to ensure party discipline. The leaders of each Parliamentary Group, plus two more from the majority party and one more from the first minority party, comprise the Political Coordination Board (Junta de Coordinación Política), a multiparty group responsible for promoting agreement on legislative initiatives, and proposing committee

Table 5.2.
Standing Congressional Committees

Senate

Agrarian Reform	Justice and Human Rights
Agriculture and Livestock	Labor and Social Welfare
Attention to Vulnerable Groups	Metropolitan Development
Budget and Public Accounting	National Auditing and Oversight
Citizen Participation	National Defense
Communication	Navy
Constitution	Population, Border, and Migration Issues
Culture	Public Education
Economic and Social Welfare	Public Safety
Economy	Radio, Television, and Film
Energy	Rules and Parliamentary Practices
Environment and Natural Resources	Rural Development
Federal District	Science and Technology
Fishing	Social Development
Foreign Relations	Social Security
Gender and Equality	Strengthening Federalism
Government	Transportation
Health	Treasury and Public Credit
Housing	Tourism
Indigenous Issues	Water Resources
Jurisdictional	Youth and Sports

Chamber of Deputies

Administration	Health and Social Security
Agrarian Reform	Human Rights
Agriculture and Livestock	Indigenous Issues
Belisario Dominguez Medal	Jurisdictional
Border Issues	Justice
Constitution	Labor and Social Welfare
Economic Development	Legislative Studies
Education and Culture	Library and Editorial Issues
Energy	National Defense
Environment, Natural Resources, and	Navy
Fishing	Population and Development
Federal District	Regional Development
Federalism and Municipal Development	Retirees and Pensioners
Foreign Relations	Rules and Parliamentary Practices
North America	Rural Development
Latin America/Caribbean	Science and Technology
Asia-Pacific	Social Development
Europe and Africa	Trade and Industrial Development
International Organizations	Transportation
Nongovernmental Organizations	Treasury and Public Credit
Gender and Equality	Urban Planning and Development
Global Parliamentary Group for Habitat	Water Resources
Government	Youth and Sports

Bicameral Committees

National Congressional Library System
National Congressional Television Channel

appointments to the Executive Committee. The president of the Coordination Board is elected by an absolute majority of its membership and is responsible for securing agreement on the legislative agenda.

The Mexican Senate also has a number of committees (*comisiones*) that specialize in specific policy areas and play an integral role in formulating bills that are then introduced to the entire body. Committees comprise no more than fifteen seats allocated according to the proportion of representation each party has in the Senate. Each committee has a president and two secretaries and can take one of two main forms: standing committees (*comisión ordinaria*), permanent committees that analyze initiatives in specific areas (e.g., trade and development, foreign relations, border issues), and ad hoc committees (*comisión especial*), that seek to investigate a specific transitory issue (e.g., state reform and promoting peace in Chiapas). Bipartisan committees can also be established for specific purposes. The most important bipartisan committee is the Permanent Commission (Comisión Permanente), which presides over matters during the legislative recess. Table 5.2 provides a full list of standing congressional committees.

The Chamber of Deputies

The Chamber of Deputies has 500 members, 300 of whom are directly elected by a plurality in single-member districts. The other 200 are drawn from party or *plurinominal* candidates elected in regional districts using proportional representation. All deputies serve three-year terms and cannot be immediately reelected, though (like senators) they can serve nonconsecutive terms. In Mexico, the lower house of Congress has the sole authority to approve the president's budget, though the Supreme Court ruled during the Fox administration that the president could issue a veto of the budget.[7] The Chamber of Deputy's power of the purse is one of the most important aspects of power sharing and checks and balances within the national government.

The Chamber is organized in the same manner as the Senate, with an Executive Committee, Parliamentary Groups, and a Political Coordination Board. The Executive Committee serves a one-year term and is made up of a president, or speaker, three vice presidents, and three secretaries. Like their counterparts in the Senate, all members of the Chamber's Executive Committee must be elected with a two-thirds majority. Each political party with at least five members in the Chamber is entitled to have a formally recognized Parliamentary Group. The Political Coordination Board comprises the party leaders and is responsible for making committee nominations, proposing the budget, and presenting resolutions to the Executive Committee.

The Chamber of Deputies has a well-established committee system that allows legislators specialize in a particular policy area (table 5.2). The Chamber's standing committees are very similar in focus to those found in the Senate (e.g., national defense, public education, environment and indigenous issues). The Fox administration also established a number of special committees to investigate issues as diverse as campaign finance and the high rate of homicide of young women in Ciudad Juarez, in the state of Chihuahua. Each committee can have up to thirty members and no deputy can serve on more than three standing committees. Since 1994, party representation in the committees has been roughly proportional to their numbers within the Chamber, and this has allowed minority parties to have an important influence on policy decisions.[8]

Mexico's Evolving Legislature

Despite the fact that the Mexican constitution clearly establishes three separate branches of government, the Mexican legislature served as a rubber stamp for presidential initiatives from the mid-1930s until 1997. As we saw above, the dominance of a single party headed by the president made it possible for the executive to effectively monopolize the electoral and legislative processes. Table 5.3 shows that until 1988, the PRI regularly won at least 75 percent of the seats in the Chamber of Deputies. Under such conditions, the president had no trouble garnering the simple majority needed to approve a bill. Members of the PRI were all too happy to support the president's legislative initiatives given that he had the power to determine the trajectory of their future in the party. Moreover, with its two-thirds majority, the PRI could single-handedly amend the constitution. Table 5.3 also shows that the PRI retained its dominance within the Chamber into the early 1990s, though its representation dropped to roughly 50–60 percent. This was still enough to allow the PRI to single-handedly approve most legislation, and the president continued to enjoy an extremely high rate of approval of executive-sponsored bills.[9] But by the late 1990s, the PRI was no longer able to win even a simple majority in either the Chamber or the Senate, and, since 2000, no party has held a majority in either house of Congress.[10]

As the PRI's dominance waned, the legislature became more active and independent. This trend began in earnest after 1997 when the PRI lost its majority in the Chamber of Deputies. Consequently, whereas the Chamber sponsored, on average, 195 public bills during each legislative session between 1988 and 1997, during the fifty-seventh legislature (1997–2000), it sponsored 566 initiatives. In the Senate, that number increased from roughly two, to 38.[11] Moreover,

Table 5.3.
Seats in Mexican Chamber of Deputies, 1976–2009

Party	L 1976–1979	LI 1979–1982	LII 1982–1985	LIII 1985–1988	LIV 1988–1991	LV 1991–1994	LVI 1994–1997	LVII 1997–2000	LVIII 2000–2003	LIX 2003–2006	LVIII 2006–2009
PRI	195	296	300	289	260	320	299	236	211	224	106
PAN	20	42	50	41	100	89	119	121	206	151	206
PRD	–	–	–	–	–	41	65	126	50	97	127
PT		–	–	–	–	–	9	7	7	6	12
PVEM	–	–	–	–	–	–	–	6	17	17	17
PC	–	–	–	–	–	–	–	–	4	5	17
PANAL	–	–	–	–	–	–	–	–	–	–	9
ASC	–	–	–	–	–	–	–	–	–	–	5
PSN	–	–	–	–	–	–	–	–	3	–	
PAS	–	–	–	–	–	–	–	–	2	–	
PPS	12	12	10	11	50	11	–	–	–	–	
PARM	11	12	–	11	33	14	–	–	–	–	
PFCRN	–	–	–	–	36	24	–	–	–	–	
PST	–	10	11	12	–	–	–	–	–	–	
PDM	–	10	12	12	–	–	–	–	–	–	
PSUM	–	–	17	12	–	–	–	–	–	–	
PCM	–	18	–	–	–	–	–	–	–	–	
PMS	–	–	–	–	20	–	–	–	–	–	
PRT	–	–	–	6	–	–	–	–	–	–	
PMT	–	–	–	6	–	–	–	–	–	–	
Indep.	–	–	–	–	1	–	8	4	–	–	1
Total:	238	400	400	400	500	499	500	500	500	500	500

Sources: Figures for 1976–2000 obtained from Yolanda Meyenberg Leycegui, "La Cámera de Diputados y la oposición en México," in *La Cámara de Diputados en México,* ed. Germán Pérez and Antonia Martínez (Mexico City: Cámara de Diputados de la H. Congreso de la Unión, LVII Legislatura, 2000). Figures for 2000–2001 obtained from Enrique Davis-Mazlum, "A Balance of Power Emerges in Mexico," *La Prensa San Diego,* September 1, 2000. Figures for 2003–2009 obtained from Mexican Chamber of Deputies website: www.camaradediputados.gob.mx.

Key for Current Party Acronyms:
ASC: Alternativa Socialdemocratica Campesina; PAN: Partido Acción Nacional; PANAL: Partido Nueva Alianza; PC: Partido Convergencia; PRD: Partido de la Revolución Democrática; PRI: Partido Revolucionario Institucional ; PT: Partido del Trabajo; PVEM: Partido Verde Ecologista Méxicana

Congress began to check the president's power. Between 1997 and 2000, President Zedillo sponsored only 29 percent of all approved bills in the Chamber of Deputies, down from 75 percent in the previous legislature (1994–1997), while the Chamber and Senate together sponsored 67.9 percent of all approved bills (up from 24 percent).[12] Equally important was the willingness of Congress to block presidential initiatives. For example, in 1998, in what was mainly a symbolic gesture of newfound legislative power, the Chamber of Deputies refused to authorize two of President Zedillo's planned trips abroad. More meaningfully, the Chamber exercised its authority to "review and approve" the budget and, in the process, challenged the president's budget proposals.[13]

That the legislature is now more active and independent than it was in the past does not necessarily mean that it has the capacity to fulfill all of its constitutional functions and responsibilities. Indeed, many scholars agree that there remain at least three main obstacles to further strengthening and improving the quality of the legislature: low congressional budgets, the ban on consecutive reelection, and the use of proportional representation to allocate 200 Chamber and thirty-two Senate seats. First, unlike legislators in the United States, members of Mexico's Congress do not have large budgets and extensive support staffs. Moreover, Mexico does not have a readily accessible store of congressional archives and other documents needed for legislative research.[14] As a result, the legislature often relies on the executive branch for information and individual legislators, as well as congressional committees, have a difficult time developing independent and thoroughly researched analyses needed to formulate effective policy initiatives.[15]

The problem of creating good legislation is compounded by the second obstacle, the prohibition on immediate reelection. While the ban on reelection is of great historical importance in Mexico, it creates at least three important problems for the legislature. [16] First, it means that members of Congress have few opportunities or incentives to gain the experience needed to be professional legislators. This is especially true within the Chamber of Deputies, where members serve a short three-year term. Three years is just enough time to learn the ropes before they are turned out for a new bunch of "freshman" deputies. Second, the ban on immediate reelection strengthens political parties at the expense of the voters. Since members of Congress cannot be reelected, voters have no chance to hold them responsible (or reward them) for their performance in office. Instead, politicians see themselves as responsible to the party, which evaluates their performance and determines the fate of political careers based on how well they uphold party discipline. Therefore, Mexican legislators tend to represent their parties' interests rather than their electoral constituents' preferences. Finally, in the context of the Mexican political system, no reelection has served to strengthen the executive because the combination of unified government, strong party discipline, and the dual role of the president as head of state and head of the party, created incentives for the legislature to defer to the executive. Given these consequences of no immediate reelection, it is not surprising that many Mexican politicians and academics have called for reforms that would eliminate the ban. And while there is considerable interest in such a proposal, especially among politicians from the PAN and the PRD, there is much less support in Mexico's general population and little agreement on what term limits (if any) should take its place.

The third obstacle to strengthening and improving the legislature is the use of proportional representation to elect thirty-two senators and 200 deputies. While the introduction of the plurinominal seats has the positive effect of ensuring minority representation in Congress, it also prevents these members of Congress from developing a strong geographic base (particularly when combined with no reelection) and gives a significant amount of influence to the parties, again, at the expense of voters who otherwise would have the ability to hold them accountable for their performance.[17] While most Mexican politicians recognize the problems associated with the use of proportional representation in their system, there is little interest in doing away with it. This stance can be attributed to the fact that many are loath to reform an institution that has awarded them (and their parties) a place within the federal legislature.

Meanwhile, though Mexican voters are often critical of the executive-legislative deadlock that has resulted in recent years, they have not necessarily elected to strengthen the president's hand vis-à-vis the legislature. Mexican voters appear increasingly disposed to split-ticket voting—dividing their ballots to elect executives and legislators from different parties—and less inclined to back the president's party during midterm elections. For example, President Fox was elected in 2000 with approximately 44 percent support from voters, while his PAN party obtained only 38 percent of the vote; hence, a significant percentage of his supporters opted not to vote for legislators from his party. Later, when the PAN tried to persuade Mexican voters during the 2003 midterm elections, they used the slogan "take the brakes off change" to insinuate that the Mexican Congress was too much of an obstacle. Yet, as is common in other presidential systems, the president's party actually lost congressional seats during the midterm elections and Fox faced even greater opposition in the legislature.

As a result of the trend toward divided government and other factors, the Mexican Congress is no longer a mere rubber stamp for the executive. In the coming years, efforts by the Congress to assert its authority will surely continue to dramatically reshape its role in contemporary Mexican politics. A key institution in determining the constitutional limits of both presidential and legislative authority will be the Mexican Supreme Court, which we examine below.

The Judiciary

Like the legislature, Mexico's Supreme Court served to refine, but above all to support, presidential initiatives, for much of the twentieth century. Until

1994, the twenty-five justices were handpicked, and could be removed only by the president. Moreover, the Court rarely considered cases of importance and did not have the power of judicial review. Hence, the Supreme Court never ruled against the interests of the president or the PRI—a practice that directly violated the democratic principle of separation of powers.

According to one scholar, there were three reasons why the judiciary was subordinate to the president: a flexible constitution, presidential control over political nominations, and lack of power of judicial review.[18] While Mexico prided itself as having a progressive constitution and an active legal process, in practice the constitution could be easily altered to suit presidential interests because the PRI held the necessary two-thirds majority in both houses of the legislature needed for an amendment. Furthermore, the president, as the head of the party, controlled the nomination (and dismissal) of political appointees in all areas of government, including the judiciary. Finally, the constitution did not grant the Supreme Court the power of judicial review on electoral matters or the ability to serve as an arbiter of intergovernmental disputes.

In 1994, the Law of Judicial Power was enacted to increase the power and independence of the judiciary. This law, introduced by President Zedillo and approved by Congress, mandated that the Supreme Court be composed of eleven justices who serve fifteen-year terms. The president nominates judicial appointments based on their legal experience and candidates must be confirmed with two-thirds approval of the Senate. These changes, together with the multiparty composition of the Senate, and the guarantee that no single party can hold more than the two-thirds majority needed to approve a presidential nominee, suggest that for the foreseeable future, the Mexican Supreme Court will operate independently and impartially in its role as the cornerstone of the Mexican legal system.

Another important change brought about by the 1994 constitutional reform was the introduction of two new powers of judicial review (see textbox 5.2). The Court now had the authority to decide the constitutionality of federal laws and international treaties with "constitutional actions," and the right to resolve "constitutional controversies," or legal disagreements among different branches and levels of government.[19] Constitutional actions require the support of 33 percent of the members of Congress (or the state legislature at the state level), the attorney general, or the leadership of any official political party (for the constitutionality of electoral laws) to send a case before the Court. Constitutional controversies can be introduced by any branch or level of government seeking arbitration in an intergovernmental dispute. These new powers give the Supreme Court the ability to veto legislation deemed unconstitutional and settle intergovernmental conflicts—two functions that were previously nonexistent in Mexico.

Textbox 5.2. Judicial Review and Activism in Contemporary Mexico

Mexico uses a "civil" or statutory legal system. This system is also known as Roman or Napoleonic Law because it is derived from the traditions first established in ancient Rome and later reinstated in parts of Europe by Napoleon Bonaparte during the early nineteenth century. Civil legal systems differ significantly from so-called common law systems, like the one used in the United States. In a civil legal system, judicial decisions are strictly interpreted as codified by legislative statute; that is, a judge makes a decision in a case solely based on his or her interpretation of the law as it is written. In contrast, judges in a common law system also take into consideration the "common" practices and precedents established by decisions in other cases. In addition to an emphasis on the law as written, common law relies on the principle of *stare decisis,* which is Latin for "let the decision stand." This principle allows judges to decide a case based on precedents established by other judicial decisions in cases that have a similar fact pattern.

Critics of civil law systems argue that such systems lack the flexibility of interpretation provided in common law systems, since legislative changes to the law may be slow in coming or otherwise politically infeasible. At the same time, some domestic critics of the common law system used in the United States have charged that U.S. judges effectively "legislate from the bench" by reshaping and even overturning the decisions of democratically elected legislators. Both civil and common law systems are widely used around the world, with varying degrees of efficiency and effectiveness. In Mexico, the combination of civil law with a U.S.-style, constitutional separation of powers creates a unique—and some might say awkward—hybrid. The U.S. judiciary was able to assert its role as a check on other branches of government with the Supreme Court's landmark decision in *Marbury v. Madison,* which provided a precedent for judicial review to determine the constitutionality of government decisions. Yet in Mexico, the judiciary has not been as free to curb the power of other branches or modify public policy through case law, in part because of its civil law tradition.

Mexican federal courts have long addressed legal controversies through the *amparo* procedure, an innovation introduced by Mexico's 1857 constitution. An *amparo*—literally a "protection"—provides an injunction blocking government actions that encroach on an individual's rights. However, a given court's decision to grant *amparo* is only binding for the parties involved in that particular case. Binding precedents can be established through the *amparo* procedure, but only after the Supreme Court or collegiate circuit courts make five consecutive and identical majority rulings on the same topic, thereby establishing a legal norm known as a *jurisprudencia.* Reforms introduced in December 1994 expanded the Supreme Court's powers of judicial review by introducing "motions of unconstitutionality" (*acciones de inconstitutionalidad*). This innovation allowed key institutional actors—the executive branch, political parties, and a designated proportion of representatives from the Senate, the Chamber of Deputies, and the Mexico City legislature—to challenge the constitutionality of legislation or other government actions. Moreover, recent decisions—including a celebrated June 2007 verdict invalidating a piece of legislation known as the Televisa Law, in which legislators blatantly favored corporate interests—signal a growing sense of independence on the part of the Mexican Supreme Court, which may suggest the beginning of a new era of judicial activism in Mexico.

The Law of Judicial Power has paved the way for greater judicial activity and independence. Since 1995, the number of constitutional actions and controversies has increased steadily. For example, in 1995, the Supreme Court heard one constitutional action and nineteen controversies. By 1998, the number of cases increased to twelve actions and twenty-nine controversies.[20] The federal judiciary has also become much more active in its attempts to promote its own institutional independence. Since 2000, it has engaged in a concerted effort to establish budgetary autonomy with a constitutional amendment that guarantees it a fixed percentage of the federal budget. It has also sought a constitutional amendment that would allow the judiciary to initiate legislation on judicial matters, and encouraged reform of the Otero Formula, a provision in Mexican law that prevents the Supreme Court's decisions from having general effects, or the establishment of legal precedent, unless they are approved by at least eight of the eleven justices.[21] So far, none of these initiatives has met with success, but they are clear indications of the Court's new role as an independent branch of the federal government.

Late in his term, President Zedillo learned firsthand what it meant to have an empowered Court. In an attempt to learn the truth behind the federal government's bailout of several banks in the mid-1990s, Congress had asked the government to release important government documents. The Zedillo administration refused and the case went before the Supreme Court. The Court ordered that the documents be released, thus redefining the limits of executive power.[22] During Fox's *sexenio* the Supreme Court has also handed down some decisions that directly contradict the president's authority. In one instance, the Court invalidated a presidential decree that sought to establish daylight savings, instead ruling that it was the responsibility of the Congress to decide Mexico's timetable. Fox suffered a more serious blow when the Supreme Court declared unconstitutional his initiative to allow private corporations to engage in the production and sale of energy to the public. The Court decided 8 to 3 that the decree violated Article 28 of the constitution, which gives the state a monopoly over the production and distribution of energy.[23] In all, the Court struck down three of the six presidential policy initiatives it heard between 1997 and 2005, indicating its willingness to exercise much greater independence than it did in the past.

The Supreme Court has also begun to fulfill its new role as an impartial interpreter of the constitution. In practice, this has meant that its decisions are based on legal principles rather than political interests or public opinion. For example, in 1998, the Court handed down a unanimous decision declaring a state electoral law in Quintana Roo unconstitutional. This marked the first time that the Supreme Court had ruled against the PRI and signaled the judiciary's willingness and ability to act as an independent arbiter.[24] More recently, the Court agreed with a lower court's decision that upheld the thirty-year statute of limitations on genocide. This ruling made it very difficult for prosecutors to bring genocide charges against former president Luis Echeverría, who has been accused of ordering paramilitary forces to fire on student demonstrators in the 1968 Tlatelolco massacre.[25]

In fact, the judiciary's activity and independence has not come without controversy. In late 2004, President Fox introduced his budget proposal for 2005. The Chamber of Deputies modified the bill to include an additional $112 billion pesos in spending. The Fox administration claimed that the spending increases were ill conceived because they were based on unrealistic income projections, and more importantly, that the Chamber had overstepped its authority to modify the budget when it voted to authorize approximately 4 billion pesos for projects that lay outside the scope of the executive's National Development Plan. In late December of that year, the Fox administration filed a constitutional controversy against the Chamber in order to block the new budget items thought to exceed congressional authority.[26] Because the Court was not in session, the case was sent to the single Supreme Court justice who was on duty during the recess.[27] He assigned the case to another justice who then ruled in the president's favor and suspended the 4 billion pesos in question. Many within the Chamber of Deputies claimed that these procedures directly violated the law on two counts: first, only the Chief Justice has the authority to make case assignments and second, the judiciary does not have the authority to modify the budget. These criticisms put the Supreme Court in the difficult position of evaluating the legality of its own actions.

At the same time, the judiciary must also work toward the establishment of rule of law. In this regard, Mexico has not changed much. Mexican citizens continue to live in a society where the law is applied arbitrarily and does not guarantee protection of individual rights. In other words, the rule of law is not institutionalized in Mexico.[28] It is extraordinarily difficult to prosecute criminals and, as a result, a large number of crimes are neither investigated nor prosecuted. Also, widespread corruption in law enforcement and the judiciary makes it even more difficult to bring criminals to justice. Because the Mexican legal system gives public prosecutors a significant amount of discretion over which crimes are prosecuted, they are easily targeted by criminals who simply buy their way out of prosecution. As Magaloni and Zepeda point out, "The victims of crime have no legal recourse when public prosecutors refuse to investigate a crime and bring charges against a suspect because prosecutors hold a monopoly over such actions. . . . Indeed, the overwhelming majority of the complaints filed before the National Human Rights Commission are related to the criminal justice system."[29]

The role of the judiciary in strengthening the rule of law is critical, and has broader ramifications for the future of democracy in Mexico. As long as the government cannot credibly protect citizens' rights and impartially protect citizens from one another's actions, it is impossible for democratic principles to become institutionalized, and Mexicans may lose what little faith they have in the government and democracy as a political goal. Moreover, without fair and predictable legal treatment of property rights, consumer protections, and basic contractual terms, private sector firms and individuals cannot conduct business transactions or make the investments necessary to promote Mexico's economic development. Hence, the longer-term strengthening of the judiciary is therefore a critical component to help guarantee the rule of law and democracy in Mexico. We take up these issues in greater depth in chapter 11.

State and Local Governments

As we have seen in the previous sections, one of the consequences of Mexico's combination of single-party dominance and *presidencialismo* is that political authority in the country became highly centralized. That is, the federal government, and more specifically, the executive branch, had a disproportionate amount of control over policy decisions, and over the resources needed to implement them. Normally, a federal system is one that has independently elected and relatively autonomous governmental entities that have differing responsibilities and levels of jurisdiction. Indeed, on paper, Mexico has had a three-tiered federal system of government since soon after its independence in 1821, but in reality relatively little authority remains to state and local governments. The fact that most major business activity occurred in Mexico City—located in the approximate center of the country—added an economic and geographic element to the country's high level of centralization. In short, in practice, Mexico looked much more like a unitary system of government—where political representatives at the local level are essentially appointed and directed by national level authorities—rather than a federal system. Because much has changed in the last thirty years in terms of the relative importance of state and local governments, it is to these areas that we now turn.

Mexico comprises thirty-one states and the Federal District (see textbox 5.3). Each state has its own constitution, and therefore a unique set of institutions, but all share the same general characteristics as the three branches of government: the executive, comprised of the governor, his or her cabinet, and supporting bureaucracy; a unicameral legislature or state congress; and a state judiciary.

Textbox 5.3. The Federal District

Mexico City, or the Federal District (DF), is the national capital of Mexico. With a population of over 20 million, it consistently ranks among the largest three cities in the world. The DF is divided into sixteen boroughs and forty electoral districts. Before 1997, Mexico City was essentially an extension of the federal government. The president appointed the head *(regente)* to implement and oversee his policy initiatives. In 1987, Congress amended the constitution to create a representative assembly charged with making some administrative decisions and advising the president on the city's policy priorities. Reforms in 1993 and 1996 paved the way for the assembly to become a true legislative body, with lawmaking and budget authority. The Legislative Assembly of the Federal District comprises sixty-six deputies, forty elected by plurality in single-member districts, and twenty-six elected by proportional representation from party lists. All deputies serve three-year terms. Furthermore, the DF's head of government is now popularly elected and serves a six-year term. The PRD has strong support in Mexico City and the first three elected heads of government of the Federal District, Cuauhtémoc Cárdenas (1997–99), Andrés Manuel López Obrador (2000–05), and Marcelo Ebrard (2006–12) were all members of this party. Two other members of the PRD, Rosario Robles (1999–2000) and Alejandro Encinas (2005–06), have also served as interim heads of government. Financially and administratively, the DF has a special status that allows it to function as a city, but with many of the same rights enjoyed by states. In practice this means that it has more powers of taxation and hence more resources for governing. In translation, it also contributes to some confusion, since its head of government is often referred to as the Mexico City mayor despite the district's special status as a federal entity. Mexico City is also unique because, despite attempts to introduce decentralization, the capital remains the country's most important political, economic, and cultural hub.

At the local level, Mexico has close to 2,500 municipalities.[30] Each municipality elects a mayor *(presidente municipal)*, and a council *(cabildo)* from a single slate for a three-year term of office.[31] The constitution grants both states and municipalities specific rights and responsibilities, though in practice, *presidencialismo* made many of these rights irrelevant. That is, like politicians at the national level, governors had few incentives to act independently—their performance was evaluated not by their popularity or use of innovation, but rather, by their ability to maintain stability and ensure overwhelming support for the PRI come election time. Governors who failed to comply or achieve this goal risked being asked to step down by the president and not advancing their career within the party. To the extent that state executives had autonomy, it was to determine who within the state would receive the resources doled out by the federal government.[32] Municipal presidents faced a similar situation, though at the local level the pressure was to demonstrate loyalty to the governor.[33]

The economic and political perils of extreme concentration became apparent in the wake of the economic crisis of the early 1980s. When Mexico nearly defaulted on its external loans, the government's first move was to reduce spending drastically and embark on a period of economic austerity. As the federal government struggled to provide even basic services, the PRI's performance legitimacy was severely damaged, and the newly elected de la Madrid administration began to call for decentralization reforms. This first round of reforms sought to clarify the rights and responsibilities, particularly of local governments, and to deconcentrate economic production and national government agencies. While de la Madrid's reforms constituted an important effort to address some of the problems associated with overcentralization, they were only mildly successful, in part because they were designed more to recapture electoral support for the PRI than to begin a coherent plan of decentralization. The Salinas administration had the same goal in mind when it introduced the Solidarity program, which was aimed to alleviate problems associated with poverty by strengthening local organizations and governments.[34] Again, this program did make some headway in empowering local authorities, and more progress in addressing poverty, but it is difficult to ignore the strategic allocation of Solidarity funds to states and municipalities or the program's positive impact on the PRI's performance in the 1991 midterm elections.[35]

More meaningful decentralization reforms would have to wait until the mid-1990s when President Zedillo introduced the most comprehensive plan for decentralization to date. The New Federalism project had a variety of aims, among them, reform of the revenue sharing system and boosting the power and autonomy of state and local governments. His motivation for this program surely stemmed from a combination of pressure by the opposition and his commitment to reforming the Mexican political system. Zedillo had to deal with an unprecedented number of demands from the opposition, which by then had a strong presence in state and local elected offices: by 1997, the PAN and PRD governed ten states and the Federal District and at least half of the thirty-one state capitals. Because many of the PAN and PRD governors and mayors of the 1990s were staunch advocates of reviving federalism and promoting democracy in Mexico, Zedillo had little choice but to grant them some concessions.[36] One of the areas of greatest concern among subnational politicians was the distribution of national revenue.

Governors and mayors have long complained about the overcentralization of financial resources, claiming that there exists an 80-16-4 split, meaning that the national government hoards 80 percent of the nation's resources, leaving a paltry 16 and 4 percent for the states and municipalities, respectively. How, they ask, can subnational governments possibly hope to address the many public policy priorities and public demands with so few resources? It is true that the federal government in Mexico controls a disproportionate amount of public revenue. But this is true in most federal systems. What is different in Mexico is that its revenue-sharing system is set up in such a way as to weaken subnational governments. The Law of Fiscal Coordination (LCF) stipulates that states and municipalities forfeit many of their tax powers (most notably, sales tax) in exchange for a share of federal revenue that is transferred to subnational governments.[37] For many states, and especially local authorities, this arrangement makes good financial sense because they do not have the bureaucratic infrastructure needed to levy their own taxes. Moreover, because federal transfers are allocated according to redistributive formulas, the system provides poorer states and municipalities with more funds than they might be able to collect on their own. Yet, while the existing tax and revenue systems may help redress regional inequalities, they create several obstacles to healthy federalism and good governance in Mexico.[38]

First, there is general unhappiness with the current revenue-sharing arrangement. In particular, wealthier states feel slighted because they invariably contribute the most tax revenue to the general fund, but receive proportionately less than their fair share. This perceived injustice stems from the national government's obligation to redistribute resources to poorer states and promote equality among its geographic regions. On several occasions, governors of wealthier states have even threatened to opt out of the revenue-sharing system unless the formulas are revised to give greater weight to the origin of tax receipts. For their part, poorer states tend to be unhappy with the status quo because they feel that even with the redistributive formulas, they never have enough resources to address their many public policy challenges. Their most commonly voiced demand is that the central government increase the overall amount of resources given to the states and municipalities.

The second problem is that the LCF allows states to determine how to allocate a portion of the federal transfer funds among their municipalities. While this provision is an important aspect of state autonomy, it has the potential to create tension between state and municipal governments, particularly when the former chooses to allocate the bare minimum or use political rather than objective criteria as the basis for distributing what constitutes, in many cases, over half of the local budget. Third, the existing tax system promotes inefficiency and overdependence on the national government and inefficient taxation. There are few incentives for states and municipalities to exercise the tax authority they do have, when it is much easier, and sometimes more lucrative, to wait for a monthly check from the federal government.[39] Finally, the current system of revenue sharing undermines government accountability. Because state and local governments have little tax authority and rely so heavily on federal transfers, governors and mayors can always claim that their administrations' shortcomings are a result of too few funds rather than incompetence or unresponsiveness.

Together, these problems have set the stage for some serious intergovernmental conflicts over resource distribution, taxation authority, and states' rights. The focus on strengthening federalism has boosted the power of subnational politicians, and events in recent years have shown that governors have effectively raised their national profiles by challenging the federal government on these issues. In fact, all of the major presidential hopefuls in 2000, and most in 2006, were former governors. However, decentralization in Mexico has some important shortcomings. In particular, some claim that strengthening subnational governments has created local strongholds for governors, many of whom wield a disproportionate amount of power and have no interest in promoting democracy.[40] Moreover, as we have seen, severe economic disparities among states persist and create tension in the federal arrangement that will not be easily resolved because they pit rich states against poor and states against municipalities. There is little doubt that these issues will be at the forefront of Mexican politics for the foreseeable future.

Conclusion

Mexico's political system has changed significantly over the past twenty years. No longer dominated by a single political party and the executive, there is now more balance among political parties and among the various branches and levels of government. The late 1990s ushered in a period of power sharing never before seen in Mexico. The three largest political parties have since enjoyed significant representation in the legislature, and as the PAN demonstrated in 2000, it is possible for the opposition to win the presidency. Furthermore, executive dominance at the national level has waned and both the legislature and the judiciary are willing and able to oppose the president on some of his highest profile policy initiatives (e.g., tax reform and the privatization of energy). Likewise, states and municipalities now exercise significantly more independence than in the past, some going so far as to challenge the federal government and even the president on matters of revenue distribution and subnational autonomy.

Does this mean that the era of *presidencialismo* and extreme centralization has ended? Many argue that returning to the past is now impossible because the PAN and the PRD are so well established that the PRI can never hope to recapture its near-monopoly on the electoral and hence the governing process. Proponents of this view could point to the many important institutional changes (e.g., empowerment of the Supreme Court and the constitutional clause that prohibits any party from holding more than 60 percent of the seats in the legislature) that have been implemented since the 1990s. As noted above, much of the reform of the Mexican political system has occurred thanks to the multipartisan composition of the legislature and the strong presence of the PAN and PRD at the state and local levels. And, while it is theoretically possible for a single party to capture the executive and a majority in both legislative bodies, the current political environment in Mexico would appear to make that development impossible. Indeed, it is much more likely that the country will continue to experience greater shared governance, with all the benefits and drawbacks that this entails.

Key Terms

Chamber of Deputies
de jure
dedazo
Executive Committee
Federal Electric Commission (CFE)
healthy distance/*sana distancia*
hyperpresidentialism/*presidencial-
     ismo*
Law of Fiscal Coordination (LCF)
Law of Judicial Power
Mexican attorney general
Ministry of the Interior
New Federalism
Otero Formula

parastatal enterprises
Parliamentary Group
party discipline
Permanent Commission
Petróleos Mexicanos/PEMEX
plurinominal seats
Political Coordination Board
proportional representation
revenue sharing
Senate
split-ticket voting
unified government

Recommended Readings

Castañeda, Jorge. *Perpetuating Power: How Mexican Presidents Were Chosen.* New York: New Press, 2000.

Ugalde, Luis Carlos. *The Mexican Congress: Old Player, New Power*. Foreword by Armand B. Peschard-Sverdrup. Washington, D.C.: CSIS Press, 2000.
Ward, Peter M., and Victoria E. Rodríguez. *New Federalism and State Government in Mexico*. Austin: University of Texas Press, 1999.

Notes

1. Matthew Soberg Shugart and Scott Mainwaring, "Presidentialism and Democracy in Latin America: Rethinking the Terms of the Debate," in *Presidentialism and Democracy in Latin America*, ed. Scott Mainwaring and Matthew Soberg Shugart (New York: Cambridge University Press, 1997).

2. This discussion draws on Jeffrey Weldon, "Political Sources of Presidencialismo in Mexico," in *Presidentialism and Democracy in Latin America*, ed. Scott Mainwaring and Matthew Soberg Shugart (New York: Cambridge University Press, 1997); and Weldon, "Changing Patterns of Executive-Legislative Relations in Mexico," in *Dilemmas of Political Change in Mexico*, ed. Kevin J. Middlebrook (London: University of London, Institute of Latin American Studies/University of California-San Diego, Center for U.S.-Mexican Studies, 2004), 133–67.

3. The Mexican presidency also enjoyed what one author has called "anticonstitutional" powers, for example, the power to declare legal or fraudulent any election results, and the ability to extend immunity to any public official. These powers stemmed from the same three conditions described above and the fact that they guaranteed that the legislature would not exercise its power of legislative review. See Luis Javier Garrido, "The Crisis of Presidencialismo," in *Mexico's Alternative Political Futures*, ed. Wayne A. Cornelius, Judith Gentleman, and Peter H. Smith (La Jolla: University of California-San Diego, Center for U.S.-Mexican Studies, 1989).

4. All of Mexico's presidents between 1946 and 1976 served as interior minister before their election, and in subsequent years the head of this agency was almost always a serious contender for the PRI's presidential candidate. This tradition continued into the Fox administration when Santiago Creel entered the presidential horse race for the 2006 election.

5. Proportional representation seats are distributed without regard to state.

6. While the PRD itself may be underrepresented, in the 2006 election it was part of a three-party coalition and when taken together, the coalition's senatorial seats do come close to matching its proportion of the national vote. It is quite common for countries to employ electoral systems that distribute seats in ways that are not perfectly proportional to the popular vote.

7. When President Fox exercised this power by vetoing the budget in 2004, there was some ambiguity about this issue. Although the Mexican presidency does have veto power, the constitution only states that it can be used on bills approved by both houses of Congress. Since the Chamber of Deputies is the only one with authority to approve the budget, some questioned the president's authority to veto the budget. See Weldon, "Changing Patterns," 146, n. 31; and David Gaddis Smith, "Mexican Congressman Prods Government with Challenges," *San Diego Union Tribune*, January 22, 2006.

8. Jeffrey Weldon, "Committee Power in the Mexican Chamber of Deputies" (paper presented at the Twenty-First Chamber of Deputies International Congress of the Latin American Studies Association, Chicago, September 1998).

9. Indeed, the presidents' bills enjoyed a success rate of 98 percent between 1988 and 1997. This was significantly better than the chamber's showing, which averaged 23.4 percent. See Weldon, "Changing Patterns," 159, tables 5.7, 5.8.

10. The PRI's representation in the Senate follows a similar pattern: Whereas the PRI consistently won 60 to 75 percent of Senate seats before 1994, its share had declined to 47 percent in 2000.

11. Weldon "Changing Patterns," 156, table 5.4.

12. The remaining 2.8 percent were sponsored by state legislatures. Weldon, "Changing Patterns," 158 (table 5.6).

13. "His Congress Says No, No, Zedillo," *New York Times*, November 9, 1997; and Sam Dillon, "Newly Elected Mexican Opposition to Fight President's Economic Plan," *New York Times*, November 9, 1997.

14. This situation has begun to change. Much of this information is now available online or in one of the congressional research institutes.

15. Roderic Ai Camp, "Mexico's Legislature: Missing the Democratic Lockstep," in *Legislatures and the New Democracies in Latin America*, ed. David Close (Boulder: Lynne Rienner, 1995).

16. This discussion draws on Jeffrey Weldon, "The Prohibition on Consecutive Reelection in the Mexican Congress," *Election Law Journal* 3, no. 3 (2004): 574–79.

17. Michael Taylor, "Constitutional Crisis: How Reforms to the Legislature Have Doomed Mexico," *Mexican Studies/Estudios Mexicanos* 13, no. 2 (1997): 299–324.

18. Beatriz Magaloni, "Authoritarianism, Democracy, and the Supreme Court: Horizontal Exchange and the Rule of Law in Mexico," in *Democratic Accountability in Latin America*, ed. Scott Mainwaring and Christopher Welna (New York: Oxford University Press, 2003), 281.

19. The law granted the same powers to state supreme courts.

20. Magaloni, "Authoritarianism," 281.

21. Jeffrey Staton, *Lobbying for Judicial Reform: The Role of the Mexican Supreme Court in Institutional Selection*, USMEX 2003-04 Working Paper Series (La Jolla: Center for U.S.-Mexican Studies, 2003).

22. Kevin Sullivan and Mary Jordan, "Mexican Supreme Court Refuses to Take Back Seat," *Washington Post*, September 10, 2000, A31.

23. For more on these cases, see Jodi Finkel, "Judicial Reform as Insurance Policy: Mexico in the 1990s," *Latin American Politics and Society*, Spring 2005, 87–113.

24. Jodi Finkel, "Supreme Court Decisions on Electoral Rules after Mexico's 1994 Judicial Reform: An Empowered Court," *Journal of Latin American Studies* 35 (2003): 777–99.

25. Kevin Sullivan, "Mexican Court Rejects Part of Genocide Appeal," *Washington Post*, February 24, 2005, A18.

26. Banamex, "Review of the Economic Situation of Mexico," Working Paper Series 81, no. 949 (2005).

27. The Supreme Court has two sessions per year: early January to mid-July and

early August to mid-December. The constitution allows a single Supreme Court justice to address emergency issues during a recess that would normally require the consideration of the full court.

28. This discussion draws on Magaloni, "Authoritarianism"; and Beatriz Magaloni and Guillermo Zepeda, "Democratization, Judicial and Law Enforcement Institutions, and the Rule of Law in Mexico," in *Dilemmas of Political Change in Mexico*, ed. Kevin J. Middlebrook (London: University of London, Institute of Latin American Studies/La Jolla: University of California–San Diego, Center for U.S.-Mexican Studies, 2004), 168–97.

29. Magaloni and Zepeda, "Democratization," 194.

30. Mexican municipalities are the rough equivalent of U.S. city governments. In 2004, INEGI reported 2,451 municipalities in Mexico. This number tends to increase slightly every year.

31. The *cabildo* is comprised of *regidores* (aldermen) and *síndicos* (trustees). The exact number of these positions depends upon the size of the municipality. Together, the municipal presidency and the *cabildo* are known as the *ayuntamiento*.

32. Peter M. Ward and Victoria Rodríguez, *New Federalism and State Government in Mexico: Bringing the States Back In*, U.S.-Mexican Policy Studies Program, Report no. 9 (Austin: University of Texas, Lyndon B. Johnson School of Public Affairs, 1999).

33. The seminal work on local government in a PRI-dominated political system is Richard Fagen and William Tuohy, *Politics and Privilege in a Mexican City* (Stanford: Stanford University Press, 1972).

34. Victoria Rodríguez, *Decentralization in Mexico: From Reforma Municipal to Solidaridad to Nuevo Federalismo* (Boulder: Westview, 1997).

35. Juan Molinar Horcasitas and Jeffrey Weldon, "Electoral Determinants and Effects of Pronasol," in *Transforming State-Society Relations in Mexico: The National Solidarity Strategy*, ed. Wayne Cornelius, Ann Craig, and Jonathan Fox (La Jolla: University of California–San Diego, Center for U.S.-Mexican Studies, 1994).

36. On the early experiences of the opposition at the subnational level, see the work of Victoria E. Rodríguez and Peter M. Ward, *Policymaking, Politics, and Urban Governance in Chihuahua: The Experience of Recent Panista Governments* (Austin: University of Texas, LBJ School of Public Affairs, 1992); Rodríguez and Ward, *Political Change in Baja California: Democracy in the Making?* Monograph Series 40 (La Jolla: University of California–San Diego, Center for U.S.-Mexican Studies, 1994); and Rodríguez and Ward, eds. *Opposition Government in Mexico* (Albuquerque: University of New Mexico Press, 1995).

37. The Law of Fiscal Coordination mandates that 20 percent of national revenue be transferred to states and municipalities.

38. For more on the challenges of creating a federal arrangement that can function amid extreme economic inequalities, see Alberto Diaz-Cayeros, "Decentralization, Democratization, and Federalism in Mexico," in *Dilemmas of Political Change in Mexico*, ed. Kevin J. Middlebrook (London: University of London, Institute of Latin American Studies/La Jolla: University of California–San Diego, Center for U.S.-Mexican Studies, 2004), 198–234.

39. States and municipalities do have some taxation authority. For example, states

can levy a tax on the sale of new automobiles and municipalities can collect property taxes.

40. In some respects, *presidencialismo* is more alive in the states than it is at the national level because some state congresses have been slower to check executive authority. For more on this issue, see Wayne A. Cornelius, "Blind Spots in Democratization: Sub-national Politics as a Constraint on Mexico's Transition," *Democratization* 7, no. 3 (2000): 117–132; and Chappell Lawson, "Mexico's Unfinished Transition: Democratization and Authoritarian Enclaves in Mexico," *Mexican Studies/Estudios Mexicanos* 16, no. 2 (2000): 267–87.

6

Political Parties and Elections in Mexico

Before 1988, any discussion of political parties and elections in Mexico inevitably centered on the PRI. During most of that period, Mexico's official party was much like the powerful hegemonic parties found in other noncommunist, single-party systems. Like the KMT in Taiwan, the People's Action Party in Singapore, the People's Democratic Party in Nigeria, and even the Democratic Party in New York's Tammany Hall era, the PRI maintained power through a combination of genuine popular support, electoral fraud, institutional manipulation, and careful coordination of organized political interests. This formula made it possible for the PRI to achieve a relatively high degree of political stability and control. In this context, political opposition was tolerated but it was largely futile because the PRI was the only party with a realistic chance of winning elections: those who spoke out against the regime were effectively marginalized, and those who truly threatened PRI power were severely repressed.

Yet the PRI never lacked detractors. Indeed, from its very inception the postrevolutionary political system had a number of vocal critics, like José Vasconcelos, David Alfaro Siqueiros, and later, Elena Poniatowska. Still, for most of the twentieth century, political opposition to the ruling party was relatively small, often disorganized, and had few resources with which to effectively challenge the PRI. As we have seen, PRI political hegemony began to erode in the late 1980s and, today, Mexico's electoral climate is highly competitive. Unmistakable evidence that the opposition had begun to make inroads against the former ruling party came in 1997, and the end of PRI hegemony was realized in 2000 with the victory of the first opposition president, Vicente Fox.

The first half of this chapter provides a detailed examination of Mexico's most important political parties, their political agendas and bases of support, and their formal organization both before and after PRI hegemony. Next we focus on the electoral process and the specific electoral institutions that contributed to the making and eventual unmaking of PRI hegemony. Finally, we close this chapter with a discussion of Mexican elections today, with particular attention to the realignment of voter preferences and the dynamics of electoral competition since the fall of the PRI. While political parties and elections in Mexico have evolved considerably from the era of single-party hegemony, some degree of uncertainty remains about the future development of Mexico's contemporary party system.

Political Parties

Like most countries in Latin America, today Mexico has a multiparty system, in which more than two significant parties compete for power.[1] However, because of the PRI's longtime dominance, Mexico's multiparty system did not become truly competitive until the 1980s, when the National Action Party (PAN) and later the Party of the Democratic Revolution (PRD) began to obtain a much greater share of the vote in elections. Until that point, Mexico's multiparty system largely comprised a wide array of smaller parties that lacked a large following, but nevertheless played an important role in legitimizing the PRI's rule. By the 1990s, political support for the PAN and the PRD grew dramatically, as support for the PRI waned and new voters became increasingly engaged in the political process. Likewise, even the relative importance of Mexico's minor parties has grown as elections have become more competitive; minor parties like the PVEM and the PT have increasingly served as vital coalition partners in electoral campaigns and legislative negotiations. Table 6.1 provides a snapshot of the most important political parties in the contemporary Mexican political arena. They are discussed in greater detail in the sections below.

The PRI

As we saw in chapter 2, the party that governed Mexico for most of the twentieth century originated from the National Revolutionary Party (PNR), which was founded in 1929 by President Plutarco Elías Calles in order to forge a revolutionary family of the disparate political and military elements that emerged victorious from the 1910–1917 conflict. By 1937, in order to more formally incorporate peasants, urban laborers, and middle-class professionals, President Lázaro Cárdenas and his followers reorganized the ruling party as

Table 6.1.
Mexican Political Parties, 2000–Present

	Convergence (for Democracy)	National Action Party (PAN)	New Alliance Party (PANAL)	Party of the Democratic Revolution (PRD)	Institutional Revolutionary Party (PRI)	Social Democratic Alternative Party (PASD)	Workers Party (PT)	Green Party (PVEM)
Spanish Name:	Partido Convergencia para la Democracia	Partido Acción Nacional	Partido Nueva Alianza	Partido de la Revolución Democrática	Partido Revolucionario Institucional	Partido Alternativa Socialdemócrata	Partido de Trabajo	Partido Verde Ecólogista de México
Year Formed / Official Registration:	1999	1939	2005	1989	1929 as PNR 1938 as PRM 1946 as PRI	2005 as PASC 2008 as PASD	1993	1993
2006 Presidential Candidate:	Andrés López Obrador	Felipe Calderón	Roberto Campa	Andrés López Obrador	Roberto Madrazo	Patricia Mercado	Andrés López Obrador	Roberto Madrazo
Platform / Ideology:	Social democracy. Favors free market economic policies but argues for the necessity of state intervention in order to ensure equality, social justice, and respect for basic human rights.	Conservative with a strong Catholic base. Committed to open market economic policy, low government spending, transparency, devolution of economic and administrative power to subnational governments.	Emphasizes education as a key element in economic development, as well as moderate state intervention in the market economy.	Leftist. Calls for the rejection, or at the very least, a re-examination of neoliberalism with emphasis on the plight of the poor. Calls for wider social welfare programs and poverty alleviation.	Variable. Rhetoric centers on revolutionary nationalism but since early 1980s, has used free market policies (e.g., privatization, deregulation, low spending) to "modernize" the country.	Promotes a progressive social democratic agenda, with strong emphasis on agrarian workers' rights. Mercado introduced an emphasis on women's rights. In 2006, the party ran under the name Social Democratic and Agrarian Alternative (Partido Alternativa Socialdemócrata y Campesina).	Socialist roots. Advocates mass participation, economic nationalism, increased redistributive public spending, and decreased economic dependence on the United States.	No clear ideology beyond environmental protection. Some emphasis on sustainable development, protection of human rights, and "just distribution of resources to guarantee the consolidation of democracy."

the Mexican Revolutionary Party (PRM), a corporatist entity that now integrated Cárdenas's nationalist agenda to defend the economic interests of the patrimony. Later in 1946, Manuel Ávila Camacho oversaw the ruling party's transformation as a civilian party, which was reborn as the Institutional Revolutionary Party. This rechristening of the ruling party was remarkably apt, since the PRI truly became a lasting and institutionalized legacy of the revolution. From its founding until its decline in the 1990s, the ruling party was an indomitable political force in Mexico.

Guided directly by the hand of the Mexican president, the ruling party provided a forum for elite power sharing and political negotiation among hierarchically organized factions (*camarillas*) and interest groups. The PRI also served as a political machine that mobilized voters in support of the regime during electoral campaigns, and with the help of fraud, ensured that electoral results reflected overwhelming popular support for the regime. So successful was this combination of functions, that for nearly three-quarters of a century, the PRI was essentially fused with the government and the two were often considered one and the same.

While the so-called official party was much more inclusive than the pre-revolutionary status quo in which political power belonged to those who could claim and enforce it, the PRI's relationship to society and its internal organization had some important shortcomings. First, although the corporatist arrangement in which the government officially recognized groups like peasants and laborers brought tangible and otherwise inaccessible benefits (e.g., access to land, wage increases, job stability), it effectively excluded any group or organization that did not join the PRI. Independent groups were at best ignored and at worst persecuted by the government, and in both cases were completely excluded from power and access to government resources. This systematic exclusion of detractors who refused to be coopted would prove to be one of reasons why the PRI saw its popularity decline, particularly after 1968.

Second, the PRI's hierarchical structure created a situation in which upward mobility within the party was determined by loyalty to the president and the party's leadership rather than by performance or merit, commitment to ideological principles, or strong connection with constituents. The *camarilla* system allowed different elite groups to circulate in and out of power, yet it also created losers, in that some individuals were passed over in the candidate selection process. Subsequently these individuals and their supporters had to be convinced, or coopted, to return to the fold. Until the 1980s, disgruntled party members almost always calculated that they were better off within the party than outside of it. However, by the mid-1980s some members came to a different conclusion because of what they perceived to be the PRI's ideological shift away from the ideals of the revolution. This schism was another factor that contributed to the weakening of the PRI after 1987, when leftist elements bolted the party and supported Cuauhtémoc Cárdenas as an alternative candidate in the 1988 elections.

By the late 1990s, the PRI confronted a much more competitive electoral environment. The reality of the situation hit the party hard and fueled its internal divisions. Again the reformers who believed that the party's future depended on its ability to adopt more democratic practices (internally and externally) found themselves at odds with the more retrograde "dinosaurs," or *prinosaurios,* who favored traditional PRI practices such as electoral alchemy. The relative strength of different PRI factions was apparent in 1999 when the party held its first ever internal primary to select a presidential candidate. Ironically, although perhaps not surprisingly, the election was marred by claims of fraud, with almost all of the precandidates claiming that irregularities had occurred during the voting process. The winner was Francisco Labastida, a former governor with little popular appeal. Despite the PRI's traditional advantage, Labastida proved no match for Fox and he received only 36.9 percent of the popular vote.

While the days of PRI hegemony are clearly over, the party is by no means dead. Indeed, although it lost the presidency in 2000, it still managed to remain the largest single party in Congress, with 42 percent of the seats in the Chamber and 46.9 percent of the seats in the Senate (see tables 6.2 and 6.3). The PRI was able to maintain a strong presence thanks in part to a loyal base made up predominantly of the poor, less educated, and rural sectors of Mexican society. Equally important, the party continued to hold over half of Mexico's thirty-one governorships. These PRI governors, no longer protected by a *dedazo*-wielding president and complete control over the electoral process, have had to learn how to operate in a more transparent and competitive political context, both within the PRI and in general state elections. In states like Chihuahua, the PRI opened itself to internal competition and often managed to produce candidates—like Patricio Martínez—who could win without the need of massive electoral fraud or illicit government assistance.

At the same time, national party leaders have worked to rebuild the PRI's national organization and to promote the party's state and local candidates. First, however, the PRI underwent a painful internal struggle as factions within the party battled for control of national leadership positions. In the internal elections for party president in 2002, former Tabasco governor Roberto Madrazo proved victorious in that struggle, in part by building on the impression that the party chose wrongly by not supporting his candidacy in the PRI's primary for the 2000 presidential election.[2] Under Madrazo's leadership, the PRI seemed poised to make a comeback in 2006. In 2003, the PRI's seat share increased slightly from 42 to 44.8 percent in the Chamber of Deputies. In 2004, it reclaimed most of the local governments in Baja California and the governorship of the state of Nuevo León, both of which had been PAN strongholds

Table 6.2.
Party Representation in the Chamber of Deputies, 2000–2006

Party	2000–2003		2003–2006		2006–2009	
	Seats	%	Seats	%	Seats	%
PRI	210	42	224	44.8	106	21.2
PAN	207	41.4	153	30.6	206	41.2
PRD	52	10.4	95	19	127	25.4
PVEM	16	3.2	17	3.4	17	3.4
PT	8	1.6	6	1.2	17	3.4
Convergencia	2	0.4	5	1	12	2.4
PNS	3	0.6				
PAS	2	0.4				
PANAL					9	1.8
PASC					5	1.0
Independent					1	0.2

Sources: David Shirk, *Mexico's New Politics: The PAN and Democratic Change* (Boulder: Lynne Rienner, 2005), Table 6.4; Camp (2003) Table 8-1; Cámara de Diputados (www.diputados.gob.mx).
Note: In 2000, the PVEM ran as part of the PAN's Alliance for Change, while the PT, Convergencia, the PNS, and PAS ran as part of the PRD's Alliance for Mexico.

Table 6.3.
Party Representation in the Senate, 2000–2012

Party	2000–2006		2006–2012	
	Seats	% Senate	Seats	% Senate
PRI	60	46.9	33	25.8
PAN	46	35.9	52	40.6
PRD	15	11.7	26	20.3
PVEM	5	3.9	6	4.7
PT	1	0.1	5	3.9
Convergencia	1	0.1	5	3.9
Independent			1	0.8

Source: IFE.
Note: In 2000, the PVEM ran as part of the PAN's Alliance for Change, while the PT and Convergencia ran as part of the PRD's Alliance for Mexico.

over the previous decade. In 2005, the PRI won three of five gubernatorial elections, thanks in large part to the national leadership's efforts to ensure victory by working with their local organizations. Many believed that the PRI's state and local victories during the Fox administration could pave the way for the PRI to reclaim the presidency in 2006, with Madrazo as a likely candidate.

However, Madrazo faced competition from other major national party leaders. Key governors and rivals who remained bitter about his takeover of the party in 2002 collectively attempted to thwart his bid for the presidential nomination by forming a coalition of allies known by the Spanish acronym TUCOM, for Everyone United Against Madrazo (Todos Unidos Contra Madrazo). To select their candidate, TUCOM members deferred to popular opinion polls, which indicated that outgoing Mexico state governor Arturo Montiel was the most popular among them to defeat Madrazo in an open primary.[3] Yet on the eve of the party's formal vote, reports of financial scandals involving Montiel and his family, including revelations of evidently illicit personal enrichment, led to the unexpected withdrawal of Madrazo's main opponent. The only remaining contender was an obscure former deputy attorney general named Everardo Moreno Cruz, whom Madrazo had previously defeated by a nearly 10 to 1 margin in the party's primary election in 2005. In the final analysis, however, the internal schism in the PRI seemed to damage Madrazo's chances of victory in 2006. Indeed, with Madrazo as its candidate, the PRI obtained an all time low of 22 percent of the vote, in part because disaffected Montiel supporters and TUCOM leaders withheld their support.

After its disastrous performance in 2006, the PRI again renewed its national leadership in February 2007, this time selecting Beatriz Paredes as party chairwoman. Paredes was the first woman ever elected as governor of her home state, Tlaxcala, in 1987. She became the third woman—after María de los Ángeles Moreno in 1994 and Dulce María Sauri in 1997—to head the PRI. Under Paredes's leadership, the PRI will face two major challenges in the coming years. First, of course, the PRI needs to regain electoral support in Mexico's contemporary political context, where candidates must appeal effectively to the electorate. Second, the PRI needs to develop its political strategy for working as an opposition party in government. As long as there is a three-way split between Mexico's political forces, the PRI can be a critical ally for either the PAN or the PRD in the legislature, at both the national and the state level. The policy positions that it adopts will therefore be highly significant in determining political outcomes in Mexico for the foreseeable future. Already we have seen that under the Calderón administration, the PRI has been willing to work with both the PAN (on social security reform) and the PRD, calling for a formal investigation of Vicente Fox, who allegedly used his position as president to illegally enrich himself.

The PAN

Without a doubt, the strongest opposition party during the twentieth century was the PAN.[4] Formed in 1939 by a group of disenchanted entrepreneurs, professionals, and activist Catholics, the PAN was meant to provide a conservative and institutionalized alternative to the official party. Its founder, Manuel Gómez Morin, represented a group that believed that the PRI's hierarchical organization and corporatist practices violated the democratic ideals of the revolution and the principle of separation of powers set forth in the constitution. Instead PAN members, or *panistas,* favored a government that promoted the common good through democracy, compassion, and protection of private property. Moreover, the left-leaning economic policies enacted by Lázaro

Cárdenas in the mid-1930s were objectionable to many in the PAN because they required a high level of state intervention in the economy. For example, *panistas* objected to the creation of *ejidos*, or collective farms, which were anathema to private property and economic efficiency, and served to dampen entrepreneurial drive in the countryside.

Another important group within the PAN was made up of Catholic activists who staunchly opposed the regime's secular character and its enforcement of the constitutional provisions that prohibited Church involvement in politics. Their mentor was Efraín González Luna, an ardent Catholic and an advocate of political humanism, a doctrine advanced by Catholic thinkers like Thomas Aquinas and Thomas More, which articulated the belief that a perfect society is possible if humans are able to maximize their true potential.[5] The social doctrine of the Catholic Church served as the moral foundation for many of the party's social policies, chief among them the importance of family and compassion for the poor. In practice this meant that the state should not intervene in areas best left to the individual, family, or local community, or rather, "As much society as possible, as much government as necessary."[6] Therefore, the role of government was to help people help themselves by providing educational and economic opportunities for self-realization.

From 1940 until the mid-1970s, the party organization's primary preoccupation was not so much ideology as it was what strategy would provide the most effective challenge to the regime. While all *panistas* agreed that the PRI's methods and ideology were illegitimate, they disagreed on whether to participate in elections. Some believed that it was necessary for the party to field candidates in order to openly challenge the PRI. Others favored nonparticipation rather than tacit approval of what were invariably fraudulent electoral contests. Disagreement on the issue together with small size and lack of resources meant that the PAN was either unable or disinclined to field candidates in all elections. Yet by the mid-1940s, the PAN consistently won a handful of federal deputy positions and at least one mayoral post.[7] Nevertheless, these electoral victories did not resolve the party's internal dispute over electoral participation. Disagreement over the issue was so severe that it prevented the party from agreeing on a candidate for the 1976 presidential election and pushed the party to the brink of extinction.

The PAN could have disappeared had it not been for the confluence of some important internal and external factors. First, the viciousness of the fight over a presidential candidate convinced many *panistas* of the need for consensus for the party's survival. Additionally, in the wake of a steep drop in oil prices in 1982, the government botched a devaluation of the peso, and nationalized the banking industry. Some industrialists and middle-class entrepreneurs, particularly in the north, perceived these events as examples of the PRI's incompetence and egregious abuse of authority, and they channeled their disgust with the regime into support for the PAN.

With a newly forged consensus to share power within the party and an expanded popular base, the PAN was poised to make solid electoral gains throughout the late 1980s and 1990s. This success was also a product of the PAN's strategy of focusing, at least initially, on local and state elections where the party had a good chance of winning. To provide an idea of the party's dramatic reversal of fortune, in 1985 there were twenty-six mayors, fifty-one state legislators, and no governors from the PAN; in 2000 those numbers had increased to 329, 299, and 9, respectively. Equally important is the fact that by that same year, the PAN governed almost 42 percent of Mexico's population.[8] Another factor contributing to the rise of the PAN was the party's decision to cooperate with the PRI on key legislative measures (e.g., the 1990 electoral reform discussed below) rather than adopt an antagonistic posture that would elicit a hostile attitude from the PRI.

Despite its electoral success in the 1990s, the PAN continues to have significant internal divisions that are sometimes at odds with one another. The PAN is a right-of-center party that advocates social conservatism (e.g., opposes abortion and homosexuality and supports traditional morality and religious education), and also free market economic policies (e.g., supports private property and self sufficiency and opposes state intervention in the economy). Its socially conservative elements are devout Catholics who, in the spirit of González Luna, believe that the purpose of the party (and government) is to defend society's moral norms and enable individuals to realize their true material and spiritual potential. Its pro-business elements are drawn from businessmen and professionals, often described as *neopanistas*, or new *panistas*, who entered the party during the 1980s and tended to place greater emphasis on winning elections than on strong ideological principles. To be sure, these divisions are not always clear cut, or necessarily at odds. For example, Manuel Espino, former-PAN party chairman (2005–2007), was named president of the Christian Democratic Organization of the Americas and also faced accusations of being a member of a secret Catholic clique called "El Yunque." At the same time, Espino was also closely aligned with the party's *neopanistas*, particularly President Fox and Santiago Creel.

Regionally, the PAN enjoys its strongest support in the business-friendly northern states (e.g., Baja California, Chihuahua, Nuevo León) and traditionally conservative central western states (e.g., Guanajuato, Aguascalientes, Querétaro). The party's core base of support comes primarily from middle- and upper-class urban dwellers who are relatively better educated and more likely to identify themselves as Catholic than most Mexicans. Yet one of the keys to the party's success in 2000 was its ability to reach beyond its traditional base of support and appeal to another type of voter: one who wanted regime change.[9] In a clear triumph of the *neopanistas* over the traditionalists, the party's strategy was to tap into popular disgust with the corruption and lack of transparency associated with the status quo. This, together with the charisma and colorfulness of Vicente Fox, convinced many voters that the PAN represented the best avenue for change. The party's hard-won gains were relatively short-lived, however. Fox's *sexenio* was characterized by congressional gridlock and few policy successes, and the party bore the brunt of the public's disenchantment with change. In the 2003 midterm elections, the PAN's share of seats in the Chamber of Deputies declined from 207 to 153.

The PAN's prospects for winning the 2006 presidential election did not seem much better. Given disappointment with the Fox administration's accomplishments and strong support for the PRD in public opinion polls, many observers expected the PAN to lose the 2006 elections. In a competitive primary, the party selected as its candidate a longtime party bureaucrat named Felipe Calderón, who defeated his better known rivals: former interior secretary Santiago Creel and former Chihuahua governor Francisco Barrio. While somewhat of a surprise to outside observers, Calderón's experience in the party established his credentials as an ideologically committed *panista*, and his ties to party leaders and staunch partisans were quite strong. However, his appeal to voters in the general electorate was weaker. Until December 2006, Calderón was a consistent third-place contender behind his PRI and PRD rivals in the general election. From January through March, Calderón gained sufficient recognition and support to rival PRI candidate Roberto Madrazo, but remained about ten points behind PRD candidate Andrés Manuel López Obrador. Then, in the last several weeks before the election, PAN candidate Felipe Calderón gained significant ground. By election day on July 2, the resulting dead heat contributed to one of the most contentious presidential elections in modern history, and by far the greatest test of Mexico's independent federal electoral authorities to date (see textbox 6.1).

Textbox 6.1. The 2006 Mexican Presidential Election

On Sunday, July 2, 2006, Mexicans headed to the polls amid great uncertainty. In contrast to virtually all of Mexico's elections of the twentieth century, this election was too close to call. In the weeks before the election, polls alternately granted the winning margin to leftist candidate Andrés Manuel López Obrador or conservative candidate Felipe Calderón Hinojosa. The one thing that was virtually assured was that, for the first time ever, the PRI would obtain third place in a presidential election. The unpopularity of Roberto Madrazo converted the 2006 presidential race into a contest between two very different options. On the one hand, Felipe Calderón Hinojosa (PAN) represented the PAN's Catholic pro-business agenda. His campaign emphasized his personal integrity and ability to promote job creation through neoliberal economic policies. Calderón was viewed by many voters as *el menos mal*, or "the lesser of two evils," when contrasted against PRD candidate Andrés Manuel López Obrador.

López Obrador, known by his initials AMLO, was a former member of the PRI who helped to create the PRD, and later lost the governorship of his home state of Tabasco to Madrazo in a fraud-ridden 1995 election. AMLO won the Mexico City mayoral race in 2000. Through ambitious public-works projects and generous social services for the poor, young, and elderly, AMLO achieved approval ratings of over 60 percent. For his opponents, AMLO also represented the specter of a newly resurgent Latin American left that promotes populism and anti-Americanism.

Until March 2006, AMLO enjoyed a comfortable five- to ten-point lead over his rivals, with a high of nearly 45 percent public support in late 2005. However, a series of negative attacks on AMLO—as well as a number of campaign blunders, such as choosing not to appear at the first of two live televised debates—ultimately changed the course of the election. Thereafter, the candidates were in a dead heat in the race for the presidency.

The technical tie in public opinion polls was reflected in an extremely narrow result on election day, with Calderón and AMLO receiving 35.8 percent and 35.3 percent of the vote, respectively. Given the close result, AMLO refused to recognize Calderón's victory, and demanded a vote-by-vote recount of all ballots; he alleged that nearly 3 million votes had been deliberately omitted from the count. However, Mexican electoral regulations did not allow for a general call for a recount, and instead required that legal challenges be made through specific charges in districts where alleged violations of electoral law had occurred. The IFE did conduct a recount of those precincts for which there was evidence of error or inconsistencies (more than 11,000), but ruled against a full recount. In the end, the federal electoral tribunal (TRIFE) did not identify sufficient votes to overturn the results of the election. Rather than accept this decision, López Obrador took the unusual step of holding a public vote before supporters assembled at the Zocalo in Mexico City and declaring himself Mexico's "legitimate president." In September, members of the PRD staged dramatic protests in Congress, successfully blocking President Fox from giving his annual report to the legislature. Later, in December, the PRD unsuccessfully tried to prevent Calderón entering the legislature to be sworn in as president. President Calderón therefore took office in a context of considerable controversy, raising questions about whether, in the eyes of many citizens, he would be able to achieve sufficient legitimacy to lead the country. While Calderón made some progress in this regard, there was still sufficient controversy in 2008 that the Mexican Supreme Court felt obliged to intervene; in August, the court ruled that referring to López Obrador as Mexico's legitimate president in television advertisements was not punishable by fines.

Calderón emerged victorious in the legal challenges that followed the contested election, but he faced the unenviable task of governing with a fractionalized and significantly polarized legislature, in which his party holds about
40 percent of the seats. This means that on issues where the PRI and the PRD
choose to unite, they can combine their strength in both houses of Congress
to hinder the president's program and block PAN legislation. Still, many analysts have noted the contrast between presidents Fox and Calderón. Fox was
widely credited as an excellent and charismatic candidate and campaigner, but
was severely criticized for his inability to work with the legislature and broker
political reforms. In contrast, while seen as a much less effective candidate and
barely winning the 2006 election, Calderón is perceived to be a more skillful
negotiator and much more savvy political operator because of his experience
in the PAN and in the legislature. Given the divisions within the legislature
and remaining criticisms of the PRD about the outcome of the 2006 election,
he will certainly need to be.

The PRD

In many ways the PRD is the antithesis of the PAN. It is a relatively young
party with a decidedly left of center ideology made up of a significant number of ex-PRIistas.[10] Yet the birth of Mexico's third major party shares at
least one similarity with the PAN: its founders were disenchanted with the
direction of the PRI. The PRD began as an electoral alliance organized by
a group of several small leftist parties and nonpartisan social movements
for the purpose of supporting Cuauhtémoc Cárdenas in his bid for the
presidency in 1988. Until 1987, Cárdenas, son of Lázaro Cárdenas, one of
Mexico's most beloved presidents, was a prominent member of the PRI.
In 1986, Cárdenas and other members of the party's left flank formed the
Democratic Current (Corriente Democrática, CD) and openly criticized the
de la Madrid administration's adoption of free market economic policies as
a betrayal of the revolution. The CD also called for the PRI to use democratic primaries, rather than the *dedazo*, to select the party's candidates—a
move that presumably would prevent the selection of another technocrat
as the party's presidential candidate. When the party rejected the proposed
internal reform, Cárdenas and others in the CD left the PRI and began to
forge the National Democratic Front (Frente Democrática Nacional, FDN),
a leftist coalition that brought together parastatal parties like the PARM
with popular movements in order to mount what would be the most serious
electoral challenge to the PRI to that point.

Garnering 31 percent of the vote, the FDN fared much better than anyone,
especially the PRI, expected.[11] With Cárdenas at the helm, it attracted voters

who yearned for a return to the past when the ideals of the revolution were supposedly alive and well. Furthermore, the Front was able to capitalize on growing dissatisfaction with the PRI. Mexico was just beginning to emerge from its most serious financial crisis and their recent economic hardship weighed heavy on many voters' minds. The PRI's candidate, Carlos Salinas de Gortari, was sure to deepen the technocratic approach introduced by his predecessor. Cárdenas and the FDN represented an alternative for voters who wanted to send a message to the PRI.

Almost immediately after the election, some members of the FDN, led again by Cárdenas, began the process of transforming the movement into a bona fide political party. But the newly formed PRD did not fare well in subsequent elections. Its vote share in the 1991 midterm elections plummeted to a mere 8 percent, and by 1994, when Cárdenas again ran for president, it recovered only some its former popularity in garnering 17 percent of the vote. As noted by Kathleen Bruhn, the PRD's decline in the early 1990s was caused by several factors.[12] First, the party comprised a number of disparate groups with different ideals and goals. While this heterogeneity was key to the FDN's success in 1988, it hindered the consolidation of the party as an organization because it complicated tasks that should have been relatively straightforward. So, for example, defining the party's platform and choosing candidates and leaders were hotly contested issues that often created further division. Moreover, these divisions also had adverse effects on the PRD's internal democracy, because the losers often claimed that the winners had triumphed through fraud. In the end, the real loser was the PRD as a whole because internal charges of fraud and corruption damaged the party's external image as a serious proponent of democracy and a viable electoral alternative.

As a young organization the PRD also suffered from a lack of institutionalization. Initially many of the party's internal rules and procedures were decided on an ad hoc basis and the arbiter of last resort was the party's leader, Cuauhtémoc Cárdenas. This method of operation, while perhaps suitable for a temporary political movement, was inadequate for a consolidated political party because, at the very least, it made enforcing rules difficult and promoted overreliance on a charismatic leader.

The internal weaknesses of the PRD were compounded by external efforts to hinder its success. Most notable of these was the PRI's campaign to undermine its leftist challenger. The PRI's bitterness toward the PRD stemmed from what many PRIistas consider Cárdenas's unforgivable betrayal by leaving, openly criticizing, and then challenging the PRI in the late 1980s. Additionally, the PRI felt threatened by the PRD's popular appeal and its attempts to woo the party's progressive elements and traditional base of support with calls for economic nationalism and attention to the poor. As a result, the PRI used state resources to harass or even harm PRD activists and gleefully publicized the PRD's internal scandals. It also used its control of the media to portray the PRD as a radical party prone to violence. For example, in the 1994 presidential campaign, a PRI television advertisement showed mob violence with burning and looting while a solemn voice suggested that a vote for change would be a vote for insecurity and instability. Finally, the PRI routinely stole elections, forcing *perredistas* to mount postelectoral challenges that further branded the party as confrontational and incapable of playing by democratic rules. Adding to the PRD's negative image was its reputation for intransigence. The party's refusal to negotiate with other parties was as much a result of the PRD's internal divisions as it was a principled stance. Regardless of the reasons, this attitude also reinforced the notion that the PRD was a bunch of wild-eyed radicals more intent on using its power in Congress to stand in the way of, rather than promote, reform and progress.

The PRD enjoyed a revival of sorts in 1997 when Cárdenas was decisively elected mayor of Mexico City with 44 percent of the vote, and it nearly doubled its share of seats in Congress. Undoubtedly, the PRD's gains in the late 1990s were due, at least in part, to the mobilization of its core base of support: the rural poor in the southern states and voters in Mexico City. But this mobilization and the party's appeal to others probably would not have occurred were it not for the fact that the 1997 elections were the first to take place after the calamitous peso devaluation of 1994. Unfortunately for the PRD, it was not able to parlay its 1997 gains into a similar showing in 2000 when Cárdenas was again the party's presidential candidate. His mediocre performance as Mexico City's mayor and lackluster campaign, together with the party's damaged reputation and popularity of Vicente Fox, meant that the PRD did not make many inroads with voters and it garnered only 16.6 percent of the national vote.

More notable was the party's showing in 2003, when, in relatively good economic times, its share of seats in the Chamber almost doubled from fifty-two to ninety-five. Indeed, this appeared to be a sign of the party's good political fortunes to come. As early as 2002, political observers had begun to note strong support for Mexico City mayor Andrés Manuel López Obrador. López Obrador's ascendancy was remarkable because it marked the first time that someone other than three-time PRD presidential candidate and party founder Cuauhtémoc Cárdenas might represent the party in a presidential election. López Obrador was a former member of the PRI who left the party with Cárdenas. He ran unsuccessfully for governor in his home state of Tabasco in 1994, an election that evidenced widespread electoral fraud favoring the eventual winner, PRI candidate Roberto Madrazo. Thereafter, López Obrador went on to become state party president in Tabasco, national party president, and finally mayor of Mexico City, all the while building a reputation for his commitment to the poor and his ability to use popular mobilization as leverage in negotiations.

López Obrador's popularity suffered somewhat during a series of corruption scandals involving some members of his administration, several of whom were caught taking bribes on videotape. Whatever support he lost, however, López Obrador recuperated when the Fox administration tried to indict him in 2005 on a minor charge for the purpose of disqualifying him as a presidential candidate. This *desafuero* or impeachment effort actually caused a dramatic increase in support for López Obrador—including a 1.2 million person march on the capitol—that led the government to drop the charges against López Obrador.

Thereafter, López Obrador continued at the head of public opinion polls until two months before the July 2 election, when suddenly his support declined to put him in a virtual tie with the PAN's Felipe Calderón. Many analysts noted that this sharp decline in support for López Obrador was the result of his own missteps and a very successful media and Internet campaign by the PAN. Similar to the efforts to discredit the PRD during the 1994 election, the Calderón campaign team's television advertisements sought to convince voters that supporting López Obrador would lead to political and economic chaos. Other advertisements sought to link López Obrador to Venezuelan President Hugo Chavez, whom many Mexicans identified with the reckless and radical left. In the end, while essentially as many Mexicans supported López Obrador as Calderón, the sharp reduction in support for the PRD illustrated the very real concern that a López Obrador victory would seriously worsen their economic situation.

Other Parties

In addition to Mexico's three major political parties, there are a number of smaller so-called third parties. As in other political systems, Mexico's small parties are unlikely to win a majority of votes in races for executive office or in district-level contests for legislative seats. However, because Mexico's federal and state legislatures (and city councils) allow for a certain degree of proportional representation, there are important opportunities for even small parties to obtain a voice in government. Also, because there is substantial public funding available for registered political parties in Mexico, small parties have access to resources that enable them to attract followers and promote their agendas in the media. As electoral competition has intensified in recent years, the importance of small parties has increased since they are now seen by the larger parties as useful strategic partners in building electoral and governmental alliances.[13]

The most successful of Mexico's smaller parties is the Mexican Ecological Green Party (Partido Verde Ecologista Mexicano, PVEM), also known as the Mexican Green Party. The PVEM has obtained a significant share of the vote—between 3 and 7 percent—in federal elections since 1994, and has been an important coalition partner for each of the three major parties in federal and state elections (see textbox 6.2). Meanwhile, other parties that have found representation in the federal legislature are the New Alliance Party (Partido Nueva Alianza, PANAL), Convergence for Democracy (Convergencia), the Social Democratic and Agrarian Alternative Party (Partido Alternativa Socialdemócrata y Campesino, PASC), and the Labor Party (Partido de Trabajo, PT). The PANAL was founded in 2005 with the support of Mexico's teachers' union, the National Union of Education Workers (Sindicato Nacional de Trabajadores de la Educación, SNTE). Indeed, the PANAL's creation appeared to be a result of the estrangement of SNTE leaders from the PRI. Aside from a general commitment to workers' rights, the PANAL does not have a well-articulated political agenda.

In contrast to both the PVEM and the PANAL, Convergencia, the PASC, and the PT do have relatively clear ideological principles and policy agendas. Indeed, all three of these parties have a leftist orientation that supports the redistribution of resources to the poorest sectors of society and calls for social justice and the respect of basic human rights. Of the three, the PT is the most reminiscent of a socialist party in its commitment to economic nationalism and rejection of free market economic policies. Meanwhile, Convergencia favors neoliberal economic strategies as long as they are tempered with some government intervention. Their ideological leanings make both Convergencia and the PT "natural" allies of the PRD; in fact, they joined the PRD's alliances in both the 2000 and 2006 national elections. The PASC is the newest of Mexico's major parties and has distinguished itself for its support progressive social policies, having supported avid feminist Patricia Mercado as its candidate in 2006.

In short, Mexico has a wide array of political parties, and the political dynamics between them are still emerging. The long-term prospects for all of Mexico's political parties have been significantly determined by the configuration of Mexico's electoral institutions. Indeed, the design of Mexico's electoral system was one of the major factors that perpetuated the PRI in power for over seven decades. A series of gradual electoral reforms, like the introduction of proportional representation, also helped to dramatically transform the Mexican political system over the last three decades of the twentieth century. In an effort to better understand the important role of electoral institutions in shaping the prospects of political parties in Mexico, we now focus on the

Textbox 6.2. Mexico's Unusual Green Party

Despite its origins as a community-based nongovernmental organization and its stated commitment to preserving the environment and promoting sustainable development, the PVEM has very weak green credentials. Indeed, the party's greater claim to fame is its involvement in corruption scandals, some of which potentially threaten rather than protect the environment. For example, in 2004, Senator Jorge Emilio González Martínez, president of the PVEM, was caught on videotape negotiating the exchange of $2 million for government permits to develop land in Cancún. The party also gained notoriety for being fined $16 million by the IFE for violating campaign spending laws in the 2000 election.

Notwithstanding the PVEM's questionable commitment to environmental causes and its dubious accounting skills, as a party organization it has demonstrated a shrewd ability to obtain power by making itself available as a coalition partner. In 2000, its partnership with PAN candidate Vicente Fox in the Alliance for Change was mutually beneficial in that it provided the PVEM with a springboard to an unprecedented number of legislative offices, and it gave the PAN a 5 percent boost that helped to win the presidency. When the alliance fell apart in 2001, the PVEM wasted no time in pairing up with the PRI for the 2003 midterm and 2006 presidential elections. Again this strategy paid off for both parties by increasing the former's seat share in the Chamber of Deputies and strengthening the latter's legislative plurality.

The PVEM's involvement in the scandals mentioned above undoubtedly hurt its credibility as a coalition partner and its popularity among voters. Equally serious is the fact that the party has no discernable platform beyond protecting the environment, and even this lacks clearly articulated goals or strategies. On the one hand, an ideological void no doubt provides important flexibility when it comes to making alliances with larger parties. On the other hand, the party runs the risk of losing popular support if voters do not feel that it stands for some coherent ideological or policy agenda. Combined, these factors make the PVEM's long-term success uncertain.

evolution of the contemporary electoral system. In so doing, we pay special attention to the reforms that created space for opposition parties to challenge, and ultimately change, the status quo.

The Mexican Electoral System

The PRI achieved its hegemonic position thanks in large part to an internal organization that facilitated power sharing among competing groups, the monopolization and clientelistic distribution of state resources, and the occasional use of electoral fraud and political repression. However, equally

Table 6.4.
Federal Electoral Laws, 1917–1977

Electoral Regulation	Party Formation/Eligibility	Representation and Terms of Office
1917 Postrevolutionary Electoral System[1]		
• National legislature confirms presidential and congressional elections • Supreme Court resolves electoral disputes • Elections overseen by municipal authorities • State level Consejos de Listas Electorales compile voter registration and define district boundaries	• Parties cannot have a religious affiliation • Must have support of 100 citizens and publish governing rules • Independent candidates allowed	• No reelection[2] • Four-year presidential term • Deputies are elected by plurality from single 4-member districts (SMD) for two-year terms • One deputy per 60,000 inhabitants, with at least two per state and one per territory/DF[3] • Senators are elected by plurality vote from SMD for four-year terms[4]
1946 Federal Electoral System		
• Established the Federal Electoral Oversight Commission, headed by minister of the interior (Gobernación) to organize and oversee elections[5] • Established National Voter Registration Agency to define districts and develop voter lists[6]	• Candidates must have support of a political party • Parties must be national with at least 30,000 supporters: 1,000 in each of two-thirds of the states and territories[7]	
1963 Party Deputy System		
		• Introduction of partial proportional representation (PR), or "party deputy" seats in the Chamber of Deputies for parties that receive 2.5 percent of the national vote.[8] • Each party with 2.5 percent gets one seat per 0.5 percent, and a maximum of 20 seats.[9] • Any party that received more than 25 percent of the national vote would receive no party deputy seats.

Table 6.4.
Federal Electoral Laws, 1917–1977

Electoral Regulation	Party Formation/Eligibility	Representation and Terms of Office
1977 (LOPPE) *Federal Law of Political Organizations and Electoral Processes* • Parties must be national with at least 65,000 supporters: 2,000 in two-thirds of states and territories • Composition of CFE changed to include a representative from government, one from each party, one senator, one deputy, and a notary public • CFE given the authority to register, deny or withdraw party registration • CFE assumes responsibility for choosing the number and composition of PR districts • Media access: Free monthly radio and TV time for all registered parties	• Any victorious party that fails to assume its posts loses its registration and vote • Parties must be national with at least 65,000 supporters: 2,000 in two-thirds of states and territories • Any victorious party that fails to assume its posts loses its registration and vote • Established two methods of party registration: • *Conditional registration* given to organizations with four continuous years of political activity. In order to obtain permanent registration, must obtain 1.5 percent of vote in national election • *Definitive registration* given to parties that submit party statutes and evidence of 65,000 members: 3,000 in one-half plus one of states, or 300 in one-half plus one of all federal electoral districts	• Number of seats in Chamber of Deputies is increased to 400, 300 SMD, 100 PR for parties that win fewer than 60 SMD, and at least 1.5 percent • In 1986, the number of seats in Chamber increased to 500, 300 SMD and 200 PR, and a governability clause gives party with highest vote (even if less than 51 percent) a majority in Chamber.

Table 6.4.
Federal Electoral Laws, 1917–1977

1. The foundations of the Mexican electoral system were established by the 1917 Mexican constitution and the 1918 Federal Electoral Law.
2. In 1927, the Mexican constitution was amended to increase the presidential term from four to six years, and to permit reelection for up to one consecutive term and unlimited reelection for nonsuccessive terms. However, in 1928, restrictions on reelection were again imposed by constitutional amendment, which allowed no reelection for presidents and governors and nonconsecutive reelection for legislative and local offices.
3. The 1928 constitutional reform later modified the representative formula to be one deputy per 100,000 inhabitants.
4. A 1933 constitutional amendment to the constitution established three-year terms for federal deputies, six-year terms for senators, and made Senate elections concurrent with presidential elections.
5. Later, under the 1954 Federal Electoral Law, the Federal Electoral Commission (CFE) or state and district counterparts (formed in 1951) was given the responsibility of settling electoral disputes.
6. With the 1954 Federal Electoral Law, the National Electoral Registry was created and empowered to define district boundaries and maintain voter lists.
7. With the 1954 Federal Electoral Law, parties were required to be national with at least 75,000 supporters: 2,500 in two-thirds of states and territories.
8. In response to PAN protests against alleged fraud in 1968 state-level elections, a 1969 constitutional amendment established that any victorious party that failed to assume its posts would lose its registration, and politicians who failed to assume their posts would have their political rights suspended for three years.
9. The 1973 Federal Electoral Law lowered the threshold for PR seats to 1.5 percent, with a modified formula awarding one seat per 0.5 percent, up to a maximum of twenty-five seats. Any party that received more than 25 percent of the national vote would receive no party deputy seats.

Table 6.5.

1990s Federal Electoral Reforms

Electoral Regulation	Electoral Competition	Representation
1990 Federal Code of Electoral Institutions and Procedures (COFIPE) • Federal Electoral Institute (IFE) replaces CFE as chief electoral authority • Led by Consejo General, which is comprised of Secretary of Government, four representatives of majority party, one senator and one deputy from majority party, one member of Congress from the opposition, and six independent members, nominated by president and confirmed by two-thirds majority in Chamber • Consejo adjudicates electoral disputes • All parties choose precinct observers • New voter registration list with photo identification card • Campaign finance: Parties receive funds in proportion to support and seats in CD; new formula for public funding for political parties; limits on campaign spending; new procedures for reporting and monitoring party finances • In 1993, the IFE was granted power to certify congressional elections **1994 Electoral Law** • Established Federal Electoral Tribunal (TRIFE); headed by Chief Supreme Court Justice and four members of the judiciary (with 2/3 approval in Chamber) to examine disputes relating to congressional elections • Independent members within Consejo General of IFE are replaced by six citizens chosen by consensus of major political parties and appointed by the Chamber • Parties must submit report to IFE that details campaign revenue and spending • Campaign finance: Establishes new campaign spending limits; limits private contributions from individuals, labor unions, anonymous donors; prohibits contributions from businesses, churches, and foreign organizations	• Coalitions must be formed well in advance of elections • No two parties can nominate a single candidate unless they form a coalition • Coalition candidates do not count toward parties' total for PR seats	• Eliminates first governability clause in favor of a formula that overrepresents the party with most victories in SMD in the Chamber, so that if winning party gets 35 percent of vote, it automatically gets 250 SMD seats plus one PR seat, for a simple majority • In 1993, the second governability clause was eliminated, and new law established that no single party can hold more than 63 percent of total seats in Chamber • In 1993, the number of Senate seats increased to four from each state for a total of 128. First-place party wins three, and the second-place party, one seat

Table 6.5.
1990s Federal Electoral Reforms

Electoral Regulation	Electoral Competition	Representation
1990 Federal Code of Electoral Institutions and Procedures (COFIPE)		
1996 Electoral Law		
• Federal District: Introduces direct election of governor of DF • Campaign finance: Allocates public campaign funds to all political parties: 30 percent are distributed equally among parties, 70 percent based on share of vote in previous election • Establishes sanctions for violating spending laws • Parties must submit annual reports on revenue and spending • Permanent commission established to oversee campaign spending and party expenditures	• Establishes independent audit of voter registration list • Legalizes participation of international election observers • IFE president is an independent citizen (rather than Secretary of Government) chosen by consensus and with two-thirds approval of Chamber • Voting rights within IFE limited to its president and eight independent electoral councilors chosen by consensus with two-thirds approval of Chamber, to serve six-year terms • Establishes Supreme Court as final arbiter of electoral results • Integrates TFE into Supreme Court bureaucracy • IFE given right to buy time slots for political party advertising • IFE monitors media for signs of bias	• Changes Senate seat allocation to two per state (64), 32 to second-place parties, and 32 on the basis of PR • Majority party in Chamber can have no more than 300 seats and number of seats cannot exceed share of vote by more than 8 percent

important was its ability to manipulate the electoral system in its favor, while coopting opposition parties to participate in and legitimate the political process. By tinkering with various electoral laws, the PRI was able to ensure that it would consistently be overrepresented in the legislature; this was a key component of *presidencialismo* and essential for the party to single-handedly amend the constitution and stay in power. Table 6.4 lists the major features of the electoral system that facilitated single-party dominance, while table 6.5 provides a chronological summary of the reforms enacted during the 1990s that alternately bolstered and then diminished the PRI's dominance. A more detailed discussion of the major institutional features of the Mexican electoral system follows below.[14]

No Reelection

The prohibition on reelection has been an almost constant feature of Mexico's postrevolutionary political system: a 1933 constitutional amendment established that the president and governors cannot seek reelection, and that national legislators and local offices can be reelected only to nonsuccessive terms. Some of the negative effects of this law, namely, weakening the link between politicians and constituents and strengthening parties at the expense of voters, were discussed in chapter 5. Yet despite these problems, and the fact that eliminating the ban would almost surely increase the quality and accountability of politicians, attempts to introduce consecutive reelection for national legislative and local offices have not elicited widespread support. One reason for this is that nearly 100 years later, the principle of no reelection remains one of the few meaningful results of the revolution. The fear that a single individual would capture the presidency along the lines of Porfirio Díaz seems an ironic one given the development of PRI hegemony, yet it is one of great symbolic import to many Mexicans.[15] Yet the ban on reelection is more than just a nostalgic throwback to the past. As an institutionalized feature of the Mexican political system, it has given rise to powerful beneficiaries with a vested interest in maintaining the status quo. Chief among its supporters are members of the old guard within the PRI who argue that introducing reelection would weaken the party by creating incentives for politicians to pay more attention to their constituents, on whom they will depend for career advancement, than to the party organization. These vested interests help explain why, even with widespread recognition among scholars and politicians that eliminating the ban would represent a step forward in Mexico's transition to democracy, it has been difficult to bring about change.[16] This is not to say that the issue is dead. Indeed, militants in virtually all of the parties have sought to make it part of their parties' platforms and as of this writing, there appeared to be some inchoate support for introducing reelection at the local level.

Party Formation

One of the ways that the PRI was able to maintain its dominant position was to make it very difficult for opposition parties to mount a strong challenge to its hegemony.[17] The Electoral Law of 1918 allowed independent candidates to run for office and created a very low threshold for party registration. But after several challenges posed by opposition parties and independent presidential candidates during the 1930s and 1940s, the regime enacted the Federal Electoral Law of 1946 to insulate the ruling party. The reform outlawed independent candidacies and required political parties to demonstrate a minimum level of national support in order to be officially recognized and participate in elections. In 1954 the threshold for party registration was raised from 30,000 to 75,000, with a minimum of 2,500 members in each of two-thirds of the federal entities. In 1973, the requirement was relaxed slightly, to 65,000, in an effort to promote greater pluralism, and hence legitimacy for the political system.[18] Of course relatively few parties were able to meet these requirements and even fewer were able to consistently maintain their financial and political independence and thus behave as a true rather than loyal opposition.

The charade of electoral competition was exposed in the 1976 presidential election when the PRI candidate, Jose Lopez Portillo, ran unopposed. As noted in chapter 4, Lopez Portillo subsequently introduced the Federal Law of Political Organizations and Electoral Processes (LFOPPE) in 1977, which sought to increase the access of smaller opposition parties by creating two methods of obtaining official registration. Organizations could apply for conditional registration, and hence participate in national elections, if they could demonstrate four years of continuous political activity. Conditional parties could obtain permanent registration if they received 1.5 percent of the national vote. Alternatively, parties established definitive registration by providing a copy of party statutes and evidence of 65,000 members, 3,000 in one-half plus one of the states, or 300 in one-half plus one of all federal electoral districts. As a result of this new law, smaller parties found it easier to participate in elections and gain a nominal level of representation. Yet the overall effect of the reform was to enhance the legitimacy of the Mexican political system by making it appear more competitive than it really was. Therefore the main beneficiary of the 1977 law was the PRI, whose hegemonic position was preserved and further legitimized.

The next important reform in the area of party formation came in 1990 in the wake of the 1988 presidential election, in which several opposition parties formed a coalition to support Cuauhtémoc Cárdenas against PRI candidate,

Carlos Salinas. The seriousness of the challenge prompted the PRI, together with the support of the PAN, to pass the Federal Code of Electoral Institutions and Processes (COFIPE), which required that joint candidates be supported by an official coalition, and that coalitions nominate common candidates for more positions than just the presidency. This new law made it less likely that parties would join forces to challenge the PRI. But the real question surrounding COFIPE was why the PAN agreed to support a law that clearly put it at a disadvantage. While *panista* support of the reform was by no means unanimous, most members serving in the Chamber of Deputies at that time agreed that the measure pertaining to coalitions would help stave off a threat from the left, something they feared would derail the country's economic progress.

The evolution of laws governing party formation and participation in the electoral arena almost always favored the PRI and helped that party maintain its hegemony. Yet clearly, these laws were not enough to keep the opposition down indefinitely. In fact, hindsight allows us to recognize that rules such as the requirement that parties demonstrate a national following actually forced opposition parties to broaden their appeal and garner the popular support that would eventually help undermine the ruling party's dominance.

Elections

Control over the election process was perhaps the most important institutional determinant of PRI hegemony. For several decades, the official party used a combination of biased electoral rules and fraud to ensure that it would win elections.[19] Before 1990, the government tightly controlled electoral process through a variety of mechanisms. For example, the minister of the interior, who was always closely linked to the president, headed the body in charge of most aspects pertaining to elections, the Federal Electoral Commission (CFE). This arrangement allowed the standing government and the ruling party to intervene directly in electoral matters, including the settlement of electoral disputes and charges of fraud. It is therefore unsurprising that the PRI was able to use fraud with impunity to ensure favorable electoral results.

One of the most notorious examples of electoral fraud was the crash of the vote tabulating system on election night in 1988. The circumstances surrounding this election, and demands of the opposition, prompted the replacement of the CFE with the Federal Electoral Institute (IFE) as the country's chief electoral authority. Despite the fact that IFE was formally separate from the government, it was hardly an independent organization, since the minister of the interior still served as its head of the IFE, and the PRI was overrepresented on the governing board. It would take further reforms to completely separate the electoral process from the government. In 1994, the governing board of the IFE was changed so that its six independent councilors would be chosen by consensus of the major political parties, rather than nominated by the president, and approved by a two-thirds majority of the Chamber. Furthermore, the reform established the Federal Electoral Tribunal (Tribunal Federal Electoral, TRIFE). The TRIFE was comprised of the Chief Justice and four other Supreme Court justices and its purpose was to examine disputes relating to congressional elections.

It is possible that no more reforms would have occurred in the short term had it not been for the guerrilla uprising in Chiapas on January 1, and the political assassinations surrounding the presidential elections of 1994. These events led newly elected President Ernesto Zedillo to call for reforms that would definitively remove the government from the electoral process.[20] Accordingly, the 1996 electoral reform made the IFE truly independent by requiring that its president be an independent citizen chosen by the Chamber of Deputies. The reform also established the Supreme Court as the final arbiter of electoral disputes and integrated the TRIFE into the Supreme Court bureaucracy. More than previous reforms, the 1996 electoral laws paved the way for all political parties in Mexico to compete on equal footing in local and national elections. It is not coincidental that the PRI lost its majority in the Chamber of Deputies in the first year that the reforms were in effect.

Legislative Representation

Electoral dominance was key to the PRI's control of the national legislature. Until 1988, the PRI consistently held at least a two-thirds majority in both houses of Congress. Indeed, the opposition's representation in Congress was so low by the early 1960s, that President Adolfo López Mateos introduced proportional representation, or party seats, to the Chamber of Deputies. With this reform, any party that received between 2.5 and 20 percent of the national vote was awarded one seat per 0.5 percent of the vote, for a maximum of twenty seats. The addition of these seats was a novel way to allow the opposition representation, all the while preserving the PRI's majority and in fact punishing opposition parties that received over 20 percent of the national vote.[21] In the aftermath of the social unrest of 1968, the threshold for plurinominal seats was lowered to 1.5 percent, and the maximum number of seats was increased to 25. Moreover, following the PRI's embarrassment in the presidential election of 1976, 100 plurinominal seats were set aside for parties that obtained at least 1.5 percent of the national vote and won fewer than 60 of the 300 single-member district seats. Again, these reforms were quite shrewd in that they encouraged the formation of many small parties, and the perception of greater representation, while at the same time ensuring that opposition parties with larger followings would never pose a serious threat to the PRI.

When the opposition began to make inroads against the PRI in the mid-1980s, the ruling party manipulated the electoral system to ensure that it would be overrepresented in the national legislature. A constitutional amendment in 1986 further increased the size of the Chamber of Deputies to 500 with addition of 100 more plurinominal seats. But while this appeared to create more space for the opposition, in fact, changes to allocation formula gave the PRI access to the proportional representation seats for the first time. Furthermore, the reform was more beneficial to the PRI than the opposition because it also guaranteed the party with the highest vote a majority in the Chamber, even if it won less than 51 percent of the national vote. As discussed in chapter 4, the governability clause meant that the PRI need only obtain a plurality in order to control the lower house of the legislature, and in fact, this is what occurred in the 1988 congressional elections, when the PRI won only 239 seats.

In 1990, the PRI was able to enlist the help of the opposition to pass the COFIPE. In exchange for the creation of the IFE as the first step toward an independent electoral authority, the COFIPE eliminated the governability clause, but replaced it with a similar arrangement in which a majority of Chamber seats was automatically awarded to the party with the most victories in single-member districts.[22] More specifically, the new law established several important thresholds: if a party won less than 35 percent or between 60 and 70 percent of the national vote, its seat share was proportional to its vote share. If it won more than 70 percent, it would automatically receive 350 seats, or a two-thirds majority. But the most important provision was the one that was most likely to apply to the PRI: a party that won between 35 and 60 percent of the national vote was awarded 50 percent plus one, or 251 seats, and two additional seats for each percentage point above 35 percent. In a second round of reforms in 1993, the Salinas administration conceded more space to the opposition with a package of reforms that doubled the size of the Senate to 128 members, but again altered electoral rules for the Chamber to favor the ruling party.[23] Thus while the opposition benefited from the addition of thirty-two Senate seats to be awarded to the second-place party in each state and the Federal District, and the elimination of the provision that prevented a party from holding more than 315 seats in the Chamber, it was nevertheless disadvantaged by a new provision that allocated the 200 plurinominal seats on the basis of each party's share of the overall vote, a move that made it easier for the PRI to claim proportional representation seats and thus protect its majority in the lower house of the legislature.[24]

By 1996, the opposition's demands for a more level playing field were strong enough to prompt the Zedillo administration to introduce a reform that virtually eliminated the possibility that the PRI would be overrepresented in the Chamber of Deputies. The new law made it impossible for the majority party's share of seats to exceed its share of the vote by more than 8 percent and capped its seats in the Chamber at 300 seats, significantly less than the 350 needed to unilaterally amend the constitution. New proportional representation allocation formulas in the Senate also made it easier for the opposition to win seats. Without a doubt the new laws played an important role in giving the opposition greater access to positions in the national legislature. Since 1997, no party has won more than a plurality in either house of the national legislature.

Media Access

Until the mid-1970s, all television and virtually all newspaper coverage of political matters favored the PRI and provided no meaningful outlet for the opposition. Close ties between government officials and owners of media outlets, combined with the widespread practice of paying kickbacks to reporters made it next to impossible for the Mexican press to have an objective or independent voice. In the aftermath of the Tlatelolco massacre and several government crackdowns in the early 1970s, many newspaper journalists began to reexamine their previous complicity and take on a more independent and critical stance vis-à-vis the government.[25] Recognizing the essential role that the media played in maintaining the PRI's dominance, and that a uniformly pro-government stance would not fly in the country's volatile political climate, the 1977 LFOPPE included provisions to allow all registered political parties free monthly television and radio time. Like many reforms of the time, this provision was more symbolic than substantial since the government, in concert with the media outlets, determined which time slots were given to the opposition. It was not until the mid-1990s, with the strengthening of the IFE, that opposition political parties had meaningful access, and could count on more objective coverage by the media. The 1996 reform gave the IFE the right to buy the time slots for party advertising and charged with monitoring the media for signs of bias, such as it did in obliging the PAN to discontinue some paid advertising that it deemed too personal an attack on López Obrador. Thus Mexicans today enjoy relatively balanced coverage of political issues. However, it cannot be said that freedom of the press is complete since journalists, particularly at the state and local level, are commonly harassed, threatened, and even killed for reporting on delicate matters such as human rights violations, drug trafficking, and political scandals.

Campaign Finance

The PRI's virtual fusion with the government bureaucracy allowed it to blur the lines between party and government resources. As such, the party developed the habit of dipping into government coffers to fund its electoral bids. Not surprisingly, this practice put the opposition at a further disadvantage and created widespread disenchantment with the PRI. Before 1987, federal election laws governed public funding for political parties, but they were vague and rarely enforced. These rules were modified and strengthened in 1987 when the Federal Electoral Code established that parties would receive public funds in proportion to their electoral returns and percentage of seats held in the Chamber.[26] Shortly thereafter, in 1990, COFIPE altered the allocation formula and introduced electoral spending limits. However, the latter were so high, that they made no practical difference in the way the PRI funded its electoral campaigns. COFIPE also established procedures for reporting and monitoring campaign spending, yet in practice, these rules were widely ignored. In 1993, limits were placed on contributions from private individuals, labor unions and anonymous donors, and churches, businesses, and foreign organizations were prohibited from giving money to Mexican political campaigns. Further reform occurred in 1996 when parties were obligated to submit annual revenue and spending reports, and Congress established that public, rather than private funds would be the most important source of campaign financing. At that time it was decided that 30 percent of all public funds would be equally distributed among political parties, and 70 percent would be distributed according to each party's vote share in the previous election.[27] Yet despite these reforms, campaign spending remains a serious problem in Mexico because the regulatory framework is not stringent enough to limit campaign contributions or provide transparency in any meaningful way.[28] As a result, Mexican elections are among the most expensive in the world, and further reform is necessary to ensure that parties are competing on equal footing.

Conclusion

Although the PRI dominated the Mexican political arena for seven decades, in the late 1980s, the opposition began to organize and compete effectively for power. By the mid-1990s, Mexico had a multiparty system and a competitive electoral system. The 2006 elections provoked perhaps the greatest test of Mexico's new democratic electoral system to date, since the PRD's refusal to recognize the results constituted a major crisis. A significant percentage of the public—over a quarter of the population—continued to express significant disillusionment with the electoral process in the months following the election. Still, upon taking over the presidency, Calderón's support increased significantly, with over half of the population generally approving of his efforts as president and—for the first time ever—more voters identifying themselves as supporters of the PAN than of any other party. The coming years therefore present an important challenge for both the PRI and the PRD, which must work to build their bases of support if they hope to successfully challenge the PAN as the new governing party in contemporary Mexican politics.

Key Terms

2006 election	PAN
camarilla	PANAL
COFIPE	Paredes, Beatriz
Democratic Current	PASC
FDN	political machine
Gómez Morin, Manuel	PRD
González Luna, Efraín	PRI
IFE	*prinosaurios*
LFOPPE	PVEM
Madrazo, Roberto	SNTE
neopanistas	TRIFE
no reelection	TUCOM

Recommended Readings

Bruhn, Kathleen. *Taking on Goliath: The Emergence of a New Left Party and the Struggle for Democracy in Mexico*. University Park: Pennsylvania State University Press, 1997.

Dominguez, Jorge I., and Chappell Lawson. *Mexico's Pivotal Democratic Election: Candidates, Voters, and the Presidential Campaign of 2000*. Stanford and La Jolla: Stanford University Press/Center for U.S.-Mexican Studies, 2004.

Middlebrook, Kevin. *Party Politics and the Struggle for Democracy in Mexico: National and State-Level Analyses of the Partido Acción Nacional*. La Jolla: Center for U.S.-Mexican Studies, 2002.

Notes

1. On party systems in Latin America, see Scott Mainwaring and Timothy Scully, eds., *Building Democratic Institutions: Party Systems in Latin America* (Stanford: Stanford University Press, 1995). For more on Mexico's political parties, see Ann Craig

and Wayne Cornelius, "Houses Divided: Parties and Political Reform in Mexico," in Mainwaring and Scully, eds., *Building Democratic Institutions.*

2. In an open election that mobilized 3 million voters nationwide, including independent members of other parties, exit polls placed Madrazo and Beatriz Paredes within a few percentage points of each other. The closeness of the election was considered a "technical tie" that provoked a full recount of all ballots and a stream of acrimonious accusations in both directions, including charges of fraud and manipulation. Paredes alleged that in several states favoring Madrazo the vote was manipulated in his favor by inflating the results and suppressing turnout among her supporters through various forms of deception.

3. The process for determining the TUCOM candidate relied on the results of polls conducted by three major firms among respondents drawn from professed party members and a representative sample of the general electorate.

4. For more on the history and development of the PAN, see Soledad Loaeza, *El Partido Acción Nacional, la larga marcha, 1939–1994: Oposición leal y partido de protesta* (Mexico City: Fondo de Cultura Económica, 1999); David Shirk, *Mexico's New Politics: The PAN and Democratic Change* (Boulder: Lynne Rienner, 2005); Yemile Mizrahi, *From Martyrdom to Power: The Partido Acción Nacional in Mexico* (Notre Dame, Ind.: University of Notre Dame, 2003); Vikram Chand, *Mexico's Political Awakening* (Notre Dame, Ind.: University of Notre Dame, 2001).

5. Shirk, *Mexico's New Politics*, 59–60.

6. Cited in Mizrahi, *From Martyrdom to Power*, 23.

7. See Shirk, *Mexico's New Politics*, 23 (figure 2.1) and 107 (figure 4.1).

8. Shirk, *Mexico's New Politics*, 110 (table 4.1).

9. Joseph Klesner argues that in the 1990s, this cleavage overshadowed ideology and created incentives for catchall behavior. In other words, it induced parties to pursue broad nonideological platforms in order to attract voters. See "Electoral Competition and the New Party System in Mexico," *Latin American Politics and Society* 47, no. 2 (Summer 2005): 103–42.

10. On the formation of the PRD, see Kathleen Bruhn, *Taking on Goliath: The Emergence of a New Left Party and the Struggle for Democracy in Mexico* (University Park: Pennsylvania State University Press, 1997).

11. This was the official figure, though many suspected that popular support for the FDN was actually higher—an accomplishment that was deliberately destroyed by the PRI's electoral shenanigans.

12. These factors are identified and discussed by Kathleen Bruhn in "The Partido de la Revolución Democrática: Diverging Approaches to Competition," in *Governing Mexico: Political Parties and Elections*, ed. Monica Serrano (London: University of London, Institute of Latin American Studies,1998).

13. This is by no means an exhaustive discussion of the Mexican opposition. Rather, it focuses on the most contemporary examples of smaller opposition parties. For a brief yet thorough discussion of the many opposition parties in postrevolutionary Mexico, see Craig and Cornelius, "Houses Divided," 266–81.

14. The 1917 constitution granted males over twenty-one years of age and married men over eighteen the right to vote. In 1947 the franchise was extended to include

women in local elections, and in 1953 in national elections. Since 1969, all Mexicans over the age of eighteen have been permitted to vote. A 2005 electoral law established the procedures for absentee voting and legalized the vote of Mexican citizens living abroad.

15. However, a recent poll suggests that Mexicans might support reelection if they knew more about its advantages. See Shirk, *Mexico's New Politics*, 213, n. 89.

16. The problems associated with the no reelection rule are discussed cogently in Taylor, "Constitutional Crisis," and Jeffrey Weldon, "The Prohibition on Consecutive Reelection in the Mexican Congress," *Election Law Journal* 3, no. 3 (1994).

17. For more on the development of Mexico's electoral institutions, see Craig and Cornelius, "Houses Divided," and Jose Antonio Crespo, "Party Competition in Mexico: Evolution and Prospects," in *Dilemmas of Political Change in Mexico*, ed. Kevin J. Middlebrook (La Jolla: Center for U.S.-Mexican Studies, University of California–San Diego, 2004).

18. Ten years earlier, the PRI had also introduced a law that would penalize parties and politicians for boycotting the system by refusing to assume their elected posts and thus damage Mexico's competitive image. The law enacted in 1963 was a response to PAN efforts to do just this in the 1958 presidential election. It stated that candidates who refused to assume their elected posts would forfeit their political rights for three years and their parties would lose their registration. Crespo, "Party Competition," 68.

19. Among the types of fraud commonly employed by the PRI were stuffing ballot boxes, buying votes, coercing voters, physically delivering citizens to the polls and monitoring their votes, allowing voters to cast more than one ballot, and including names of the deceased on voting lists.

20. Crespo, "Party Competition," 73.

21. No party ever passed the 20 percent threshold while the law was in effect. The PAN came the closest in 1973 but still fell short by five percentage points. See Shirk, *Mexico's New Politics*, 22–23.

22. The creation of the IFE was not the only concession that the PRI granted to the opposition in exchange for its support of COFIPE. Equally important for the PAN was the fact that the government agreed to recognize *panista* victories in state and local elections. A similar concession was not made to the PRD, and not surprisingly, that party refused to support the passage of the COFIPE.

23. Salinas's motivation for the electoral reforms of the early 1990s was also driven by his desire to show the world that Mexico was becoming more democratic. The state of Mexico's democracy was of particular interest to the U.S. Congress, which was hotly debating whether to ratify NAFTA.

24. Crespo, "Party Competition," 71.

25. For a thorough discussion of the political role of Mexico's media, see Chappell Lawson, *Building the Fourth Estate: Democratization and the Rise of a Free Press in Mexico* (Berkeley: University of California Press, 2002).

26. Mony de Swann, Paola Martorelli, and Juan Molinar Horcasitas, "Public Financing of Political Parties and Electoral Expenditures in Mexico," in *Governing Mexico: Political Parties and Elections,* ed. Monica Serrano (London: University of London, Institute of Latin American Studies, 1998), 157.

27. Chand, *Mexico's Political Awakening*, 273; de Swann et al., "Public Financing," 159.

28. For an account of how these problems affected the 2006 election, see Todd Eisenstadt and Alejandro Poiré, "Campaign Finance and Playing Field 'Levelness' Issues in the Run-up to Mexico's July 2006 Presidential Election" (working paper presented at the Center for U.S.-Mexican Studies, University of California–San Diego, October 5, 2005), http://repositories.cdlib.org/usmex/eisenstadt_poire.

7

Mexican Political Culture

After hundreds of years of authoritarian or semiauthoritarian rule in Mexico, are Mexicans ready for democracy? Many scholars believe that certain political values, civic attitudes, and participatory behaviors are necessary to consolidate and sustain democratic governance. Yet some have suggested that Mexican society lacks these attributes, and instead exhibits a customary adherence to hierarchical leadership structures, patronage networks, and political subservience, dating as far back as the conquest. Such assertions dramatically oversimplify a very complex problem and must be viewed with caution. In the worst cases, claims that Mexicans are naturally inclined to authoritarianism result from stereotypes, ethnocentric biases, or other inappropriately subjective standards. Nevertheless, it is important to explore the dimensions of Mexico's political culture—widely shared political orientations—and evaluate its relevance in explaining contemporary political outcomes. For example, in a country where four in five people identify themselves as Catholics, it makes sense to ask how religious beliefs factor into Mexicans' political considerations. Likewise, since many scholars feel that certain political behaviors—such as high rates of voter turnout—can positively reinforce democratic governance, what can we make of current trends in Mexico? Or, to the extent that people have strong positive opinions or expectations regarding Mexican political institutions, what does this say about the quality of democracy? This chapter explores the multiple facets of Mexican political culture, first, by defining the concept and discussing its importance for stable democracy. The focus then turns to two important indicators of the country's democratic health, Mexicans' attitudes toward politics and their political behavior.

Studying Political Culture in Mexico

Political culture is an overarching concept used to describe a collective set of values and beliefs, norms and behaviors, and attitudes and feelings about politics. Individuals acquire these orientations toward the political system through a prolonged process of socialization—beginning in their families and communities—and through the day-to-day accumulation of information and experiences through education (which varies by level and type), religious affiliations, peer networks, occupation, political organizations, media, and similar influences. Naturally, historical context and events may factor heavily into people's political attitudes. We saw in previous chapters, for example, how key events like the Mexican revolution, the 1968 student massacre, and the 1985 earthquake became important events that shaped the political viewpoints of many millions of Mexicans. For many political scientists, the influences of political socialization and different historical experiences on a society's political culture must be carefully studied through comparative analysis to understand the differences among countries.

The first major comparative study of Mexican political culture was conducted by Gabriel Almond and Sidney Verba in *The Civic Culture*, published in 1963. Mexico was one of the five countries studied, also including the United States, the United Kingdom, Germany, and Italy. Through analysis of cross-national survey data, the authors were attempting to identify and categorize different types of political culture, and how they contributed to specific regime types.[1] In general, Almond and Verba's findings supported those of previous, smaller studies: that is, they found that Mexicans were largely parochial and narrowly self-interested in their political attitudes, and therefore tended to be apathetic or distrustful with regard to politicians and public institutions. In this regard, Mexico was found to be similar to Italy and different from the United States and the United Kingdom, whose citizens were more politically aware and engaged. The major conclusion of this study was that having a civic culture—where citizens were active and involved in politics—helped to promote democratic governance, while the lack thereof contributed to authoritarianism. Based on these findings, the authors claimed that stable democracy was much more viable in the United States, the United Kingdom, and to a lesser extent Germany, than in Italy or Mexico.

Almond and Verba's study was a landmark for understanding political culture because it was the first systematic, comparative study to employ large cross-national surveys. Indeed, subsequent empirical studies commonly have been modeled on this seminal piece. Like *The Civic Culture*, many of these studies have found that Mexicans held values and attitudes that at least demonstrated political apathy and alienation, if not actively contributed to support for authoritarian leaders, single-party hegemony, and centralized political control.[2] Hence, while the findings of later studies exhibited important variations in Mexican political attitudes, in general, they tended to support the notion that the Mexican personality was predisposed toward characteristics and behaviors, such as paternalism, subservience, and subornation. Consequently, many authors concluded that Mexicans are predisposed to accept authoritarianism and unlikely to challenge the status quo.

Yet the notion of political culture involves highly amorphous and intangible concepts and requires observers to generalize across many individual perspectives. Hence social scientific research in this area is fraught with analytical difficulties, and raises important methodological questions (see textbox 7.1). For example, given that people's thoughts about politics are often very complex—and may even have internal contradictions—can we truly measure and analyze their viewpoints with any degree of certainty? Given Mexico's regional diversity and social disparities, can we talk realistically about a single Mexican political culture? For many scholars such questions make it difficult, and even controversial, to conduct social scientific research about political culture. Indeed, critics frequently argue that studies of political culture are too imprecise, too methodologically flawed, and often too biased to be of much analytical value. Even when well designed, studies of political culture may be subject to overgeneralization or false causal connections. Hence, a focus on political cultural analyses may lead to stereotyping, or exaggerated claims about the salience of beliefs, attitudes, and norms in determining political outcomes.

Textbox 7.1. Studying Political Culture: Chicken or Egg?

One of the main problems associated with the study of political culture stems from the fact that it is very difficult to ascertain whether political culture is what drives political behavior and outcomes (e.g., propensity to vote, party affiliation, policy preferences, support for democracy, etc.); or whether political culture is instead shaped by social norms and values, socioeconomic characteristics and institutions (e.g., belief in equality, education levels, political parties). Assuming Mexicans do indeed hold authoritarian values, is this the cause or effect of centuries of nondemocratic governance? When people are subject to repression, they tend to act obsequiously or face the real possibility of persecution. It is also difficult to believe that political culture is a determining factor precisely because values and belief systems are very slow to change. Hence if culture has causal relevance, how can we explain relatively sudden changes in political outcomes, such as Mexico's democratization in the 1980s and 1990s? Many critics of political cultural analysis feel that beliefs, norms, and attitudes, while they should not be ignored, cannot be attributed sole—or even primary—causal significance for macrolevel political outcomes like the ultimate success or failure of democracy.

Many early studies of Mexican political culture had significant shortcomings that cast doubt on the validity of their findings and brought well-deserved criticisms. For example, in some cases, early survey questionnaires administered by foreign researchers contained translation errors that probably affected the way Mexicans responded to the questions posed to them.[3] Another problem is that the effort to generalize findings about political culture beyond a sample population can lead to erroneous conclusions about the population as a whole.[4] Even in much larger national and cross-national surveys, it is important to be careful about the generalizations made. For instance, in past studies, researchers frequently tended to underrepresent Mexico's rural population and focus instead on urban areas that were easier to reach.[5] Understandably, in order to fully assess a country's political culture, researchers must make an effort to carefully identify the key cleavages and differences that distinguish various sectors of the population.

Modern studies continue to struggle with the significant methodological challenges of systematically gauging political culture.[6] Still, careful study of Mexican political culture can provide useful insights. Such analysis can help us better understand how people think about politics, what their preferences are with regard to political outcomes, and how they behave and express themselves politically. For example, one consistent finding that has borne out fairly consistently across different studies is that education levels and gender are important determinants of political attitudes. Also, males and more highly educated Mexicans are more likely to be interested in and actively participate in political activities.[7] Other studies have substantiated early findings that most Mexicans distrust politicians and politics, and that low-income citizens are less likely to expect fair treatment by government officials and institutions (e.g., local bureaucracy, law enforcement).[8] However, it is important to take into consideration the limits of such research, and how these results should be interpreted. Below, we consider these issues as we evaluate three major aspects of political culture in Mexico: values and belief systems, norms and behaviors, and attitudes and feelings. In the process, we consider the major trends found in Mexico, and how they are relevant to the country's political development and contemporary democratic politics.

Mexican Values and Belief Systems

Many social scientists interested in political culture focus on how values and belief systems can shape political and economic outcomes.[9] Values and beliefs are perhaps best understood as the philosophical frameworks or the worldview that determine people's priorities, goals, and notions about how things should be. In politics, people often interpret—and act on—ideas, information, and events depending on how these conform to relatively well established belief systems and values. When values and beliefs are based on a system of ideas—such as a religion or ideology—they tend to generate rather consistent patterns in terms of people's interpretation of the world, and their behavior. Yet some people may also act entirely without regard to specified principles; such pragmatism might also be considered a belief system in itself.

What is important is that—to the extent that they are measurable—widely shared values and belief systems can have political significance since they help observers determine (and perhaps even predict) what people think is important, what they want, and how they may behave. But how and to what extent are values an important determining factor in Mexican politics? What values and beliefs are perceived to have an important role in Mexican political culture, and what demonstrable influences do they have in terms of actual trends and outcomes? Below, we consider the historical origins of Mexican values and belief systems, as derived from the country's Spanish colonial heritage. Subsequently, we consider the emergence of democratic values in contemporary Mexico.

The Legacies of Spanish Colonialism and the Mexican Revolution

Some observers believe that democracy has been slow to develop and is relatively weak in Latin America because of the cultural legacies of Spanish colonialism. According to this view, Spanish colonizers introduced political, social, and economic institutions (e.g., viceroyalty, the Catholic Church, and mercantilism) that reified hierarchy within the bureaucracy and society, and instilled authoritarian values and beliefs.[10] Together, these influences institutionalized social and political inequality and absolutism, and effectively taught Mexicans that they had no right to govern themselves. Yet, while there is no doubt that Spanish colonialism had deep and lasting influences in Mexico, it is more difficult to explain exactly how it continues to affect Mexican politics today, more than five hundred years later.

How, for example, could Mexico transition from autocratic rule to democracy in just a few decades if the legacy of colonialism were so strong? It is likely that Mexican attitudes in the twentieth century were more directly affected by education (or lack thereof), and by the ability of the PRI and government to politically socialize citizens with the use of mass media and by manipulating symbols of the revolution.[11] The PRI sought to embody the revolution in name and in fact; in the process, the ruling party also shaped public attitudes about the system. In its rhetoric, faithfully transmitted through the public education system and mass media outlets, the government consistently emphasized that the PRI embodied the spirit of the revolution and that national unity and strong presidential leadership helped lead Mexico forward with industrialization and high rates of economic growth, as well as broad social programs, including free public education and land reform.[12]

This strategy worked well for much of the twentieth century. For reasons already discussed, however, the regime's legitimacy began to falter in the late 1960s and subsequent decades. It is no coincidence, then, that Mexican political attitudes began to change during the same time period: levels of political interest and participation, as well as commitment to democratic values increased.[13] By the late 1980s, for example, the number of Mexicans with an interest in politics was on par with that of countries like Germany and the United Kingdom, and there was a much greater willingness among all Mexicans to discuss politics. Furthermore, Mexicans of all ages and socioeconomic circumstances expressed pride in their country and were more likely than in the past to favor rule of law over strong leadership.[14] Most important, as education levels grew, and as the PRI's ability to monopolize sources of information diminished, Mexicans illustrated increasingly democratic impulses by voting for candidates of the opposition.

Emerging Democratic Values in Contemporary Mexico

The steadily growing strength of democratic values is evident in a study conducted in 2004, which found that 40 percent of Mexicans expressed support for government institutions and democratic principles (e.g., protection of civil rights like free speech), while another 40 percent supported either government institutions or democratic principles. The remaining 20 percent opposed the government and did not agree that civil rights should be guaranteed to all citizens.[15] While these numbers may not seem impressive initially, it is important to note three things. First, they are in fact high when compared to other countries in the region: Mexico ranked third in support for stable democracy among Latin American countries. Second, democratic ideals and practices are not formed overnight. The 40 percent of Mexicans whose attitudes reflect only partial support for democracy may well be in the process of adopting more favorable attitudes toward the whole of democracy. Third, that Mexicans support democracy as much as they do is remarkable given that the same study found that 67 percent of all respondents felt that corruption among politicians was widespread in Mexico.

These findings reinforced earlier research conducted in 2002 by the U.N. Development Program, which also found that Mexicans have developed stronger support for democracy.[16] In this study, Mexicans were asked a series of questions to ascertain their orientations toward democracy. Fifty-four percent of Mexicans were found to prefer democracy over economic well-being, compared to 30 percent who did not and 15 percent who expressed ambivalence. Again, while these numbers do not appear, at first glance, to reveal a strong commitment to democracy, according to the U.N. survey, there is as much or more support for democracy in Mexico as in Costa Rica and Chile, often cited as two of the region's strongest democracies.

These indicators are encouraging, since they suggest that Mexico is no longer hindered by antidemocratic values and beliefs. In fact, given how quickly support for democracy has grown—within the course of a single generation—it is quite possible that Mexicans' core values and beliefs were not a causal factor, but rather a symptom of authoritarian rule. At the very least, these aspects of Mexican political culture have proved sufficiently malleable to change along with Mexico's larger process of democratization. Yet even so, assuming that values and beliefs are causally relevant—significant in facilitating or undermining democracy—what might help to sustain and strengthen current trends in Mexican support for democratic governance? One hypothesis is that the region-wide shift to democratic rule in Latin America might positively reinforce domestic support for democracy in Mexico. This assumes, however, that the current wave of democratic rule will endure for the foreseeable future, and that Mexican values and beliefs about democracy are somehow shaped by these international trends. Both assumptions are, of course, subject to debate. Perhaps a more convincing hypothesis is that the performance of democratic governance—and Mexicans' own sense of political efficacy—will be the primary determinant of continued Mexican support for democracy over the longer term, whether for better or worse. In this sense, Mexicans' basic support for democracy may be strongly linked to the emerging political norms and attitudes about politics to which we turn in the next two sections.

Political Norms and Behaviors in Mexico: From Clients to Constituents

Is it customary in your community, as it was during the heyday of New York City's Tammany Hall, to vote "early and often"? Or, more likely, do nearly half of the people in your community prefer to spend their time doing other things, rather than turn out to vote at all? Do you participate actively in sport teams, civic organizations, and neighborhood groups that help weave a tight social fabric in your community? Or do you spend most of your time isolated from your neighbors, whose names you barely know? Many scholars think that your answers to such questions may reveal a great deal about the political dynamics of your community, since they provide information about norms and behaviors that may encourage or detract from democratic political life. Norms and behaviors constitute regular but informal standards or patterns of political conduct. Like formal political institutions, norms may constitute widely acknowledged standards or rules of conduct. Yet norms are informal in the sense that they are not codified, and in some cases may not be openly discussed or even consciously recognized. Norms may reflect deeply held values and beliefs such as those noted above, as well as opinions and attitudes about what constitutes acceptable social conduct.

For much of the twentieth century, Mexican political culture was strongly influenced by norms and behaviors that reinforced autocratic rule of the PRI. As we have noted in earlier chapters, the corporatist arrangement that coordinated and controlled disparate societal interests under auspices of the revolutionary party deeply influenced political behavior. By designating official labor, peasant, and middle-class interest groups, and hand-selecting their leaders, the PRI was able to become highly inclusive, and at the same time maintain a paternalistic orientation toward society. This institutional arrangement was successful at uniting the revolutionary family, and provided access and representation to groups that otherwise might have remained outside the system. However, the corporatist system worked against the development of independent interest groups and the principle of political equality because it wholly excluded those groups and individuals that were not officially sanctioned by the government. Thus corporatism was instrumental in shaping Mexican political attitudes because citizens quickly learned that there were few benefits to challenging the PRI or the system, and that the only way to obtain access to government resources was to play by the PRI's rules.

In general, the system also produced two kinds of political strategies for Mexicans: one that required accepting the status quo and becoming part of the system by supporting the PRI in exchange for resources and political access, and another that required forgoing those benefits in order to challenge the PRI and its methods. Interestingly, it was not uncommon for Mexicans to have similar political attitudes regardless of which strategy they pursued. That is, by the 1980s, both supporters and critics of the system tended to distrust politicians and the system as a whole. Many supporters felt that the system and the PRI had let them down by not delivering promised goods, while detractors viewed the status quo as undemocratic, ineffective, and corrupt.

Recurring economic crises and mismanagement undermined the PRI's corporatist and clientelistic system by severely reducing its ability to dole out public resources. As a result, people began looking for new methods of accessing the system. Although today only minor vestiges remain of the former corporatist system, patron-client relationships are still ubiquitous. Many Mexicans have been socialized to believe that personal relationships with people in positions of power are the most effective means of accessing the political system. So, although outright voter fraud and blatant intimidation are now quite rare, it is still common for both politicians and citizens to eschew political institutions and government bureaucracy in favor of private clientelistic relationships.

Civic Behavior in Contemporary Mexico

What has fundamentally changed in Mexico is the degree of influence that clients now have vis-à-vis their patrons. The advent of political competition through free and fair elections has dramatically increased the relative power of voters as "clients," and exposed their "patrons" to greater political vulnerability. Whereas the PRI's political clients once gladly traded votes and signs of support for minor offerings from the ruling party's political candidates, today's candidates must clamor to attract the support of more discerning voters who have many choices—and perhaps better offers—before them.

Indeed, for most of the twentieth century Mexican voters did not have a real choice when they went to the polls because the PRI was assured victory in nearly every election, and voting was rarely a free enterprise. Under these circumstances, voters often went to the polls out of fear that failure to vote for the PRI would restrict their access to important resources (e.g., union jobs, agricultural credit, basic services); or conversely, voters supported the PRI because they received something tangible in return (e.g., food, clothing, attention to a local problem). For these and other reasons, PRI supporters tended to be very loyal to their party, faithfully supporting all of its candidates, election after election.[17] To the extent that Mexicans supported the opposition, it was almost always an effort to express dissatisfaction with the ruling party by casting a protest vote. However, as the PRI's legitimacy faltered during the 1980s, partisan loyalty declined and voters began to support candidates who could defeat the PRI and to focus on policy issues such as free trade and foreign investment. This was particularly true of the 2006 election, which was centered on two starkly different candidates and their opposing policy platforms.

Although the absence of reliable electoral data makes it difficult to generalize about Mexican voting behavior before 1988, it is clear that in the short span of a single generation, Mexican voters embraced democratic participation and learned to be highly informed and sophisticated voters.[18] For example, in the 1988 election, which marked the first opportunity for voters to make a meaningful choice at the polls, it was mainly the PRI faithful who cast their votes for Salinas.[19] In general these people tended to be less educated females who lived in rural areas. Those who chose to oppose the PRI then had to make a choice between the PAN and Cuauhtémoc Cárdenas. Supporters of the former were more likely to be from urban areas in the north, to support neoliberal economic policies, and to attend church regularly, while Cárdenas supporters were both rural dwellers and members of the urban working class, and particularly inhabitants of Mexico City. The common denominator in this eclectic group appears to have been opposition to free trade and foreign investment.

In the 1994 presidential election, party loyalty was again very important: 65 percent of those who voted for the PRI said they always voted for the same party, and 75 percent of those who voted for Salinas also voted for Zedillo. Loyalty was also important for the opposition: over two-thirds of all voters supported the same parties in 1988 and 1994.[20] Yet while the PRI appeared to be relatively secure among its base before 1994, the growing popularity of the opposition and the devastating effects of the 1995 peso crisis drastically eroded the size of its loyal base. The 1997 midterm elections were an important bellwether in this regard: when the PRI won only 39 percent of the seats in the Chamber of Deputies, a severe decline from its vote share of 60 percent in 1994.

The PRI was not the only party to see a decline in voter loyalty. After 1997 voters became increasingly undecided, and by 2000, fewer than half of all Mexican voters identified with any party. More recent survey data show this number has continued to decline: in 2004 only 28.3 percent claimed that they belonged to a specific party and always voted for that party.[21] Furthermore, they could no longer make assumptions about who their supporters were, because traditional socioeconomic and demographic characteristics such as levels of education, gender, occupation, income level, or even region, were no longer reliable predictors of partisan support.[22] Thus it appears that by the late 1990s a significant portion of the Mexican electorate was willing to support different parties from one election to the next, and this makes election outcomes much more uncertain than in the past. Uncertainty is a positive development for Mexico. Combined with an impartial and transparent electoral process, it creates incentives for citizens to pay more attention to politics, and for politicians to pay more attention to citizens, and to go to the polls on election day. Indeed, Mexico has seen relatively high rates of voter turnout since the onset of democratization in the late 1980s. Unlike the past when the perception of electoral fraud damaged the credibility of the system and increased abstentions, most Mexicans now eagerly participate in the electoral process (see figure 7.1).

Moreover, this new dynamic has heightened the importance of campaigns and personality-based politics. Indeed with smaller loyal party bases both the personal characteristics and media campaigns were important influences on Mexican voting behavior in the 2000 and 2006 elections. For example, in 2000, the PRI's base was smaller and the number of undecided voters was higher than it had been in the past. Among these undecided voters, traditional indicators like levels of education, income, and gender were unreliable predictors of voting behavior. Moreover, the availability of unbiased news coverage and

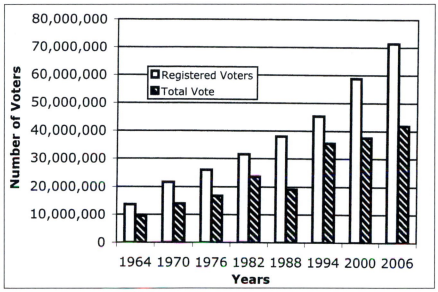

FIGURE 7.1   Registered Voters and Voter Turnout in Mexican Presidential Elections, 1964–2006

Source: International Democracy and Electoral Assistance, http://www.idea.int/vt/country_view. cfm?CountryCode=MX

the nationally televised debates worked in Fox's favor because they allowed him to project a positive image of a straight-talking, no-nonsense professional with the gumption to promote real change. Meanwhile, his negative advertisements highlighted Labastida's political and personal shortcomings and thereby helped convince undecided voters to support the PAN. Also of critical importance was the fact that Fox's campaign increased voter turnout among PAN sympathizers, while many traditional supporters of the PRI chose to stay home on election day.[23] Like the 2000 election, candidates and media campaigns were at the forefront of the 2006 presidential campaign. However, unlike previous elections, policy issues were more important in the 2006 presidential election. The two frontrunners, Calderón and López Obrador, presented opposing economic platforms and voters cast their ballots based on which plan they felt was best for Mexico's future.

Clearly, as one scholar observes, Mexicans are making the transition from clientelism to citizenship.[24] The earlier mentioned U.N. Development Program survey provides important evidence that Mexicans are much more politically engaged than they were in the past. For example, 81 percent of the sample reported voting in the 2000 election, 59 percent reported contributing to or active engagement in civic or religious organizations, 40 percent participated in at least one collective demonstration, and 22 percent had contacted a government representative. Just under 30 percent reported doing all of the above.[25] Mexicans' attitudes toward the voting process have also improved. Of the small number of respondents who did not vote (19 percent), nearly 9 percent of them tried to but were unable to cast votes because they lacked the proper documents, had expired documents, or did not appear on the rolls. Seventy-three percent were either in agreement or very much in agreement that elections offer real options to choose among parties, and two-thirds agreed or very much agreed that voting allows citizens to influence political events. Less than 3 percent of respondents claimed that voting offers no option, is a farce, or makes no difference.[26] This is a significant change from the past when the vast majority of Mexicans felt that elections were a sham.

Mexican Attitudes and Public Opinion

Political attitudes and public opinion reflect individuals' current views and feelings—their psychological or emotional orientations—in relation to political phenomena, actors, and events. People's political attitudes may also include specific policy preferences regarding such things as capital punishment, abortion, or universal health care. Or they may have to do with the person's gut feeling about a politician or idea. Unlike the deeply held values and beliefs that evolve over longer periods of time to shape an individual's political perspective, attitudes and opinions can often change quite rapidly in response to experiences, circumstances, and the revelation of new information. For example, a voter's opinion about a given candidate depends not just on their agreement or disagreement with her philosophical positions—often derived from well-entrenched values and beliefs—but also on feelings toward that candidate based on daily observations: how the candidate responds to a verbal attack, whether the candidate makes a witty and timely remark, and to what degree a candidate makes a fool of herself on television.

Like all people, Mexicans have strong opinions about policies, politicians, and the political process in general. With democratization, citizens have become more forthcoming about their political attitudes, and public opinion polls and surveys are now prevalent. Virtually every day, it seems, a newspaper or polling firm has released the results of its latest survey: about the names Mexicans most prefer for their children, about their feelings regarding relationships, or who is their favorite musician or *cantante*. So too it is with regard to questions about Mexican politics. Growing interest and technical capability among academics, newspaper companies, private polling firms, and even po-

Table 7.1.
Mexicans' Trust in Their Political Institutions, July 2006

	High/Some Confidence (%)	Little/No Confidence (%)
Catholic Church	82	17
Army	74	24
Priests	74	25
Television news	66	33
National Human Rights Commission	61	36
Presidency	57	39
Newspapers	56	41
Federal Institute for Elections	52	44
Legislature	35	55
Judges and magistrates	38	56
Political parties	33	63

Source: Adapted from Parametría, "Confianza en Instituciones," Carta Paramétrica, July 2006, www.para-metria.com.mx.

litical parties have produced some interesting findings about Mexican views and feelings about politics and political issues. [27]

So how do Mexicans feel about politics and their political leaders? What do Mexicans care about in terms of public policy, and what do they expect from democratic governance? How do their attitudes and opinions change over time and what impressions do they have of the performance of democratic governance? These are questions of critical importance in any democratic political system, or at least for policy makers who wish to gauge and respond effectively to public concerns. In recent years, a plethora of data and information has become available to evaluate contemporary Mexican attitudes about politics. We may try to glean something about Mexico's political culture, for instance, by looking at attitudes toward the government. As mentioned earlier, surveys and polls suggest that while many Mexicans express support for democracy, they remain fairly skeptical with regard to contemporary government institutions and political leaders. Indeed, when asked in July 2006—in the immediate aftermath of the recent presidential elections—how much confidence they had in the president, national Congress, the judicial system, and other key institutions, in several cases, barely half of the respondents expressed confidence in these institutions (see table 7.1).[28]

Still, it is worth remembering that Mexicans' confidence in democracy is not significantly lower than in other countries in Latin America. In the U.N. Development Program's survey of democracy in the region, no respondents in any Latin American country expressed that they had substantially more than "a little" confidence in government and politicians.[29] Hence, it is difficult to say that Mexican skepticism about contemporary political leaders and

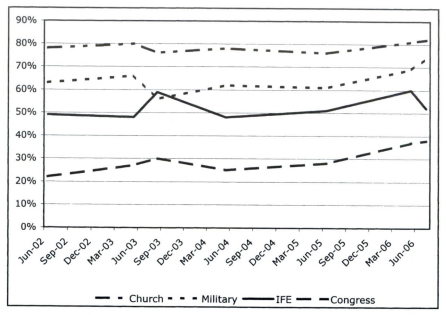

FIGURE 7.2   Public Confidence in Key Institutions, 2000–2006
Source: Parametría

institutions is tantamount to a lack of support for democracy, or at least it suggests less support than in other emerging democracies. Moreover, it is also important to note that public opinion can be fickle, and that polls generally provide only a snapshot of respondents' sentiments at a given point in time. Indeed, if we look at approval and disapproval ratings of four key institutions from table 7.1, we see in figure 7.2 that results for the same pollster (Parametría Polling) varied somewhat for the IFE over the course of the Fox administration. Meanwhile, public confidence remained constantly high for the Church, and grew measurably for both the Congress and the military over the same period.

Similar variation can be found in the president's approval ratings (see figure 7.3). As in many countries, Mexicans' feelings about many different aspects of politics are often projected—rightly or wrongly—on the head of government. Hence presidential approval ratings may also provide an indicator of public opinion about the political, social, and economic direction of the country. However, notwithstanding the many challenges Mexico faced in early 2007—lingering divisions from a controversial election and smoldering political unrest in Oaxaca—public approval of the Calderón administration improved over the two years of the new president's term, thanks in large part to widespread support for his involvement of the military in Mexico's drug

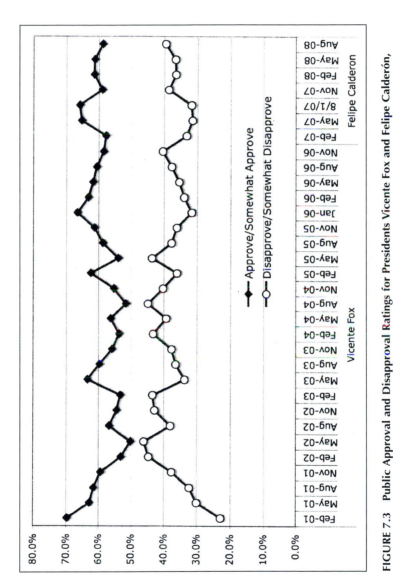

FIGURE 7.3   Public Approval and Disapproval Ratings for Presidents Vicente Fox and Felipe Calderón, 2000–2008

Sources: Data for February 2001 through August 2006 from "Evaluación de Gobierno: Presidente Vicente Fox," August 2006. Data through December 2006 from Mitofsky-Roy Campos Tracking Poll, "Evaluación de gobierno," March and June 2007. Data through November 2007 from Mitofsky-Roy Campos Tracking Poll, "Evaluación Ciudadana: Felipe Calderón al Cumplir Un Año de Gobierno," November 2007.

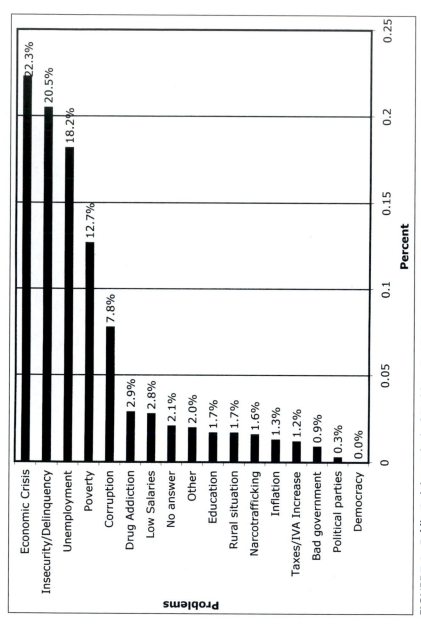

FIGURE 7.4   Public Opinion: Principal Problems in Mexico, Average 2000–2006
Source: Consulta Mitofsky, "Evaluación Final de Gobierno," November 2006.

war and higher levels of spending on public advertising than seen under the previous administration. Whether Calderón will continue to maintain such favorable ratings remains to be seen. If Fox's experience is any indication, Calderón may well experience the same fluctuation in public support as his predecessor. Generally, the more people who perceive that government represents their best interests, the more likely people are to have a favorable view of politics. To the extent that Calderón and other elected officials are prudently responsive to such shifts in public opinion, this may be a good thing for Mexican democracy.

Mexico's elected leaders need to take into careful consideration the issues that Mexicans feel are most important, and the policy preferences that they express. In this regard, Mexicans tend to express some clear and consistent priorities and concerns in surveys and public opinion polls. In recent years, depending on how they are defined, the top two broad concerns regularly expressed by Mexicans relate to economic conditions and the justice system. Specifically, over the course of the Fox administration, the two issues that Mexicans most regularly identified among their top policy concerns were "economic crisis" (22.3 percent) and "public insecurity" (20.5 percent) (see figure 7.4). If we combine the economic crisis with other related issues—unemployment, poverty, low salaries, inflation, and taxes—we see that an average of 58.5 percent of respondents identified economic concerns as Mexico's top problem over the course of the Fox administration. In contrast, on average, more recent concerns about public insecurity and related rule of law concerns—corruption, drug addiction, and drug trafficking—represented the top concern for about 32.8 percent of the population over the same period.

These results are hardly surprising, since economic difficulties have been a major challenge in Mexico over the last few decades, while the country's rule of law concerns are relatively recent. Still, given that Mexico enjoyed modest economic development over the course of the Fox administration, it is notable that many Mexicans continued to feel concerns about the effects or prospects of economic crisis, more so than any other pressing policy problem, even poverty. This makes it more understandable why Mexico's economic situation was a major concern when voters went to the polls in 2006, and perhaps explains why appeals based solely on poverty alleviation were not sufficient to sway voters. Mexicans appear especially concerned about ensuring longer-term economic stability and job creation, two issues heavily emphasized by Felipe Calderón when he ran as a candidate for Mexico's presidency.

At the same time, because they reflect the average sentiments of the public over a six-year period, these figures mask somewhat a slight decline from 2001 to 2004. Concerns about crime and violence increased noticeably in the last years of the Fox administration, due largely to the outbreak of significant levels of drug-related violence beginning in 2005. In both 2005 and 2006, over 25 percent of Mexicans polled identified crime and public insecurity as their top concern, more than any other single policy problem. It is hardly surprising that—despite campaign appeals based on improving Mexico's economic situation—the Calderón administration embraced a law and order policy agenda from the outset and gained high marks as a result. Still, for longer-term success, it will likely be important for Calderón to address the economic concerns of Mexicans as well.

Conclusion

Not surprisingly, Mexicans distrusted a system that, at least until recently, was overwhelmingly associated with fraud, corruption, and impunity. After decades of living in the PRI-dominated system in which election rigging, raiding public coffers, and manipulating voters was common and even expected, how could Mexicans trust or embrace their political system? Yet as we have seen, attitudes and consequently political behavior have changed significantly since the late 1980s. Generally speaking, Mexicans are now more willing to talk about and participate in the political process. They are also more inclined to believe in the value and superiority of democracy. The electorate is more sophisticated in its ability to use elections to reward and punish politicians and parties, and thereby hold them accountable for their actions.

Undoubtedly, these changes are the result of the confluence of a number of different factors. The role of education is likely to be key. On the whole, Mexicans are better educated than they ever were in the past. Basic education and higher literacy rates have increased people's understanding of the political system and their rights and responsibilities in a democracy. Another important factor is access to information. While print media are still relatively expensive and have small circulations, access to political information is widely available on television—which is by far the preferred medium in Mexico.[30] Moreover, although in the past all press coverage was notoriously biased in favor of the PRI and government, many mass media outlets are now much more independent. Therefore, citizens have access to alternative viewpoints and sources of information. Finally, the increased transparency and competitiveness of the political system have fostered greater confidence that citizen participation has a real impact. Political reform and the creation of an impartial Federal Electoral Institute have gone a long way to convincing voters that they have meaningful choices and that votes will be counted accurately.

Many Mexicans remain distrustful of public institutions, democracy, and politicians, and adhere to clientelistic practices. But as we have shown in this chapter, Mexicans have also become significantly more democratic in their orientation. There is little reason to believe that authoritarian attitudes and behavior will return to past levels, nor is it necessary for them to disappear entirely in order for Mexico to continue on its road to democracy. The majority of Mexicans continue to demand transparency and accountability; equally important, they continue to assume the responsibilities of democratic citizenship. Provided the institutional means to make such demands—free and fair elections, open access to information—it is quite likely that they will continue to do so.

Key Terms

attitudes and opinions
citizenship
Civic Culture
legacies of Spanish colonialism
Mexican political values
norms and behaviors
party loyalty
policy concerns

political culture
presidential approval ratings
public opinion
socialization
values and beliefs
voter turnout
voting behavior

Recommended Texts

Almond, Gabriel A., and Sidney Verba, eds. *The Civic Culture Revisited.* Newbury Park: Sage, 1989.

Camp, Roderic Ai. *Politics in Mexico: The Democratic Consolidation.* 5th ed. Oxford: Oxford University Press, 2007.

Domínguez, Jorge, and James McCann. *Democratizing Mexico: Public Opinion and Electoral Choices.* Baltimore: Johns Hopkins University Press, 1996.

Notes

1. Gabriel Almond and Sidney Verba, *The Civic Culture* (Princeton, N.J.: Princeton University Press, 1963).

2. In one study of Mexican children, for example, Rafael Segovia found that presidents were more admired for their ability to maintain order than for their ability to fulfill the will of the people. *La politización del niño mexicano* (Mexico City: El Colegio de México, 1975), 58.

3. A related problem even in country surveys using a single language often forces respondents to have an opinion about issues that they have not seriously considered but are deemed relevant by pollsters. Hence, even when questions are carefully crafted, survey responses can sometimes reflect gut reactions or glib thoughts, rather than deeply held beliefs and attitudes.

4. Most of the earliest studies of Mexican political culture used a psychological approach to study a relatively small, regionally specific group. While such studies can provide rich insights, researchers must be careful not to exaggerate the larger relevance of such studies. See, for example, Erich Fromm and Michael Maccoby, *Social Character in a Mexican Village* (Englewood Cliffs, N.J.: Prentice-Hall, 1970); Richard Fagen and William Tuohy, *Politics and Privilege in a Mexican City* (Stanford: Stanford University Press, 1972); Rafael Segovia, *La politización del niño mexicano*. Ann Craig and Wayne Cornelius provide an insightful review of these and other studies in "Political Culture in Mexico: Continuities and Revisionist Interpretations," in Gabriel Almond and Sidney Verba, eds., *The Civic Culture Revisited* (Boston: Little, Brown, 1980), 325–83.

5. In the 1963 Almond and Verba study, the rural sector represented two-thirds of the entire population but was ignored. Today, rural dwellers represent only a quarter of the population but remain less likely than their urban counterparts to have access to basic public services, have regular contact with government institutions, and have opportunities to participate in politically active organizations.

6. For example, another problem with evaluating political culture is that researchers assume they can properly interpret people's internal motivations based on how they respond to survey questions and other forms of external observation. This assumes that survey respondents fully understand the questions they are being asked, and whether they accurately (and sincerely) communicate their responses.

7. See Alberto Hernández Medina and Luis Narro Rodríguez, *Como somos los mexicanos* (Mexico City: Centro de Estudios Educativos, 1987).

8. Craig and Cornelius, "Political Culture," 371–78.

9. For example, Protestantism is said to have played a direct role in the development of capitalism. See Max Weber in *The Protestant Ethic and the Spirit of Capitalism* (New York: Scribner's, 1958).

10. For example, Wiarda (1973) asserts that Latin American political culture—including a tendency toward authoritarianism and corporatism—is attributable to the legacy of an "a peculiarly Iberic-European tradition dating from approximately 1500, with a political culture and socio-political order that at its core was essentially two-class, authoritarian, traditional, elitist, patrimonial, Catholic, stratified, hierarchical, and corporate." Howard J. Wiarda, "Toward a Framework for the Study of Political Change in the Iberic-Latin Tradition: The Corporative Model," *World Politics* 25, no. 2 (1973): 209.

11. Wayne Cornelius and Jeffrey Weldon, "Politics in Mexico," in *Comparative Politics Today: A World View,* ed. Gabriel Almond, G. Bingham Powell, Kaare Strom, and Russell Dalton (New York: Pearson Longman, 2004).

12. Ilene V. O'Malley, *The Myth of the Revolution: Hero Cults and the Institutionalization of the Mexican State, 1920–1940* (New York: Greenwood, 1986).

13. Jorge Domínguez and James McCann, *Democratizing Mexico: Public Opinion and Electoral Choices* (Baltimore: Johns Hopkins University Press, 1996), chap. 2.

14. It is important to point out, however, that when asked whether "a few strong leaders would do more for Mexico than all the laws and talk," 54 percent of all respondents agreed. This suggests that during the mid-1990s, roughly half of the population still believed that strong leadership is more effective than laws and institutions. See Domínguez and McCann, *Democratizing Mexico*, 41, table 2.7.

15. Jorge Buendía and Alejandro Moreno, *La cultura política de la democracia en México, 2004: México en tiempos de competencia electoral*. This study surveyed 1,556 Mexicans over the age of eighteen in 130 randomly selected areas. It has a margin of error of +/-2.5 percent.

16. *Democracy in Latin America: Towards a Citizens' Democracy* (New York: United Nations Development Program, 2004). This survey was conducted in 2002 and interviewed 1,210 adults in predominantly urban areas. Therefore the opinion of rural populations is necessarily underrepresented.

17. Small parties like the PAN also had very loyal bases, despite their minor role in the political system.

18. There is a plethora of work on Mexican voting behavior, for example, Domínguez and McCann, *Democratizing Mexico;* Jorge Domínguez and Alejandro Poiré, eds., *Toward Mexico's Democratization: Campaigns, Elections, and Public Opinion* (New York: Routledge, 1999); Jorge Domínguez and Chappell Lawson, eds., *Mexico's Pivotal Democratic Election* (Stanford: Stanford University Press/La Jolla: University of California–San Diego, Center for U.S.-Mexican Studies, 2004); Jorge Buendía, "The Changing Mexican Voter, 1991–2000," in Kevin Middlebrook, ed., *Dilemmas of Political Change in Mexico*, 108–29; Alejandro Moreno, *El votante mexicano* (Mexico City: Fondo de Cultura Economica, 2003).

19. Domínguez and McCann demonstrate that in 1988, voters made their decisions in a two-step process. First, they made a strategic choice about whether to support the PRI. This decision was based on the voters' assessment of the PRI's strength and whether altering the status quo would be disruptive or beneficial. Voters who opted for the opposition then chose a candidate based either on their perception of which candidate had the best chance of defeating the PRI, or, in some cases, on their assessment of which candidate best represented his norms and beliefs. Domínguez and McCann, *Democratizing Mexico*, chaps. 3–4.

20. Domínguez and McCann, *Democratizing Mexico*, table E-3, p. 206.

21. U.N. Development Program, *Democracy in Latin America*, 236.

22. Alejandro Poiré, "Retrospective Voting, Partisanship, and Loyalty in Presidential Elections: 1994," in Domínguez and Poiré, eds., *Toward Mexico's Democratization*, 24–56; and Beatriz Magaloni, "Is the PRI Fading? Economic Performance, Electoral Accountability and Voting Behavior in the 1994 and 1997 Elections," in *Toward Mexico's Democratization*, 203–36.

23. On media coverage of the 2000 election, see Chappell Lawson, "Television Coverage, Vote Choice, and the 2000 Campaign"; in Domínguez and Lawson, eds., *Mexico's Pivotal Democratic Election*, 187–210; Alejandro Moreno, "The Effects of Negative Campaigns on Mexican Voters," in *Mexico's Pivotal Democratic Election*,

243–68. On voter turnout, see Chappell Lawson and Joseph Klesner, "Political Reform, Electoral Participation, and the Campaign of 2000," in *Mexico's Pivotal Democratic Election,* 67–87.

24. Jonathan Fox, "The Difficult Transition from Clientelism to Citizenship: Lessons from Mexico," *World Politics* 46, no. 2 (1994): 151–84.

25. U.N. Development Program, *Democracy in Latin America,* 224–25.

26. U.N. Development Program, *Democracy in Latin America,* 233–35.

27. Just as there are methodological problems with studying political culture, there are a number of difficulties associated with studying public opinion. For example, the choice to include a particular question and omit another, the wording of a question, the method used to collect the data, the qualifications and attributes of the surveyors, the size and attributes of the sample population, and so on, all play important roles in determining the quality of the information gathered by any given survey or poll.

28. "The question asked was, In a scale like the one is used in the school where 0 is nothing and 10 is a lot, please tell me how much do you trust in . . . ?" Consulta Mitofsky, "Confianza en Instituciones," *National Home Survey,* July 2005, 3.

29. U.N. Development Program, *Democracy in Latin America,* 247.

30. According to UNESCO media statistics, there was approximately one television set to every four Mexicans in 2003.

8

Interest Representation

Workers, Women, and Indigenous People

Previous chapters have shown that one of the keys to Mexico's political stability and the PRI's longevity was its ability to incorporate a broad array of interests into the party. Indeed, unlike most parties in Latin America, the PRI's malleable ideology, corporatist institutions, and control of vast state resources allowed it to convince, coopt, or coerce groups and individuals (who under other circumstances might have been detractors), to support or at least tolerate the regime. However, democratization has significantly altered the relationship between the state and society: whereas the complex corporatist arrangement created a top-down structure in which interests were aggregated and groups were represented through direct links to the ruling party (and hence the government), interest groups must increasingly compete on the basis of their organizational capacity and political capital. This move toward greater pluralism may strengthen democracy by promoting political equality and equal access.

Although state-society relations have changed dramatically in the past two decades, there remain some vestiges of the past that continue to exert influence on the political arena. This chapter looks at the experience of three important interest group—labor, women, and indigenous people—within this context. It examines the historical trajectory of each group's political role and evaluates its current status in Mexico's nascent democracy. The discussion demonstrates that these groups have achieved varied levels of formal representation, access to resources, and political clout. As a result, they have varying approaches to and levels of influence and representation in the mainstream political system. We conclude with some thoughts on the necessity for government and society to promote greater equality and inclusion if Mexico is to improve and deepen its democracy.

Organized Labor

As in other Latin American countries during the early twentieth century, the labor movement in Mexico grew increasingly active and organized, partly in response to changing industrial conditions and partly because international syndicalist and communist ideologies inspired a higher level of worker consciousness and activism. Pressure from industrial and agricultural workers during the revolution had led the drafters of the 1917 constitution to enshrine highly progressive protections for labor such as standard daily work hours, minimum wages, and the right to strike.[1] In the aftermath of the revolution, Mexico's leaders aligned themselves with labor groups as they sought to consolidate their political power. Over time, presidents Obregón, Calles, and Cárdenas managed to coopt labor into supporting the government's political positions and economic policies. The result was that the Mexican state exercised a high degree of control over Mexico's labor unions. This control was institutionalized in the Federal Labor Law of 1931, which sought to protect the rights of workers and laid the legal groundwork for the state to actively play a role in worker-employer relations.

Eventually it would become clear that the state's efforts to articulate the interests of labor tended to prioritize the interests of the government over those of workers. The 1930s and 1940s saw the creation of several new state institutions designed to enforce existing labor laws and mediate conflicts between workers and employers.[2] For example, the Ministry of Labor and Social Welfare (Secretaría del Trabajo y Previsión Social, STPS) used its oversight capacity to advance workers' rights, but as part of the president's cabinet it also facilitated the institutionalization of the government's tutelary role vis-à-vis labor.[3] Although labor technically had the autonomy to organize and articulate its own demands, the Mexican government, with the use of its labor laws and the STPS, established the legal terms for forming unions, enacting strikes, and negotiating with employers. Workers could form unions at any time, but they were not eligible to strike or negotiate unless they met basic organizational requirements and were officially recognized by the government. Even officially recognized unions had to follow government-regulated procedures for contract negotiations and strikes. Thus the government's ability to grant a union official recognition—and to establish the rules of the game—formed the basis of the corporatist arrangement with organized labor, and allowed the state to assert considerable political control over workers.

Why would workers and labor unions acquiesce to such government control? Some might argue that they had little choice since the government repressed "independent" unions and any who rejected the government's corporatist arrangement. This claim accurately captures reality, but over the longer term two conditions were critical to sustaining worker support of government control. First was the postrevolutionary regime's ability to deliver important general benefits for labor, including a commitment to an economic model that provided low inflation, protection for domestic industries, and continuous growth from the 1940s through the 1960s. Members of officially recognized labor unions benefited not just from the job opportunities created by a vibrant and growing economy, but also from access to government-subsidized housing, health care, and basic consumer goods. Given these advantages to union membership, many workers supported the regime even when it restricted their individual and organizational autonomy. Why labor continued to support the PRI when economic crises reduced or eliminated many of the perks they previously enjoyed is not clear. Indeed, the working class bore the brunt of the economic turbulence of the 1980s and 1990s, including unemployment, price increases, and falling wages.

Labor's loyalty to the PRI during hard times can be explained by the second important element of its corporatist arrangement with organized labor: the cooptation of union leaders and organizations. The government granted union leaders tangible benefits, including government positions, political influence, and state subsidies to sustain their organizations. In return, they were expected to deliver the consistent support of labor for the PRI at the polls and at political rallies, and a compliant workforce for pro-government businesses. A worker who wanted access to scarce jobs, promotions, or perks associated with a particular job or industry had to demonstrate loyalty to the union's leadership. Above all, loyalty was demonstrated by accepting the word of the boss, even if it meant a wage freeze, benefit cutbacks, or layoffs. Individuals who rejected this arrangement were ousted from unions, and unions who refused to play by the government's rules were denied access to jobs, wage increases, and even protections afforded by the constitution and federal labor code. [4]

As noted earlier, two labor confederations—the Mexican Regional Labor Confederation (Confederación Regional Obrera Mexicana, CROM), and the Confederation of Mexican Workers (Confederación de Trabajadores de México, CTM)—held privileged positions as the official representatives of the labor force in Mexico's postrevolutionary corporatist system. Each of these deserves to be described in some detail.[5] From its foundation in 1918 and into the late 1920s, the CROM was Mexico's dominant labor union. The CROM was created with the explicit support of Carranza who, despite his reputation as a pro-business politician and his repression of labor groups in 1916, sought to coopt the support of organized labor for the constitutionalist government. Ultimately, under the leadership of Luis Napoleón Morones, the CROM betrayed Carranza by supporting Alvaro Obregón's presidential bid in 1920. The CROM and its political wing, the Mexican Labor Party, became a critical source of support for both Obregón and Calles in the 1920s.

The CROM's influence was illustrated by, and significantly tied to, the political fortunes of Morones, who became a federal deputy in the Mexican Congress and was later named secretary of industry, commerce, and labor (1924–1928) in the Calles administration. Morones quickly acquired a reputation for avarice and political ambition, revealed by a fortune in ill-gotten wealth and by his presidential aspirations. Indeed, Morones's downfall came when his aspirations clashed with Obregón's and he overtly opposed the former president's bid for reelection. Soon after, Morones resigned from his cabinet position and the CROM's influence waned rapidly. Calles's successor, Emilio Portes Gil, had been an outspoken critic of the CROM, and during his administration he enacted a sweeping purge of its members from the government. The CROM was eventually eclipsed by the rise of other aspiring organizations during the 1930s, including several formed by defectors from its own organization.

The CTM, the ultimate beneficiary of the CROM's rapid decline, was born of these diverse labor unions, which were woven together by Lombardo Toledano, a disaffected former CROM member, a lawyer, and a Marxist intellectual. Toledano was one of several gifted leaders of his generation—known as the Seven Sages (*Siete Sabios*)—who emerged from the National Autonomous University of Mexico (UNAM) and went on to make major contributions to Mexico's postrevolutionary development. It was at UNAM where Toledano first began his union activities, helping to organize other professors. As a member of the CROM and the Mexican Labor Party he went on to serve in political positions as governor of Puebla and as a federal deputy (1925–1928) during the Calles administration.

However, in 1932, Toledano defected from the CROM and, building alliances with non-CROM unions, started his own labor organization, which he referred to as the "purified CROM." Under Toledano's leadership, these unions combined in 1933 to form the General Confederation of Mexican Workers and Farmers (Confederación General de Obreros y Campesinos de México, CGOCM), which began to organize a series of strikes over the next several years. The CGOCM changed its name in 1936 to become the Confederation of Mexican Workers (CTM). That same year, the CTM provided essential support to the Cárdenas administration against former president Calles, who was fiercely critical of the intensifying activism of the Mexican labor movement. Labor's support for President Cárdenas proved decisive in forcing Calles's exile and in negotiating a resolution to strikes by railroad and electrical workers that had provoked the crisis. With tremendous gratitude to Toledano, President Cárdenas made the CTM the primary representative of the labor sector—finally displacing the CROM—when he reorganized the ruling party.

Wary of granting too much power to the CTM, Cárdenas prevented it from representing government employees and encouraged the development of a separate union for agricultural workers, the National Farm Worker Confederation (Confederación Nacional Campesina, CNC). Meanwhile, the CROM and independent labor unions continued to provide alternative sources of representation within the corporatist system. However, there is no doubt that the CTM became the most powerful representative of organized labor. The CTM's ability to ensure the compliance of workers and guarantee electoral support for the PRI made it an essential pillar within the regime for the remainder of the twentieth century.

Perhaps no other individual so embodied the CTM's role within the regime and the cooptation of the Mexican labor movement in general as Fidel Velázquez, who helped found the CTM and served as its undisputed and iconic leader for over six decades. Fidel Velázquez got his start as a milkman and union organizer under the CROM. Like Toledano, he eventually broke with the CROM, and together with several others formed his own union, the Mexico City–based Workers Sindicalist Confederation of the Federal District (Confederación Sindical de Trabajadores del Distrito Federal, CSTDF). When Toledano invited the CSTDF to join under the umbrella of the CGOCM, the prominent place he offered to Velázquez created significant tensions with rival labor and communist groups. Still, when Toledano's term as head of the CTM ended in 1941, President Manuel Ávila Camacho—who eschewed labor radicalism—supported Velázquez as Toledano's replacement. Over the coming years, Velázquez asserted his control over the CTM by slavishly aligning himself with the government and ruthlessly isolating potential rival interests.

In 1946, with the final reorganization of the ruling party as the PRI, the CTM's place as the primary representative of the labor sector was further institutionalized. Velázquez helped consolidate this position by working with the government to suppress rival leaders and organizations over the next decade. Velázquez even ousted Toledano from the CTM in 1948, as its former leader was fiercely critical of Ávila Camacho's more conservative successor, Miguel Alemán Valdés. Velázquez's remarkable survival skills in politics—and in life—made him one of the most powerful and visible PRI figures until his death at the age of ninety-two in 1997. His loyalty to the PRI and the system was steadfast across numerous crises and intermittent ideological shifts. Toward the end of his reign, Velázquez came to personify the fossilized old guard of the PRI, the "dinosaurs" or the *PRI-nosaurios*. Thanks to Velázquez and union bosses like him, organized labor became a means for Mexico's corporatist state to incorporate, coopt, and exercise political control over the masses.

Labor and Neoliberal Reform

Despite the close relationship between labor leaders and the PRI, the economic position of organized labor steadily declined during the 1980s and 1990s. In the aftermath of serious economic crises during those decades, the government often adopted economic policies that were detrimental to the interests of the working class. For example, drastic reductions in government spending led to job cuts, wage freezes, price increases, and reduced benefits even for those belonging to sanctioned labor unions. Yet leaders like Velázquez were often more loyal to the PRI than they were to their own constituents. Moreover, because the economic crises were so severe, rank-and-file union members had little choice but to accept the meager concessions offered by the government, lest they risk their economic livelihood.

Moreover, Mexico's move away from the use of protectionism and state-led economic development during the 1980s meant that the state's relationship with labor would necessarily change. The new neoliberal approach to economic development called for cutting tariffs on imports, reducing government subsidies in most areas, and the privatization of state-owned enterprises. As Middlebrook points out, "The closing or privatization of state-owned enterprises eroded what had long been the principal advantage of some of Mexico's largest and most influential unions: the ability to use their political leverage to win concessions from state managers in negotiations over wage and fringe benefit levels and contract terms."[6] Thus organized labor lost on two counts: the economic crisis meant that the government had fewer resources (e.g., jobs, wage increases, fringe benefits) to hand out, and the new economic development strategy expressly reduced both the state's role in regulating the economy and the privileged position of Mexico's labor unions in the revolutionary family.

Labor's gradual decline was also facilitated by President Salinas (1988–1994), who made a concerted effort to reform state-labor relations. The relationship between Salinas and labor was strained from the beginning by the fact that the CTM was clearly opposed to deepening Mexico's shift to a neoliberal economic model, and therefore chose to back Salinas's opponent, Alfredo del Mazo, to be the PRI presidential candidate in 1988.[7] Once in office, Salinas shrewdly bestowed favor on those labor leaders willing to accept his policy changes and ruthlessly purged those who did not. For example, he had Joaquín "La Quina" Hernández Galicia, the leader of the petroleum workers union, arrested, and forced the resignation of the longstanding leader of the National Education Workers Union (SNTE) to make way for a new leader more receptive to decentralizing the public education system. Additionally, he praised and held up as models those unions that were willing to accept redefinition of worker-employer relations, such as the Mexican Telephone Workers Union, which accepted privatization of the industry and agreed to more flexible work rules and the linking of wage increases to productivity (rather than cost of living). In exchange, TELMEX protected most union jobs and gave union members stock options.[8] Meanwhile, despite his belief that the market should be the determining force for wages, employment levels, and working conditions, Salinas used the government's power to limit strikes, intervene in negotiations between workers and employers, and minimize wage increases. For example, the Economic Solidarity Pact that Salinas negotiated between the government, labor, and the private sector was critical to bringing inflation under control during the late 1980s and early 1990s, but required major sacrifices from workers. Still, while labor's influence and privileges clearly declined during the Salinas *sexenio,* some unions were able to maintain their influence as long as they were willing to accept the new rules of the game. Indeed, Salinas could not afford to completely alienate labor, since this sector's support was still essential for political stability—especially in the face of neoliberal reform.

Labor in Contemporary Mexico

With labor's gradual decline during the 1980s and 1990s, unions lost members and mobilization strength. Years of economic crisis and restructuring led to declining real wages and job losses that made union membership much less attractive than it had been in previous decades. For example, by the early 1990s there was virtually no difference in the average wages earned by union and nonunion workers, and the modest wage increases that unions did manage to secure were still well below the rate of inflation.[9] Furthermore, the economic crises led to hundreds of thousands of job losses, which reduced the opportunities for labor organizations. Even after the country began its economic recovery in the late 1990s, most of the union jobs created lacked security and benefits—reinforcing the notion that union membership no longer guaranteed the perks of the past.

Meanwhile, the PRI's electoral losses and the rise of the PAN in contemporary Mexico ensured that organized labor would not regain its former privileged position.[10] Whereas the CTM generally held about ninety seats (as PRI deputies) in the Chamber of Deputies in the 1970s and 1980s, after 2000 they have never won more than nineteen seats, suggesting that even within the PRI, labor's influence has declined.[11] Furthermore, like many members of the PAN, Vicente Fox was highly critical of traditional state-labor relations, not only because of his ideological conviction that the state should play a very limited role in negotiations between labor and management, but also for the obvious political reason that organized labor's support was essential to the PRI's hegemony. Therefore comprehensive reform of the labor code became as one of his policy priorities and his cabinet organized a roundtable on the modernization of labor relations. This forum brought together representatives from official and independent trade unions as well as from business and government to discuss how they might collectively agree on changes to redefine the relationship between the state and labor. Not surprisingly, the CTM opposed dramatic changes to the status quo. Ultimately Fox did relatively little during his tenure to challenge the CTM's waning but still appreciable power. Certainly any attempt to radically alter state-labor relations would have met with the disapproval of the opposition-dominated Congress. But it is also undeniable that, recent changes in the CTM's influence notwithstanding, all presidents, regardless of their partisan affiliation, still depend on the CTM and other cooperative labor organizations to maintain control over their rank and file in order for Mexico to enjoy political stability and attract foreign investment.

Calderón's approach to labor is not as dramatic as that of Fox, who specifically mentioned labor reform as one of his major goals. Nonetheless, Calderón has included among his priorities several initiatives that will have a direct impact on state-labor relations (e.g., increasing the transparency and accountability of PEMEX, support for small and medium-size businesses, and pension and health care reform). Therefore, to the extent that he envisions changing state-labor relations, it will probably occur slowly, indirectly, and in a piecemeal fashion. The one area where Calderón has demonstrated a strong connection to labor is in his solid working relationship with Esther Elba Gordillo, the former head of the SNTE, Mexico's largest teachers' union.

The SNTE was founded in 1943 from the various regional teachers' confederations then in existence. Although it has experienced internal factional splintering in recent years, the SNTE maintains an impressive 1.3 million members and remains the largest teachers' union in Latin America. Former SNTE leader Esther Elba Gordillo maintains significant influence over the organization, and in recent years has established important ties to the Calderón administration. Gordillo helped to found the New Alliance Party (Partido Nueva Alianza, PANAL), which ran Roberto Campa as its 2006 presidential candidate. However, some analysts suspect that Gordillo used her influence with the SNTE to support Calderón's candidacy, providing a critical block of votes in the hotly contested election. Whether Gordillo was as influential in the election as perceived, Campa and members of her family benefited from high-level positions in the Calderón administration. During Calderón's first years in office, she certainly appeared likely to be a key player in any efforts to overhaul Mexico's public education system.

Women in Mexico

As is common throughout Latin America and other parts of the world, Mexican society has traditionally been characterized by male dominance. This tendency is often described in Mexico as *machismo*, the celebration (and in some cases glorification) of masculine power and virility. The cultural norms of machismo hold that men possess the superior qualities of intelligence, strength, and virility, all of which make them better suited for positions of power. Meanwhile, the corresponding cultural norm for women is *marianismo*, the expectation that women should occupy a subordinate position at home and in society. *Marianismo* portrays women's place as being in the home—wives, mothers, sisters, and daughters—where they are expected to embody virtue, humility, and sacrifice, and comport themselves with obedience and dignity. Needless to say, under these norms, women are traditionally expected to be apolitical members of society. Hence, for many years, a woman who demonstrated an interest in politics was seen at best as overstepping her bounds, and at worst, a "social danger."[12]

Although this traditional understanding of gender roles persists among some Mexicans, women's roles gradually changed throughout the twentieth century. Of course, peasant and working-class women had long worked as laborers and domestic servants. Yet as early as the 1920s, it eventually became socially acceptable for even middle-class women to enter the workforce, as long as they practiced traditional women's trades such as nursing or education. By the 1950s, women were also commonly employed in factory jobs; by the 1960s and 1970s, women emerged as pivotal members, if not leaders, of labor unions, social movements, and neighborhood associations.

In the 1980s, Mexican women's economic and political roles began to change dramatically in the wake of the country's economic crises, when families had to look for new strategies for survival. Women of all ages entered the workforce, both formal and informal, in order to help provide basic necessities for their families. At the same time, many women also began to play a more active role in household decision making. These gains helped create the foundation for increased female participation in all aspects of the political sphere. Today Mexican women are present in all sectors of economic and political society, from entrepreneurs in the informal economy and local community activism, to highly educated professionals and national-level politicians. However, like their counterparts in most countries of the world, Mexican women still lag behind men when it comes to holding positions of power.

Economic Status of Women

Women make up just over half of Mexico's population (51.2 percent) yet in almost every respect, women are underrepresented and disadvantaged. Economically, women are more likely to be employed in the service sector, an economic sector in which wages are relatively low. Additionally, jobs in this area are vulnerable to economic downturns, and are often part of the informal economy and therefore lacking important benefits like health care and social security. The National Women's Institute (Instituto Nacional de la Mujer, INMUN) estimated for the period 2003–2004 that 59.8 percent of women worked in jobs that did not provide benefits.[13] Women in Mexico are also more likely to be paid less than men. Table 8.1 shows that inequality occurs at every income level. Whereas 11.7 percent of all men receive a salary of at least five times the official minimum wage, only 7.9 percent of women earn similar wages. At the other end of the spectrum, 46.1 percent of women earn two times or less than the official minimum, while only 35 percent of men fall into this category.

Because women in Mexico make up a greater percentage of the population, live longer, and tend to be paid lower wages, they are more likely than men to be poor.[14] Whether as a cause or a consequence of the former, women are also less likely to be educated. According to INEGI, in 2000, 7.5 percent of Mexican males over the age of fifteen were illiterate, while 11.4 percent of Mexican females in the same age group were also illiterate.[15] Furthermore, while women make up approximately 48 percent of all college graduates, overall, this represents a small number of women since college graduates make up only about 10 percent of Mexico's population.

Table 8.1.
Wage Differentials between Men and Women in Mexico, 2004

Income Level	% Women	% Men	Differential
None	11.8	6.4	5.4
Minimum wage	19.0	14.0	5.0
Between 1 and 2 times the minimum	27.1	21.0	6.1
Between 2 and 5 times the minimum	30.3	42.0	−11.7
Five times the minimum or more	7.9	11.7	−3.8
Not reported	3.9	4.9	−1.0
Total	100	100	

Source: Adapted from INMUN, *Cuarto informe de labores,* 2004–2005, Cuadro 1.1, p. 15.

Thus women are far from equal in contemporary Mexican society. Yet there is little doubt that today, Mexican women are important actors in the political sphere as community leaders, members of nongovernmental organizations, government bureaucrats, party activists, and politicians. In order to understand how they have come to play such an active role in politics, we must examine the trajectory of the women's movement in Mexico.

The Mexican Women's Movement: Historical Overview

Despite the fact that the constitution of 1917 was one of the most socially progressive of its time, it was blatantly sexist. Claiming that they lacked the capacity to participate in politics, the framers of the constitution refused to extend voting rights to women. Universal suffrage was not present in Mexico until 1953, when women were granted the right to vote in national elections. Yet long before that time, women were politically active in Mexico. As noted in chapter 2, women actively participated in the revolution as spies, arms smugglers, and *soldaderas* (a combination of companion, cook, laundress, nurse, and soldier) for the rebel armies.[16] Women from the upper social classes formed clubs and organizations to support leading figures in the revolution, like Francisco I. Madero and Venustiano Carranza. After the revolution, women also played an important role in organizing and participating in political campaigns and women's political groups such as the Mexican Feminist Council (CFM) and the Mexican section of the Pan-American League. The former sought to unite feminism and socialism, while the latter's goal was to promote women's civil rights.[17]

According to scholar Victoria Rodríguez, a unified women's movement first emerged in 1935 through the Sole Front for Women's Rights (Frente Unico Pro Derechos de la Mujer, FUPDM), an organization that brought together women (and women's organizations) from a variety of ideological and socioeconomic backgrounds and lobbied for equal voting rights and a variety of other social reforms concerning children and indigenous women.[18] FUPDM efforts to obtain a constitutional amendment to extend voting rights to women appeared to have been successful in 1939 when such an initiative was ratified by all of Mexico's states. However, the PRI-controlled Congress blocked the amendment out of fear that enfranchised women would overwhelmingly support the PAN's candidate in the upcoming presidential election. This move, along with President Manuel Ávila Camacho's (1940–1946) antipathy toward the movement and its goals, was a serious setback, but the FUPDM remained active and grew in size and popularity throughout the 1940s. With the election of Miguel Alemán (1946–1952), the movement was rewarded with the right to participate in local elections and female political appointments to posts within the PNR's new configuration called the Institutional Revolutionary Party. Unsatisfied with a partial victory, the FUPDM continued to press its demands with Alemán's successor, Adolfo Ruíz Cortines (1952–1958).[19] This paved the way for an amendment that granted women full political rights. Congress ratified the amendment in 1953.

After the victories of the early 1950s, the women's movement essentially went dormant until the late 1960s when it reemerged and, like many other social movements, worked to raise awareness about social and economic discrimination as well as inequality in Mexico. Yet during this period the women's movement was far from unified: women were divided by class, race, and urban/rural differences. As Rodríguez explains, in the 1970s, "the bulk of feminist activity was confined to small consciousness-raising groups comprised of . . . middle-class, educated women from Mexico City."[20] These groups focused primarily on three main issues: reproductive rights, violence against women, and freedom of sexual choice.[21]

During the 1970s and 1980s feminists were active in a number of areas, pressing for new laws to protect women's reproductive rights and establishing publications, academic programs, and support organizations (e.g., shelters, rape crisis centers). Much of this activity, especially in the aftermath of the economic crisis of 1982 and the devastating earthquakes in Mexico City in 1985, was incorporated into a larger movement to protest the government's neglect of the poor, lower, and middle classes. In other words, women's political activism broadened its focus to include issues that often had a disproportionate effect on women, rather than remain narrowly focused on women's issues. To be sure, there have always been a number of feminist organizations in Mexico that actively pursue specifically gender-based policies (e.g., better health care for women, laws protecting victims of sex crimes, legalization of abortion), but on the whole, Mexican women tend not to separate these issues from their broader political interests.

This trend continued into the 1990s, and the women's movement continued to encompass a variety of goals, including more government attention to poverty, crime, and violence, better access to education, as well as legislation to promote social and economic equality in the workplace, and efforts to promote greater female participation in politics. Perhaps the truest testament to women's progress in the political sphere is the fact that many so-called gender issues are now incorporated into mainstream politics.[22] In 2007 the Mexico City Assembly passed a law making abortion legal and free in Mexico City for women over the age of eighteen during the first twelve weeks of pregnancy. While the measure remained highly controversial, it passed due to the efforts of a broad array of women's organizations, and because it enjoyed support from the general population in the capital and male city assembly members.[23]

Women's Participation in Political Parties

Women have significantly increased their role in Mexican politics by joining the ranks of political parties. All political parties in Mexico count on women as members, activists, and loyalists, yet until the mid-1990s, it was uncommon for women to hold positions of power within party organizations and rare for women to represent their parties as candidates for public office. This situation has changed somewhat, thanks in part to the recognition that women have long played an important role in party activities, and in many cases are as well suited as their male counterparts for public office. But women have also been given a boost by an electoral law passed by the IFE in 2000, which requires that women constitute a minimum of 30 percent of candidates from each party.[24] Without a doubt, this gender quota has contributed to an increased number of women running for political office in Mexico. Whereas women accounted for only 25 percent of all national-level candidates in 1997, in 2000, they accounted for 34 percent. In the 2000 elections for the Chamber of Deputies, women accounted for 38 percent of all candidates.[25] However, there is no provision that specifies where women should be positioned on a party's electoral list. As a result, it is common for parties to place female candidates to the lowest positions on a list and thus dramatically reduce their chances of winning a seat.[26] This practice reflects the common belief that most women are weak candidates because they possess inferior experience, because they lack qualifications, or simply because of sexism.

The gender quota law notwithstanding, the three major parties in Mexico have differed significantly in their willingness to nominate female candidates and allow women to serve as party leaders. The PRD adopted a 30 percent quota in 1994, long before the IFE made it mandatory for all parties, and stipulated that every third candidate (on the party list) should be female. This rule prevented the party from relegating women to unelectable positions.[27] Moreover, the PRD's quota required that women have at least 30 percent representation in the party's executive committee. Table 8.2 shows that thanks to this rule, the PRD was the only party to meet the IFE's standards in 2000. Moreover, it is common for women to serve in the PRD's highest positions of power. For example, Amalia García was the party's president from 1999 to 2002, followed by Rosario Robles. Robles also represented her party as Mexico City's mayor in 1999.[28]

Within the PRI, women have also had success in obtaining leadership positions. María de los Ángeles Moreno and Dulce María Sauri both served as the party's president, and Socorro Díaz Palacios and Esther Elba Gordillo served in PRI's second highest position of secretary-general. However, in general, women face significant obstacles to advancement within the party. For ex-

Table 8.2.
Percentage Representation of Women in the National Executive
Committees of the PAN, PRI, and PRD

Year	PAN	PRI	PRD
2000	20	21.9	33.3
2002	35.5	26.2	36.4
2004	36.5	20.8	26.1

Source: Instituto Nacional de las Mujeres, *Informes de Labores,* 2001–2002, 2003–2004, 2004–2005. More recent figures suggest that in 2008 female representation in the executive committees of the PAN and PRI was 25 percent, while women made up 45 percent of the PRD's CEN.

ample, despite having adopted a gender quota in 1997, the PRI regularly ignored the quota or relegated women to inferior positions on electoral lists, or women were chosen as candidates for districts and cities of little importance to the party. Furthermore, as table 8.2 shows, the PRI has had difficulty meeting its 30 percent quota for female representation in the party's CEN.

Of the three major parties, the PAN is the only one that did not adopt a gender quota before 2000 and has never had a female party chairperson. However, in the late 1990s, it was the only party to increase its female representation in Congress, and after 2000 it greatly increased the representation of women in the party leadership.[29] Thus women appear to have fared about as well (or as poorly) in the PAN as their counterparts in other parties. Now that the gender quota is in effect for all parties, the PAN, like the PRI, has found ways around it. For example, women within the party complain that they are chosen as candidates only in districts where the party's chances of winning are slim to none.[30] Another common practice is for women candidates to run as an alternate candidate (*candidato suplente*) to the principal candidate. Alternates assume office only if the "real" candidate resigns or is unable to serve the full term of office.[31]

Clearly, all three parties can do much more to promote women within their organizations, since none has consistently upheld the 30 percent rule when it comes to women in leadership positions within the party. In this sense the parties' outward support for women belies the stronger belief that women are inferior political candidates. While some women may indeed be weaker because they lack the experience or training of their male counterparts, this is not always the case. Ironically, in order for women to gain the experience they need, the parties must be willing to give them the opportunity to lead the party and run for office. So far, these opportunities have been scarce.

Given that women face such serious obstacles to advancement in their own parties, it is hardly a surprise that they are also underrepresented in government. Figure 8.1 demonstrates that the number of women in the Mexican legislature has increased at a steady rate. In 2003, the percentage of female legislators

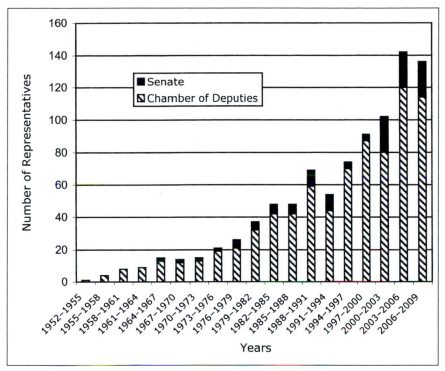

FIGURE 8.1 Female Representation in the Mexican Legislature, 1952–2009
Sources: Victoria E. Rodriguez (2003), Table 4.1 and www.cameradediputados.gob.mx, www.senado.gob.mx

reached an all-time high at 120 deputies (24 percent) and 27 senators (21.1 percent). Yet women still make up a relatively small minority of national legislators, and while these numbers are significant and compare favorably to most other countries in the Americas, including the United States, they fall considerably short of the IFE's goal of 30 percent, and an even farther cry from 51 percent, the share of women in Mexico's population. Moreover, women who are elected to the legislature tend to sit on less influential committees which have traditionally been deemed more appropriate for women (e.g., Gender and Equity, Culture, Civil Protection, Health, and Social Development).[32]

In contrast to the other areas of government, women have a long and impressive history of representation in the Mexican judiciary. The first female was appointed to the Supreme Court in 1961, and by the late 1980s, women comprised roughly 10 percent of the judicial branch's top officials. These numbers continued to increase in the 1990s, when women accounted for 19 percent of Supreme Court justices, 15 percent of federal magistrates, and 24 percent of judges.[33] The number of women declined somewhat after the reorganization of the judiciary in 1995. In 2008, only two of eleven members of the Supreme Court were female: Justice Olga María del Carmen Sánchez Cordero, and Justice Margarita Beatríz Luna Ramos.

Like most countries, Mexico has never elected a female head of state, and only five women have ever run for president as minor party candidates. The three major parties' unwillingness to consider a female presidential candidate, and the relatively poor showing of the female candidates who have run, suggest that (1) the women who have run for president were not strong candidates and (2) many Mexicans may be reluctant to elect a woman as their leader. This is not to say that women are absent in the executive branch. Between 1976 and 2007, ten women have served as cabinet ministers.[34] The first major appointment was made in 1998, when Ernesto Zedillo chose Rosario Green as Mexico's first female secretary of foreign relations. Vicente Fox appointed three women to his cabinet, but only one occupied a top-tier position as the head of social development. Felipe Calderón's cabinet improved on this slightly with four female cabinet appointees, including those in two top positions: Georgina Kessel (energy secretary) and Patricia Espinosa Castellano (foreign secretary).[35]

If women have been underrepresented at the national level, the problem is more severe in state and local governments. Only a handful of women have been governors, and nationally, women rarely comprise more than 15–20 percent of state legislators.[36] Female representation at the municipal level is even more disappointing. Between 2000 and 2005, only 3.5 percent of mayors, and less than 20 percent of city council members, were women.[37] One small recent advance for women is that whereas in 1995, female mayors tended to govern smaller, more impoverished municipalities, by 2004, they were equally likely to be found in larger municipalities with higher average levels of income and living standards.[38]

Although women are clearly underrepresented in Mexico's formal political institutions, they have played pivotal roles in other forms of political activity. For example, since the 1970s, women have actively participated in a wide variety of neighborhood associations and urban popular movements. In many cases, these women did not start out with the idea that they were engaging in political activism. Rather, they found that government actions (e.g., failure to provide housing or basic public services) hampered their ability to uphold their everyday responsibilities as homemakers and therefore decided to take action. Because most of these women were unfamiliar with, or unwilling to go through, formal government channels to register their complaints, they turned to community activism. As Bennett explains, "The fact that poor urban women do not have interlocutors representing their interests within the formal political structures has forced them either to use public protest as their channel of communication with government decision makers or to create urban movements that can represent their collective voice."[39]

Women's involvement in urban and social movements led to a number of notable accomplishments, both small and large. For example, small groups and neighborhoods successfully petitioned local governments for health clinics, waste disposal, and access to land and housing. One particularly high-profile victory occurred in the mid-1980s, when women in the city of Monterrey used a variety of forms of public protest to force the national government to extend basic water services to those areas of the city without access to the main water system.[40] Such community activism has been important not only because, in many cases, it led the government to address key citizen demands, but also because it gave women valuable political experience.[41] That women became accustomed to voicing their demands and, equally important that society became familiar with female activists, likely facilitated the entry of Mexican women into formal politics.

Hence, the past twenty-five years have seen women take on new and important political roles in Mexico. No longer confined to the home or to religious service, women now enjoy many of the social and political freedoms that they lacked in the past. This is not to say that machismo is a relic of the past. Indeed, it is alive and well in many aspects of Mexican society, and women continue to face obstacles to political advancement. Yet it is important to recognize Mexican women's accomplishments in this area, which are many and of great significance. Unfortunately, the same cannot be said for Mexico's indigenous people, who on the whole, remain excluded from positions of power at the state and national level. It is to this group that we turn next.

Indigenous People and Ethnic Identity

In a country where bloody conquest fused two very different cultures and erased much of the past, there is much debate about how to define "indigenousness" in Mexico. Most Mexicans have indigenous ancestry and many see the indigenous as synonymous with the peasantry. Still, the government has adopted a fairly straightforward definition: to be considered indigenous, an individual must be a native speaker of an indigenous language. Using this definition, it is estimated that Mexico is home to roughly 6 million people from eighty-five different indigenous language groups.[42] While dwarfed by the country's population of mestizos—people of mixed European and indigenous ancestry—Mexico's current indigenous population is markedly increased from the 1930s, when the indigenous population was estimated at only 2.3 million. As a result of this relatively recent increase, most indigenous people (52.6 percent) are young, under the age of thirty. Yet currently, indigenous Mexicans still represent just 7.1 percent of the total population.

Moreover, while Mexico's indigenous population has relatively high numbers when compared with other countries in the Americas, they do not constitute a strong political force. In fact, they occupy the lowest rung in society because they are disproportionately poor, uneducated, and disenfranchised. Most indigenous people reside in rural areas in the southern states of Oaxaca, Yucatán, Chiapas, Guerrero, Puebla, Campeche, and Quintana Roo, and work as unskilled laborers, earning some of the lowest wages in the country.[43] Indeed, in 2000, approximately 27 percent earned less than the national minimum wage, and 28 percent earned between one and two times the minimum wage.[44] Roughly half of the indigenous population lives in dwellings with dirt floors, no running water, and uses firewood (rather than a gas or electric stove) to prepare meals. Nearly three-quarters live in communities with no access to health care, garbage collection, or sewer systems. Furthermore, among Mexico's indigenous people over the age of fifteen, the illiteracy rate is 44 percent, much higher than the national average of 9 percent. Only 16 percent have completed elementary school and nearly one-third (31.1 percent) have never had a formal education.[45]

The reality of Mexico's indigenous people is stark: they live in deplorable conditions and are, in many ways, geographically and socially marginalized from the modern aspects of Mexican society. Compounding and, some would argue, causing their socioeconomic hardship is the fact that racist attitudes toward indigenous people are prevalent in Mexico.[46] Many of the same stereotypes that have plagued minority groups elsewhere—such as Native Americans and African Americans in the United States—are applied to indigenous people in Mexico, so that it is not uncommon even for educated, middle-class Mexicans to believe that indigenous people are intellectually and socially inferior to those of mixed or European ancestry. Indeed, in the same way that there exists in the United States a plethora of jokes and beliefs about the laziness, drunkenness, and ineptitude of particular racial and ethnic groups, many Mexicans recount personal experiences and urban legends about the idiocy of "Indios," and frequently treat indigenous people with disdain.[47] Meanwhile, it is still common for mass media, employers, and people generally to express a preference for taller, lighter-skinned, fine-featured individuals than is the norm among indigenous people. People with indigenous features are a rarity on television programs and advertisements, and when they do appear, they are invariably cast as servants, lower-class characters, and miscreants. Similarly, some employers still openly solicit job applicants based on their physical appearance, requiring a minimum height, light skin, and European facial features.

That Mexico's indigenous peoples are, in effect, second-class citizens comes as no surprise given their long history of subjugation. As we saw in chapter 1, the Spanish colonizers enslaved the native populations and considered them important only insofar as they represented an economic resource. Yet ironically, indigenous people had more rights under Spanish rule than they did immediately following independence. In the colony of New Spain, indigenous peoples were considered wards of the Crown or the Church and as such enjoyed some protections. For example, they were given some measure of local autonomy and so were able to maintain a number of their social and political customs. In addition, indigenous people had the right to own property and access to the General Indian Court, which settled many cases in favor of indigenous plaintiffs.[48] However, the constitutions written after independence did not preserve these rights, in large part because liberal reformers sought to modernize and assimilate indigenous people, and therefore eliminated what few paternalistic protections they had under the Crown. Indeed, one of the negative consequences of the Ley Lerdo enacted by the government of Benito Juárez was that it forced the auction of *ejidos*, the communal lands that belonged to indigenous communities. Since the wealthy were the only ones in a position to buy the lands, they increased their share of holdings and many indigenous people were forced to become laborers on lands they previously owned.[49] Indigenous people fared even worse under the rule of Porfirio Díaz and his *científicos*, whose inequitable economic policies cemented indigenous people as the lowest class in Mexican society.

Postrevolutionary Indigenous Representation

In the constitution of 1917, indigenous people did little better—in spite of the fact that they played an integral role in many aspects of the revolution. For although they gained the right to own *ejidos*, and indigenous men technically enjoyed the same political rights as other men, the constitution did not explicitly recognize indigenous people or grant them specific rights based on their identity. The latter concession would have officially granted indigenous people the right and opportunity to maintain their cultural and political autonomy. Instead, the Revolutionary constitution, like its postindependence predecessors, sought to promote a single Mexican identity. And while such a move made good sense for a country coming out of a revolution and seeking national unity, it proved to be problematic for Mexico's indigenous people whose reality was rooted in social, economic, and political inequality.

After the revolution, the government adopted a somewhat bipolar stance vis-à-vis the country's indigenous population. On the one hand, it sought to celebrate indigenous people in Mexico's new postrevolutionary identity as part of the "cosmic race" combining European and other heritages.[50] On the other hand, the new regime continued to impose largely European-style standards and norms, and focused mainly on assimilating indigenous peoples as Mexicans. Particularly in the 1920s, the federal government made a concerted effort to expand public education to include rural and indigenous areas as a means of assimilation, bringing previously excluded groups into society by providing free basic education.[51] And although many indigenous people undoubtedly benefited from this effort, for many, education came at the expense of their cultural identities because the curriculum was taught exclusively in Spanish and inculcated Western norms and values.

Inclusion in the postrevolutionary political system also meant relinquishing cultural identities in favor of class-based identities. Thus, indigenous people became indistinguishable from peasants, or individuals who depended upon their labor and access to land for economic survival. As peasants, many of Mexico's indigenous people were brought, or coopted, into the corporatist arrangement as members of the National Peasant Confederation (CNC), the sectoral organization recognized by the PRI to increase access to land and otherwise represent peasants' political interests. Initially, peasants fared relatively well in this system: by 1940 approximately 75 million acres were redistributed, mostly in the form of *ejidos*.[52] Most of this land was redistributed by President Cárdenas, who was committed to making the revolution's goal of agrarian reform a reality. Unfortunately for the peasants, subsequent presidents did not share Cárdenas's commitment to this goal, and the CNC's ability to negotiate land reform waned steadily after 1940.[53] Thus to the extent that indigenous peasants had formal representation within the political system, they always bargained from a position of weakness. Moreover, it would be misleading to say that indigenous interests were represented in this system because access to resources (e.g., land, jobs, credit) was mediated by local caciques who often were leaders chosen by the government (rather than elected locally) and who used violence and intimidation to ensure support of the regime rather than function as true representatives.[54] Also, indigenous people may have filled the same economic niche as peasants, but their interests were much more diverse. Of equal importance were the issues of self-determination and the right to maintain their cultural and linguistic identities, yet there were no political institutions for articulating these interests. Finally, in the decades since the end of the revolution, indigenous Mexicans have very little to show in the way of social, economic and political advances.

As we saw earlier, they remain the poorest, least educated, and most marginalized sector of Mexican society, and the prevalence of racism contributes to public disdain for indigenous peoples and limits efforts to address their plight. Therefore, it is hardly surprising that many indigenous people eschewed formal political institutions and chose instead to use alternative forms of political expression

and activism. As early as the 1940s, indigenous groups began to form autonomous organizations in an effort to achieve the political ends that eluded them as
part of the PRI's corporatist arrangement. While some organized themselves in
nonviolent political movements, like the COCEI (see textbox 8.1), others opted
for armed conflict.[55] Below, we examine one of the most significant and best
known indigenous rights movements in contemporary Mexican politics.

Textbox 8.1. COCEI

One of the most successful indigenous political movements in contemporary Mexican politics is the Coalition of Workers, Peasants, and Students of
the Isthmus (Coalición Obrero, Campesina y Estudiantíl del Istmo, COCEI),
which formed in Juchitán, Oaxaca, in the early 1970s in response to the
government's systematic repression and exploitation.[1] This group of Zapotec indigenous people used grassroots activism to resist the PRI, protesting
the fraudulent election of government-chosen leaders, exploitative government programs, and the lack of basic public services. The COCEI used
strikes, marches, occupations of government offices, and negotiation to
improve the living and working conditions of Juchitecos. Thanks to widespread popular support and its solid, Zapotec-based identity, the coalition
withstood military intervention and political assassinations, and emerged
as a formal political player in the early 1980s. Its track record was strong
enough to pressure the government to recognize its victory in the 1981
municipal elections. After a two-year interlude in which the COCEI was
forced out of office, the organization has governed Juchitán continuously,
either in coalition with a political party or alone, since 1986. The COCEI's
tenure in office has not been perfect, due to government repression, bitter
internal divisions, and its own political failures. Yet overall, the COCEI has
succeeded in protecting the Zapotec language, culture, and land. Furthermore, it has significantly improved the living and working conditions in
Juchitán—accomplishments that likely would not have occurred had the
PRI maintained its hold on the city. COCEI's approach was to put pressure
on government authorities in order to gain entrance to the political system
on its own terms.

[1] Jeffrey Rubin is a leading scholar on the COCEI. This textbox draws on his work, especially "Popular
Mobilization and the Myth of State Corporatism," in *Popular Movements;* and *Decentering the Regime:
Ethnicity, Radicalism, and Democracy in Juchitán, Mexico*, ed. Foweraker and Craig (Durham, N.C.:
Duke University Press, 1997).

The EZLN

Other indigenous political movements have rejected the system altogether.
Such is the case with the Zapatista Army of National Liberation (Ejército

Zapatista de Liberación Nacional, EZLN).[56] On January 1, 1994, Mexico rang in the New Year with the shocking news that an indigenous army wearing ski masks had taken over several towns and attacked an army base in the southeastern state of Chiapas. The EZLN was made up of disaffected Mexico City intellectuals working with local indigenous men and women from the Lacandon highland region of Chiapas to spark what they believed would be a radical social and political change in Mexico (see textbox 8.2).[57]

Textbox 8.2. Women in the EZLN

Women have played an important role in the EZLN, occupying a wide range of positions from military commanders and combatants to local community organizers. Their incorporation stemmed from a combination of factors, including a strong regional tradition of community organizing and the EZLN's stated commitment to the economic and political equality of human beings, regardless of gender. The influence of the women Zapatistas was such that a document titled "Women's Revolutionary Law" accompanied the EZLN's initial statement of principles and demands, which called for the political, economic, and social equality of women by stating that women have, for example, the right to decide the number of children they will bear, the right to education, the right not to be mistreated by family members or strangers, and the right to hold military rank in the revolutionary armed forces. To be sure, the incorporation of women as equals in the EZLN and its local councils was not uncontroversial within the indigenous communities themselves. Indeed, many men and women resisted adopting and accepting these new roles. Nevertheless, within the organization women have achieved a level of parity that is uncommon in many other aspects of Mexican society. And while it would be an overstatement to assert that the EZLN has single-handedly improved the position of indigenous women, many women in those communities now express greater self-confidence, a willingness to participate in public and political life, and self-determination in the home.

Source: Lynn Stephen, "Gender and Grassroots Organizing: Lessons from Chiapas," in *Women's Participation in Mexican Political Life,* ed. Victoria Rodríguez (Boulder, Colo.: Westview, 1998).

The timing of the EZLN rebellion was not a coincidence. They chose the date in part because it coincided with the first day that NAFTA went into effect: an agreement that would ostensibly bring Mexico great economic rewards by boosting international trade. Yet many in Mexico perceived the agreement to be detrimental to the interests of the peasantry, which would lose access to land once it was privatized to encourage the production of cash crops.[58] In the minds of the Zapatistas and many indigenous peoples, the developments of the early 1990s were the latest in a long line of government efforts to subjugate and marginalize Mexican indigenous people.

Rather than accept their fate, the Zapatistas declared war on the Mexican government, which they called an "illegal dictatorship," and released a declaration stating the rationale for the uprising and their goals: "work, land, housing, food, education, independence, liberty, democracy, justice, and peace."[59] (See textbox 8.3.) With an army of approximately 2,000 people, some armed with AK-16s, M-16s, or Uzis, and many more armed with more rudimentary weapons such as shotguns, the EZLN took over the government offices in seven cities in Chiapas, attacked an army base, kidnapped a former governor, and freed prisoners from a local prison. President Salinas responded by sending in 12,000 troops. With the help of armored vehicles and air strikes, the Mexican military forced the Zapatistas to retreat into eastern tropical forests and lowlands. In all, approximately 150 people were killed. On January 12, President Salinas proposed a cease-fire and agreed to negotiate with the EZLN if they laid down their arms.[60]

Textbox 8.3. First Declaration from the Lacandon Forest

Hoy decimos basta! Today we say enough is enough! To the people of Mexico: Mexican brothers and sisters: We are a product of 500 years of struggle: first against slavery, then during the war of independence against Spain led by insurgents, then to promulgate our constitution and expel the French empire from our soil, and later [when] the dictatorship of Porfirio Díaz denied us the just application of the Reform laws and the people rebelled and leaders like Villa and Zapata emerged, poor men just like us. We have been denied the most elemental education so that others can use us as cannon fodder and pillage the wealth of our country. They don't care that we have nothing, absolutely nothing, not even a roof over our heads, no land, no work, no health care, no food, and no education. Nor are we able freely and democratically to elect our political representatives, nor is there independence from foreigners, nor is there peace nor justice for ourselves and our children.

Excerpt cited in George Collier and Elizabeth Lowery Quaratiello, Basta! Land and the Zapatista Rebellion in Chiapas (Oakland, Catif.: Institute for Food and Development Policy, 1994), 2.

The peace talks between the government's Commission for Peace and Concordance (Comisión de Concordia y Pacificación, COCOPA) and the EZLN's leadership, the Committee of the Clandestine Indigenous Revolution (Comité Clandestino Revolucionario Indígena, CCRI) began in February. Under the aegis of Bishop Samuel Ruíz, a noted advocate of indigenous rights, the talks commenced with Manuel Camacho Solís, a well-respected negotiator representing the government, and an EZLN spokesperson operating under the alias of Subcomandante Marcos, representing the Zapatistas and their supporters. In just two weeks, the two sides drew up thirty-two tentative accords. Each side then took the accords to their respective constituencies for approval. Three months later, Zapatista supporters rejected the accords, refused to give up their arms, and called for a national convention as the only meaningful alternative to overhaul the Mexican political system. An uneasy truce remained in effect until February 1995, when newly elected President Zedillo announced that they had unmasked the Zapatista leader, Subcomandante Marcos, believed to be a former professor named Rafael Sebastián Guillén Vicente. Though the government issued an order for his arrest, the army failed to apprehend Marcos, and the Mexican government renewed talks with the Zapatistas in September of that year.

After five months of negotiations, the two sides agreed to the San Andrés Accord on Indigenous Culture and Rights, an agreement that acknowledged the need for the right of self-determination, territorial autonomy, and recognition of customary laws of indigenous peoples. In December 1996, the CO-COPA, together with a congressional commission, drafted a bill to incorporate key elements of the San Andrés Accord into new legislation. Initially, the Zapatistas agreed to the new drafts, but became disillusioned when Congress dragged its feet on recognizing indigenous autonomy and customary laws and insisted on amending the proposal. The EZLN rejected the subsequent draft and broke off all negotiations with the government. Neither side appeared willing to back down from its demands or reinitiate the peace process until December 1997, when government-supported paramilitary forces killed forty-five Zapatista supporters at a prayer meeting in the village of Acteal. Domestic and international pressure forced the resignations of the governor and the minister of the interior and compelled the Zedillo administration to introduce a watered down version of the COCOPA legislation in the Senate in March 1998. The initiative went nowhere and talks did not resume again until three years later.

In early 2001, Vicente Fox extended an olive branch by removing some military installations in Chiapas and reintroducing the original (1996) CO-COPA bill in the Senate. For their part, the Zapatistas organized a march to Mexico City to rally popular support and demonstrate their willingness to negotiate with the new administration. The Zapatour elicited an outpouring of public support and EZLN representatives were invited to present their case to the legislature. Subsequent negotiations produced a constitutional amendment that recognized the rights of indigenous peoples, but did not ensure protection for self-government, collective land rights, control of natural resources, customary law, or collective legal rights.[61] Therefore, although the Fox administration claimed that it had successfully solved the

Chiapas "problem," the Zapatistas and many indigenous peoples felt that the new legislation was largely symbolic.

Since 2001, the Zapatistas have remained largely silent. Their followers, about 20,000 people, live in self-governed communities in Chiapas. They do not allow police or government officials to enter the land, but they are closely monitored by the Mexican army. Periodically Subcomandante Marcos has issued statements, usually condemning local and national politicians and the political process more generally. In late 2005 he again lashed out against all three political parties, but singled out the PRD for its harshest criticism. Dismissing the PRD's previous show of support and solidarity, Marcos called the party "the left hand of the right" and its presidential candidate, Andrés Manuel López Obrador, a traitor to the goals of the true left. In January 2006, the Zapatistas emerged from their communities unarmed in order to launch a six-month peaceful tour of the country. The purpose of the campaign was to design a new political order from the ground up by meeting with ordinary people and leftists who are similarly disillusioned with the formal political system. To date, it is not clear what kind of political alternative this move-ment offers since Marcos has stated that it will not field candidates in local and national elections. Instead, Subcomandante Marcos, who, beginning in 2006, asked to be called "Delegate Zero," said his aim is to reiterate the nega-tive effects of free trade and capitalism and the need for democracy and social justice. Others claim that the tour was an effort to shore up popular support so that the rebel group would have more negotiating power with the new Calderón administration. So far this has not matrialized.

Although most social and guerrilla movements have been unsuccessful at achieving many of their goals, their activities and continual presence during the past decade have had the effect of raising awareness about the plight of Mexico's indigenous peoples. Additionally, the government has made address-ing poverty in indigenous regions a higher priority. Both the Zedillo and Fox administrations increased public spending on infrastructure, education, and other basic services in Chiapas and other states with large indigenous popula-tions. And while increased funds have not, by themselves, gone far to address the underlying causes of many of the problems that prompted the Zapatista rebellion, they have improved the quality of life of some indigenous com-munities. Moreover, for many, they are a formal acknowledgment that the government systematically neglected Mexican indigenous people during the twentieth century.

National legislative reform has been slow and difficult, and ultimately disappointing for many involved. As noted above, the laws passed by the Mexican Congress in 2001 were a far cry from the more progressive pro-posals drafted by the COCOPA. However, there has been some success at the state level. For example, in the mid-1990s, the state of Oaxaca, which has been at the forefront of establishing and protecting indigenous rights, enacted reforms that guarantee the ability of indigenous communities to govern themselves using "customary practices" or *usos y costumbres*. These practices have their roots in pre-Hispanic and colonial times and allow communities to choose their leaders in an assembly and to use common-law judicial norms for conflict resolution.[62] Currently the state of Oaxaca allows 418 municipalities to use these practices, and they greatly enhance indigenous autonomy.[63] Although some other states also recognize customary practices as legitimate and necessary, none has the legal framework established in Oaxaca.

Conclusion

All three of the groups discussed in this chapter made important inroads into the political sphere in the twentieth century. Of the three, organized labor was clearly the most successfully represented in the postrevolutionary political system. Obviously not all in the working class benefited from the system, since the PRI rewarded only those willing to play by its rules and support it unconditionally, but the corporatist arrangement between the state and organized labor gave Mexican workers access to jobs and benefits that they otherwise may not have had. In return, labor became one of the PRI's most important pillars of political support. However, two severe economic crises, the adoption of the neoliberal economic model, and the decline of the PRI during the past two decades have threatened the gains made by all workers, regardless of their union affiliation or lack thereof. Therefore Mexican workers may find that the best strategy for exerting political influence in the twenty-first century is to present a large and united front capable of effectively articulating its interests in an increasingly plural political environment. Without a doubt, democratization is putting pressure on Mexican leaders to reform the outdated corporatist system and begin to level the playing field so that all labor organizations and interest groups have equal access to the political arena. At the same time, it is clear that those same leaders, regardless of partisan affiliation, benefit from keeping the remnants of the corporatist system intact. Thus, the future of state-labor relations is unclear.

For their part, Mexican women and indigenous people must continue to break down barriers and destroy stereotypes that prevail in Mexican society if they are to become equals in politics and in society. Although Mexico is among the Latin American countries with the best representation of females in government, women still constitute a small minority of Mexican politicians. Their underrepresentation is due to a combination of a lack experience, fewer opportunities, and commonly held beliefs among many Mexicans that women are less capable of leading and governing. Moreover, like women everywhere, Mexican women must struggle with personal and societal expectations that they fulfill their responsibilities as wives, mothers, and homemakers, in addition to any career they may choose.

Similar to many women in Mexican society, indigenous people have found formal political institutions unresponsive to their needs and have, out of necessity, opted for different forms of political expression. However, even these efforts have produced only occasional and limited success, and, on the whole, Mexico's indigenous people are severely underrepresented in the formal political system. If Mexico is to deepen its democracy, it must find ways to fully incorporate workers, women, and indigenous people (as well as other groups) in egalitarian and meaningful ways. At the same time, it is incumbent on members of these groups to continue to challenge the status quo and actively participate in the political arena. Without a commitment to individual equality and equal political access, it is difficult to see how pluralism, and indeed democracy, can flourish in Mexico.

Key Terms

candidato suplente

Coalition of Workers, Peasants, and Students of the Isthmus (COCEI)

Commission for Peace and Concordance (COCOPA)

Committee of the Clandestine Indigenous Revolution (CCRI)

CROM

CTM

Delegate Zero

ejidos

Federal Labor Law of 1931

García, Amalia

gender quotas

General Indian Court

Ley Lerdo

machismo

marianismo

mestizos

Mexican Feminist Council (CFM)

Moreno, María de los Ángeles

Morones, Luis N.

National Peasant Confederation (CNC)

National Teachers Union (SNTE)

National Women's Institute (INMUN)

San Andrés Accords

Sauri, Dulce María

soldaderas

Sole Front for Women's Rights (FUPDM)

Subcomandante Marcos

Toledano, Lombardo

usos y costumbres

Velázquez, Fidel

Zapatista Army of National Liberation (EZLN)

Recommended Readings

Labor

Middlebrook, Kevin J. *The Paradox of Revolution: Labor, the State, and Authoritarianism in Mexico.* Baltimore: Johns Hopkins University Press, 1995.

Women in Mexico

Bennett, Vivienne. *The Politics of Water: Urban Protest, Gender, and Power in Monterrey, Mexico.* Pittsburgh: University of Pittsburgh Press, 1995.
Rodríguez, Victoria. *Women in Contemporary Mexican Politics.* Austin: University of Texas Press, 2003.

Indigenous People and the Zapatistas

Collier, George, with Elizabeth Lowery Quaratiello. *Basta! Land and the Zapatista Rebellion in Chiapas.* Oakland, Calif.: Institute for Food and Development Policy, 1994.
Harvey, Neil. *The Chiapas Rebellion: The Struggle for Land and Democracy.* Durham, N.C.: Duke University Press, 1998.
Rubin, Jeffrey. *Decentering the Regime: Ethnicity, Radicalism, and Democracy in Juchitán, Mexico.* Durham, N.C.: Duke University Press, 1997.
Weinberg, Bill. *Homage to Chiapas: The New Indigenous Struggles in Mexico.* New York: Verso, 2000.

Notes

1. Article 123 also established workplace conditions, overtime pay, health and safety standards, educational facilities for workers, work contracts, and labor conciliation and arbitration boards. See Kevin J. Middlebrook, *The Paradox of Revolution: Labor, the State, and Authoritarianism in Mexico* (Baltimore: Johns Hopkins University Press, 1995), 47.

2. Control over labor unions was considered essential not only for general political stability but also for promoting the government's economic model. See chapter 9.

3. Middlebrook, *Paradox of Revolution*, 51–55.

4. This discussion is not meant to imply that all workers or unions were quiescent. In a number of instances labor in particular industries challenged state-labor relations, with differing results. For example, in the 1970s, automobile industry unions fought for and won greater internal democracy and autonomy from the CTM.

5. This discussion draws on Middlebrook, *Paradox of Revolution*, chap. 3.

6. Middlebrook, *Paradox of Revolution*, 256.

7. Once President de la Madrid's choice of successor was made clear, several prominent labor leaders committed the unpardonable sin of backing PRI renegade Cuauhtémoc Cárdenas. See Middlebrook, *Paradox of Revolution*, 293.

8. Middlebrook, *Paradox of Revolution*, 295–96.

9. Graciela Bensusán, "A New Scenario for Mexican Trade Unions: Changes in the Structure of Political and Economic Opportunities," in Middlebrook, ed., *Dilemmas of Political Change in Mexico*, 248–50.

10. Neither the PAN nor the PRD has established a strong link to organized labor in the wake of the PRI's decline.

11. Bensusán, "New Scenario," 254–55.

12. Cited in Carmen Ramos Escandón, "Women and Power in Mexico: The Forgotten Heritage, 1880–1954," in *Women's Participation in Mexican Political Life*, ed. Victoria Rodríguez (Boulder: Westview, 1998), 89.

13. INMUN, *Cuarto informe de labores, 2004–2005*, 15.

14. INMUN, *Quinto informe de labores, 2005–2006*, 39.

15. INEGI, "Población de 15 años y mas y porcentaje de la misma que es alfabeta por entidad federative según sexo, 2000."

16. Michael Meyer, William Sherman, and Susan Deeds, *The Course of Mexican History*. 7th ed. (New York: Oxford Press, 2003), 533.

17. Ramos Escandón, "Women and Power in Mexico," 92.

18. This discussion draws on the work of Victoria Rodríguez, *Women in Contemporary Mexican Politics* (Austin: University of Texas Press, 2003), 98–101.

19. Ruíz Cortines's close friendship with a prominent feminist, Amalia Caballero de Castillo Ledón, convinced him to support female participation in all aspects of the political system.

20. Rodríguez, *Women in Contemporary Mexican Politics*, 104.

21. Lamas, cited in Rodríguez, *Women in Contemporary Mexican Politics*, 104.

22. In Rodríguez's words, "The 'woman' question of yesteryear is now a part of the organizational and official discourse." Rodríguez, *Women in Contemporary Mexican Politics*, 110.

23. The bill passed 46 to 19, with the opposition coming mainly from members of the PAN. Yet despite the overwhelming margin of victory, the bill sparked national and international opposition and condemnation. James McKinley Jr., "Mexico City Legalizes Abortion Early in Term," *New York Times*, April 24, 2007.

24. Gender quotas are not uncontroversial. Supporters argue that they are the only way to give women opportunities they deserve. Detractors argue that they are discriminatory and unnecessary. See Rodríguez, *Women in Contemporary Mexican Politics*, 178–84.

25. INMUN, *Cuarto informe de labores,* table 1.11, p. 58.

26. Kathleen Bruhn, "Whores and Lesbians: Political Activism, Party Strategies, and Gender Quotas in Mexico," in *Electoral Studies* 22, no. 1 (2003): 101–19.

27. Bruhn argues that the PRD adopted the quota, in part, because of the pressure of women activists within the party. See "Whores and Lesbians."

28. Robles was chosen to take over for Cuauhtémoc Cárdenas when he left the position to launch his presidential campaign in 1999.

29. Roderic Camp, "Women and Men, Men and Women: Gender Patterns in Mexican Politics," in *Women's Participation in Mexican Political Life*, ed. Victoria Rodríguez (Boulder: Westview, 1998), 184–85.

30. Rodríguez, *Women in Contemporary Mexican Politics*, 182.

31. Although more women may have run for office in 2000 and 2003, the majority of them were designated alternates. In Mujeres, *Cuarto informe*, table 1.11, p. 58. See also Bruhn, "Whores and Lesbians."

32. Rodríguez, *Women in Contemporary Mexican Politics*, 145.

33. Camp, "Women and Men, Men and Women," 168.

34. In Mujeres, *Cuarto informe*, 60.

35. Women have been somewhat successful in mid- and low-level administrative positions in all three branches of government. Yet given that promotions in Mexico have traditionally been based on connections and loyalty rather than merit, women have rarely advanced through the ranks of the executive's bureaucracy to assume influential posts.

36. It is important to note, however, that in a number of states and in the Federal District, women regularly made up between 20 and 30 percent of the local legislatures. INMUN, *Cuarto informe*, 59; *Quinto informe*, 41.

37. Mayors and city council members are elected on a single party slate. The party determines both who is eligible to run as a candidate and where she is ranked on the list. INMUN, *Quinto informe de labores*, 40.

38. INMUN, *Cuarto informe*, 62.

39. Vivienne Bennett, "Everyday Struggles: Women in Urban Popular Movements and Territorially Based Protests in Mexico," in *Women's Participation*, 117.

40. Vivienne Bennett skillfully recounts the events leading up to this victory in *The Politics of Water: Urban Protest, Gender, and Power in Monterrey, Mexico* (Pittsburgh: University of Pittsburgh Press, 1995).

41. From inception, women who participated in these groups outnumbered men, yet the latter almost always occupied leadership positions. This dynamic began to change in the 1980s, when women began to assume leadership roles of their own organizations. See Bennett, "Everyday Struggles," 123.

42. The most widely spoken indigenous languages are Náhuatl, Maya, Zapoteco, Mixteco, Tzotzil, Otomí, and Tzetzal.

43. INEGI, "Estadísticas a propósito del día internacional de las poblaciones indígenas, datos nacionales," www.inegi.gob.mx (accessed February 4, 2006).

44. National Commission for the Development of Indigenous Peoples (CDI), www.cdi.gob.mx/indicadores (accessed February 7, 2006).

45. There are significant differences in literacy and education levels by geographic region, urban-rural communities, and between men and women. INEGI, "Estadística a propósito del día internacional de las poblaciones indígenas," 5–6.

46. Indigenous people are scorned because they constitute the largest and most visible minority group in Mexico, but they are by no means the only ones subject to racism. Negative attitudes toward people of African, Lebanese, Asian, Gypsy, and Jewish descent are also prevalent.

47. Slang words for stupidity, tackiness, and low class are commonly derived from words that refer to indigenous people.

48. Meyer et al., *Course of Mexican History*, 200.

49. Lynn Foster, *A Brief History of Mexico* (New York: Checkmark, 2004), 134.

50. Jose Vasconcelos, a Mexican intellectual, argued that miscegenation would lead to the creation of a superior "cosmic race."

51. This was also the case in U.S. attempts to "assimilate" Native American peoples. See Vine Deloria and Clifford M. Lytle, "American Indians in Historical Perspective," in *American Indians, American Justice* (Austin: University of Texas, 1983); and Stephen Cornell, "They Carry Their Lives . . .," in *Return of the Native* (New York: Oxford University Press, 1988).

52. Meyer et al., *Course of Mexican History*, 576.

53. The power of the CNC declined due to a combination of factors, among them the desire to protect private property and the economic crisis of the 1980s.

54. The government also used these leaders in order to pit indigenous communities against one another by selectively providing resources to some and not others. As a result, vicious rivalries among ethnically similar communities persist to this day.

55. The ineffective, corrupt practices of the CNC also prompted peasants to organize independent agrarian unions to press for land redistribution. See Neil Harvey, "Peasant Strategies and Corporatism in Chiapas," in Joe Foweraker and Ann Craig, eds., *Popular Movements and Political Change in Mexico* (Boulder: Lynne Rienner, 1990).

56. A number of excellent books analyze the Zapatista uprising: George Collier, with Elizabeth Lowery Quaratiello, *Basta! Land and the Zapatista Rebellion in Chiapas* (Oakland, Calif.: Institute for Food and Development Policy, 1994); Neil Harvey, *The Chiapas Rebellion: The Struggle for Land and Democracy* (Durham, N.C.: Duke University Press, 1998); and Andres Oppenheimer, *Bordering on Chaos: Mexico's Roller-Coaster Journey toward Prosperity* (New York: Little, Brown, 1996).

57. Although the EZLN was organized by well-educated mestizos from Mexico City (most notably Subcomandante Marcos), its leadership and base, not to mention its goals, are drawn primarily from Mayan communities in Chiapas.

58. Article 27 of the Mexican constitution provided for land reform and established and protected peasants' access to *ejidos*, or communally owned lands. After the Salinas administration's 1992 reform of Article 27 in search of greater efficiency and productivity in the agricultural sector, these lands could be privatized and commercialized. Indigenous people bore the brunt, since *ejidos* constituted roughly 60 percent of the land in indigenous communities and were vulnerable to pressure to sell their property.

59. Cited in Rodolfo Stavenhagen, "Mexico's Unfinished Symphony: The Zapatista Movement," in Joseph Tulchin and Andrew Selee, eds., *Mexico's Politics and Society in Transition* (Boulder: Lynne Rienner, 2003), 112.

60. The EZLN was not the first indigenous effort at resistance in Chiapas. Bill Weinberg, *Homage to Chiapas: The New Indigenous Struggles in Mexico* (New York: Verso, 2000).

61. Luis Hernández and Laura Carlsen, "Indigenous Rights: The Battle for Constitutional Reform in Mexico," in Middlebrook, ed., *Dilemmas of Political Change*, 451–52.

62. This custom is also called the cargo system. Hernández and Carlsen, "Indigenous Rights," 443.

63. However, it should be noted that the use of *usos y costumbres* is not without its problems. For some shortcomings, see Hernández and Carlsen, "Indigenous Rights," 447. See also Laura Carlsen, "Autonomía indígena y usos y costumbres: La innovación de la tradición," *Chiapas* 7 (1999), www.ezln.org/revistachiapas/No7/ch7carlsen.html (accessed January 23, 2006).

III

KEY DOMESTIC POLICY ISSUES

9

Mexico's Political Economy

Mexican Economic Development

Many people in the United States are unaware that Mexico has the world's twelfth largest economy. Nor do they typically realize that the Mexican economy has long been considered among the strongest and most successful in the developing world: between 1940 and 1970, it grew at an average annual rate of over 6 percent.[1] Indeed, Mexico benefits from tremendous natural wealth, major manufacturing zones, and cosmopolitan cities with highly sophisticated centers of art and culture. Yet paradoxically, for all of its success, Mexico's progress was impeded by deep and recurring economic crises in the 1970s, 1980s, and 1990s, further exacerbating long-standing problems such as poverty and severe income inequality. That economic modernity and widespread endemic poverty coexist, often within the space of a city block, is one of Mexico's greatest inconsistencies. Understandably, such problems are what contributes to our frequent misperceptions of Mexico as an economically backward country. Most important, these issues raise the question of why Mexico's periods of economic success have not been sustainable, and why prosperity has failed to penetrate all segments of society.

In this chapter, we address these issues first by examining the various models used to promote economic growth and development. In this chapter we emphasize that these economic models' inherent characteristics often contributed as much to income inequality as they did to raising living standards. We will also explain why Mexico has repeatedly enjoyed periods of incredible economic growth only to be followed by devastating crises, and comment on the challenges the country faces in pursuing a sound economic future.

Models of Development

In a broad sense, Mexico's trajectory of economic development followed global shifts occurring in the nineteenth and twentieth centuries (see figure 9.1). Mexico's economic development is therefore similar to that of many Western countries, especially in Latin America. At different times between independence and the current era, Mexico has embraced varied levels of state involvement in the national economy. From the colonial period until the late 1870s, Mexico's economy was, like most of Europe's, mercantilist in orientation, in which first the Crown and later the Mexican government had a high level of involvement in economic transactions. During the Porfiriato, the country again followed Europe's lead and embraced a liberal economic approach that emphasized the importance of free trade and foreign direct investment. In the 1940s, Mexico, like many developing countries, adopted import substitution industrialization (ISI), an inwardly focused state-led plan designed to insulate the national economy from the pressures of the global market during the Great Depression. In the wake of the debt crisis of the 1980s, Mexico later adopted a liberal approach that once again called for reducing the role of the government in the economy by promoting fiscal austerity, privatization, and free trade. Mexico's shift toward neoliberalism coincided with the worldwide trend toward greater globalization and economic integration. Thus today, as in the past, Mexico's economic model is as much a product of global incentives and pressures as it is reflective of an independent choice made by its leaders.

Early Historical Development: Mercantilism and Porfirian Liberalism

Mexico's early economic history was dramatically shaped by the legacies of colonial mercantilism. Mercantilism was characterized by the extraction of natural resources for the benefit of the Spanish Crown, severe restrictions on trade, and the resulting development of a dependent relationship in relation to the mother country. After independence in 1821, Mexico suffered the withdrawal symptoms of its political and economic separation from Spain. In this context, economic and political instability became mutually reinforcing, as government budget deficits, enormous foreign debt burdens, and severe

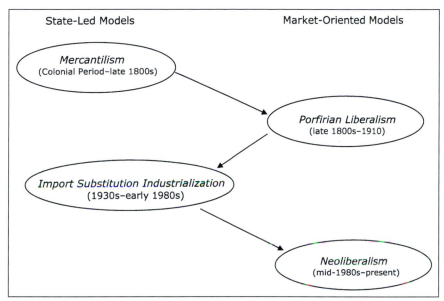

State-Led Models | Market-Oriented Models

Mercantilism
(Colonial Period–late 1800s)

Porfirian Liberalism
(late 1800s–1910)

Import Substitution Industrialization
(1930s–early 1980s)

Neoliberalism
(mid-1980s–present)

FIGURE 9.1 Mexico's Economic Models

currency instability contributed to half a century of political conflict, foreign military interventions, and armed uprisings. In this context, the lack of political stability and government funds made it difficult to invest in the infrastructure needed to develop the Mexican economy.

The long period of political stability generated by the dictatorship of Porfirio Díaz (1876–1910) finally enabled Mexico to achieve significant economic progress. Díaz's undisputed political authority and ability to impose order allowed his regime to employ a multipronged strategy that combined protectionism with massive amounts of foreign investment and the development of critical infrastructure to promote economic development in Mexico. At the same time, the export-oriented economic model that was in place at the turn of the century reified and exacerbated income inequality, and thereby helped sow many of the seeds that would erupt in Mexico's revolution in 1910. Mexico's export-oriented model of economic development was based primarily on the domestic production of agricultural goods (e.g., henequen, wood, hides, coffee, cattle, cotton, sugar, vanilla) and precious and industrial metals (e.g., gold, silver, copper, zinc, graphite, lead, antimony) for export to other countries.[2]

The Díaz regime introduced the export-oriented model using a combination of economic policy tools. First, it imposed high protective tariffs (ranging from 50 to 200 percent of product value) on foreign goods entering the country. This made imports more expensive and therefore less attractive to Mexican consumers. He also adopted the silver standard, pegging the peso to silver, which helped (at least in the short term) to stabilize the Mexican currency. Together these measures—tariffs and a stable currency—gave domestic entrepreneurs incentives to offer competitively priced, locally produced goods and therefore encourage the formation of domestic industries. Although Mexicans began to invest more in the domestic economy, their role in promoting economic growth and development paled in comparison to that played by foreigners. Díaz encouraged a flood of foreign investment into the Mexican economy by eliminating obstacles (e.g., taxes, extraction fees, export duties) and creating incentives for foreigners to finance Mexico's economic growth.[3] In less than twenty years, Mexico watched foreign investment increase from 100 million pesos in 1884 to 3.4 billion in 1911.[4]

However, the Porifirian economic model presented several important problems for Mexican society. First, although the Mexican economy was much larger and more productive in 1910 than it had been thirty years earlier, it was still highly dependent on the ebbs and flows of the international economy. Since foreign capital played such an integral role in the country's economy, it was extremely vulnerable to events that would prompt foreign investors to remove their money. While much of the foreign investment was fixed and therefore could not easily be removed (e.g., real estate and infrastructure), it was nevertheless possible and relatively easy for foreigners to withdraw existing or withhold future funding with little or now warning. Additionally, as an export-based economy, Mexico was highly vulnerable to the drop in prices of its goods. This reinforced the country's vulnerability to economic downturns, which often happened virtually overnight. Mexico learned firsthand the extent of its vulnerability when a worldwide economic downturn that began in 1907 reduced demand for Mexican products. The problem was exacerbated by a related drop in the price of important commodities like silver, and soon Mexico found its export earnings drastically reduced.

As a result of these trends and heavy infrastructure investment, Mexico's foreign debt grew tremendously during the Porfiriato, more than doubling from 193 million pesos in 1896 to nearly 590 million pesos in 1911.[5] Reduced export earnings and impending loan payments to foreign banks put an enormous amount of pressure on the Díaz regime to find an alternative source of revenue. The solution was to raise taxes on the middle class—a measure that was met with considerable dissatisfaction and did relatively little to resolve the country's financial problems.

Further complicating Mexico's economic situation was the fact that the influx of foreign capital had an inflationary effect on the domestic economy.

Indeed, the cost of living steadily increased but wages and economic opportunities did not keep pace with inflation. Despite record economic growth, overall real wages in Mexico therefore actually fell 25 percent between 1898 and 1911. The drop in real wages was steepest for agricultural workers who made up two-thirds of the workforce. Additionally, by 1910 fewer Mexicans had access to private or communal property than at any other time in the country's history. Instead, most of the peasantry was forced into debt peonage on large haciendas that produced food and other agricultural products mainly for export rather than foodstuffs for domestic consumption.[6] Thus despite all of the contributions that the export-oriented economic model of the Porfiriato made toward Mexican economic development, it also had a deleterious effect on the quality of life of the average Mexican, maintaining and exacerbating poverty, high rates of illiteracy, widespread malnourishment, and low life expectancies. Without a doubt, the severe economic inequality of the Porfirian system contributed to the discontent that fueled the Mexican revolution, which ultimately gave way to an entirely different approach to managing the economy.

Economic Nationalism and State-Led Growth

The Mexican revolution slowed growth and development for almost thirty years. The country's capacity for production was severely hampered by the reduction in the size of the population (about 1 of 15 died) and many of the nation's industries and much of its infrastructure were largely destroyed during the multi-year conflict. Political unrest had also frightened foreign investors and therefore significantly reduced Mexico's most substantial source of capital. Therefore the first two decades following the Mexican revolution presented serious economic difficulties for the country. As political stability began to develop in the late 1920s, the Great Depression hit. The global economic crisis had dramatic effects on Mexico: exports decreased drastically as demand for Mexican goods dropped, foreign capital (which had started to return) once again dried up, and as a result, Mexico's GDP declined to its lowest levels in twenty years. Of course, these events had serious consequences for the lives of ordinary Mexicans: lack of capital meant that job opportunities were scarce, government services were virtually nonexistent, and labor and social unrest were rampant. Therefore, when Lázaro Cárdenas assumed the presidency in 1934, he faced several formidable economic, as well as political, challenges.

Many of Cárdenas's most significant economic policies (e.g., redistribution of land, expropriation of petroleum) were inextricably linked to his efforts to bring about greater distribution of resources and economic nationalism at the expense of foreign investors and the domestic private sector. But Mexico's shift to a more inwardly oriented economic model was also the result of external factors over which it had no control. More specifically, with the outbreak of World War II in 1939 and subsequent U.S. involvement in 1941, Mexico began to experience a "natural" shift in trade patterns. As Europe and the United States focused on war making, they had fewer economic and human resources for the production of food, textiles, and materiel. Consequently the demand for Mexican exports increased substantially and helped revive levels of economic growth not seen since the Porfiriato. At the same time, Mexico had to find a way to acquire the vast array of finished manufactured goods that it normally imported from countries that were at war. This necessity prompted the development of domestic industries to produce Mexican substitutes for value-added manufactured products as diverse as industrial metals, machinery, consumer goods, and furniture. This practice of substituting domestically produced products for goods that were formerly imported is known as import substitution industrialization (ISI) (see textbox 9.1). ISI became Mexico's principal economic development strategy—one that would be used for roughly forty years and produce both astounding economic growth and devastating economic and social failures.[7]

Textbox 9.1. ISI: A Cure for Underdevelopment?

The reorientation of Mexico's economy in the 1930s and 1940s from an export-based model to one that promoted domestic industrialization was influenced in no small measure by world events such as the Great Depression and World War II. However, the decision to deepen ISI in the 1950s and 1960s was also influenced by prevailing wisdom in the region about the nature of Latin American "underdevelopment." A number of Latin American economists and intellectuals advocated ISI as a method of promoting development: an outcome that had never materialized with export-oriented economic models. They argued that only by establishing domestic industries capable of producing manufactured goods demanded by local consumers, and diversifying their economies, would developing countries be able to break out of their dependency on industrialized countries.

These dependency theorists claimed that Mexico's (and other Latin American countries') lack of development was the direct result of being exploited by the core—industrialized countries like the United States, which purchased raw materials at relatively low prices and used them for the manufacture of finished goods that they then sold back at a premium to countries like Mexico. Thus a dual dependency was created: the developing country depended on the industrialized country as a market for its raw materials, but it similarly depended on it for value-added imports that it could not produce at home. If Latin American countries developed their own industries, they would diversify their economies, become more productive, reduce their vulnerability to price drops in export commodities, and be less dependent on the core for their economic survival.

ISI helped many developing countries achieve many of these goals for a time. However, the model required the use of expensive technology, high trade barriers (e.g., tariffs, export subsidies, industrial incentives), loose monetary policy, and tax breaks (for domestic producers), all of which required an extraordinary amount of capital from the government. Had the model sustained the momentum it produced in the early phase of its implementation, the resulting economic growth might have offset the dislocations that occur after prolonged use of such expensive policy tools. Unfortunately for Mexico and much of Latin America, the model became exhausted once the relatively small domestic markets were saturated with manufactured goods, and economic growth was no longer sufficient to underwrite further investment in the enterprise. Latin American countries had few options because local products could not compete on international markets (high levels of protectionism drastically reduced the competition needed to improve their quality and lower their price abroad) and the price of many of their export commodities was variable. In order to avoid a larger economic crisis, most countries in the region chose to deepen ISI, or focus on the production of different, generally more durable industrial goods. Yet this move required even more capital and led to a frenzy of borrowing from international lending institutions. While debt financing can be a good strategy for promoting economic growth and development, the inherent flaws of ISI combined with high levels of government spending on wages, social programs, and public services, as well as several external factors such as the oil shocks and the global recession of the 1970s that brought with it higher interest rates, came together to undermine many of the economic gains that ISI had brought to Latin America.

As mentioned earlier, between 1940 and 1970, Mexico enjoyed an average increase in GDP of over 6 percent. This period of incredible growth and development is known as the Mexican Miracle and is even today an enviable accomplishment for any country. How was Mexico able to produce such miraculous economic success? Without a doubt, much of the explanation lies in a decision by the Mexican government to reinforce its new economic approach and promote industrialization.

The adoption of ISI in the 1940s marked the beginning of Mexico's industrialization process. Before that time, the economy was almost exclusively based on the extraction and production of raw materials. The ISI model required a significant amount of involvement by the state, which provided much of the necessary investment capital for developing domestic industries from scratch. President Manuel Ávila Camacho (1940–1946) and his successors made a concerted effort to promote industrialization using these policy tools not just because it represented a promising strategy for Mexican economic growth and development, but also because it was an important step toward establishing the performance legitimacy, or popular support based on solid economic gains, of the ruling party, and thereby consolidating its political dominance.

The implementation of ISI faced some early challenges when, for example, World War II ended and the demand for Mexico's exports dropped, while the demand for imports rose simultaneously—often to supplement domestic industries with foreign intermediate goods. In response to this crisis, the presidential administration of Miguel Alemán Valdés (1946–1952) worked to sustain this new formula for economic development by developing policies to ensure continued ISI. This formula involved several related elements: the development of state-owned enterprises in heavy industry (e.g., oil and petrochemicals, steel, automobiles); increased governmental expenditures on much-needed infrastructure (e.g., roads, communications, ports, dams, irrigation) to further promote domestic development; higher import restrictions (e.g., tariffs, quotas) on finished consumer goods to make them less competitive with domestically produced alternatives; reduced import restrictions on intermediate and capital goods to supplement domestic industrial production; and, counterintuitively, foreign direct investment (FDI) in important economic sectors.

Investment was a critically important aspect of Mexico's ISI model because it introduced much needed capital and made available cutting-edge technology and professional training that otherwise would have been absent. However, unlike FDI in the Porfirian era, investment encouraged under ISI was highly regulated by the state. For example, the government required that transnational companies operating in Mexico use locally produced inputs, train workers and managers, and transfer critical technologies to local industries. Moreover, foreign firms were prohibited from wholly owning production facilities and operations in Mexico. This policy, described as Mexicanization, required a majority of local ownership. Despite such unfavorable terms, many foreign companies continued to invest in Mexico because it was the only way to have access to the domestic market without the high tariffs placed on imported goods. Furthermore, there were a number of loopholes for getting around local ownership requirements.[8] Another form of FDI that was unique to Mexico's version of ISI was the establishment of the *maquiladora*—or assembly plant—industry along the border with the United States.[9]

Another challenge for the ISI model was that, by the 1950s, rapid economic growth and investment, increased government spending, and loose monetary policy combined to produce high levels of inflation, as the increased availability of money caused prices to rise dramatically. In response, the administration of President Adolfo Ruiz Cortines (1952–1958) moved to stabilize economic development, first by devaluing the peso in 1954 (and pegging the value of the

Mexican currency to the U.S. dollar at a rate of 12.5 pesos to the dollar), and then carefully managing its money supply and government expenditures to maintain that exchange rate.[10] The managed exchange rate required Mexico to significantly tighten its monetary policy, which helped to curb inflation. At the same time, devaluing the peso also spurred tourism and exports, since Mexican goods and services were now more attractive to foreigners.[11] In this way, the government's policy of stabilizing development (*desarrollo estabilizador*) bolstered the ISI model, and enabled Mexico to take advantage of a worldwide period of postwar economic growth and prosperity during the 1950s and 1960s.

However, for all of its success at producing economic growth, Mexico's economic formula had important limitations.[12] For example, while ISI brought important benefits—specialized training, better job opportunities, higher wages, better access to services like health care and education, and improved standards of living—such benefits were generally limited to specific sectors of the economy (e.g., industrialists), individuals and groups (e.g., managers and officially recognized labor unions), and urban areas. In an effort to improve the lot of the masses, the government of Adolfo López Mateos (1958–1964) made a concerted effort to more widely redistribute the proceeds of the miracle. Indeed, the strength of the economy during López Mateos's *sexenio* allowed him to expand the national social security system, initiate health and immunization campaigns, create public housing facilities, improve educational opportunities, and redistribute 30 million acres of land—more than any other president since Lázaro Cárdenas. López Mateos was also the first president to seriously enforce the policy of Mexicanization, either nationalizing or requiring Mexican ownership in several key sectors (including telecommunications, petrochemicals, mining, and automotive inputs). For his efforts to broaden the positive effects of Mexico's economic growth and his nationalist policies, López Mateos is fondly remembered in the country's political memory.

Still, over the course of the 1950s and 1960s, the significant gap between rich and poor continued to grow dramatically, and sluggish growth for middle-income sectors left many dissatisfied with the Mexican miracle. This underlying dissatisfaction, which became manifest during President Gustavo Díaz Ordaz's term (1964–1970), fueled strikes and demonstrations by doctors, insurgent labor unions, and more memorably the 1968 student movement, and was ultimately attributable to the shortcomings of Mexico's economic strategy.[13] By the 1960s, Mexico had passed the supposedly easy phase of ISI, which focused on fostering high-value-added manufactured and consumer goods, using protective tariffs that prevented foreign competition and government subsidies that gave domestic producers a boost. During this phase, however, Mexico's domestic production of industrial and commercial inputs—the backward linkages that support manufacturing—was only weakly developed.

Instead, the government actually encouraged large domestic manufacturers to obtain inputs from abroad, by lowering tariffs on those imports (while protecting finished products).[14] By moving to the more difficult second stage of ISI, Mexico might have developed more midlevel and semiskilled jobs.[15] However, without such opportunities, the Mexican economy was unable to meet the rising expectations of the generation of the 1960s.

At the same time, like the U.S. dollar, Mexico's currency was becoming over-valued—unduly expensive in relation to other currencies—constraining the purchase of Mexican exports abroad. An overvalued currency is a common oc-currence and can be corrected by floating or devaluing the currency to reflect its true value. As noted above, however, from 1954 on Mexico maintained a fixed rate of exchange relative to the dollar, which was itself fixed at a rate of $35 to an ounce of gold (established at Bretton Woods in 1944). By the 1960s, the strength of the dollar was being undermined by large U.S. trade and fiscal deficits; with more dollars circulating in the international economy, the real demand for U.S. currency was lower than the fixed rate of exchange.[16] To address this problem, the United States would need to (1) adjust the value of the dollar to actual levels of demand or (2) dramatically improve its balance of payments by spending less money abroad. That happened in 1971, when the United States opted to do both, breaking from the gold standard and imposing a hefty 10 percent tariff on all U.S. imports.[17] The result was a significant slowdown in the international economy, and a serious blow to Mexico. On the one hand, without the gold standard as an anchor, the initial fluctuations of the dollar affected currencies that were pegged to it (like the peso), creating broader instability and inflation that disproportionately hurt the lower and middle classes. On the other hand, the new tariff on U.S. imports further deteriorated the demand for Mexico's products in the United States (its most important trading partner).[18]

Thus Luis Echeverría's administration (1970–1976) faced the difficult task of restabilizing the economy and finding new ways to promote growth and development. Echeverría's approach combined continued use of many ISI policies, but supplemented it with what he called "shared development" poli-cies such as higher wages for workers and price controls on basic food items like tortillas, beans, and milk; invested in public works like schools, health clinics, a credit program for small farmers, and rural infrastructure; and na-tionalized the important telephone and tobacco industries. Increased govern-ment spending to finance these projects had to come from somewhere, and in the wake of an economic downturn, Echeverría had little choice but to borrow capital from abroad. In the short term, his strategy paid off and economic output nearly matched the heady days of the miracle. However, the president's move to increase the role of the state in the economy and to eliminate some of the subsidies and other privileges formerly extended to industrialists alienated the business class and increasingly they removed their capital from the country—further undermining Mexico's prospects for economic recovery.

When Echeverría left office in 1976, the Mexican economy was in crisis. Federal and trade deficits created a severe imbalance in the budget, two devaluations left the peso at only half its previous value, and inflation was up 30 percent. The IMF had placed stringent restrictions on Mexico, virtually eliminating international loans as a source of much needed capital. Rational investors, both foreign and domestic, had taken their money elsewhere (capital flight), and ordinary Mexicans were facing extraordinary hardship. Even food was in short supply: agricultural production was depressed and Mexico was forced to import basic food products, which further exacerbated its balance of trade problems. Hence it was abundantly clear by the mid-1970s that the miracle was over.

When Echeverría's successor, José López Portillo, took office, he initially adopted a conservative economic outlook. López Portillo's strategy for economic recovery was in line with IMF strictures, including drastic cuts in government spending, floating the peso until it reached a stable rate of exchange, and guarantees to entice investors back to Mexico. Yet, Mexico was soon able to break with such austerity measures when the discovery of vast new petroleum reserves was announced in early 1977. Now Mexico had a chance not only to escape financial crisis but, in López Portillo's terms, chart a new and promising course for the future by "administering abundance." Indeed, with 60 billion barrels in proven reserves and 250 billion in potential reserves, oil paved the way for economic growth that far outstripped levels attained even during 1950s and 1960s: petroleum exports increased exponentially, from $500 million in 1976 to a whopping $13 billion in 1981, and the Mexican economy grew 8 percent annually.[19]

Determined to avoid the inflationary and dislocating effects of petrolization of the economy, the López Portillo administration implemented a gradual approach that called for a moderated pace of extraction and export. The intention was to use oil proceeds to finance further industrialization—a move that would simultaneously ensure that Mexico not become overly dependent on oil exports, and would provide a solid industrial foundation and diverse economy capable of fueling Mexico's development in the long term. To that end, the Industrial Development Plan was launched in 1979. Continuing the ISI model, its aim was to use tax breaks, subsidies, and energy discounts to encourage the creation of eleven new industrial zones that concentrated on the production of expensive inputs such as steel, petrochemicals, machinery, and capital goods, and thus eliminate the need to import them from abroad. It was believed that the industrialization project would also allow the government to address some of the country's most pressing social issues by producing enough jobs to absorb Mexico's burgeoning population and providing resources to be used in promoting rural development.

Given the ambitiousness of these goals, Mexico required more capital than the country actually had on hand.[20] Yet this was not a problem thanks to the high price of oil, Mexico's seemingly endless supply of petroleum reserves, and the eagerness of private banks and international lending agencies such as the World Bank to make loans guaranteed by future oil earnings. For its part, Mexico was eager to borrow because interest rates were very low and it had valuable collateral with which to guarantee its debts.

An unfortunate confluence of national and international factors turned Mexico's dreams of oil wealth into an economic nightmare. Domestically, the oil boom brought millions of new jobs and investment, but rapid economic growth also increased the rate of inflation, which undermined the already limited effects of price controls. Subsidies on basic food items and other cost of living expenses (e.g., housing and public services) increased substantially.[21] Additionally, rampant corruption and mismanagement at all levels of government and the bureaucracy hindered the success of the López Portillo administration's development project, as massive amounts of resources were siphoned off by politicians and bureaucrats or diverted to important political actors lining their own pockets.

Meanwhile, Mexico's balance of payments deficit grew exponentially during the same period because it had borrowed so heavily to jump-start oil and other industries as well as increase investment in development. This situation ultimately led to two significant problems: debt and devaluation. First, Mexico's foreign debt almost tripled, from approximately $30 billion to $80 billion in 1982, or 18 percent of the country's GDP, earning Mexico the dubious distinction of being the world's second-most indebted country (after Brazil). When world interest rates rose and oil prices plummeted in 1981–1982, Mexico's export earnings fell far short of government expectations and the government was forced to borrow even more money abroad to cover the shortfall.[22]

Second, by the early 1980s, the peso had become overvalued as a result of the imbalance of payments. As Mexico attempted to cope with its sudden debt crisis, further borrowing and increased capital flight exacerbated that imbalance. With rapidly dwindling foreign reserves and mushrooming debt, López Portillo initially refused to devalue the peso, vowing that he would defend Mexico's national currency "like a dog." Yet the administration ultimately had little choice but to devalue the currency (twice), causing the peso to lose nearly three-quarters of its value. This severely decreased the already declining purchasing power of ordinary Mexicans, who found it even more difficult to make ends meet.

The devaluations also prompted even greater capital flight as investors, foreign and domestic alike, sought to protect the value of their capital by moving it out of the country. To control the mass exodus of capital, the government froze foreign currency accounts and put strict controls on the amount of currency that could be exchanged, angering the business community—long a supporter of the López Portillo administration. Finally, the devaluations had the effect of increasing the amount owed to foreign creditors who had made most of the loans in dollars. With such a severe economic downturn in a short period of time, it was not long before Mexico simply ran out of dollars. The debt crisis officially began on August 15, 1982, when the Mexican government publicly announced that it would no longer be able to make payments on its debt—a move that sent shock waves through the international financial community, which was faced not just with the prospect of an $80 billion default, but with the much larger threat of a $700 billion mass default if other countries in similar conditions followed suit.[23] Just two weeks later, in his final national address, President López Portillo stated that capital flight was the primary culprit in the crisis and, to eliminate the threat it posed to the future of the country, announced that all private banks would be nationalized. While the bank nationalization was popular among the middle and lower classes who believed that the business class should share responsibility for the crisis, it created a serious rift between the private sector and the PRI regime that would take almost a decade to heal.

When López Portillo assumed the presidency in 1976, he was hailed as the pragmatic and sober influence that was needed to resolve the serious crisis left behind by Luis Echeverría. Yet in 1982, Mexico's economic situation was drastically worse than it had been six years earlier. Economic growth had dropped to zero, inflation was running in the triple digits, and Mexico had no way to begin to repay its multibillion dollar foreign debt. Thus Mexico ushered in what became known as the "lost decade," nearly ten years of economic stagnation.

Neoliberal Reform and Economic Restructuring

López Portillo's successor, Miguel de la Madrid Hurtado (1982–1988), had to find a way out of the mire that left Mexico, once an international darling, now a virtual pariah. De la Madrid's response to the crisis demonstrated his belief in the superiority of a free market or neoliberal economic model for bringing about stability and growth. The neoliberal economic model, which emphasized a laissez-faire approach, was also known as the "Chicago School" economic model or the "Washington Consensus" (see textbox 9.2). De la Madrid's first move was to accept the terms of a rescue package put together by the IMF, which included new loans to enable Mexico to resume payments on its debt. However, the package simply bought the country more time to pay the interest on its previous loans; it did not in any way reduce the total amount that Mexico owed to foreign creditors. In exchange, de la Madrid agreed to implement a series of economic reforms that would first stabilize the economy and then restructure its orientation to promote higher levels of growth.

Textbox 9.2. Neoliberalism

Neoliberalism refers to an economic perspective that advocates a free market approach to economic development, and was believed by some to be a way to promote the emergence of democratic politics. Because it was strongly advocated by economists from the University of Chicago and policy-makers in Washington, D.C., it is also known as the "Chicago School" model or "Washington Consensus" approach. Unlike ISI, which requires high levels of state investment and involvement in the economy, the neoliberal strategy reflects the belief that the government should play a minimal role in the economy. The cornerstones of the neoliberal approach are stabilization, structural adjustment, and trade liberalization.

Stabilization refers overall to tightening the money supply in order to create the conditions necessary for the other two components of neoliberalism. Reducing the money supply generally requires devaluing currency, freezing wages, reducing government spending on wages (i.e., laying off workers) and public services (e.g., health care, education, infrastructure), and making it difficult and expensive to borrow money by tightening credit and raising interest rates. Reducing the money supply has the overall effect of improving the balance of trade and the fiscal deficit by making exports cheaper and imports more expensive.

Structural adjustment is the next step and is aimed at reducing the government's role in the economy. In particular, structural adjustment is meant to shift a wide array of economic activities, such as the distribution of goods and services, from the public to the private sector. In practice it requires that government "privatize" or sell to private investors, services (e.g., health care, education, and utilities) and industries (e.g., energy, banking, telecommunications) that it may once have controlled. The logic here is that the private sector in an open market economy is more efficient and more productive because it must respond to the pressures of competition (both domestic and international). The end result is therefore posited to be more efficient production methods, higher-quality outputs, lower prices for consumers, and greater overall economic stability, since the government no longer has the responsibility to provide services or underwrite industrial development.

Trade liberalization is the final component and means shifting away from protectionism in order to promote trade and attract foreign investment. By reducing (and ideally eliminating) tariffs, subsidies, quotas, and bureaucratic restrictions, governments again curtail their involvement and instead allow the international market to determine the allocation of resources. Countries achieve greater gains from trade by basing the production of exports on their comparative advantage and importing those goods they cannot produce efficiently. Thus exports and foreign investment become the engines of economic growth.

Chief among the reforms was cutting back on public spending to reduce the budget deficit and control inflation. This required the government to lower or even eliminate "unproductive" expenditures such as food subsidies, pensions, and public services. In all, de la Madrid managed to cut government spending by a third, but the budget cuts disproportionately affected the poor and working classes who most relied on public programs. After another devaluation in 1986, the peso again lost nearly half its value and Mexicans had even less purchasing power than before. Equally devastating was the introduction of a new 15 percent value-added tax (VAT) tacked on to nearly all goods. This sales tax, together with increased income taxes, was supposed to add $10 billion to government coffers, but as a flat tax, it marked an additional way that the lower classes were forced to bear the brunt of the crisis. Another of the IMF's conditions for providing emergency loans was that Mexico become more open to international trade. During the ISI era, tariffs and other trade barriers were used with alacrity to insulate domestic producers from the effects of foreign competition. While these protectionist measures fostered the development of domestic industries, they ultimately resulted in inefficient production methods and goods that had difficulty competing on the world market. The new approach called for the Mexican government to reduce trade barriers in order to introduce competition that would result in higher quality goods and greater world demand for Mexican manufactured goods.

The reforms helped bring inflation under control, at least temporarily, but they also led to a recession as real wages and income fell, unemployment rose, the cost of basic food items like tortillas, beans, milk, eggs, and cooking oil increased by roughly 25 percent, and living standards generally declined. Moreover, even when inflation was in check, Mexico was still unable to achieve economic growth. Another drop in oil prices depressed export earnings and domestic industrialists faced difficult and sometimes insurmountable obstacles to competing on the world market, thus leading to a decline in productivity and general economic stagnation. Meanwhile, the government had pledged to spend 53 percent of the federal budget to repay the debt, leaving very little with which to stimulate economic investment and growth. Hence in a sad and ironic twist mirroring the success of the miracle years, the Mexican economy shrank by an average of 6 percent every year between 1982 and the early 1990s.[24]

Rather than reverse course in the face of what was at most a tepid success and at worst the beginning of failure, the de la Madrid administration deepened the use of austerity in an effort to further stabilize the economy and reduced the role of the state in the economy in order to spur economic growth. In addition to larger cuts in public spending, de la Madrid began to sell off many state-owned enterprises to private interests, arguing that the private sec-

tor was much better suited to efficient production. He also signed on to the
General Agreement on Tariffs and Trade (GATT) in 1986 in order to commit
Mexico to reducing its trade barriers and leveling the playing field for foreign
imports. Nevertheless, for all of the economic restructuring that had taken
place, and the sacrifices made by ordinary Mexicans, it appeared that Mexico
had made very little progress by the end of de la Madrid's term: public debt
remained high at 19 percent of GDP, inflation was up again, to 143 percent,
and the Mexican stock market had nearly collapsed in 1987.[25] In other words,
the debt crisis very nearly outlasted the de la Madrid administration.

As de la Madrid's term came to a close in 1988, the memory of severe
economic hardship was still fresh in the minds of most Mexicans who
were appreciably worse off than they had been six years before. Under the
circumstances, it would not have been surprising if de la Madrid's successor had chosen to abandon the neoliberal approach in favor of a radically
different alternative. However, because the country was still beholden to international loans and their conditions, and because the incoming president,
Carlos Salinas de Gortari, was equally committed to neoliberalism, Mexico
stayed the course.

As de la Madrid's minister of budget and planning, Salinas had master-
minded much of the administration's economic policies. Therefore, when he
became president, Salinas had no intention of altering his approach. Instead,
he implemented a strategy designed to encourage long-term investment in
Mexico—a key component of the neoliberal economic model. His first step
in this direction was to initiate talks with commercial banks to make Mexico's
debt burden more manageable. By July 1989, Salinas had succeeded in lowering the country's annual payments and reducing Mexico's debt by $48.5
billion.[26] This achievement, combined with Salinas's reprivatization of the
banks and other industries, went a long way toward restoring confidence in
the private sector.[27] Hence, in the short term these measures spurred capital
repatriation, and in the long term they made it less likely that the country
would again be undermined by massive capital flight.

Meanwhile, on the domestic front, the Economic Solidarity Pact was beginning to bear fruit. The pact was an agreement made by government, labor,
agriculture, and business to work together to promote economic stabilization. The government pledged to further tighten monetary policy and reduce
protectionism but would keep wages fixed. For their part, labor agreed not to
strike for higher wages, and agriculture and business agreed not to raise prices
on their goods and services. The economic pact produced quick and positive results, as inflation declined and GDP began to grow. Soon inflation was
under control, domestic interest rates had decreased, foreign reserves were
higher, and GDP was growing steadily. To most observers, it appeared that

Mexico had returned from the brink of collapse and achieved the impossible: a stable, healthy, and growing economy.

In this context, in August 1990, Salinas announced his intention to pursue what became the most renowned component of his neoliberal project: a free trade agreement with the United States and Canada, known as the North American Free Trade Agreement (NAFTA).[28] The details surrounding NAFTA are discussed in chapter 13; here we note that the treaty was important not only because it gave Mexico the means to attract foreign investment and pursue export-driven growth. It also committed the country to the neoliberal approach, since an international treaty would be very difficult for future administrations to overturn. This institutionalization of free market reforms served to deepen both domestic and international confidence in Mexico, so much so that between 1990 and 1994, Mexico became the second-largest recipient of private investment in the world.

Unfortunately, beginning in 1994, the inflow of foreign capital began to reverse, and by the time Salinas left office later that year, the peso had become grossly overvalued, leading to yet another major devaluation and economic crisis. How could this have happened if presidents de la Madrid and Salinas had taken all the prescribed steps to bring Mexico the stability and growth attributed to the market-based economic reform? The answer is that, in some senses, the neoliberal policies worked too well and were not properly managed. That is, Salinas's confidence-boosting measures encouraged a huge influx of foreign capital investment, which offset once persistent trade imbalances, increased Mexico's foreign reserves, and helped curb inflation. The government tried to sustain that investment, and the peso's value, by selling short-term, dollar-denominated treasury bonds called *tesobonos*, which paid a high rate of interest to investors. The drawback was that keeping investment in Mexico became more difficult over time, especially as a series of domestic and international events led to the gradual withdrawal of foreign capital over the course of 1994. That year, an increase in U.S. interest rates, the Zapatista uprising, and several high-profile political assassinations led investors to pull their money out of Mexico. The withdrawal of foreign capital caused Mexico's foreign reserves to dwindle, naturally contributing to an overvalued peso, and pressure to adjust the value of the currency to actual market demand. Ironically, Salinas had refused to devalue the peso because he was afraid it would spark further capital flight, and destroy all of the confidence in Mexico's economy that he had worked so hard to build. These were unacceptable risks in 1994, since the U.S. Congress was heatedly debating whether or not to ratify NAFTA—Salinas's crowning achievement. Also, devaluation would bring about more economic hardship for Mexicans, something Salinas found unacceptable in an election year (see textbox 9.3).

Therefore, the Salinas administration refused to accept the economic and political risks of devaluation and in so doing, virtually guaranteed that Mexico's next economic crisis would be worse than those that had come before.

Textbox 9.3. Backlash against the Washington Consensus

The triumvirate of stabilization, structural adjustment, and trade liberalization was adopted throughout Latin America in the aftermath of the debt crisis and acquired the moniker "Washington Consensus" because it formed the foundation for conditions required by U.S.-based banks and private lending institutions for loans. Countries in need of loans to offset problems with the trade balance, shortfalls in foreign reserves, and unstable currencies had little choice but to implement fiscal austerity, reduce state involvement in the economy, and lower trade barriers. And while in many cases these policies did help promote stability and growth, they also made life very difficult for the middle and lower classes, since neoliberal policies substantially increase the cost of living (with higher prices, lower wages, and more unemployment), drastically reduce public services and programs on which these classes disproportionately depend, and displace workers in many sectors of the economy. Thus the Washington Consensus was blamed for causing severe economic hardship for the vast majority of Latin Americans. Not surprisingly, politicians, especially those on the left side of the political spectrum, were quick to capitalize on the growing opposition to policies that "forced the poor to repay the sins of the rich." Indeed, many attribute the recent wave of leftist electoral victories in places like Argentina, Brazil, Chile, Uruguay, Bolivia, and Venezuela to the backlash caused by the region's adoption of neoliberalism in the 1990s.

Less than three weeks after assuming the presidency, Ernesto Zedillo was forced to devalue the peso or face economic collapse. In just two weeks, the peso lost 30 percent of its value and the value of the Mexican stock market was cut in half. Foreign reserves dropped by $4 billion and Mexico once again found itself on the verge of economic collapse. The Zedillo administration, still wet behind the ears, exacerbated the situation by not sending clear signals about the course of action it intended to pursue, and thus creating even greater instability. Much of this was precipitated by the circumstances surrounding Zedillo's selection as Salinas's successor: as a distant second choice, and indeed the only viable choice after the assassination of Luis Donaldo Colosio, Zedillo was widely perceived as a weak leader with neither the authority nor political acumen to govern. This led all influential groups both within and outside the PRI to try to apply pressure to the administration for specific policies that would protect their interests.

However, Zedillo chose to stick with the neoliberal approach of his predecessors, not just because he too was a U.S.-trained technocrat, but also because this assured Mexico assistance from the United States. The Clinton administration, together with the IMF, orchestrated a $47 billion bailout that used future earnings from the export of oil as collateral. In exchange, Zedillo agreed to reintroduce Mexico to the harsh realities of fiscal austerity. The results were predictable: Mexico avoided economic collapse but began a deep recession that saw GDP decline by 6 percent and real wages drop by more than 10 percent. What was less predictable was that the recession was relatively short-lived, lasting only eighteen months, and that Mexico, to the surprise of many, demonstrated not only that it was able to repay the loans, but also that it was able to do so ahead of schedule. Yet serious problems remained, most notably in the banking sector.

In the aftermath of the peso crisis interest rates shot up, effectively increasing the amount of outstanding debt owed to Mexican banks. Already finding it difficult to adjust to the increased cost of living, debtors were now faced with interest rates as high as 100 percent on their outstanding loans.[29] Further complicating matters from the banks' perspective was the fact that Mexico lacked the legal mechanisms to force debtors to repay their loans. The result was an impending catastrophe that threatened to bring down the banking sector and the Zedillo administration was forced to orchestrate a bailout. The solution was the creation of the Savings Protection Banking Fund (Fondo Bancario de Protección al Ahorro, FOBAPROA), a government agency that bought out many of the banks' bad loans for a total of $65 billion. While FO-BAPROA helped breathe new life into the Mexican banking sector, the decision to bail out the banks raised the hackles of many, who viewed it as a thinly veiled attempt to save the nation's largest lending institutions who had lent too much and taken too many risks during the Salinas administration.[30] Critics were also enraged by the Zedillo administration's decision (and Congress's approval) to convert the outstanding loans, equivalent to 15 percent of GDP, into public debt.[31]

Persistent weaknesses in the banking sector notwithstanding, Zedillo achieved what few thought was possible: he stabilized the Mexican economy. By the end of his *sexenio*, the current account was more balanced, inflation was under control, the exchange rate had stabilized, government spending was in check, the foreign debt was shrinking, and macroeconomic growth was restored: in the final year of Zedillo's term, GDP grew by 6.6 percent, and Mexico had managed to recapture some of its former economic glory. Thus Ernesto Zedillo, the unlikeliest of heroes, not only brought Mexico back from the brink but charted a course toward macroeconomic stability and growth. When Vicente Fox took office in late 2000, he "inherited one of the healthiest economies in Mexican history" and therefore had an unprecedented opportunity in Mexico's recent experience, namely, to begin his term without the need to address impending economic collapse.[32] Accordingly, Fox arrived with ambitious plans for promoting economic development, including greater investment in infrastructure and education, and support for small businesses. Moreover, he promised annual GDP increases of 7 percent.

Yet curiously, these auspicious circumstances were not sufficient to ensure Fox's success. Why not? This question is particularly relevant not only because Mexico's economy was already very strong in 2000, but also because much of Fox's personal success stemmed from his strong performance as an executive at Coca-Cola, one of the world's most successful multinational firms. The answer has at least three components. First, Mexico and the world suffered a serious economic downturn in the aftermath of September 11, 2001. Second, even without this event, Fox would have encountered problems because he was not particularly shrewd in the way he pursued many of his economic goals. Third and relatedly, many of his proposed plans were so sweeping in their design that they were bound to encounter resistance in the legislature.

For example, one of Fox's first high-profile ventures was an overhaul of the tax system. His first proposal, introduced in April 2001, aimed to increase tax revenue by extending the 15 percent federal value-added tax (VAT) to include most of the goods and services that were previously exempt (e.g., food, most medicines, school tuition, books, public transportation, and medical/health services). Reform of the VAT purportedly would have reduced evasion and increased much-needed tax revenue. Yet the Fox administration was unsuccessful in this and subsequent tax reform efforts because it was unable to convince the opposition to support an initiative that appeared to create a significant burden for the poor and the working and middle classes.[33] Also important, however, was Fox's failure to consult or negotiate the terms of the fiscal reform bill with any group outside of his cabinet. In the end, Fox's failure to push through tax reform became emblematic of his approach to a number of intractable economic problems. Rather than trying to strong-arm Congress into passing wide-ranging reforms that threatened myriad entrenched interests, Fox would have been more successful had he focused on implementing small, incremental changes that fall entirely within the scope of executive authority. For example, he might have streamlined the bureaucracy necessary for starting a business, or created a greater role for the private sector in building and maintaining infrastructure.[34]

Overall, the Fox administration worked hard to maintain Mexico's economic stability and these efforts largely paid off. At the end of Fox's term Mexico enjoyed a balanced budget, mild inflation, a healthier banking sector, a stable peso, and a growing stock market. However, these accomplishments were overshadowed by sluggish growth—GDP averaged less than 2 percent annually between 2001 and 2006—very low job creation, and Mexico's drop to the number three most important source of imports to the United States.[35] Therefore while Felipe Calderón's government inherited a fundamentally sound economy, it was left to address the shortcomings of the Fox administration in order promote further economic growth and development. In his first years in office, Calderón managed to steer a steady course, with the Mexican economy doing relatively well even in the face of a U.S. recession, a falling dollar, inflationary pressures, and a global financial crisis. The problem of addressing Mexico's deeper economic challenges remains daunting, however.

Mexico's Future Economic Challenges

After Mexico's miraculous economic recovery from the peso crisis and its ability to weather the severe economic downturn that happened after 9/11, many proponents of neoliberalism claimed that ten-plus years of economic restructuring had made the Mexican economy much more stable and resilient. While there is little doubt that Mexico is now better able to bounce back from deep economic shocks, the past two decades have also revealed that the country still faces several important economic challenges in the twenty-first century. First, as with any export-based model, the Mexican economy is vulnerable to exogenous shocks that reduce the price or demand for its exports. This is particularly true for Mexico, since the vast majority of its exports are sold to one country: the United States. Mexico is also vulnerable because it relies so heavily on oil for its revenue—roughly 37 percent of the country's revenue comes from the export of petroleum. While a significant drop in oil prices on par with those of the 1980s does not seem likely, Mexico's oil output, and therefore oil export income, has declined significantly. If Mexico is going to avoid another catastrophe precipitated by its dependence on petroleum, it must take action now.

There are at least two potential solutions to this problem. The first is the highly controversial (and unpopular) option of privatizing the petroleum industry. PEMEX, the national petroleum company, is a bloated and corrupt bureaucracy sorely in need of rationalization and modernization. Some argue that privatizing the industry and welcoming foreign investment is the only way to rapidly update Mexico's production facilities so as to be able to more quickly and efficiently tap into the country's 12.9 billion barrels of proven reserves, much of which is located in inaccessible areas such as the deep waters of the Gulf of Mexico. Yet privatizing an industry that is widely considered to be integral to Mexico's independence and sovereignty will be no small task. In accord with the majority of the population, the PRD and many members of the PRI have consistently opposed privatization and foreign control of the petroleum industry. Indeed, in 2008 the PRD led the charge against Calderón's energy reform proposals which, while not fully privatizing the petroleum industry, would have taken initial steps to introduce private sector participation and increase competition in the energy sector. Another possible approach is to invest more in the development of other economic sectors to offset the decline in oil revenue and diversify Mexico's export earnings. But this too is difficult, expensive, and only likely to produce results in the medium and long term. Therefore, it is probably in Mexico's best interest to promote industry reform (even if privatization is not forthcoming) and diversification of exports in order to ensure a steady stream of revenue in the future. Just how to accomplish this is one of the Calderón administration's most formidable challenges.

The second possible way to reduce oil dependence and promote economic development is to increase tax revenue. Of the twenty-nine members of the Organization for Economic Cooperation and Development (OECD), Mexico ranks last in the amount of revenue it collects from businesses and private citizens. While most OECD states collect roughly 30 percent of GDP from tax receipts, Mexico's tax revenue hovered around 10 percent in the late 1990s and increased only slightly to 12 percent during Fox's term. The recent increases are laudable but still fall short of the 15 percent that is considered necessary for a government to provide basic public services and infrastructure. Therefore, if Mexico is going to reduce its dependence on oil and maintain macroeconomic stability, it must find a way to increase its tax income—no small task given that, at least until recently, there was no taxpaying culture in Mexico. Indeed, businesses and citizens alike had few incentives to contribute to coffers they knew were used to enrich politicians rather than promote the public good. Calderón has worked to succeed where Fox failed, designing a set of reforms to increase tax receipts, and working with the multiparty Congress to achieve a consensus on fiscal reform. The fiscal reform package approved in September 2007 achieved this goal, resulting in significant increases in new revenue to allow government spending on infrastructure, energy subsidies, and education.

A related challenge for Mexico is the emergence of the informal economy, particularly in the aftermath of the crises of the 1980s and 1990s. As formal employment opportunities disappeared and the cost of living increased, Mexicans were forced to find new economic survival strategies. For many this meant emigrating to the United States. Many of those who stayed became self-employed, setting up taco stands, selling wares in areas with high pedestrian traffic or at makeshift marketplaces, working as domestic servants and day laborers, and so on. These kinds of economic activities allow millions to make a living or cover periodic budget shortfalls. However, they take place as personal arrangements among citizens and as such are not taxed or regulated by the government. The result is that the government loses out in valuable revenue generated by the informal economy, and, as we discuss further in chapter 10, citizens are vulnerable to exploitation and economic instability.

Further plaguing Mexico's economic future is the presence of several highly influential domestic monopolies and oligopolies. In theory, privatization of firms leads to greater efficiency and competitiveness since entrepreneurs, rather than government bureaucrats, must respond to market forces in order to stay in business. However, in Mexico the sale of industries previously owned by the state led to the creation of private monopolies (most notably in telecommunications and broadcasting) and oligopolies (cement, airlines, financial sector). This creates a number of problems. First, Mexican consumers suffer from the absence of competition. As an example, Mexicans pay some of the highest telecom rates in the world because Telmex controls 94 percent of Mexico's landlines.[36] Furthermore, domestic monopolies have the overall effect of making the country less competitive on the international market. Notorious for using domestic legal loopholes to protect their market dominance, Mexican monopolies have been able to keep out foreign competitors, and this has the potential to undermine investment and growth. While nearly everyone acknowledges the problem that monopolies pose to the economy, mustering the political will to challenge their power, particularly in the broadcasting industry, may be very difficult indeed.

Also pressing is the dire need for creating higher-paying jobs. Like many of his predecessors, Fox pledged to create a million jobs a year during his *sexenio*—the number needed to absorb the number of Mexicans entering the workforce. Yet Fox was unable to keep his promise, only coming close to the 1 million in the last year of his administration. For his part, Calderón proclaimed himself the "jobs president," thus suggesting that he would focus at least as much attention on the issue as his immediate predecessor. With Fox's dismal performance in this area, Calderón may well do better. But it is important to point out that what Mexico needs is not just jobs but permanent jobs that pay workers enough to live on. Temporary work and miserly wages may succeed at temporarily lowering the unemployment rate and reducing the size of the informal economy, but they will do little to provide the solid economic base that the country needs to grow. Whether Calderón will be able to succeed where many before him have failed is uncertain. What is clear is that unless Mexico can make significant strides in this area, it will continue to lose millions of its hardest-working, most entrepreneurial-minded citizens as they look for better economic opportunities in places like the United States.

Finally, Mexico must find a way to maintain its competitive edge in trade and industry. For many years Mexico was the prime destination for multinational firms that wanted access to lower labor wages and lower transportation costs on goods destined for the U.S. market. Today, wages in many parts of Central America, and particularly China, are far lower than those paid in Mexico. In many cases, the wage differentials are large enough to offset increased shipping costs that are invariably incurred when goods are transported from more remote locations. Moreover, national governments all over the world are much savvier at attracting the attention of multinationals looking for new locations for their production facilities. Without its traditional comparative advantages, Mexico must find other ways to remain competitive. Of particular concern is Mexico's relatively low levels of investment in science and technology; it ranks last among OECD countries in this category. Without sufficient resources in these areas, it will be impossible for Mexico to increase its productivity, promote innovation, and otherwise remain competitive in the global economy. Clearly there needs to be a greater focus on promoting industries and products for which there is high demand in emerging markets like China, if Mexico is going to redefine its economic niche and maintain its comparative advantage. Countries that can tap into a market as large and with as much potential as China's are much more likely to be successful in the future than those that remain focused on traditional markets like the United States.

All of these issues present significant challenges for Mexico's economic growth and stability. There is little doubt that Mexico must work more aggressively to chart its course for the future. Unless it develops a sound and coherent strategy for promoting economic development, the gains of the past ten years are sure to erode over time. Yet perhaps the biggest challenge that Mexico currently faces is how to distribute economic gains more equitably. As we have noted throughout this chapter, Mexico has enjoyed periods of impressive growth, yet much of the population has failed to benefit from the country's economic success. The "miracle" years of ISI favored the domestic business class but left behind many in the working class and the countryside. The neoliberal economic model appears to have taken no less a toll on ordinary Mexicans: stabilization, structural adjustment, and trade liberalization required the government to enact policies that made life very difficult for most Mexicans. The combined effects of high unemployment, stagnant wages, reduced government services, and higher prices made economic survival a constant struggle. This hardship, difficult in the best of times, was dramatically worsened by the peso crisis of the mid-1990s. If Mexico hopes to achieve true economic development and reinforce its democratic gains, it must address its severe income inequality and myriad problems associated with widespread poverty. It is to these issues that we turn in chapter 10.

Key Terms

Alemán Valdés, Miguel
Camacho, Manuel Ávila
capital flight
debt crisis
Díaz Ordaz, Gustavo
Echeverría, Luis
economic restructuring
Economic Solidarity Pact
export-oriented growth
foreign direct investment (FDI)
FOBAPROA
import substitution industrialization (ISI)
inflation
informal economy
López Portillo, José

lost decade
Mexican Miracle
NAFTA
neoliberal economic policies
oil reserves
PEMEX
performance legitimacy
petrolization
privatization of banks
Ruíz Cortines, Adolfo
shared development
stabilizing development
tax reform
tesobonos
value-added tax (VAT)
Washington Consensus

Recommended Readings

Hansen, Roger. *The Politics of Mexican Development*. Baltimore: Johns Hopkins University Press, 1974.

Lustig, Nora. *Mexico: The Remaking of an Economy*. Washington, D.C.: Brookings Institution, 1992.

Notes

1. By way of comparison, the U.S. economy, the largest and most diverse in the world, had an average annual growth rate of just 3 percent between 2000 and 2005.

2. Mexico was not the only country to employ the export-oriented model. It was used almost exclusively in Latin America and many other parts of the developing world at least until the 1930s.

3. As noted in chapter 1, the belief that foreigners ought to play a central role in Mexico's economic development was partly grounded in the culturally biased (if not racist) view of Díaz and the *científicos*, who believed that Europeans were inherently superior to other peoples. Hansen, *Politics of Mexican Development*, 18–20.

4. The countries most heavily invested in Mexico were the United States, Great Britain, and France, though each country concentrated its investments in different sectors. The United States was primarily invested in railway construction and mining. British investments were also heavily concentrated in railroad infrastructure, as well

as in mining and the public services sector. Meanwhile, France focused its capital on banking, public debt, industry, and commerce. See Hansen, *Politics of Mexican Development*, 16–17.

5. Brian Hamnett, *A Concise History of Mexico* (Cambridge: Cambridge University Press, 1999).

6. Hansen, *Politics of Mexican Development*, 23–29.

7. The ISI model was used widely throughout Latin America. For a concise description of the model and an assessment of its effects in the region, see Patrice Franko, *The Puzzle of Latin American Economic Development* (Boulder: Rowman & Littlefield, 2007), chap. 3.

8. One of the most common was to pay a Mexican citizen for the use of his name, a *prestanombre* that served as a front for a foreign firm yet gave the appearance of local ownership.

9. The *maquiladora* industry is discussed in greater detail in chapter 13.

10. A significant prior devaluation occurred in 1949.

11. The combination of infrastructure development and the peso devaluation made Mexico an attractive tourist destination for U.S. citizens. Newly constructed airports, roads, hotels, and the relative affordability of Mexico in the 1950s spurred tourism from the United States, which would eventually become one of Mexico's most important sources of international capital.

12. Further exacerbating the problem was the fact that Mexico had one of the highest rates of population growth in the world in the 1960s, thus making it less likely that economic growth alone would lead to an improved standard of living.

13. Exemplifying the discontent among middle sectors was the doctors' strike that occurred at the outset of Díaz Ordaz's term. Some doctors were arrested and beaten before they agreed to go back to work. Díaz Ordaz also had to resort to hard-line tactics to deal with insurgent labor groups, notably oil workers and Mexico City truck drivers. Raul Trejo Delarbe and Anibal Yanez, "The Mexican Labor Movement: 1917–1975," *Latin American Perspectives* 3, no. 1 (1976): 133–53.

14. For example, while Mexican refrigerator producers benefited from protective tariffs, they tended to import cheap inputs—things like motors or refrigeration components—from abroad.

15. The entrenched political interests of larger manufacturing industries—which benefited from the status quo and the accessibility of cheaper, high-quality foreign inputs—made it difficult to move toward the domestic development of input production.

16. In the United States, high consumer spending, increased public sector spending on social welfare programs, and military expenditures during the Vietnam War combined to create a significant U.S. imbalance of payments.

17. Thomas D. Lairson and David Skidmore, *International Political Economy: The Struggle for Power and Wealth*. 3rd ed. (Belmont, Calif.: Thomson-Wadsworth, 2003).

18. The tariff—along with the weaker dollar—also contributed to the general slowdown in the global economy, as the power of U.S. consumers to purchase foreign goods declined.

19. Rene Villarreal and Rocio de Villarreal, "Mexico's Development Strategy," *Proceedings of the Academy of Political Science* 34, no. 1 (1981): 97–103; Thomas Skidmore and Peter Smith, *Modern Latin America* (New York: Oxford University Press, 2005), 283; Lynn Foster, *A Brief History of Mexico* (New York: Checkmark, 2004), 212.

20. Although Mexico's oil deposits were at one time expected to surpass those of Saudi Arabia, in the early days of the boom it was ill equipped to capitalize on its treasure because the industry was in disarray. Thirty-five years under national control had taken their toll: the necessary technical expertise, training, modern equipment, and adequate infrastructure were all absent. Therefore, the government had to make significant investments in modernizing the industry before it could fully exploit its oil reserves. See Judith Adler Hellman, *Mexico in Crisis*. 2nd ed. (New York: Holmes & Meier, 1988), 74–76.

21. Even though the oil boom created millions of jobs, it fell far short of creating enough jobs to substantially reduce unemployment, especially in rural areas.

22. Global interest rates increased significantly as the United States sought to tighten its money supply to get a handle on stagflation—inflation at a time of low growth.

23. Although Mexico was the first to announce its inability to service its debt, many other countries in Latin America and elsewhere found themselves in similar circumstances. Low prices for many export commodities combined with heavy indebtedness to finance ISI and rising international interest rates made it nearly impossible for even relatively strong economies like Argentina's, Brazil's, and Venezuela's to make good on their loans. See Franko, *Puzzle*, 97–98.

24. Foster, *A Brief History of Mexico*, 215.

25. Skidmore and Smith, *Modern Latin America*, 285.

26. This goal was achieved with the help of U.S. Treasury Secretary James Brady. The so-called Brady Plan allowed highly indebted countries like Mexico to reduce their debt with "buybacks" in the secondary market, structure repayment over a longer period of time, or take out new loans from the IMF. See Franko, *Puzzle*, 97–98.

27. The government's sale of industries that were previously owned by the state brought in much-needed capital to the public coffers and arguably improved the efficiency of the industries by placing them in private hands. Yet equally important is the fact that the sell-off benefited a select group of Mexican entrepreneurs that had ties to the Salinas family. For example, Carlos Slim, a Mexican businessman, purchased the formerly state-owned telecommunications company, Telmex, at well below market price and converted it into a privately held monopoly.

28. The United States already had a free trade agreement with Canada. The latter agreed to become part of NAFTA in the hopes of retaining its privileged access to the U.S. market, not so much because it had a compelling interest in free trade with Mexico.

29. One interesting political outgrowth of this development was the formation of El Barzón, a middle-class grassroots organization that put pressure on the banks and the government to allow some leeway in the repayment of increased debt that occurred when the value of their savings declined and interest rates on their outstanding debt (credit card, mortgage, car payments, etc.) shot up after the devaluation.

30. Mexicans were incensed by the fact that many of the loans were made to un-creditworthy but politically well connected business interests who gambled that the government would not allow a mass default.

31. Russell Crandall, "Mexico's Domestic Economy: Policy Options and Choices," in *Mexico's Democracy at Work: Political and Economic Dynamics*, ed. Russell Crandall, Guadalupe Paz, and Riordan Roett (Boulder: Lynne Rienner, 2005), 71–72.

32. Alfredo Coutino, quoted in Marla Dickerson, "Fox Not Shy in Touting Record," *Los Angeles Times*, March 21, 2006.

33. It launched a second effort at reforming the VAT in 2003, but Congress again defeated it.

34. See Edna Jaime, "Fox's Economic Agenda: An Incomplete Transition," in *Mexico Under Fox*, ed. Luis Rubio and Susan Kaufmann Purcell (Boulder: Lynne Rienner, 2004).

35. Adding insult to injury was the fact that Mexico was displaced by China, its biggest economic rival, as the United States' number two source of imported goods.

36. Marla Dickerson, "$49 Billion Is Slim's Pickings in Mexico," *Los Angeles Times*, March 9, 2007.

10

Poverty, Inequality, and Social Welfare Policy

First-time visitors to Mexico are often struck by images of economic hardship—such as street children selling gum and ramshackle shanty housing—which confirm their preconceptions about Mexico as a poor country. Yet what many visitors find, often to their surprise, is that Mexico is also a country of tremendous wealth. In 2007, Mexico's US$1.2 trillion gross domestic product (GDP) edged out both North Korea and Canada.[1] Mexico is also home to Carlos Slim, the telecommunications magnate who was ranked in July 2007 as the world's richest man (a position he has alternately shared in recent years with Bill Gates and Warren Buffett). Mexico's cosmopolitan cities—Mexico City, Monterrey, Guadalajara—boast fabulous hotels, chic restaurants, high-priced shopping districts, and luxury automobile dealerships. Wealthy Mexicans travel to Disneyland and Sea World for vacation, and send their children to expensive private schools. Because of this disparity, visitors often come to the simple, not completely inaccurate conclusion that Mexico's poverty and inequality are the result of government corruption and unfair privileges in Mexican society. But the dimensions and causes of poverty and income inequality in Mexico, as elsewhere, are complex and require careful analysis in order to better understand and address them.

In this chapter, we consider the nature of poverty and inequality in Mexico, and their implications for the country's overall economic development. In the first part of this chapter, we will try to understand what factors have contributed to the persistence of poverty and income inequality during an era of expanding international trade and economic productivity. In the second part of this chapter, we will examine the different approaches to promoting social welfare in Mexico, and how they have changed over the last two decades. In the process, we will discuss the major contemporary Mexican government programs and policies that have been developed to deal with poverty and inequality. What emerges from this discussion is a clear indication of the enormity and complexity of Mexico's greatest challenge, and a look at the ways in which Mexico's contemporary leaders have responded to the needs of society. Throughout, we offer considerations of how these challenges will factor into Mexico's longer term process of democratic consolidation.

Understanding Poverty and Inequality

What does it mean to be poor in Mexico? This is a difficult question because the concept of poverty is relative. What one person considers to be poor economic conditions in a particular country (or even in a given community) may actually be relatively better than those considered poor in another. For example, a poor person living in the United States may have access to services—clean running water, electricity, medical vaccinations, public housing, and cable television—that are not available to many of the world's poorest citizens. At the same time, the relative cost of goods may vary significantly from one region or country to another. Thus poor people living in Mexico—who earn much less money than their counterparts in the United States (where the poverty rate in 2007 was set at about $18,000 annual income for a family of four)—may also find it far less expensive to meet their basic needs for food, housing, medicine, and so on.

How then can we begin to analyze poverty and inequality in Mexico? When is a person considered poor? How is inequality manifested in Mexico's economy, and with what implications? In Mexico, as in the United States, poverty is often defined according to household income from wages and other income-based measures, such as GDP per capita. Yet such measures capture only part of what it means to be poor. Economists therefore ‘ also evaluate other factors that indicate the quality of life and degree of inequality for people who are economically disadvantaged. As we discuss below, both income-based and qualitative measures show a relatively high rate of poverty and inequality in Mexico compared to the United States and other developed countries.

Additionally, income distribution in Mexico approaches the most unequal in the world: while the wealthiest quintile (20 percent) of the population owns roughly 60 percent of the country's resources, the poorest quintile claims a paltry 3 percent of the national income. Nowhere is the disparity more evident than in a comparison of Carlos Slim with an ordinary Mexican citizen.

Slim, a Mexican tycoon, owns a broad array of Mexican companies, including telecom, retail and department stores, restaurants, a banking and insurance firm, and an airline. The Slim fortune was estimated in 2007 to be almost $50 billion, a sum that represented nearly 6 percent of Mexico's GNP. In contrast, an ordinary Mexican earns approximately $10 a day, has no health insurance, does not own a car, and is unable to finish high school, let alone have access to a college education. Therefore when considering Mexicans' economic well-being, it is essential to take into account the distribution of wealth in the country.

Income-Based Measures of Poverty and Inequality

One common income-based definition of poverty in Mexico is centered on the country's daily minimum wage, which is set at about double the cost of a minimum basket of goods, or about US$4.50 per day.[2] Because there is significant variation in the cost of living across Mexico's different geographic areas, the daily minimum wage varies accordingly.[3] Depending on which regional rate is used, any Mexican household that survives on less than the local minimum wage is generally considered to be poor or marginalized (*marginalizado*). Those Mexican households earning incomes less than the cost of a minimum basket of goods—or roughly half the poverty line—are often described as living in extreme poverty.[4] According to these definitions, approximately 40 percent of Mexicans live in poverty, while roughly 28 percent live in extreme poverty.[5]

Since the cost of living can vary significantly from place to place, it is common for income to be adjusted for purchasing power parity (PPP).[6] Controlling for PPP in GDP per capita, we can see that Mexican citizens earn far less on average (about US$7,310 annually per household) than U.S. citizens (about US$43,740 annually for a family of four). Indeed, despite Mexico's ranking as having the 12th highest GDP, relative to its population Mexico ranks 71st in terms of GDP/PPP per capita.[7]

Of course, GDP/PPP per capita is only a measure of the average income for a country. That is, it merely reflects a country's total national income relative to population size. It does not account for the actual distribution of income in a country. To measure income distribution, economists often refer to a country's Gini coefficient. The Gini coefficient is a measure of inequality in the distribution of wealth, and is represented on a scale of 0 to 1 (which is sometimes converted to a scale of 0 to 100). A score of 0 represents perfect equality of distribution, while a score of 1 (or 100) represents total inequality. In 2007, overall economic inequality in Mexico was among the worst in the world, with a Gini score of 46.1 out of 100, placing it 91st out of 126 countries. By comparison, the

Table 10.1.
Distribution of Family Income by Gini Index among Key Latin American and Caribbean Countries

Country	Gini Score (1–100)	World Ranking
Nicaragua	43.1	81
Mexico	**46.1**	**91**
Venezuela	48.2	98
Costa Rica	49.8	100
Argentina	51.3	107
Dominican Republic	51.6	108
Peru	52.0	109
El Salvador	52.4	110
Ecuador	53.6	111
Honduras	53.8	112
Chile	54.9	113
Guatemala	55.1	114
Panama	56.1	115
Brazil	57.0	116
Paraguay	58.4	118
Colombia	58.6	119
Haiti	59.2	120
Bolivia	60.1	121

Source: World Bank 2007, *World Development Indicators 2007,* Washington, D.C.
Note: A Gini score value of 0 represents absolute equality; a value of 100 absolute inequality. World ranking out of 126 countries rated.

Gini coefficient for the United States was 41 in the same year—it was ranked 71st worldwide in 2007—while the average coefficient for other Latin American and Caribbean countries was about 53.4.[8] (See table 10.1.)

While income-based measures give us an approximation of how much money people have at their disposal, they tell us less about the circumstances in which they live. For this reason, some economists have suggested trying to find other ways to measure poverty, including other dimensions that impact a person's basic quality of life. Indicators such as infant mortality rates, the percentage of the population with access to potable water, and the life expectancy of citizens can provide useful measures of quality of life. We describe such indicators as qualitative measures of poverty, and provide greater consideration of what they tell us about Mexico below.

Qualitative Measures of Poverty and Inequality

In addition to being a relative concept, poverty is also a multidimensional problem, going beyond the mere lack of income. In other words, being poor also implies additional circumstances, largely as a result of having lesser access to basic services than most other people in an economy. Poor people are often deprived of proper prenatal care, vaccinations, adequate shelter, nutritious food, education, regular medical attention, and access to lifesaving medicines. As a result, poor people often have a much lower quality—and a shorter length—of life. In fact, in the words of one economist, "poverty kills."[9] For this reason, it is important to draw on a wider range of qualitative indicators—the actual living circumstances of people—that help us to understand the dimensions of poverty and inequality in Mexico.

Economists in the Fox administration sought to further elucidate the problem of poverty by developing a more complex scale of indicators that incorporated both income-based and qualitative measures. The poverty index developed by Fox's Technical Committee for Poverty Measurement identified three distinct categories or levels of poverty: inadequate nutrition (*alimentaria*), inadequate access to health and education (*capacidades*), and inadequate material resources (*patrimonio*).[10] First, nutritional poverty refers to people whose earnings are considered inadequate to cover their basic nutritional needs. The second measure—which also includes those individuals suffering from nutritional poverty—extends to those who do not have adequate access to education and health care. Finally, the third measure focuses on those individuals who, in addition to the first two categories, also lack access to basic material needs, in terms of shoes, clothing, shelter, and public transportation. Using these measures, the Fox administration achieved a somewhat more nuanced—and disturbing—assessment of poverty in Mexico than that based solely on the minimum wage. Using this measure, Fox officials found that an estimated 45 percent of households (and 53 percent of individuals) lived in poverty in 2000.

One alarming finding was that a much higher proportion of Mexico's rural population had a lack of access to basic nutrition (34 percent), health care, and education (41 percent), and material resources (60 percent) than urban dwellers. Indeed, people living in urban areas were one-third as likely to lack basic nutrition, less than half as likely to lack access to health care, and just over half as likely to be lacking in basic material needs as the 25 percent of Mexicans living in rural areas (see table 10.2).

Regardless of whether a quantitative or qualitative measure of poverty is used, it is clear that the proportion of Mexico's population living in poverty is about average for Latin America. At the same time, the percentage of poor people living in Mexico is significantly higher than in the United States, where poverty rates have remained close to 12.5 percent—or about 1 in 8 persons—over the last two decades. Why, given its relative economic strength, does Mexico have such high poverty levels and such tremendous inequality? Below, we consider in greater detail the factors that have contributed to pov-

Table 10.2.
Measurements of Poverty during the Fox Administration

Type of Poverty	Percentage of Households		Percentage of Individuals		
	2000	2004	2000	2004	2005
National					
Nutrition	18.6	13.7	24.2	17.3	18.6
Health/Education	25.3	19.8	31.9	24.6	25.6
Material Resources	45.9	39.6	53.7	47.0	47.8
Urban					
Nutrition	9.8	8.7	12.6	11.0	10.3
Health/Education	16.2	14.2	20.2	17.8	16.2
Material Resources	37.4	34.2	43.8	41.0	39.0
Rural					
Nutrition	34.1	22.3	42.4	27.6	32.4
Health/Education	41.4	29.4	50.0	35.7	40.6
Material Resources	60.7	48.8	69.3	56.9	62.4

Sources: Adapted from Aguayo, *Almanaque Mexicano*, 2007. Table 3.1 in Juan Pardinas, "Fighting Poverty in Mexico," in *Mexico under Fox*, 69. www.sedesol.gov.mx.

erty and inequality in Mexico, which helps shed light on some of the possible policy solutions for improving the quality of life in Mexico.

Empirical Trends in Poverty and Inequality in Contemporary Mexico

Over the course of the twentieth century, the quality of life for most Mexicans improved. This was particularly true during the early years of the economic miracle, when unemployment declined, wages increased, and the levels of inequality diminished. Yet even in this era of economic prosperity, poverty was not eliminated because many of the improvements in income brought by economic growth were accompanied by other changes. For example, like many developing countries, Mexican development has been accompanied by steady population growth throughout the twentieth century. By 2005, Mexico's population of roughly 103 million was more than seven times larger than its population of 13.6 million in 1900. Much of the population explosion occurred during the middle part of the century, in the heyday of the economic miracle and throughout the 1970s. Thus, although the economy was expanding during this period, so was the size of the population. Therefore, greater national wealth did not necessarily mean better conditions for everyone.

Currently the vast majority of the population (64 percent) is between fifteen and sixty-four years of age. Although this age group will continue to make up the bulk of the population in the short term, the country is expected to undergo a demographic shift, as decreased family size reduces the number of youngsters and the percentage of seniors aged sixty-five and older increases to roughly 25 percent (up from its current level of 6 percent) of the population by midcentury. This shift will undoubtedly place a greater strain on Mexico's economy and government services as its baby boom generation moves into retirement. Indeed, as we discuss below, Mexico has already begun to brace for this challenge by significantly reforming its pension system.

Another critical aspect of Mexico's economic development and social transformation over the twentieth century has been the rapid rate of urbanization in the postwar era, and the greater demands that this has placed on Mexico's urban infrastructure, educational institutions, and social welfare services. In 1950, 57.4 percent of the population lived in rural areas; this number declined to 34 percent by 1980, and then to 25 percent in 2000. New urban dwellers were drawn to jobs and higher wages in major metropolitan areas, or otherwise compelled to move by the decline of Mexico's traditional agricultural sector.[11]

This metropolitan demographic shift helped to improve living standards for many Mexicans by providing greater employment opportunities and access to basic services that may have proved scarce in the countryside. This, in turn, provided a high degree of legitimacy to the PRI government for much of the mid-twentieth century. However, with the series of economic crises and devaluations that Mexico experienced beginning in the 1970s, the living conditions and relative wealth of many Mexicans deteriorated significantly.[12]

During the lost decade of the 1980s, unemployment soared, and inflation drove up prices while wages stagnated. Mexico's subsequent economic restructuring brought further job losses in uncompetitive industries (notably agriculture). Those who remained employed saw the steady deterioration of their wages due to soaring inflation over the course of the decade. Subsequent currency volatility further diminished the buying power of Mexican wages. In sum, during the 1980s and 1990s, real wages declined nearly 40 percent, while the minimum wage lost nearly 70 percent of its purchasing power. Although middle incomes improved significantly in Mexico over the 1990s (especially in northern Mexico), by the end of the decade the buying power of Mexico's poor was still less than a third of what it had been in 1980.

Because so many factors contributed to poverty in Mexico, it is not surprising that there exists more than one *type* of poverty in Mexico. First, for many poor people in contemporary Mexico, poverty is a chronic problem. That is, poverty is a systemic and multigenerational condition for some families, related to their lack of access to basic economic opportunities. As noted above, poor people often lack access to basic health care and nutrition, decent housing, adequate education, formal employment, and capital or credit for investments that would significantly improve their quality of life *and* enable them to participate more effectively in the economy. In terms of demographic patterns and geographic distribution, chronic poverty has particular characteristics in Mexico. For example, rural and indigenous people have been consistently overrepresented as a share of Mexico's impoverished population over many generations. In addition, women and children are especially prominent among the chronically poor; this is in part because women have significantly lower earning potential than men, and because poor people are likely to have more children than average. Hence, on the whole, Mexicans who are ethnically indigenous, rural, young, and female are more likely to find themselves in poverty; those who are male urban dwellers with European backgrounds are much less likely to find themselves in chronic poverty.

In addition to being a chronic problem, poverty also frequently takes on a second manifestation in Mexico. That is, poverty can also be the result of a significant change in economic circumstances, or what some economists refer to as transitional poverty.[13] In other words, individuals who were previously not considered poor may suddenly experience a worsening in their economic situation due to a sudden crisis: unemployment, rising prices, or the death of the family breadwinner. While the effects of transitional poverty can be less discriminating than those of chronic poverty, people who are already at the lower end of the economic spectrum are certainly more vulnerable than others. For example, because the minimum wage is ultimately determined by policy makers, the purchasing power of the minimum wage earners may not rise consistently with the rate of inflation. Similarly, when the peso is devalued relative to other national currencies (like the dollar), the rising cost of imported goods can quickly spiral out of reach. In such cases, while a person might be considered above Mexico's nominal poverty line, they may suddenly have less purchasing power than they once did.

Both chronic and transitional poverty raise important questions about democracy in Mexico. First, we must consider how poverty—whether chronic or transitional—played a role in Mexico's long period of single-party hegemony under the PRI, and whether changes in the economic conditions contributed to its prolonged process of democratization. As we have argued in earlier chapters, the PRI actively catered to Mexico's chronically poor population throughout its long period of political dominance. In fact, the ruling party dramatically improved the living conditions of poor people during Mexico's midcentury economic miracle, earning important performance legitimacy for the PRI regime as a result. Not surprisingly, the PRI tended to draw significant support at polls from poor voters.

Why did the poor continue to support the PRI even as Mexico's economic situation worsened during the 1980s and 1990s, when the PRI's performance legitimacy appeared to dissipate? It may be that the poor—especially the chronically poor—could be easily enticed to report to PRI rallies and even sell their votes in exchange for various forms of political patronage and direct material benefits, such as sandwiches, T-shirts, hats, and even washing machines. At the same time, as Vivienne Bennett argues, the relative decline in economic conditions for persons living in extreme and chronic poverty—such as a *campesino* living off the land—might have been very different than for urban middle class and moderately poor Mexicans suddenly thrust into transitional poverty by economic shocks.[14] If so, those who experienced transitional poverty may have been more likely to mobilize in support of the political opposition, whether voting for PAN mayors and governors in the mid-1980s or for Cuauhtémoc Cárdenas in 1988. In this way, poverty and economic hardship may have had simultaneously divergent effects on the PRI's support base, and on the process of democratization.

A second and related question regarding the politics of poverty—and especially inequality—in Mexico is how it may bear on the future of democratic governance, as well as the policies of democratic governments. Advocates of modernization theory argue that a large middle-class population is beneficial to democratic governance, because middle-class voters tend to have characteristics that promote active political participation, such as higher levels of education and a larger stake in the outcome of government policies. If this is the case, then Mexico's large poor population could be a barrier to democratic governance, insofar as they may be vulnerable to political manipulation and lack commitment to democratic participation. At the same time, even if the millions of poor Mexicans prove to be highly democratic in their orientation, the country's extreme levels of inequality skew political outcomes in favor of the few extremely wealthy Mexicans who can buy access to power, and thereby corrupt the political system. What is clear for now, as we saw in the 2006 elections, is that the issue of poverty and inequality is an issue of great concern to a significant portion of the electorate. This is a fact that Mexican policy makers can ill afford to ignore.

As they design Mexico's future social welfare policies, it will be necessary for Mexican politicians to consider the nature of poverty, and its causes. As we have discussed, whether a person is the victim of chronic or transitional poverty will likely require policy makers to develop different policy approaches to improve the overall macroeconomic situation and to provide assistance to alleviate the effects of a temporary crisis. Tackling complex, ingrained patterns of poverty may require longer-term, multifaceted strategies. For example, some programs seeking to alleviate the symptoms of multigenerational poverty may focus on providing access to basic services, such as food assistance and medical care. Other policy makers may seek to increase the accessibility of grants and loans for making longer-term investments (e.g., housing).

Still others emphasize the need for targeted, long-term programs to increase educational quality and access for the children of poor families. Below we consider the policy prescriptions employed in recent decades, and their implications for combating poverty and reducing inequalities in Mexico.

Reforming Social Welfare Policy in Mexico

Social welfare policies are government programs that seek to provide assistance to members of society who cannot meet their own basic needs. Governments provide this safety net because they seek to maximize the overall welfare of society. Effective social welfare policies accomplish this goal by making sure that fewer members of society suffer undue hardship, more individuals can make positive contributions to the whole of society, and fewer people are inclined to cause harm to society. To accomplish these goals, most social welfare programs seek to provide assistance that helps level the economic playing field. Such policies often provide food, health care, housing, education, and job training to those who need assistance.

In effect, social welfare programs are the manifestation of what many political scientists and policy analysts refer to as the welfare state. The notion of the welfare state emerged during the early- and mid-twentieth century, as governments in industrializing societies wrestled with the political demands of newly empowered workers, as well as the challenges of economic crises in a much more complex and interconnected global economy. As we have seen in earlier chapters, Mexico's revolutionary government was, in fact, one of the first to formally embrace a strong caretaker role for the state. Numerous provisions of the 1917 constitution commit the state to the provision of overall societal welfare, such as education and health care. However, it was not until the 1930s, during the administration of Lázaro Cárdenas, that the Mexican government adopted policies seriously committed to the protection of social welfare; even then, progress toward meeting the basic needs of society was limited over the coming decades.

One explanation why Mexico's welfare state has been ineffective in reducing poverty may be a significant lack of policy continuity across administrations, or political manipulation by the ruling party for many years. There has been a particular tendency in Mexico for each new presidential administration to eliminate or otherwise reconfigure the social welfare programs of their predecessors. In most cases, Mexican presidents then endeavored to place their own stamp on Mexican social welfare policy by introducing new programs, scope, or emphasis in order to create mechanisms for clientelistic distribution of resources that would consolidate their own political power.

The frequent alterations to Mexico's social welfare policy can be seen in the historical development of the two main government cabinet-level agencies that address these issues: the Ministry of Social Development (Secretaría de Desarollo Social, or SEDESOL) and the Ministry of Health (Secretaría de Salud). Today, the secretaries of both agencies report to the president and oversee a large bureaucratic organization with a wide variety of programs. The names, functions, and significance of many of these programs have varied over time, as nearly every new president renamed or otherwise attempted to redefine the direction of Mexican social welfare policy. The secretary of social development was originally created under another title in 1959 to promote the development of public works projects. The agency continued to deal with housing, public works, and ecological projects under various titles until 1992, when it was again renamed and made generally responsible for dealing with poverty alleviation and social assistance.[15] The Ministry of Health was created in 1938 to provide general social welfare assistance. However, by the 1980s, the social welfare functions of the agency became more specialized in public health, and in 1992 the agency was renamed with that as its sole mission, and other social welfare programs were gradually transferred to SEDESOL.[16] Examples of several recent programs overseen by both agencies are listed in table 10.3.

Alterations to Mexican social welfare policy have not been solely based on reorienting political and societal loyalties. In recent decades there have been important differences in the design—and underlying philosophical approaches—of social welfare programs in Mexico. In the process, recent modifications to social welfare policy in contemporary Mexico have begun to

Table 10.3.
Social Welfare Programs Operated by SEDESOL and the Secretary of Health

SEDESOL	*Secretary of Health*
Adult Education Program	IMSS (Mexican Institute of Social Security)
Micro-Region Development Program	ISSSTE (Public Employee Insurance
"Habitat" Housing Assistance Program	Program)
Youth for Mexico	Medical Insurance for a New Generation
3-to-1 Migrant Remittances Program	Popular Security (Seguro Popular)
DICONSA (Food Assistance Program)	National Institute of Medical Sciences and
LICONSA (Milk Purchasing Program)	Nutrition
FONART (Artisan Assistance Fund)	National Rehabilitation Institute
FONHAPO (Rural Housing Program)	National Cancer Institute
INDESOL (Social Investment Program)	INFOGEN (Birth Defects Prevention Program)
FONHAPO (Popular Housing	Woman's Health Program
Assistance Fund)	Migrant Health Program
OPORTUNIDADES (Opportunity	SISESIA (Infancy and Child Services
Program)	Program)
	CNEGYSR (Reproductive Health Program)

significantly reshape the state's relationship to society, and expectations about the role of government in providing for individual well-being. Below we consider traditional state-centered approaches to social welfare policy in Mexico, as well as recent innovations emphasizing a greater role for public-private partnerships, in the provision of social welfare. In particular, we focus on the key antipoverty programs that exemplify this shift in approaches in Mexico.

Traditional Social Welfare Programs

Beginning in the early- and mid-twentieth century, Mexican social welfare programs sought to provide universally accessible redistributive benefits to the needy through intensive government involvement. The Mexican government established a wide range of programs—administered by SEDESOL and other agencies—to provide food assistance, universal medical care (for formally employed workers), and pensions for the elderly. The Mexican government's social welfare programs reflected the progressive orientation of the revolution, with universally accessible benefits for the poor. In Mexico, some critics viewed such social welfare programs as wasteful forms of patronage intended to build support for the PRI regime (highly susceptible to official corruption). Often such programs merely alleviated the symptoms of poverty, and proved ineffective as long-term solutions to the problem.

Mexico's National Company for Popular Subsistence (Compañía Nacional de Subsistencias Populares, CONASUPO) provides a useful example. Founded in the 1960s, CONASUPO provided public subsidies for the production and distribution of staple foods like beans, rice, wheat, and corn (including tortillas). The fiscal crisis of the early 1980s led the government to gradually scale back support for CONASUPO, and by the 1990s it had significantly reduced its subsidies for most food products except beans and corn. The urgency to dismantle the food subsistence program increased in the fall of 1998, due to a major scandal involving former CONASUPO official Raúl Salinas, brother of former president Carlos Salinas. A U.S. Department of Justice investigation alleged his possible involvement in money laundering activities through the program. By the end of the year, the Mexican Congress decided on the total liquidation of this program.

CONASUPO was essentially replaced by two separate programs operated by the Ministry of Agriculture, Livestock, Rural Development, Fishing, and Food (Secretaría de Agricultura, Ganadería, Desarrollo Rural, Pesca y Alimentación, SAGARPA) to help subsidize agricultural production. The first program was called Alianza—the name was later modified by the Fox administration to be Alianza Contigo—and provides subsidies and financial assistance for the purchase of farm implements and irrigation. The second program is called PROCAMPO, and provides direct subsidies to protect farmers to offset international competition from foreign agribusinesses that receive subsidies from their governments, particularly those from the United States.[17] Thus the Mexican government essentially continues to provide subsidies for farmers and Mexican consumers—especially for corn and widely consumed corn-derived products like tortillas—which creates ample political support for these programs. President Calderón learned how strongly such subsidies are supported during his first few months in office, when he initially refused to offset agricultural price increases in early 2007 (see textbox 10.1).

Textbox 10.1. President Calderón and the Tortilla Conflict

The issue of food subsidies became a contentious one for President Felipe Calderón, who attempted to reduce the deep divisions following the 2006 election by pledging to make fighting poverty his first priority. Yet when Calderón initially refused to offset the increase in the price of corn—the principal ingredient in tortillas, an indispensable staple of the Mexican diet—during his first few months in office, his pledge to help the poor seemed disingenuous. Calderón later negotiated a voluntary price cap on corn in which producers and retailers agreed not to allow corn to be sold above forty-five cents a pound. Still, while Calderón supporters widely viewed this pact to be in keeping with his promise, his critics were incensed by the fact that the cap still allowed the price of corn to increase. Moreover, the higher price of tortillas was just one of many signs of inflation: between January 2006 and January 2007, the price of tortillas increased 40 percent, eggs were up 46 percent, sugar had increased by 26 percent, and rice cost 15 percent more. In response, a broad coalition of groups, including members of Congress from the PRD and PT, as well as peasant organizations, civic groups, and unions, organized a series of public demonstrations, the largest attracting tens of thousands of supporters, to call for the systematic reintroduction of price controls on basic food items. Notably marginalized from the demonstrations was Andrés Manuel López Obrador, who was forced to speak after the main event had ended rather than taking center stage. Still, while López Obrador's support seemed seriously diminished, Calderón's ability to address the needs of Mexico's poorest citizens will no doubt remain a critical challenge throughout his term. If Calderón fails to do so, support for the political opposition could grow significantly by the next election.

Moreover, in addition to food subsidies, the Mexican government provides an array of other broadly accessible social assistance, such as the national housing program known as INFONAVIT (which assists workers in saving and obtaining loans to buy a home) and the health care and pension system described later in this chapter. Such programs fit the model of traditional social welfare programs, but have increasingly seen important modifications that reduce or otherwise significantly alter the government's role in welfare service provision. To understand this shift, we now turn to look at the new trend toward market-oriented social welfare programs.

Market-Oriented Social Welfare Programs

Beginning in the late 1980s, Mexican policy makers gradually began to shift away from the use of traditional social welfare programs. Faced with enormous fiscal deficits, massive foreign debt, and spiraling inflation, Mexican policy makers sought to dramatically reduce public sector spending as part of the country's neoliberal economic restructuring. As we saw in the previous chapter, the shift toward fiscal austerity was partly the result of the pressure from the United States and international organizations like the World Bank and the International Monetary Fund, and the ascendancy of neoliberal economic policies that focused on market-driven policies and reduced state intervention.

In this context, reducing or eliminating government social welfare programs was one way that Mexican policy makers believed they could effectively respond to these multiple pressures. Yet, reducing public sector spending on social welfare policy also presented potential domestic political risks. As we saw above, throughout the decade, ordinary Mexicans were adversely affected by economic crisis, and—with the PAN gaining ground and new opposition forming on the left—the PRI government hoped to avoid losing political support for the regime. Hence, at the outset of his term, President Carlos Salinas introduced a new plan to address Mexico's social welfare needs, while also steering the country toward a different sort of public assistance.

In 1989, Salinas introduced the National Solidarity Program (Programa Nacional de Solidaridad, PRONASOL), also known simply as Solidaridad, as a complement to his aggressive neoliberal economic agenda. PRONASOL provided direct government funds or transfers to be used for the development of public works projects and social welfare programs, which had important political implications for building PRI support. Moreover, the type of projects—which included the construction of roads, water filtration plants, hospitals, clinics, recreational facilities, classrooms, and schools—was not particularly unique or distinct from populist or traditional social programs. However, it was the nature of its implementation that made PRONASOL emblematic of a new emphasis in social welfare policy programs emerging not only in Mexico, but also worldwide. Such programs placed greater emphasis on individual and community participation as the state's partners in the provision of social welfare, both as a way to reduce costs and to ensure a greater sense of personal responsibility among beneficiaries. Rather than providing universal benefits—such as universal access to health care or old-age pensions, even for those who can afford to pay their own way—this new brand of social welfare policy sought to ensure greater efficiency through the targeting of benefits. In the case of PRO-NASOL, the Salinas administration required local communities and stakeholders to form project committees, and required that the beneficiaries of public works projects contribute their own labor, materials, or money to each project. In many ways, PRONASOL was considered an important innovation in government social welfare programs, and marked an important shift in the underlying philosophical approach toward social policy in Mexico.

PRONASOL emphasized the decentralization of social welfare distribution, more efficient targeting of individual communities, and greater civic participation and social responsibility in its programs. Yet, at the same time, critics charged that PRONASOL in fact perpetuated strong central control, since in many cases its resources went directly to local communities, bypassing state and local governments. The program was also widely criticized because some projects were perceived as wasteful or blatant evidence of corruption. While the program led to the construction of many important infrastructure projects, PRONASOL funds were famously used to construct impractical projects in communities that had more obvious social needs; many poor indigenous communities, for example, received regulation-size basketball courts through the program. Finally, substantial amounts of money were evidently misappropriated, or went into lucrative contracts for government cronies who produced inadequately constructed projects. Not surprisingly, members of the political opposition claimed that Solidarity committees were thinly veiled extensions of the PRI, intended to bolster the party's lagging support in an era of economic crisis.

When President Ernesto Zedillo took office in December 1994, his administration was particularly sensitive to the charges of political manipulation that had been applied to PRONASOL, and hoped to develop an alternative program that would again reshape Mexican social policy. However, key constituencies continued to support the program and, more importantly, the monetary crisis Zedillo faced at the outset of his term delayed major innovations until August 1997, when he introduced a new program called Progresa and began gradually dismantling PRONASOL. Progresa was a $155 million dollar program intended to address the problem of extreme poverty through education, health care, and nutritional supplements. One of the main features of the program was direct cash stipends or scholarships (ranging from around $10 to $100 U.S. dollars per month) made to low-income families—especially in carefully selected indigenous and rural communities—to keep their children in school. The program had a special emphasis on providing education for females, whose families were awarded higher stipends for keeping their daughters in the program. Tested initially in nine states during the previous year, the program was expanded to serve 1.9 million families at the national level over the course of 1997–1998; by the end of his term, the program grew to reach 2.4 million families.[18]

Critics of Progresa—including then presidential candidate Vicente Fox—pointed to its failure to address the challenge of economic development, its perpetuation of a dependent state-society relationship, and the potential for political manipulation. That is, such critics viewed Progresa as a poor substitute for promoting economic growth and development. They also suggested that the Zedillo administration was able to use the program to manipulate public opinion in poor rural communities in favor of the PRI.[19] Progresa reached approximately 40 percent of rural Mexican households by the end of Zedillo's term, and some recipients feared the program would be abolished if the PRI lost the 2000 elections.[20] In response to such criticisms, the Zedillo administration could point to Mexico's significant economic recovery and a restoration of growth by the end of his term. Also, Progresa was meticulously designed to ensure that participants were selected on the basis of need, and not by political considerations.

In the end, Progresa proved extremely popular, given its impact in such a large number of households (reaching over 13 percent of the population in 53,000 communities by the end of Zedillo's term).[21] The program also enjoyed substantial legitimacy and support from international organizations like the World Bank and the Inter-American Development Bank, which lauded its efforts to break the cycle of multigenerational chronic poverty through education. In fact, in 2002, the Inter-American Development Bank announced the approval of its largest loan ever to Mexico: US$5 billion for the multiphase, six-year expansion of Progresa to cover urban areas and increase coverage of previously ineligible families. Hence, whatever criticisms Fox made of the program during the presidential campaign, his administration had strong incentives to continue and expand Progresa. Fox did choose to rename the program, which was now called Oportunidades, and gave more of the population access to its benefits. By the end of 2006, coverage extended to five million families—double the participation under Zedillo—from 2,441 municipalities in all 31 Mexican states and the Federal District.[22]

The Calderón administration opted to continue the Oportunidades program, which has continued to receive ample international recognition; indeed, in April 2007, New York Mayor Michael Bloomberg made headlines when he announced that he would implement a local program modeled on Oportunidades. Again, in the grand scheme, Oportunidades represents an interesting hybrid program of the two contrasting models of social welfare provision that have predominated in recent years. Like most traditional social welfare programs, Oportunidades emphasizes universal accessibility and the provision of handouts in the form of transfers and direct welfare benefits to people in need. Yet, like PRONASOL and the other market-oriented programs that have emerged in recent decades, Oportunidades seeks to help others help themselves by requiring that participants fulfill specific obligations in order to receive its benefits. Policy analysts will likely need more time to evaluate the staying power and effectiveness of this model, and whether it can ultimately help break the cycle of multigenerational poverty.

Key Challenges for Improving Social Welfare in Mexico

Our discussion of social welfare policy has so far focused primarily on social assistance programs that alleviate poverty. While such programs are an important part of the social welfare function of the modern state, they are not the only means—or necessarily the best way—to reduce poverty and promote overall social well-being. In most countries, the state's role in facilitating economic development, as well as providing other universal services—such as education, health care, retirement pensions for the elderly—arguably provides much greater overall social welfare than a reliance solely on direct assistance to the poor. With this in mind, President Fox emphasized the need for government programs that promote long-term economic development as a solution to poverty and inequality in Mexico. His administration introduced a series of programs—the Plan Puebla-Panamá, PRONAFIM, and Contigo Manos a la Obra—that were intended to promote job creation and economic development.

One of the flagship programs of the Fox administration was the Plan Puebla-Panamá, a regional development project that was intended to expand and improve infrastructure in Mexico's underdeveloped south and all through Central America. The underlying rationale of the plan was that Mexico's poorest regions (and neighboring countries to the south) suffered from a lack of connectivity to domestic and world markets. The Fox administration argued that, without adequate highways, ports, airports, and telecommunications infrastructure, these areas were prevented from taking full advantage of the opportunities of the global economy.[23] To implement the plan, Fox sought to work with his counterparts in Central America, and—importantly—to attract matching funding from private sector and international financial institutions.

Yet, the Plan Puebla-Panamá suffered important setbacks. First, the program faced significant criticism—especially by the Zapatista rebel movement—charging that the plan would simply continue and exacerbate the exploitation of the indigenous peoples by further exposing them to the ravages of the global economy. Second, the Fox administration's plan depended in large part on the government's ability to increase its own financial resources through a major fiscal reform. The failure of Fox's fiscal reform package early in his term made it difficult to secure the necessary matching funding from the private sector and international organizations in order to follow through with the plan. In succeeding Fox, President Felipe Calderón expressed his interest in continuing efforts to implement the Plan Puebla-Panamá, which could benefit from the successful fiscal reform package introduced early in his term.

In recent years, a second policy innovation intended to create jobs for the working poor has been the use of microcredit lending. Limited access to capital presents a serious obstacle to economic advancement for poor people. While the wealthy can reinvest their accumulated wealth to make financial gains, the poor must often scrape by to survive. Without access to loans and credit, the poor are unable to initiate their own microenterprises (such as a local taco business) or make larger personal investments that build equity and improve their quality of life (such as purchasing a home). In developing countries like Mexico, obtaining such loans is difficult because banks lack assurances that the loans will be properly repaid. For these reasons, many economists and international organizations have increasingly advocated programs that assist poor people by providing access to credit, often with loans as small as $50 to a few hundred dollars provided on a very short-term basis. Such programs not only help people to address short-term emergencies, but can serve as a means to jump start new business ventures.

During his presidential campaign, Vicente Fox promised to initiate a lending program that would provide the means to start microenterprises, which he referred to as *changarros* (a slang term for a small business). The microcredit program Fox introduced in 2001 was called the National Microbusiness Financing Program (Programa Nacional de Financiamiento al Microempresario, PRONAFIM). By August 2006, PRONAFIM had distributed approximately $660 million in microcredit loans.[24] Although the program did not reach all would-be borrowers and some borrowers had difficulty repaying the loans, those households that participated in the program had measurable gains in spending on education, health, and recreational activities by loan recipients. These results that seem to indicate at least preliminary benefits from participating in the program. [25] Further studies of PRONAFIM and other microcredit programs will be needed to evaluate its long-term impacts. In the meantime, the Calderón administration has maintained the program in place.

Finally, another recent approach to promoting economic development for the poor has centered on microregions, where Fox hoped to create special economic development zones, especially in poor areas. Under the slogan "With You: Hands at Work" (*Contigo, manos a la obra*)—the Fox administration sought to coordinate public-private partnerships between private businesses, universities, and communities to stimulate economic opportunities in 250 development zones in 17 states and 476 poor municipalities throughout Mexico. The program succeeded in attracting participation from CEMEX (Mexico's largest cement company) which provided concrete at reduced cost for paving dirt floors, as well as from the prestigious Monterrey Technological Institute and Microsoft, which donated computing equipment and training in these development zones. Yet the Contigo program also directed resources to other forms of poverty alleviation, health care, and education, such as access to basic nutrition, vaccinations, and Spanish-language lessons in indigenous communities.

Perhaps the best known Contigo initiative was the 3-for-1 migrant remittance program (Programa 3x1 Para Migrantes), which the Fox administration initiated in 2002 in an effort to leverage the billions of dollars sent back by migrants to their home communities in Mexico each year. Most money sent back to Mexico by migrants is intended to help out their families back home, putting food on the table, assisting with home improvements, sending children to school, and the like. But some experts have noted that the economic development effects of such cash transfers are limited, since they are not channeled into long-term economic development projects. The 3-for-1 program tries to address this issue. For every peso migrants contributed to the 3-for-1 program, the federal, state, and local governments invested one peso each in matching funds for projects that to help improve those communities. By 2005, the government estimated that the program had benefited over 4 million people, distributing nearly $20 billion in investments to migrant-sending communities. Projects included social assistance programs, highway and street paving projects, electrification, and other local improvement projects, with 76 percent of federal funds for the program concentrated in five moderately poor migrant-sending states: Jalisco, Zacatecas, Guanajuato, Michoacán, and San Luis Potosí (in order of spending).[26] It is not clear that these projects will have long-lasting effects; some may be mere white elephant projects that do relatively little to promote economic development. For another, most migrant remittances are directed by individuals to support their families; getting migrants to contribute to public goods is more difficult, since it does not provide a direct personal benefit. Hence, experts still disagree as to whether migrant remittances truly can (or should) be harnessed for economic development purposes.

What is clear is that in recent years, policy makers have increasingly emphasized innovative approaches to solving poverty through strategies that emphasize economic development. This shift may be particularly representative of Mexico's larger political transformation, in that the country's new governing party—the PAN—has a strong business orientation. In the longer term, critics may also raise questions about the effectiveness of these strategies in addressing poverty; the longer-term benefits of PAN policies may have more significant benefits for moderately poor states (like the ones that benefit from the 3-for-1 program), and members of the lower middle class who may be better positioned to take advantage of these programs than the extremely poor.[27] Yet to turn such criticisms into a political advantage, PRI and PRD opponents of the PAN will need to develop an alternative set of policies that successfully engages the poor and, ideally, helps to improve their conditions.

Reforming Education, Health Care, and Social Security

In addition to strategies that improve economic development opportunities as a means of combating poverty, policy makers and experts have also increasingly pointed to the need for reforms in Mexican education. At the same time, the Mexican government has recently tried to expand and modernize the provision of health care and retirement pensions, to better address the basic needs of society. Below we briefly outline the current systems in place, the areas for improvement, and recent or pending reforms in these areas.

Education

Mexico's constitution guarantees all citizens access to a basic education. Like the United States, Mexico has multiple levels of education, including primary school, secondary or middle school, and preparatory or high school. Unlike in the United States, however, two-thirds of Mexican children aged three to five also attend preschool, which generally consists of three grades, corresponding to the child's age.[28]

All told, approximately 91 percent of students enrolled at these levels attend public schools. Mexico has a number of alternative programs to provide access to primary education, including adult education programs and bilingual/bicultural programs for many of Mexico's numerous indigenous dialects and cultures. Since 1993, a secondary education—the equivalent of U.S. middle school—has been obligatory for all persons aged twelve to sixteen who have completed primary education. Students over age sixteen are eligible to study in facilities designed for vocational studies or in adult-oriented secondary education programs. Together, preschool, primary, and secondary education constitute what Mexican officials describe as the basic education required by the constitution; approximately 25 million students (or 77 percent of all students) are enrolled at this level, with approximately 1.1 million (67 percent) of Mexican teachers working in basic education.

Preparatory (*preparatoria*) education is the Mexican equivalent to U.S. high school.[29] While preparatory school is typically required for entrance to university and professional schools, it is neither obligatory nor guaranteed. Approximately 3.6 million Mexicans attended preparatory schools in 2005–2006, though this represented a relatively small proportion (only about 11 percent) of total student enrollment in the Mexican education system (see figure 10.1). Since 1990, however, there has been a modest increase in the proportion of students attending early childhood education and higher levels beyond basic or middle school education. The largest increases can be seen in the proportion of students going to preschool (up from 10.9 percent in 1990 to 13.8 percent of total student enrollment in 2005) and preparatory school (up from 8.4 percent in 1990 to 11.3 percent of all student enrollment in 2005). These trends are especially promising because of the perceived long-term benefits of preschool—including better student retention, performance, and socialization—and the potential for increased advancement to higher education.[30] However, meeting the obligatory requirements of preschool established by law while ensuring a high level of quality is likely to prove challenging; in 2007, the Ministry of Education reported difficulties in ensuring full preschool enrollment for all Mexican children, due to a lack of adequate teachers and facilities.[31]

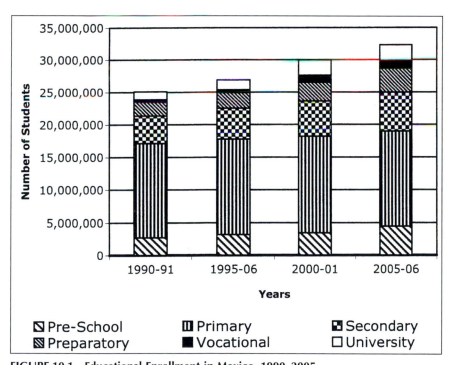

FIGURE 10.1 Educational Enrollment in Mexico, 1990–2005
Source: "Sistema Educativo de los Estados Unidos Mexicanos, Principales Cifras, Ciclo Escolar 2005–06," Secretaría de Educación Pública, Dirección General de Planeación y Programación, Unidad de Planeación y Evaluación de Políticas Educativas.

Mexican higher education (*educación superior*) is provided by university, vocational, and other specialized educational programs. The objective of higher education is to promote the development of professionals in various areas of science, technology, culture, and other specialized fields. While higher education programs may be either public or private, the vast majority of students at this level attend public universities. This reflects the fact that public universities tend to be much more affordable than private universities. For example, for many years there was virtually no cost—students paid a few U.S. cents per year—to attend the National Autonomous University of Mexico (Universidad Nacional Autonoma de México, UNAM), the largest university in Mexico, with over 200,000 students. In fact, when university officials tried to introduce higher fees in 2000, students and faculty waged a massive 291-day strike to protest, essentially shutting down classes. Government troops reclaimed the campus on February 6, 2000, arresting about 700 people and drawing accusations of minor abuses. The campus was reopened the following week, but authorities declined to follow through on their plan to significantly increase fees; today, UNAM's annual tuition rates typically amount to several U.S. dollars, depending on the student's major. By comparison, college tuition and fees range between US$11,000–12,000 annually to attend the privately run Monterrey Technological Institute (ITESM) or the Western Technological Institute for Higher Studies (Instituto Tecnológico de Estudios Superiores del Oriente, ITESO) in Guadalajara.[32] Since Mexican universities typically do not have on-campus dormitories, these rates do not include room and board.

Mexico's total budget for education now represents about 7.1 percent of GDP (US$54 billion).[33] Despite the government's significant role in financing education in Mexico, schools that depend on public funding are supposed to be free from political influences. Yet critics point to important areas open to government intervention in shaping the content and tone of public education. For example, many claimed that during its rule, the PRI regularly manipulated national history to favor itself. Similarly, though publicly funded universities are intended to be autonomous or independent from the Mexican government, on some occasions university officials have faced significant government intervention.[34] For example, since the PAN has gained control over the federal government, members of the PRI and PRD have worried about possible religious influences and moralism in public and university education.

Much remains to be done to improve the quality and degree of access to Mexico's education system. As illustrated by the low proportion of students who go on to attend high school and higher education, there are disturbing patterns of unequal access to education in Mexico. While the national illiteracy rate was about 8 percent in 2006, many northern and urban states enjoyed much lower rates than average: Baja California (1.4 percent), the Federal

District (2.7 percent), and Nuevo León (2.8 percent). At the same time, poor southern states suffered the worst rates of illiteracy in the country: Guerrero (18.2 percent), Oaxaca (18.3 percent), and Chiapas (19.4 percent).[35] Many experts believe that addressing such inequities is critical as a means of alleviating poverty and promoting economic development. Still, important questions must be asked about the kind of educational reforms that are needed, and specifically how improved educational opportunities will be translated into opportunities for better employment and compensation.

How these questions are addressed will have important implications for contemporary democratic politics in Mexico. First, one obvious implication for Mexican democracy is that an educated populace may foster a more politically active and responsible electorate. Educated voters are usually more likely to turn out at the polls, and are often more in tune with political issues; uneducated voters are sometimes left out or—even worse, some fear—easily misled. Improvements in education may therefore make for better and more participatory democratic politics overall. Second, over the next decade, the state of education in Mexico will likely have corresponding implications for Mexico's political parties as they compete for votes. Indeed, advances in education arguably may have favored the PAN's gradual rise to power, especially in the well-educated north, while the PRI long depended on its ability to draw support from (or exploit) poor and uneducated voters. The PRI has learned how to compete for the support of Mexico's educationally advanced northern voters, but at the same time, there appears to be significant competition between the PRI and the PRD for the voters in Mexico's underprivileged southern states. The implications of this dynamic are unclear. Furthermore, it remains to be seen whether improved rates of education in these states—combined with better economic opportunities—will lead more southern voters to consider supporting the PAN.

Health Care and Social Security

Health care is an important policy area that has major social welfare implications, and bears importantly on any discussion of poverty and inequality in Mexico. The Mexican government has long played an important role in the provision of social security services including health care, disability, life insurance, and retirement benefits, and today provides coverage of some sort to approximately 80 percent of the population. Most public medical and retirement services are provided through the Ministry of Health that was created in 1943, when the Mexican government was beginning to embrace a much greater role for the state in the provision of social welfare. The main public health-care services overseen by the Ministry of Health are distinguished by whether recipients are public or private employees. Government employees and their families are covered by either federal or state-subsidized health-care programs. Federal employees pay approximately 8.5 percent of their salary to the social security insurance program of the Institute of Security and Social Services for Government Employees (Instituto de Seguridad y Servicios Sociales de los Trabajadores del Estado, or ISSSTE), while state and municipal employees are covered by state-level programs. All other formally employed Mexicans similarly pay into the Mexican Social Security Institute (Instituto Mexicano del Seguro Social, or IMSS) insurance program.[36]

IMSS is a much larger program than ISSSTE, since coverage extends to all affiliated private sector employees, their spouses, children, and parents of the primary affiliate. Both IMSS and ISSSTE also play a much broader role than the U.S. social security system, delivering a variety of health-care services, unemployment insurance, pensions for retired and disabled persons, life insurance, and programs for day care, recreation, culture, and the arts.[37] Finally, in addition to the 47 percent of the population covered by the programs mentioned above, there are a variety of other public and private health-care services available in Mexico. Thanks to a major health system reform in 2003, the Ministry of Health provides some direct services to the other half of Mexico's population who are self-employed, unemployed, or not employed in the formal sector.[38] In addition, the Comprehensive Family Development Program (Desarrollo Integral de la Familia (DIF), for example, is a decentralized government agency operated at the federal, state, and local levels to provide a wide array of services for families. At the same time, there are a variety of private and nonprofit medical care programs in Mexico. For those who are self-employed or can afford private health coverage or attention, private prepay insurance programs and fee-for-service medical care are available; indeed, this roughly 3 percent of Mexicans (mostly with relatively high socioeconomic status) has access to some of the most skilled medical professionals in the world. Generally speaking, both public and private medical services, as well as prescription drugs, are comparably more affordable than in many developed countries. Indeed, it is common along the U.S.-Mexican border, for example, for U.S. citizens to travel south to Mexico to obtain cheaper health services and medicines.

Despite this seemingly extensive infrastructure and accessibility for health care and social security, there are important limitations to Mexico's system that are germane to any discussion of poverty and inequality. First, as noted above, there can be a significant distinction in the quality of care provided by public and private medical services. While this is generally true in many public health-care systems, the degree of inequality in Mexico makes the gap in the quality of private-public medical services particularly severe. Indeed, as Knaul and Frenk note, the World Health Organization ranked Mexican health care

51st out of 191 countries in 2000, but scored Mexico much lower (144th) on the issue of financial equity in the health-care system.[39]

Second, the Mexican health-care system is not easily accessible to many Mexicans. While the system theoretically provides universal coverage to all public and private sector employees, the reality is quite different. Because a large number of Mexicans—possibly as many as 40 percent—are employed in the informal sector, their wages are not typically reported to the government and employers do not pay into Mexican social security. Because these individuals are not eligible for ISSSTE or IMSS social security coverage, the Ministry of Health operates a variety of programs—including the Popular Insurance Program (Seguro Popular) and IMSS-Oportunidades—that endeavor to provide support for this significant portion of the population.

To make matters worse, it became increasingly apparent during the 1990s that the IMSS pension system for formal employees was headed toward bankruptcy. Like other pension programs, IMSS relied on payroll deductions from employee wages to ensure that they will continue to receive income during their retirement. Like the United States, Mexico is in the midst of a major generational change that will significantly impact the functioning of its pension programs over the next two decades. Population growth and mortality rates in both countries have fallen significantly since World War II and the number of people paying in to the system has declined, while the number of people needing its benefits has increased. Furthermore, increased life expectancy, which is now over seventy, also means that pension recipients now require benefits for a longer period of time.[40] Adding to this urgent demographic reality was the fact that significant problems, including evasion in payroll contributions, weakened the financial structure of the pension program.[41]

In this context, Mexican public officials have attempted to make several major reforms, beginning with a series of modifications to the pension system and, more recently, with significant reforms to the public health care system. First, beginning in the early 1990s, the Mexican government attempted to address the pension problem by increasing the amount of workers' IMSS contributions, and by introducing a new program for worker pensions, known as a employer-defined contribution plan, in 1992. This employer contribution program, known as the Retirement Savings System (Sistema de Ahorro para el Retiro, SAR), required that employers contribute 2 percent of a worker's salary to an individual retirement account (IRA) managed by Mexican banks for the employee.[42] Drawing on these investments, SAR was intended to help to supplement IMSS pension contributions and bolster an individual contributor's retirement income. However, the SAR program experienced significant problems, including poor regulation, confusion, and excessive concentration in the management of accounts.[43] In 1997, reforms to the SAR introduced a new employee-defined contribution program in which not only employers but all formally employed workers were now required to make mandatory fixed payroll allocations into privately operated pension fund plans. The perceived advantage of the 1997 reforms was the potential for private financial institutions—also known as Retirement Fund Administrators (Administradores de Fondos Para el Retiro, AFORES)—to generate significantly greater returns and better service for pensioners.[44] Indeed, based on experiences in other Latin American countries, the AFORES program was viewed by many observers as a successful model for retirement pension management, and a way to boost Mexico's domestic savings rate.[45]

During the Fox administration, however, Mexico's public health care and social security system continued to suffer from a lack of coverage for uninsured persons. In 2003, an estimated 20 percent of the Mexican population did not have access to health and social security coverage of any kind.[46] By comparison, an estimated 15 percent of the U.S. population—including 30 percent of all people living in poverty (and one in nine children)—did not have any health-care insurance at that time, and depended primarily on pay-as-you-go care or emergency medical coverage. Moreover, Mexico's pension system also evidenced some problems in the administration of AFORES (including high operating costs, commissions, and fees), the relatively low amount of contributions to retirement accounts, and—perhaps more significantly—a lack of portability for workers wishing to transfer their pension funds from one employer to another. During President Fox's term, a major reform was passed in 2003 to expand health-care coverage from the 47 percent covered by IMSS and ISSSTE to an additional 11 million uninsured families, or roughly 50 million Mexicans. This reform created the System for Social Protection in Health (Sistema Nacional de Protección Social en Salud, SNPSS), and its centerpiece—the Popular Insurance program—with the goal of expanding universal coverage to all uninsured Mexicans by 2010.[47]

Upon taking office, President Calderón declared public health and social security to be a continuing priority for his administration, with a special emphasis on increasing overall coverage and equity within the existing system. At the start of his term, Calderón significantly increased the budget for health-care programs and announced a major initiative to provide universal access to all Mexicans born at the start of his administration on December 1, 2006. In addition, his administration announced plans to significantly expand the functions of the Popular Insurance program to better and more rapidly expand coverage to those currently uninsured. Calderón also rolled out new mobile health programs to provide medical services in poor and remote rural areas, and a series of new hospitals and clinics to be opened throughout the country during his term. Finally, in his 2006–2012 National Development

Plan, Calderón specifically targeted the 100 poorest municipalities of the country for special efforts to improve access to social welfare programs, as well as improved opportunities for economic development.[48]

Later, in March 2007, Calderón proposed significant reforms to the government pension program, ISSSTE, that were approved the next month. The ISSSTE reform signaled the Calderón administration's ability to negotiate with the opposition-dominated legislature, as well as vital support that Calderón enjoyed from some labor allies who favored the benefits that the reform would bring to government employee teachers.[49] The ISSSTE reform was the first part of Calderón's plan to expand changes to other areas of the social security system, by expanding coverage available to independent workers (including those employed in the informal sector), increasing the required contributions to pension programs, and by allowing the possibility to roll over or move pension plans between different employers. His legislative success in passing the reform appeared to boost Calderón's overall public approval ratings, and brought very favorable responses from the private sector and the international community.[50] Still, whether Calderón's efforts result in continued improvements to Mexico's health care and retirement benefit system will require further evaluation over the longer term.

Conclusion

In short, despite Mexico's economic strengths—and even tremendous prosperity—the country's continued development depends on improving the lot of poor Mexicans. Better distribution of wealth and opportunities would enable them to make a greater contribution to the overall economy. To some degree, Mexico has made progress toward this end, particularly as the economic turmoil of the 1980s and 1990s has subsided in recent years. Indeed, recent Mexican government strategies to promote social welfare have focused significantly on promoting economic development, both at the regional and grassroots level. This emphasis appears to be yet another reflection of the new emphasis on the state's role as a facilitator—and not the direct caretaker—of both the economy and social welfare.

At the same time, there has been an important shift away from traditional government policies for promoting social welfare, toward new market-oriented policies that promote greater individual responsibility and opportunity. For some, this shift in the Mexican approach to poverty represents a transition away from cumbersome, state-centered programs that encouraged clientelistic abuse and welfare dependency. The measures used by the Fox administration to evaluate poverty suggested a marked improvement over the course of his term, with a reduction in poverty to only 40 percent of households (and 47 percent of individuals) by 2004. Still, the shift away from traditional social welfare policies has fierce critics. For them, the new orientation of social welfare programs in Mexico and the dismantling of the social safety net places the actual burden of poverty alleviation on Mexico's poor, and remains unproven as a means to promote long-term economic development. Indeed, despite Fox's claims of reducing poverty, large numbers of Mexican people ultimately felt dissatisfied with his performance in delivering greater economic prosperity.

The 2006 presidential election presented a choice between two very different visions of how Mexico would address poverty and inequality: AMLO's left-leaning approach emphasized redistribution and assistance to the poor—"for the good of all, first the poor" (*por el bien de todos, primero los pobres*)—versus Calderón's more conservative vision that emphasized creating jobs and new opportunities. Now Calderón's administration may be well poised to make important advances toward achieving some of the unrealized goals of the Fox administration, such as bolstering the government's fiscal revenues for investment in infrastructure and revamping Mexico's education system. Even if he is successful, tackling poverty and inequality, and improving the quality of life for all Mexicans, will remain a challenge for some time to come. How these issues are handled will undoubtedly also hold major implications for contemporary Mexican democracy, both in terms of future political outcomes and the ability of the country's millions of poor voters to participate as full and active democratic citizens.

Key Terms

AFORES	Ministry of Education
chronic poverty	Ministry of Health
CONASUPO	Oportunidades
Contigo (Manos a la Obra)	Plan Puebla-Panamá
demographic shift	poverty
employee-defined contribution	Progresa
employer-defined contribution	PRONAFIM
GDP per capita	PRONASOL/Solidaridad
Gini coefficient	purchasing power parity
IMSS	qualitative measure of poverty
inequality	retirement savings system
INFONAVIT	social welfare policy
ISSSTE	SEDESOL
marginalized	SNPSS
minimum wage	transitional poverty

Recommended Readings

Cook, Maria Lorena, Kevin J. Middlebrook, and Juan Molinar Horcasitas. *The Politics of Economic Restructuring: State-Society Relations and Regime Change in Mexico*. La Jolla, Calif.: Center for U.S.-Mexican Studies, 1994.

Dresser, Denise. *Neopopulist Solutions to Neoliberal Problems: Mexico's National Solidarity Program*. La Jolla: Center for U.S. Mexican Studies, 1991.

Middlebrook, Kevin J., and Eduardo Zepeda. *Confronting Development: Assessing Mexico's Economic and Social Policy Challenges*. (Stanford, Calif.: Stanford University Press, 2003).

Notes

1. World Bank, World Development Indicators Database, July 1, 2007.

2. Mexico's 1917 constitution explicitly mandates the establishment of a minimum wage. The minimum is set by the National Minimum Wage Commission according to the price of a basket of food products.

3. The minimum wage for the north and in tourist areas (about US$4.50 per day) is slightly higher than that in other regions (e.g., the center, $4.37 per day and the south, $4.25 per day). Currency conversion based on the July 2007 exchange rate of roughly 10.8 pesos to the dollar.

4. This is a different definition of extreme poverty than the one used by the United Nations, which sets the rate as those persons earning less than one dollar per day.

5. One problem with measuring poverty in this way is that wages may not represent all of a household's sources of income. In Mexico, many poor people often earn money through ways that are not easily monitored by the government, such as working as a street vendor or a domestic servant. Income from this vast "informal" economy is not registered.

6. This measure of purchasing power is usually indexed to the U.S. dollar, and represents the relative value of income, controlling for the cost of living.

7. World Bank, World Development Indicators Database, July 1, 2007.

8. World Bank Data, PovCal Net, http://iresearch.worldbank.org/PovcalNet/povcalSvy.html (accessed July 21, 2007).

9. Julio Boltvinik, "Welfare, Inequality, and Poverty in Mexico," in *Confronting Development: Assessing Mexico's Economic and Social Policy Challenges,* ed. Kevin J. Middlebrook and Eduardo Zepeda (Standford, Calif.: Stanford University Press, 2003).

10. Juan Pardinas, "Fighting Poverty in Mexico: Policy Changes," in *Mexico under Fox*, ed. Luis Rubio and Susan Kaufman Purcell (Boulder: Lynne Rienner, 2004), 65–86; Aguayo, *Almanaque Mexicano*, 2007. See also the SEDESOL website.

11. See Dorte Verner, "Activities, Employment, and Wages in Rural and Semi-Urban Mexico," World Bank Policy Research Working Paper 3561 (April 2005). Table 2.1, p. 7.

12. Mexico was not alone in this experience. By the early 1990s, the number of persons living in poverty in Latin America nearly doubled from 78 million in 1982 to 150 million in 1993. By the mid-1990s, the number of poor people climbed to 210 million; a proportional increase in the number of poor people from 35 percent in the 1980s to 41 percent in the 1990s. According to some analysts, Latin American income disparities became the worst in the entire world in the 1990s. See Roberto Patricio Korzeniewicz and William C. Smith, "Poverty, Inequality, and Growth in Latin America: Searching for the High Road to Globalization," *Latin American Research Review* 35, no. 3 (2000): 9.

13. Sara R. Gordon, "Nuevas desigualdades y política social," in *Las políticas sociales de México al fin del milenio, diseño y gestión*, ed. Rolando Cordera and Alicia Ziccardi (México: Coordinación de Humanidades, Facultad de Economía and Instituto de Investigaciones Sociales, UNAM, 2000), 57–70.

14. Vivienne Bennett, "The Evolution of Urban Popular Movements in Mexico between 1968 and 1988," in *The Making of Social Movements in Latin America* (Boulder: Westview, 1992), 240–59.

15. The agency was formerly the Ministry of Public Works (1959–1976), the Ministry of Human Settlements and Public Works (1976–1982), and the Ministry of Urban Development and Ecology (1982–1992). It received its most recent title and mission under President Salinas.

16. The Ministry of Health was predated by the Ministry of Wellness and Hygiene in the 1920s and 1930s, when the primary functions of the agency were focused on health. However, when the Ministry of Social Assistance (Secretaría de Asistencia Social) was created in 1938, it took on many public health functions. In 1940, the agency was renamed the Ministry of Health and Welfare (Secretaría de Salubridad y Asistencia, SSA) until it was given its current title in 1982.

17. PROCAMPO website, www.aserca.gob.mx, (accessed July 28, 2007).

18. Rose Spalding, "Early Social Policy Initiatives in the Fox Administration" (paper presented at the Twenty-Third International Congress of the Latin American Studies Association, Washington, D.C., September 6–8, 2001), 4.

19. Academic analyses found mixed support for this claim, since the program definitely targeted poor families but also appeared to produce important political benefits for the PRI in statistical analysis. Alina Rocha Menocal, "Do Old Habits Die Hard? A Statistical Exploration of the Politicisation of Progresa, Mexico's Latest Federal Poverty-Alleviation Programme, under the Zedillo Administration," *Journal of Latin American Studies* 33 (2001): 513–38.

20. According to Spalding, Fox and his close advisers believed that Progresa had been used as a "stick" to threaten voters, who were told that if Fox was elected they would no longer receive its benefits.

21. Spalding, "Early Social Policy Initiatives," 4.

22. See "Padrón Inicial Correspondiente al Ejercicio Fiscal 2007," www.oportunidades.gob.mx.

23. Given costly fees and inefficiencies in port operations, for example, some leather producers in León, Nicaragua, might find themselves at a competitive disadvantage to conduct business with Mexican footwear producers in León, Guanajuato.

Were those barriers removed through improved port operations, mutually beneficial gains from trade could result.

24. These figures are based on preliminary data from the start of the program in 2001 to July 2006, as posted on the PRONAFIM website, www.pronafim.gob.mx (accessed July 18, 2007).

25. David Arellano Gault, Victor G. Carreón Rodríguez, Gustavo A. Del Angel Mobarak, and Fausto Hernández Trillo, "Evaluación de Resultados del Programa Nacional de Financiamiento al Microempresario (PRONAFIM) Correspondiente al Ejercicio Fiscal 2006," Evaluación Parcial: Enero—Agosto de 2006, Centro de Investigación y Docencia Económicas, A.C., 83.

26. According to external analyses funded by SEDESOL, in terms of distribution, the program made its largest investments in poor, high–migrant sending communities. Servicios Profesionales Para el Desarrollo Económico (SEDESOL), "Tablados de Información de Gabinete," *Evaluación Externa del Programa 3x1 Para Migrantes*, 2005.

27. Interestingly, similar criticisms were made of U.S. progressive reformers who toppled political machines like New York's Tammany Hall and laid the foundation for conservative local governments in much of the postwar Southwest. See Amy Bridges, *Morning Glories: Municipal Reform in the Southwest* (Princeton, N.J.: Princeton University Press, 1997); see also Stephen Erie, *Rainbow's End* (Berkeley: University of California Press, 1988).

28. This is due to a 2002 constitutional amendment, which made it obligatory to attend preschool—the equivalent to kindergarten in the United States—beginning in 2004 for age five, in 2005 for age four, and in 2008 for age three. "Sistema Educativo de los Estados Unidos Mexicanos, Principales Cifras, Ciclo Escolar 2005–06," Secretaría de Educación Pública, Dirección General de Planeación y Programación, Unidad de Planeación y Evaluación de Políticas Educativas, 41.

29. Preparatory or baccalaureate school is frequently referred to as "middle" school education (*educación media superior*) but is essentially equivalent to U.S. high school.

30. Statistical analyses carried out in the United States and Latin America show that those who attend preschool have increased high school graduation rates, improved performance on standardized tests, reduced crime and delinquency, lower rates of teen pregnancy, and better economic opportunities. Albert Wat, "Dollars and Sense: A Review of Economic Analyses of Pre-K," *Pre-K Now Research Series*, Washington, D.C., May 2007; Filip Schiefelbein, "Efecto de la educación pre-escolar sobre el rendimiento a fines de primaria en Argentina, Bolivia, Colombia y Chile," *Revista Latinoamericana de Estudios Educativos* 7 (1982): 9–41.

31. Sonia del Valle, "Fallan en kínder: La SEP no tiene maestros suficientes para dar cumplimiento a la ley de educación que en 2008 hará obligatorio cursar tres años de preescolar," *Reforma*, August 7, 2007.

32. Tuition calculations are based on majors in political science and international relations; tuition in other majors (e.g., law) may vary. UNAM, *2006 Agenda Estadística*, Dirección General de Planeación, www.planeacion.unam.mx. For a useful discussion of UNAM and its historical development, see Robert A. Rhoads, "Power and Politics

in University Governance: Organization and Change at the Universidad Nacional Autonoma de Mexico," *Journal of Higher Education* 76, no. 2 (2005): 234–37. Data for ITESO obtained from website, www.uia.mx.

33. "Sistema Educativo de los Estados Unidos Mexicanos," 201.

34. Imanol Ordorika, *Power and Politics in University Governance: Organization and Change at the Universidad Nacional Autonoma de Mexico* (New York: Routledge Falmer, 2003).

35. "Sistema Educativo de los Estados Unidos Mexicanos," 27.

36. Eligibility for pension benefits begins after a defined period of approximately ten years or 500 weeks of formal employment. Gloria Grandolini and Luis Cerda, "Mexico: The 1997 Pension Reform in Mexico," *World Bank*, April 22, 1998, 5.

37. Because of its strong research emphasis, the Ministry of Health is a useful place for obtaining national- and state-level Mexican health statistics. It maintains a website at www.salud.gob.mx. Statistics are also available from the Mexican Foundation for Health, www.funsalud.org.mx.

38. Enrique Rios, "The Mexican Health Care System: A Federal Perspective" (presentation at the Trans-Border Institute, August 2006), www.sandiego.edu/tbi/events.

39. Overall spending on health care amounted to only 6.1 percent of GDP, or about $360 per person, a figure below the average for Latin American countries. Spending on health care in Mexico varied widely by state, with the richest states spending five times as much on health care as poor states. Felicia Marle Knaul and Julio Frenk, "Health Insurance in Mexico: Achieving Universal Coverage Through Structural Reform," *Health Affairs* 24, no. 5 (2003): 1467–69.

40. L. Jacobo Rodríguez, "In Praise and Criticism of Mexico's 1997 Pension Reform," *Policy Analysis*, April 14, 1999.

41. See Grandolini and Cerda, "Mexico," 6.

42. This pension reform was first implemented in 1992 and modified through new congressional legislation beginning in 1995. Furthermore, the Mexican Central Bank guaranteed private banks a 2 percent minimum annual rate of return on these accounts. Federal Reserve Bank of Dallas, "Pension Reform in Mexico," *Financial Industry*, Third/Fourth Quarter 1996, 2.

43. Grandolini, and Cerda, "Mexico," 9–11.

44. Olivia S. Mitchell, "Evaluating Administrative Costs in Mexico's AFORES Pension System," Pension Research Council Working Paper 99-1, January 1999, 33.

45. Similar reforms had been implemented in Chile in 1981 and Argentina in 1994. While the savings rate fell slightly in Argentina, in Chile domestic savings went from 16 percent to 29 percent of GDP from the mid-1980s to the early 1990s. Federal Reserve Bank of Dallas, "Pension Reform," 1–4.

46. Regarding Mexico's uninsured population, see Grandolini and Cerda, "Mexico," 4.

47. See Knaul and Frenk, "Health Insurance in Mexico," 1468.

48. *Plan Nacional de Desarrollo, 2006-2012,* www.presidencia.gov.mx (accessed July 21, 2006).

49. See Emilio Zebadúa, "Seguridad social, pasado y futuro," *El Universal*, May 11, 2007; Artemio Ortiz, "Por qué rechazar la nueva ley," *El Universal*, May 11, 2007.

50. Ricardo Jiménez, "Riesgo país, en su menor nivel del año," *El Universal*, May 29, 2007.

11

The Rule of Law in Mexico

In July 2004, dressed in white and marching peacefully through the nation's capital, over a quarter million people convened at the Mexico City *zócalo* to protest the elevated levels of crime and violence the country experienced beginning in the mid-1990s. Nonetheless, months later, in October 2004, continued public frustration over this crisis boiled over into a nationally televised lynching of three federal police officers whom locals suspected of illegal activities. In September 2005, a special federal envoy in Ciudad Juárez declared that police incompetence or corruption had hindered the investigations of the alleged serial murders of more than 350 women. That same year, public pressure from civic groups obliged the government to finally investigate the so-called *mataviejas*, serial killings of dozens of elderly women in Mexico City. In the aftermath of the 2006 elections, violence between local protesters and state police in Oaxaca forced the government to deploy heavily armed federal forces to secure the state capitol. In July 2007, rebel groups claimed responsibility for several explosions of major PEMEX natural gas pipelines throughout the country.

Each of these examples illustrates serious rule of law challenges in contemporary Mexico, and raises questions about the coercive authority of the Mexican state in the face of escalating levels of crime and violence. Indeed, several of these examples also disturbingly illustrate that if public authorities do not respond effectively to address these challenges, citizens may take the law into their own hands. While Mexico experienced significant increases in the relative levels of crime over the course of the 1990s, experts contend that the country's rule of law challenges extend beyond a mere public safety problem. Rather, they see these problems as a crisis of public insecurity resulting from chronic inadequacies of the Mexican criminal justice and judicial system, including limited training, insufficient resources, and outright corruption. In other words, Mexico's public authorities have proved ill equipped (at best) to address increases in crime and (in the worst cases) were systematically involved in criminal activities themselves.

Unfortunately, serious rule of law challenges are not unique to Mexico; other emerging democracies—such as Brazil, Russia, and South Africa—have struggled with severe problems of crime, violence, and corruption that detract from democratic governance. Indeed, in terms of governmental performance, providing basic public safety and compliance with its laws ranks near the very top among the responsibilities of any state. But for democratic governments, in particular, ensuring that the enforcement of the law is just, accountable, and effective constitutes the essence of the rule of law. Therefore, we consider Mexico's rule of law challenges to include not only preserving public order and compliance with the law, but also ensuring that public authorities are beholden to the law and that citizens have access to justice under the law. Indeed, without these latter two elements, democratic politics cannot reasonably function.

This chapter addresses the problems of crime and violence in contemporary Mexico in this context. The first half discusses the importance of rule of law for a healthy democracy and the inability of Mexico's judicial system to deal adequately with the recent public security crisis. We then address Mexico's most pressing rule of law challenges and its prospects for justice sector reform. Throughout this chapter, we try to illustrate the important relationship between democracy and the rule of law, since they provide mutually reinforcing support for one another.

Democracy and the Rule of Law in Mexico

Does the rule of law exist if some actors in society regularly and flagrantly violate the law; that is, when there is a high rate of crime? Can there be rule of law in authoritarian regimes, where dictators and soldiers can violate the law with impunity? Is there rule of law when the law itself is blatantly unjust, as when discriminatory laws were enforced under Nazi Germany, South African apartheid, or U.S. Jim Crow legislation? Answers to these questions can vary widely, since societal standards and evaluations of the rule of law differ over time and from country to country. Still, it is clear that these questions touch on fundamental aspects of the rule of law, as it is commonly understood in scholarly literature on the topic. That is, many definitions of the rule of law incorporate several key presumptions: that actors in society are mostly beholden to the law (e.g., individual crimes are prevented or punished), that representatives of the state are also generally held accountable under the law (e.g., punished for corruption), and that there is typically access to justice under the law (e.g., equal treatment under the law, due process, and human rights protections).[1]

Hence, in trying to define the rule of law, we focus on three key components: order, accountability, and access to justice. Yet, while our analysis focuses primarily on criminal justice, on the legal responsibilities of the state, and on the legal rights of citizens, it is important to note that the rule of law is not limited to these issues. Nor is the provision of the rule of law solely a function and reflection of state power. Governmental regulation and civil legal protections in Mexico—such as corporate oversight, contract enforcement, and property rights—also contribute to the enforcement of law and order. At the same time, civil society and individual communities play a major role in promoting the rule of law.

However it is conceptualized, essential elements of the rule of law were effectively absent for much of the twentieth century during PRI rule. Criminals could act with a degree of impunity because of ineffective law enforcement, or because they could negotiate agreements with corrupt public officials. The hegemonic and clientelistic nature of PRI rule also meant that there were few checks against abuses of state power, and a tendency to utilize public positions and resources for personal advantage. Rare but sometimes severe instances of repression—as well as systematic violations of due process and human rights—further compromised access to justice in Mexico during the PRI regime. Yet at the same time, the PRI also achieved a certain degree of equilibrium and control, effectively contributing to a relative degree of order. Indeed, the country appeared to experience a continuous net decrease in criminal activity—as measured by the number of suspects charged with certain crimes—from the 1940s well into the 1970s (see figure 11.1).[2]

Mexico's Public Insecurity Crisis

Clearly it is possible to have economic success and a smoothly functioning political system without the rule of law. But with the demise of the PRI came increased attention to the weaknesses of Mexico's judicial system and many calls to revamp it. These efforts gained momentum in the 1980s and 1990s when Mexico experienced a sharp increase in certain forms of crime, especially robbery and theft.[3]

During this period, there were innovative forms of crime carefully coordinated by small-scale organized crime.[4] For example, in Mexico City,

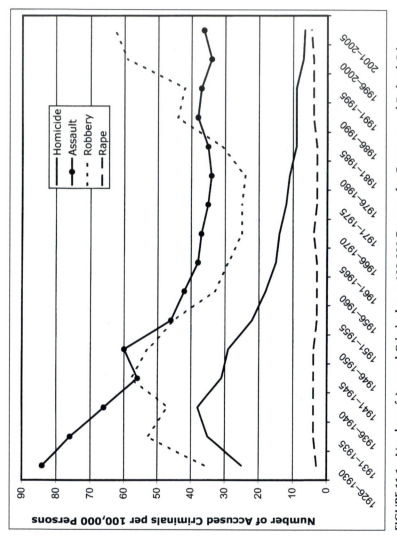

FIGURE 11.1 Number of Accused Criminals per 100,000 Persons, for Common and Federal Crimes, from 1926 to 2005 (Homicide, Assault, Robbery, and Rape)

Source: Data on accused criminals (presuntos delincuentes) compiled from INEGI by Pablo Piccato from 1926 to 2001 and from 2001 to 2005 by David Shirk and Rommel Rico.

many taxi drivers and their passengers became victims of armed assailants who forced them to go to automatic teller machines and withdraw the maximum daily amount allowed by their banks (typically around US$300). Such incidents were referred to as an express kidnapping (*secuestro express*), since assailants held their prisoners for only a few hours, sometimes waiting until after midnight in order to make possible a second maximum daily withdrawal.

What factors contributed to Mexico's dramatic increase in violent crime during this period? The most obvious factor was the effect of major economic crises. Beginning as early as the 1976 peso devaluation and spiking in the mid-1980s during the debt crisis and again after the 1994 peso devaluation, Mexico saw increased rates of crime. That is, Mexico's public insecurity crisis coincided with the fiscal and monetary crises—and the subsequent economic restructuring—that brought increases in unemployment, inflation, and inequality during the 1980s and 1990s.

Although the economic crises served as catalysts for sharp increases in crime, the problem ran much deeper and reflected serious shortcomings within society and a true public insecurity crisis. Beginning in the mid-1990s, several notorious incidents contributed to a pervasive sense that the rule of law in Mexico was rapidly coming undone. Still unsolved plots resulted in the high-profile assassinations of PRI party president Francisco Ruiz Massieu, and PRI presidential candidate Luis Donaldo Colosio. In addition, there were hundreds of unsolved series of femicides (*femicidios*) in Ciudad Juárez, Mexico's largest border city (located just across from El Paso, Texas). At the same time, elevated numbers of homicides in some states resulted from feuds among rival drug-trafficking organizations—especially in northern Mexico—and labor and land tenure disputes that provoked protests and violent conflicts in places like Chiapas and Oaxaca. In addition to these high-profile examples, Mexicans found themselves barraged on a daily basis by gruesome, full-color images of violence—alarming crime stories of rape, assault, and murder—in the so-called red page (*nota roja*) journalism of daily newspapers and media broadcasts.

Despite an apparent leveling off in Mexico's crime rate after 2000, citizens' perceptions of public security as a primary national problem continued to increase over the course of Fox's term, and for the past several years, Mexicans have regularly expressed negative impressions of the entire criminal justice system: many felt that law enforcement is part of the problem, with over 35 percent of Mexicans identifying police corruption as an urgent problem.[5] Hence, a second major contributing factor in Mexico's public insecurity crisis was the inability of the Mexican justice system to adequately respond to escalating crime and violence.

Inadequacies of Mexico's Judicial System

Systemic resource limitations, inadequate professional training, procedural and organizational inefficiencies, and corruption are serious problems throughout Mexico's law enforcement, judicial, and security institutions that seriously compromise the rule of law. Mexican crime experts like Guillermo Zepeda, author of the book *Crime without Punishment* (*Crimen Sin Castigo*), point to the abysmal performance of the criminal justice system in obtaining reports of criminal activity, investigating those crimes, and prosecuting cases efficiently with due process of law. Indeed, according to crime victimization surveys at the start of the Fox administration, only about 25 of 100 crimes were reported because of the intense distrust and lack of confidence Mexicans felt toward police and other public authorities. Of those 25 reported crimes, only 4.6 were actually investigated; and of those crimes, only 1.6 (35 percent) resulted in the filing of criminal charges against a suspected criminal (*presunto delinquente*).[6]

Two factors contribute to the public's lack of confidence in the criminal justice system. First, as discussed in chapter 5, civil law systems like Mexico's frequently draw on Roman Law and an inquisitorial model of criminal justice, which derive from historical and cultural factors in civil law systems that placed the judiciary in the position of gathering evidence and making determinations of guilt or innocence on behalf of the state. In Mexico, public prosecutors (*ministerio públio*) and the judicial police (*policía judicial*) have oversight over criminal investigations, and an active role in levying charges against the accused before the court. As in other civil law systems, the court requires compelling indications of guilt in advance of trial and sentencing, and the accused is often held in detention prior to sentencing. Indeed, in Mexico, voluntary pretrial release of the accused (e.g., through bail bonding) is rare. Thus, while many civil law systems theoretically maintain a presumption of innocence prior to the verdict of the court, defendants in such systems are commonly viewed as guilty until proven innocent. Moreover, because Mexican court procedures rely more on written than oral presentation of information—and do not currently use jury trials—criminal procedure lacks the degree of transparency and public scrutiny found in other systems.

Second, Mexico's high rates of criminal impunity and (conversely) low rates of acquittal are also exaggerated by ineffective criminal investigations, weak criminal defenses, and even occasional police and prosecutorial misconduct (including the use of torture and forced confessions). Since access to bail is extremely restricted and police investigations and prosecutions suffer enormous case backlogs, criminal defendants who had not been sentenced accounted for an estimated 40 percent of Mexico's 240,000 inmates in 2007. Not surprisingly, many prisoners complain of their prolonged confinement and severe overcrowding.[7] In many cases, defendants languish in prison for many years before their guilt or innocence has been determined.

Given the system's ineffectiveness in these areas, many victims of crime and their communities express dissatisfaction with the lack of access to justice in Mexico. In one survey, less than 20 percent of Mexicans said that they would expect the justice system to provide a fair trial and due process. Unfortunately, many of these expectations came to fruition. Of those who had used the justice system (only 25 percent of the sample), half felt that they received neither a fair trial nor a prompt resolution and 33 percent reported major problems with the process or being asked for a tip.[8] Furthermore, many Mexicans do not feel that civil rights are widely respected. When asked how frequently the vulnerable groups in society have their rights respected, most Mexicans do not perceive equality before the law to be the norm. While 55 percent believed that women always or nearly always had their rights respected, fewer than 10 percent felt that poor and indigenous people were ever treated fairly.[9]

In some cases, crime victims experience a double victimization when they attempt to report crimes, since police investigators are often ill trained to deal with the posttraumatic stress of victimization and—in the worst cases—may even ask victims to pay a bribe for a speedier investigation of their case. However common such scenarios may be, they contribute to the general sense that crime victims have little access to justice in Mexico, and suggest that there are pervasive and systemic problems that must be addressed by comprehensive rule of law reforms. To better understand these problems of access to justice, as well as the related challenges of maintaining order and governmental accountability, in the next section we examine some of the major rule of law challenges in Mexico that have come to symbolize the failures of the Mexican criminal justice system to address public concerns: drug trafficking, corruption, and crimes against women.

Major Rule of Law Challenges in Mexico

Below we discuss three major rule of law challenges that illustrate the difficulty of providing order, accountability, and access to justice in contemporary Mexico. Our examination of drug trafficking addresses perhaps the most violent and visible evidence of the absence of rule of law in Mexico, and provides a foundation for understanding related bilateral issues discussed in chapter 13. Our treatment of corruption illustrates how the weakness of rule of law is often rational and self-perpetuating. The serial murders in Ciudad Juárez mentioned above are explored in greater detail below to provide a case study in problems of access to justice in Mexico.

Drug Trafficking

Since the 1990s, ordinary Mexicans have been overwhelmed with regular media reports of killings and assaults committed by drug traffickers and gangs involved in producing and transporting cocaine, methamphetamine, and other narcotics primarily for consumption in the United States. In 2007 alone there were on average at least six drug-related murders in Mexico per day, and so far that number has been even higher in 2008. Clearly the illegal drug trade reinforces the weakness of Mexican authorities and the judicial system more generally. For although Mexican and U.S. government efforts to combat drugs sometimes yield high-profile arrests and seizures targeting the major cartels, lucrative narco-trafficking operations yield such enormous profits—with estimated net earnings in excess of $140 billion annually in North America—that drug cartels often have greater resources at their disposal than the law enforcement agencies that combat them. High-powered weaponry—including automatic assault rifles and rocket-propelled grenade launchers—are often purchased in the United States legally or on the black market, and smuggled back into Mexico where private possession of guns is illegal. The bodyguards, enforcers, and hit men employed by the strongest cartels are generally compensated far more lucratively than law enforcement agents.

Indeed, drug trafficking organizations in Mexico and along the border frequently take advantage of the relatively low salaries and low levels of professionalism among law enforcement agents and public officials, offering a combination of bribes and threats—silver or lead (*plata o plomo*)—which contributes to the corruption or intimidation of law enforcement. While such problems are most widespread and acute in Mexico, a number of important cases of corruption have been found even in U.S. law enforcement, suggesting that the effects of organized crime in North America are transnational in nature. Finally, recent trends also suggest that drug production and trafficking is having another undesirable effect. Mexican citizens are themselves increasingly consuming drugs, bringing many of the serious social problems that accompany drug addiction and abuse. In short, drug trafficking presents major challenges for the rule of law and for society in general in contemporary Mexico. In the post-9/11 context, helping Mexico overcome these challenges holds special importance for the United States, since making the border region more secure and ensuring effective border enforcement has become a higher priority to U.S. national security and overall self-interest.

Understanding how Mexico came to be a major producer and the primary transit point for drugs imported to the United States requires some consideration of the long-term evolution of the so-called war on drugs. It is easy to forget that consumption of narcotics was largely unregulated at the start of the twentieth century. Indeed, drugs like heroin, cocaine, and marijuana were consumed regularly not only for recreation but as "snake oil" remedies for a wide variety of illnesses. Immigrants to the United States played an integral part in establishing the linkages and networks of transport and distribution for narcotics, both before and after drugs were criminalized in the United States in the 1920s and 1930s. Late-nineteenth-century production and distribution of narcotics to the United States originated largely from Asia (particularly China) but later shifted to Europe and the Middle East. By the mid-twentieth century, drug trafficking operations—primarily for heroin—were largely controlled by the Cosa Nostra, Italian mobsters with ties stretching from Turkish producers to French refiners and ultimately into U.S. markets.

This so-called French Connection was broken in the late 1960s, thanks to successful law enforcement efforts and to the relocation of drug production and flows. By the 1970s and into the 1980s, shifting preferences made cocaine—a white powder refined from coca leaf—the drug of choice among U.S. consumers. This led to the development of highly sophisticated trafficking networks from the Andean region, where coca grows naturally (primarily in Bolivia and Peru) and is consumed liberally as an herbal remedy for altitude sickness, through Colombia and into the United States. Colombian cartels based in the cities of Medellín and Calí achieved a level of remarkable influence, audacity, and even social prestige. Indeed, the notorious cartel drug lord Pablo Escobar effectively bought a seat in Congress and cultivated a reputation as a folk hero for Colombia's poor. Over a year and half after escaping from jail in July 1992, Escobar was killed in a U.S.-aided operation by Colombian law enforcement. Although the Medellín cartel was briefly succeeded by the Calí cartel, Escobar's death signaled the decline of the Colombian cartels.

Historically, Mexico had been an important but low-level supplier of drugs to the United States, notably products like marijuana and opium that were home-grown in places like the Golden Triangle of Michoacán, Sinaloa, and Guerrero. During the heyday of the Colombian cartels, most Andean product was moved into the United States via the Gulf of Mexico to Miami. However, as U.S. interdiction efforts in the Gulf gained ground, the Colombians increasingly relied on Mexican supply networks into the United States. With the disintegration of Colombia's major cartels in the late 1980s and early 1990s, there was a shift in control of the transport and distribution of drugs by the Mexican cartels.

Mexico's cartels have since been divided into regional operations based in Tijuana, Ciudad Juárez, Sinaloa, and the Gulf of Mexico. The Tijuana cartel, operated by the seven brothers, four sisters, and other relatives of the Arellano Félix family, was by far the most notorious of Mexico's narco-trafficking organizations. Responsible for numerouos killings—including prosecutors and police—the Arellano Félix organization achieved even greater infamy for its assassination of Cardinal Posadas Ocampo in Guadalajara in 1994. Allegedly a case of mistaken identity, the incident provoked rumors of connections between the church and drug traffickers that were further fueled by the film *El Crimen del Padre Amaro*. The Tijuana cartel was the direct outgrowth of the trafficking operations originally established by Miguel Angel Félix Gallardo. An uncle to the Arellano Félix siblings, Félix Gallardo was Mexico's most powerful drug trafficker during the 1980s, and controlled the Ciudad Juárez cartel. However, after his arrest in 1989, he was replaced by Amado Carrillo Fuentes, the so-called Lord of the Skies, who helped pioneer Mexican airborne smuggling routes into the United States for the Colombians. After Carrillo Fuentes mysteriously died—or not, some speculate—on the operating table of his plastic surgeon in 1997, rivalries between the Arellano Félix cartel and the Juárez cartel resulted in ten years of intermittent feuding and violence. In 2002, the assassination and arrest of the two leading Arellano Félix brothers—Ramón and Benjamín, respectively—and rival trafficker Osiel Cárdenas significantly deteriorated the Tijuana and Gulf cartels.

Unfortunately, Mexican and U.S. law enforcement successes against the Arellano Félix and Gulf cartels appeared to strengthen the hand of their rivals, notably the so-called Golden Triangle Alliance comprising the Sinaloa cartel—operated by Ismael Zambada and escaped drug lord Joaquín "El Chapo" Guzmán—and its allies in Chihuahua and Durango.[10] This resulted in a wave of violence beginning in 2004: the retaliatory murder of half a dozen Matamoros prison guards; the brazen assassination of Nuevo Laredo's police chief only hours after being sworn in; hundreds of drug-related homicides that year; a series of kidnappings by masked commando units known as Zetas comprising corrupt former military personnel employed by Osiel Cárdenas from his jail cell. In response to these events, U.S. Ambassador Tony Garza issued two State Department warnings for visitors traveling to Mexico. These were followed by the closure of the U.S. consulate in Nuevo Laredo in what Garza described as a U.S. effort to punish Mexico.[11] Nonetheless, the violent drug war persisted at unprecedented levels, with a series of gruesome beheadings of narco-traffickers and police officers in Baja California and Guerrero. Narco-violence continued to escalate through the next several years, with over five thousand drug-related killings from 2005 through midyear 2008, including hundreds of government officials who died in the line of duty.

Irrational drug violence is, of course, a manifestation of "rational" cutthroat competition between rival criminal business organizations operating without a balance of power. A balance may be established among organized crime syndicates, either deliberately or tacitly, as these organizations establish their control of territory and sectors in a given market either by negotiation or brute force.

When the equilibrium among such organizations is destabilized by successful law enforcement efforts or internal feuds, the resulting power vacuum leads to elevated levels of violence. In this sense, law enforcement's successes (and losses for preexisting cartels) may facilitate gains for rival, up-and-coming organizations. This cycle of equilibrium and instability has resulted in periods of intense competition and violence between rival organizations.

We will return to this issue later in this chapter and again in chapter 13, but for now it is important to emphasize the negative impact that the drug trade has on Mexican society. For although Mexico's drug trafficking and violence has remained relatively contained, in some areas (e.g., Tijuana) drug-related violence has increased dramatically and created fear among residents for their safety. Furthermore, recurring cycles of drug violence have detracted from Mexico's public security situation and contribute to public impressions that authorities do not have a monopoly on the means of coercion. Even worse, as noted above, the pervasive influence of organized crime syndicates contributes to the corruption of Mexican law enforcement—including both the military and civilian police—up to the highest levels. Likewise, there have been allegations that some Mexican politicians have ties to drug trafficking, with such charges levied against the PRI's presidential candidate Francisco Labastida in 2000 and more recently against several candidates, including the PRI's 2007 Baja California gubernatorial candidate Jorge Hank Rhon. Hence, it is now quite appropriate that we turn to consider the issue of corruption in Mexico.

Corruption

Corruption is a prominent aspect of U.S. citizens' perceptions of Mexico. But what do we mean by corruption? Experts often distinguish political or official corruption (abuse of public office for private gain) from other forms of illegal or dishonest conduct that may occur in society, such as white-collar crime, money laundering, or cheating on college exams. Transparency International's Corruption Perception Index (CPI) measures corruption among public officials by rating a given country's "perceived levels of corruption, as determined by expert assessments and opinion surveys." With a CPI score of 3.5 out of 10 in 2007, Mexico's score ranks about average for Latin America, but well below countries like Finland (9.4), the United Kingdom (8.4), Germany (7.8), Japan (7.5), the United States (7.2), and Chile (7.0).[12]

It is also important to note that ongoing corruption, both official and other forms, negatively impact average Mexicans and Mexico's overall economic development.[13] Indeed, the high economic costs of corruption, impunity from the law, and a general lack of transparency are substantiated by research on other countries in Latin America and the rest of the developing world.[14] But why is corruption detrimental to society? This is a complicated question but for our purposes, there are at least three elements to the explanation. First, in the context of the rule of law, corruption makes it possible for some to live outside the scope of the law. Once this precedent is set, everyone has an incentive to bypass or simply ignore the law, making it essentially irrelevant and society chaotic. Second, corruption undermines the principle of equality and directly hinders transparency and accountability, all elements that are essential for a well-functioning democracy. Third, corruption has the potential to limit a country's overall economic development because it functions as an arbitrary tax that benefits a few at the expense of society as a whole. Thus in societies where corruption is rampant, people are much less likely to trust government and official institutions, and governments are less likely to be successful in their efforts to promote economic development.

How can we explain why corruption is so pervasive in Mexico? Many analysts give credence to the idea that cultural factors—the core values, attitudes, belief systems, and behavioral norms of Mexican society—contribute significantly to corruption. According to this view, Mexicans developed ingrained patterns of corruption because of norms and behaviors derived from the legacies of Spanish colonialism—in which corrupt personal enrichment was widely practiced at the expense of the Crown. These patterns of behavior are said to contribute to a lack of socially responsible values, leading Mexicans to be more prone to the shortsighted pursuit of self-interest than respect for the interests of society at large.

While there are no doubt Mexicans, and people of all nationalities, who fit this description, clearly this is not an intrinsic characteristic of Mexican political culture. If these values are present in Mexican society it is rather a result of informal systems (such as clientelistic networks) or formal institutional failures (such as no reelection) that lead to rational, albeit undesirable incentive systems and patterns of behavior. The pattern and practice of official corruption in Mexico was linked to practices institutionalized under the PRI and earlier authoritarian governments.[15] In such a context, it is often difficult for even the most well-intentioned person to avoid participating in corrupt practices. As we noted above, the politicians and police who accept bribes from drug traffickers often take the more logical of two choices: silver over lead. On the other hand, most Mexicans abide by the law and do not try to bribe police when they go to other countries like Spain and the United States, which have lower rates of corruption. Meanwhile, some U.S. citizens have been known to engage in corrupt practices (like bribing police) when they go to Mexico. This suggests that corruption may be driven by larger, systemic factors, rather than by intrinsically held beliefs and value systems. In other words, a motorist is more likely to acquiesce to corrupt practices—like fixing a speeding ticket by bribing a traffic cop—if that will prove significantly less burdensome than surrendering one's driver's license, appearing in court, or paying a fine. Also, a police officer or judge is likely to be much more susceptible to corruption if they have received little training or vetting before obtaining the job, if they are poorly paid, and if there is little likelihood of being caught. Indeed, in some cases, politicians and police may themselves be victims in a larger chain of corruption, in which their supervisors require them to generate a quota by collecting bribes. For this reason, except in rare instances—such as the case of former Quintana Roo Governor Mario Villanueva, who was arrested and extradited for alleged ties to narco-trafficking—it is often difficult to build a case to implicate high-level officials for drug-related corruption. In short, Mexico's ability to combat corruption will no doubt depend on its ability to reduce the relative costs for those seeking to subvert the law, both by better compensating public officials and by increasing the probability of punishment for those who make or take bribes.

Victims' Rights

In October 1992, the ravaged body of a fifteen-year-old girl named Gloria Rivas was found abandoned in the desert, one of the first to be discovered in an apparent wave of killings of women and girls that today numbers at least 350 in the Mexican border metropolis of Ciudad Juárez. Most of the victims in the so-called Ciudad Juárez femicides shared common characteristics with Gloria. That is, most victims tended to be young and attractive, with dark skin and dark hair; and most were poor or working class (many of whom worked in assembly plants or *maquiladoras*). When families and activists first began to report and denounce the murders, they were often shocked to find that government officials reacted lethargically or even with hostility. Activists alleged that police sought to cover up their own incompetence or even possible involvement in the murders, and that government officials along with the business community tried to downplay the number of murder victims in order to prevent a negative image for the city.

Meanwhile, the patterns of violence, sexual assault, mutilation, and discarded bodies found in many of the murders generated a wide range of theories. Some believed that the murders were the result of a lone psychopathic killer, while others pointed to underground pornography rings, human trafficking/sexual slavery, organ harvesting, recreational killing by young men from wealthy families looking for an adrenaline rush, victory celebrations by drug traffickers, and satanic cult rituals. Several factors contributed to the murders and to the failure to resolve the situation. The fact that many of the victims came from poor backgrounds meant that they and their families did not have adequate education, information, or other basic necessities (transportation and telephones) to fully access the justice system. The very fact that the victims were poor also contributed to the initial lack of official attention to the problem. Meanwhile, the political manipulation of the investigation into the murders by officials from the major political parties in the state of Chihuahua (the PAN governed the city, while the PRI governed the state) clouded the lines of accountability and the extent of the problem.

Of particular concern, however, was the lack of professionalism and also the ineffectiveness of Mexican law enforcement in solving these crimes. On the one hand, insufficient training, inaccurate identification of victims and suspects, the lack of DNA testing facilities, and the excessive caseloads of investigators point to pervasive problems of police training and resource capacity; on the other hand, the covering up of evidence and the lack of political will proved illustrative of the widespread problems of corruption and impunity in Mexico. Feminist activists and scholars like Irasema Coronado and Kathleen Staudt at the University of Texas–El Paso also pointed to the deprecation of women in general as a contributing factor to the Juárez femicides and other violence against women along the border. Negative and misogynistic portrayals of women in popular and traditional culture in both Mexico and the United States, they argue, sometimes perpetuate the idea that the women are victims of their own choices. Indeed, some police and city officials suggested to families of victims that the women dressed inappropriately or were prone to other promiscuous behavior, and therefore somehow invited the attacks. However, such attitudes gradually gave way because families, community activists, and nongovernmental organizations pressured the government to do something. International pressure, thanks in part to news coverage and documentary films like *Señorita extraviada*, also helped promote greater attention to the issue.[16]

In March 2003, the Ciudad Juárez femicides were addressed at the United Nation's Forty-Seventh Annual Commission on Women, which was soon followed by a major report on the issue by Amnesty International. While the murders continue, some progress has resulted from these efforts. In 2005, President Vicente Fox appointed Guadalupe Morfín as a special commissioner to investigate the crimes. Unlike two previous commissioners appointed during Fox's term, Morfín uncovered a pattern of official incompetence, corruption, and abuse that included torture of suspects to achieve forced confessions from individuals later acquitted of any wrongdoing. Meanwhile, prolonged political pressure led the Chihuahua state legislature to approve a massive justice sector reform introduced in 2006 by Governor José Reyes Baeza Terrazas. This reform introduced new legal innovations—like oral trials to provide greater transparency, efficiency, and swiftness—to help make the administration of justice more transparent and efficient (see textbox 11.1). At the same time, national and international crime experts have begun to introduce training and modern forensics procedures to help authorities more effectively investigate and prosecute crimes.

Textbox 11.1. Chihuahua's First Oral Trial

In June 2007, the state of Chihuahua held its first oral trial, with the case of Anselmo Chávez Rivero, a man charged with the rape of two minors. Chávez was of indigenous descent and required courtroom interpreters during the trial, as he and other witnesses testified in their native Tarahumara language. Chávez was originally arrested before Chihuahua introduced its new criminal code and trial procedures in 2006. Those reforms significantly modified Chihuahua's inquisitorial system, introducing elements from the accusatorial system—such as oral trials—used in common law systems like the United States.' When Chávez was given the option of trial under the new procedures, he agreed. Ironically, his conviction under the new reforms reportedly resulted in a longer sentence—twenty years—than if he had been prosecuted under the old system (which would have resulted in an eight-year sentence). The Chávez trial marked a new era not only for Chihuahua's justice system, but also for the rest of Mexico. Many legal experts hope that similar criminal justice and trial procedure reforms introduced in other states throughout the country will significantly enhance the rule of law in Mexico over the coming decades.

Source: Luis Alonso Fierro, "Dictan primera sentencia en juicio oral," *El Diario de Chihuahua*, July 18, 2007.

Still, with so many unresolved cases, it will likely take many years to sort out the botched investigations and achieve some resolution for the victims' families. In the meantime, Chihuahua serves as an unfortunate illustration of the problem of access to justice in Mexico, and demonstrates the urgent need for modernizing and improving its justice system. To some extent, the initial unwillingness of authorities to respond to the demands of victims suggests that achieving the rule of law requires a certain degree of public pressure and mobilization. In this sense, democracy shares yet another important link to the rule of law. Whether protecting the rights of victims or the accused, both democracy and the rule of law require active vigilance and participation from civil society. Below we consider how Mexico's new democratically elected governments have responded to public pressure for rule of law reform.

Rule of Law Reform Efforts in Mexico

Given these recent trends, what is the prognosis for the short and long term and what are the possible strategies to address major ongoing challenges? At first blush it would appear that the prospects for meaningful reform are dim because there are so many entrenched interests, including police, lawyers, and judges, prepared to fight to maintain the status quo. Reform has also been held up by charges that would-be reformers are trying to Americanize justice in Mexico. Thus although President Zedillo's reforms of the late 1990s did manage to insulate the Supreme Court from political influence, and to introduce new merit criteria and oversight for other federal judicial appointments, they stopped short of addressing general concerns regarding systemic backlogs, delays, and ineffectiveness in the justice system. These problems became more severe with the rising levels of crime and violence in the years that followed.

Legislative deadlock has served as an additional obstacle to further reform. In April 2004, President Fox proposed a package of reforms that, if passed, would have produced a major overhaul of the Mexican criminal justice system.[17] Fox's proposed changes included the unification of federal police forces, the autonomy of prosecutors from executive power, and the creation of a separate criminal justice system for minors. The reform package also attempted to introduce major procedural changes, including police investigation of crimes, stronger provisions for the presumption of innocence until proof of guilt, the use of oral argument in trial proceedings, and the possibility of plea bargaining. Finally, Fox's proposals sought to require increased professional qualifications for key legal actors in Mexico, particularly defense attorneys.

All of these proposed changes were intended to generate greater transparency, stronger protections for both victims and defendants, and more efficient and swift administration of justice (see table 11.1). Critics of the Fox reform package pointed to the impracticability of the massive changes proposed as well as the financial costs and potential hazards of importing foreign legal concepts into the Mexican criminal justice system, and ultimately the reforms failed to gain the approval of the legislature.[18] Nevertheless, this reform package remains important because it laid out a comprehensive blueprint for justice sector reform in Mexico, and because it initiated a constructive dialogue. In fact, all three major presidential candidates adopted fairly similar positions on justice sector reform issues. Most important, the fact that the PAN retained the presidency meant that key elements of the Fox reform package could be implemented over the course of the Calderón administration. Indeed, in March 2008, four years after Fox introduced his original proposal, Congress approved a sweeping reform initiative introducing major innovations—like oral trials and alternative dispute resolution mechanisms—in the Mexican criminal justice system over an eight-year period. Advocates hope the reform will bring about greater transparency, efficiency, and fairness.

Table 11.1.
Perceived Advantages of Key Justice Sector Reforms

Oral/Accusatory Proceedings	*Alternative Dispute Resolution*
• Can be more efficient than written proceedings	• Voluntary role for opposing parties in resolution of a controversy
• Neutrality in the collection and presentation of evidence	• Can be more flexible and expeditious than court proceedings
• Arbitrating role for the judge allows greater impartiality	• Fewer legal technicalities and less need for lawyers in the procedure
• Opportunities for presentation and questioning of evidence by the defense	• Relatively low cost for the parties and the courts
• Transparency and public access in court proceedings	• Opportunity for reducing subsequent animosity between the parties

The new reform package builds on some important advances in recent years. For instance, Fox was successful in gaining legislative support for an access to information law (akin to the Freedom of Information Act in the United States), which has already promoted transparency and greater accountability in the short time it has been on the books. In 2003 the Fox administration also enacted legislation designed to reform the civil service to decrease corruption and improve the quality and effectiveness of governance. Ideally, this will give citizens greater confidence in Mexico's political institutions and the rule of law. Furthermore, many of the elements introduced by the new federal-level justice reform package—oral trials, alternative dispute resolution mechanisms, and mediation of legal disputes—have already been implemented at the state level. Indeed, by the passage of the federal reform in 2008, an impressive wave of reforms in these areas had already been implemented in states like Chihuahua, Coahuila, Oaxaca, and Nuevo León. In 2007, Chihuahua demonstrated its efforts to modernize its criminal justice system by hosting the first oral criminal trial in Mexico; other reforms have greatly accelerated criminal procedure while improving other aspects of due process in the state (see table 11.2).

Meanwhile, the past few years have brought economic stability and modest growth, which appear to have contributed to a leveling, or even a decline, in certain criminal activities (e.g., petty theft) associated with unemployment and other forms of temporal economic hardship. Of course maintaining an upward economic trajectory over the long term is paramount if this accomplishment is to hold. Economic development goals must be focused not merely on aggregate growth and job creation or on poverty alleviation through social assistance, but also on reducing the gap between rich and poor that contributes in a variety of ways to crime, violence, and other social maladies in Mexico.

Table 11.2.
Introduction of Judicial Reforms in Key Mexican States through June 2007

State	Oral Trials	Mediation Initiated
Aguascalientes	Under consideration	December 2004
Baja California Sur	n.a.	January 2001
Campeche	n.a.	*
Chihuahua	December 2006	June 2003*
Coahuila	Under consideration	July 2005
Colima	n.a.	September 2003
Distrito Federal	n.a.	August 2003
Guanajuato	n.a.	May 2003
Mexico State	January 2006	March 2003
Nuevo León	February 2007	*
Oaxaca	September 2007	April 2004
Puebla	n.a.	December 2001
Querétaro	n.a.	September 1999
Quintana Roo	n.a.	February 1999
Sonora	n.a.	*
Tabasco	n.a.	*
Zacatecas	January 2009	n.a.

Source: Lourna M. Marquez-Carrasquillo and David A. Shirk, "Justice Reform in Mexico: New Possibilities at the State Level?" *TBI Border Brief*, September 15, 2007.
Note: "n.a." indicates that reforms were not applicable. An asterisk (*) indicates that a law has been introduced, but procedures may not be in place and/or further information was unavailable at the time of this brief. States that have no major reforms in place or under consideration include Chiapas, Durango, Guerrero, Hidalgo, Jalisco, Michoacán, Morelos, Nayarit, San Luis Potosí, Sinaloa, Tamaulipas, Tlaxcala, Veracruz, and Yucatán.

As difficult as it is, reforming the justice system may actually be less challenging than combating organized crime and drug trafficking. Antidrug efforts that seek to dismantle and eliminate organized crime syndicates are sometimes successful. For example, in December 2006, when President Felipe Calderón took office, he cracked down on drug trafficking organizations by sending 7,000 troops to the Pacific states of Michoacán and Guerrero, as well as 3,000 troops to the city of Tijuana. The presence of the army led to a number of important arrests and the confiscation of millions of dollars' worth of illegal drugs. Moreover, Calderón took the unprecedented step of extraditing to the United States fifteen high-level narco-traffickers, including Gulf cartel leader Osiel Cárdenas, who were wanted in the United States on drug charges.

Despite the overwhelming popularity and success of these efforts, many Mexicans remain wary. Other major law enforcement efforts against narco-trafficking organizations occurred with similar fanfare at the start of previous presidential administrations, only to taper off and demonstrate transience of their benefits. Indeed, if historical trends are any guide, the elimination or even serious reduction of drug trafficking is not on the intermediate horizon.

Instead, it is much more likely that the arrest and extradition of key leaders during the past few years has encouraged aspirants from the major cartels to engage in violent battles to establish their dominance and a new balance of power. Once a new balance is reached, society may see a decline in violence, but this hardly means that the problem will be solved.

Another problem stems from Calderón's decision to mobilize federal troops for the purpose of combating narco-trafficking. While his options are certainly limited, his efforts to establish law and order by using military power constitute a serious gamble. The militarization of counterdrug efforts has raised recurring concerns about possible military human rights violations and corruption.[19] Presently, the military is one of the most respected institutions in Mexico, but its corruption and/or violation of civilian rights could seriously diminish its prestige in the public eye, and leave Mexico without any effective weapons in the fight against drug traffickers.

Therefore it is virtually certain that the Calderón administration and future governments in both Mexico and the United States will continue to face the challenge of how to eliminate the drug trade in the foreseeable future, while Mexico will continue to struggle with the externalities of the drug trade on society and on its justice system. The only long-term solutions are prohibitively costly in either economic or political terms, and many present their own problems. For example, legalizing illicit drugs is not politically popular on either side of the border, and in any event, would probably not eliminate black markets or drug violence. Increasing the costs of operation (e.g., through tougher domestic law enforcement and interdiction efforts) could force drug trafficking organizations to move their production and transit operations elsewhere (e.g., South Asia and Southeast Asia), but at what cost to the governments and for how long? Finally, decreased consumer demand in the United States because of changes in preferences or successful drug education efforts would effectively undermine the drug trade, but achieving this goal has so far been elusive.

Conclusion

Clearly there is no silver bullet to strengthen the rule of law in Mexico. This is because promoting the rule of law—especially in the area of governmental accountability and responsiveness—is not merely about reducing crime. It is not a policy output but rather a process that must be continually refined in a democratic system. In the United States and elsewhere, political competition and the alternation of political parties in elected office proved essential to reform over the last century. It is reasonable, therefore, to expect that democratic competition will be a driving force for justice sector reform in

Mexico, even though the absence of reelection is a serious impediment to both accountability and responsiveness. Yet so long as the serious rule of law challenges discussed above persist, justice sector reform will undoubtedly remain among voters' top priorities. Politicians will be under pressure to make changes that reflect the public will.

In the short term, confronted with overwhelming and immediate challenges, it is easy to fall prey to self-fulfilling pessimism. A longer-term view, though, offers the advantage of an obtainable horizon and reachable goals. What is certain is that Mexico's domestic efforts cannot result in rapid improvements in the rule of law and reductions in transnational organized crime without cooperation, support, and constructive engagement from the United States. Indeed, while keeping in mind nationalist concerns about the protection of sovereignty, addressing Mexico's crime and drug challenges cannot be considered a solely Mexican concern. The negative externalities of Mexico's "unrule" of law have clear and direct effects on U.S. citizens and interests, including U.S. tourists who travel to Mexico each year, U.S. nationals residing in Mexico, and the billions in annual business conducted with Mexico. Moreover, the pervasiveness and strength of transnational organized crime networks in Mexico—and the lack of integrity in the Mexican law enforcement and security apparatus—has raised serious concerns that Mexico could become a transit point for terrorists and weapons to enter the United States. Hence, while not the explicit focus of this discussion, U.S. collaboration with Mexico to address these problems is not only greatly needed, but also in the direct national and strategic interest of the United States. The following chapters will address these issues.

Key Terms

access to justice	justice sector reforms
accountability	*nota roja*
alternative dispute resolution	oral trials
Ciudad Juárez killings / femicides	order
corruption	*plata o plomo*
Corruption Perception Index (CPI)	public insecurity
criminal impunity	Roman Law
drug trafficking	rule of law
express kidnapping	Sinaloa cartel
Golden Triangle	suspected criminal
Gulf cartel	Tijuana cartel
Juárez cartel	victims' rights

Recommended Readings

Bailey, John, and Jorge Chabat. *Transnational Crime and Public Security: Challenges to Mexico and the United States.* La Jolla, Calif.: Center for U.S.-Mexican Studies/University of California–San Diego, 2002.

Cornelius, Wayne A., and David A. Shirk, eds. *Reforming the Administration of Justice in Mexico.* La Jolla, Calif.: Center for U.S.-Mexican Studies, 2007.

Zamora, Stephen, José Ramón Cossío, Leonel Pereznieto, José Roldán-Xopa, and David Lopez. *Mexican Law.* Oxford: Oxford University Press, 2005.

Notes

1. Daniel Kaufman, *Misrule of Law* (Washington, D.C.: World Bank Institute, 2001); Rachel Kleinfeld Belton, *Competing Definitions of the Rule of Law: Implications for Practitioners,* Carnegie Papers Rule of Law Series (Washington, D.C.: Carnegie Endowment for International Peace, 2005); José María Maravall and Adam Przeworski, eds., *Democracy and the Rule of Law* (Cambridge: Cambridge University Press, 2003).

2. There are important problems with crime data collection in Mexico, including low rates of reporting by victims and sometimes inaccurate reporting by government agencies. Nevertheless, the data give us a useful snapshot of how crime rates in Mexico have varied over time.

3. Wayne A. Cornelius and David A. Shirk, eds., *Reforming the Administration of Justice in Mexico* (La Jolla, Calif.: Center for U.S.-Mexican Studies, 2007).

4. Others were not particularly innovative. In 1999, for example, when they were graduate students, the authors of this book fell victim to a classic small-time theft operation at Mexico City's northern bus station. While rushing through the terminal, the two were politely informed by a cunning thief that there was ketchup on the back of Shirk's shirt. While he went to clean the mess, an accomplice distracted Edmonds and stole her laptop! Unlike the authors, however, most of Mexico's countless victims do not benefit from the security of travelers' insurance, which in this case enabled Edmonds to recover her losses and finish her dissertation.

5. Transparency International, 2007, www.transparency.org.

6. Once charges were levied, however, a defendant's odds of being sentenced proved extremely high. An estimated 1.2 out of 1.6 (75 percent) prosecutions were brought to trial and 1.1 (92 percent) of those 1.2 crimes resulted in sentences. G. Zepeda Lecuona. *Crimen sin castigo: Procuración de justicia penal y ministerio público en México* (Mexico, D.F.: Centro de Investigación Para el Desarrollo, A.C. Fondo de Cultura Económica, 2004).

7. Azaola and Bergman, "Crime and Punishment in Mexico: Insights from the Mexican Prison System," in Cornelius and Shirk, eds., *Reforming the Administration of Justice in Mexico* (La Jolla, Calif.: Center for U.S.-Mexican Studies, 2007). See also "News Report," *Justice in Mexico Project,* January 2007 (www.justiceinmexico.org).

8. U.N. Development Program, *Democracy in Latin America,* 261–65.

9. U.N. Development Program, *Democracy in Latin America,* 258.

10. Trahan, Jason, Ernesto Londoño, and Alfredo Corchado, "Drug Wars' Long Shadow," *Dallas Morning News*, Tuesday, December 13, 2005.

11. Althaus et al., "Border Travelers Warned of Violence," *Houston Chronicle*, January 27, 2005; "Mexico Scolds U.S. Ambassador for 'Punish' Boast," *Houston Chronicle*, August 18, 2005.

12. Mexico ranks seventy-second in the world, tied with Brazil, China, and India, among others. Transparency International, 2007, www.transparency.org.

13. Transparencia Mexicana, *Encuesta Nacional de Corrupción y Buen Gobierno*, 2001, 2003, 2005, www.transparenciamexicana.org.mx/ENCBG.

14. For example, pioneering work by Peruvian economist Fernando de Soto has illustrated the cumulative negative effects of government corruption and excessive bureaucratic red tape as inhibitors of effective, transparent public administration that have inimical effects on economic development and basic quality of life.

15. See Alan Knight, "Corruption in Twentieth-Century Mexico," in *Political Corruption in Europe and Latin America* (New York: St. Martin's, 1996); S. D. Morris, *Corruption and Politics in Contemporary Mexico* (Tuscaloosa: University of Alabama Press, 1991).

16. Kathleen Staudt and Irasema Coronado, "Binational Civic Action for Accountability: Antiviolence Organizing in Cd. Juárez-El Paso," in Cornelius and Shirk, eds., *Reforming the Administration of Justice in Mexico* (La Jolla: University of California–San Diego: Center for U.S.-Mexican Studies, 2007).

17. Fox's justice reform package comprised six new laws, reforms to eight existing laws, and several constitutional amendments to achieve three types of changes: structural, procedural, and professional. Mexican Embassy in the United States, http://portal.sre.gob.mx/usa, and www.seguridadyjusticia.gob.mx (accessed October 27, 2005).

18. For a full critical appraisal of President Fox's initiative, see "Análisis Técnico de la Propuesta de Reforma al Sistema de Justicia Mexicano," especially the appendix, at www.usmex.ucsd.edu.

19. The militarization of the drug war in Mexico has existed since President Miguel de la Madrid first declared narco-trafficking to be a national security problem for Mexico in 1987. Maria Celia Toro, "Mexico's War on Drugs," in LaMond Tullis, ed., *Studies on the Impact of the Illegal Drug Trade* (Boulder: London: Lynne Rienner, 1995).

IV

MEXICAN FOREIGN RELATIONS

12

Mexican Foreign Policy

The nature and evolution of Mexico's state formation has had a profound effect on its relationships with other countries and its position on the world stage. Earlier we discussed the establishment of the colony of New Spain—a possession that the Spanish empire acquired in its quest to expand its territorial and natural resource holdings abroad. Spain's imperialist actions were a response to intense competition from England and France for power and influence. After winning its independence in 1783, the United States joined the so-called European Game and sought to extend its territorial reach, lest its European rivals gain an advantage in the Western Hemisphere.[1] It was this fiercely competitive environment that Mexico encountered upon winning its own independence in 1821. The U.S. efforts to expand west and south, together with a firm belief in its manifest destiny, placed its interests in direct conflict with those of Mexico. Not willing to cede regional dominance to the United States, England and France continued their efforts to influence events in Mexico well into the twentieth century. Therefore, Mexico spent much of its early history trying to maintain its territorial integrity and political and economic independence from a number of larger, stronger states, including its northern neighbor.

The end of World War II ushered in a new global distribution of power that pitted the United States against the Soviet Union in the Cold War, which featured a bipolar international system characterized by two dominant actors of roughly equal strength and diametrically opposed ideologies. The shift from several dominant actors to just two with competing ideologies narrowed the foreign policy choices for countries like Mexico, which lacked the power to challenge the status quo. In effect, all states were forced to choose between the United States and its belief in the superiority of capitalism, and the Soviet Union and its commitment to communism. Tepid support for one was generally seen as an endorsement of the other, and this mind-set made it virtually impossible for a country like Mexico, with its geographic proximity to the United States, to maintain an independent foreign policy agenda. Yet in spite of these constraints, or maybe even because of them, Mexico managed to assert its independence without ever posing a true threat to U.S. hegemony or national interests.

The breakup of the Soviet Union in the early 1990s ended the Cold War. Without an ideological rival or a military equal, the United States became the world's only superpower. However, late in the twentieth century, strong economic challenges from the European Union, Japan, and eventually China made it necessary for the United States to strengthen its ties to other countries in the Western Hemisphere and appreciate Mexico's economic importance. These changing dynamics gave Mexico the opportunity to redefine its relationship not only with the United States, but also with the global community. This chapter explores the trajectory of Mexican foreign relations, past and present. The first section provides an historical overview of relations with the United States and sets the stage for the next chapter's analysis of the most salient bilateral policy issues: migration, trade, and security. The second section discusses Mexico's leadership in the Americas and its evolving role as a global player. The chapter concludes with an analysis of how the emergence of democracy has altered the foreign policy making process in Mexico.

Mexico's Relationship with the United States

Mexico's geographic location means that its fate is inextricably linked to that of the United States. The two countries share a 2,000-mile border and inevitably share a number of common interests. Yet their geographic contiguity has never guaranteed mutual respect or cooperation. From Mexico's perspective, the United States has historically endeavored to extend its influence south of the border and dictate the outcomes on issues of mutual interest. This view, while neither entirely true nor entirely unfounded, is rooted in the power asymmetries between the two countries. The United States, by virtue of its size and economic and military might, is the most powerful country in the world and is capable of dominating its relationships with most other countries. Mexico is no exception: with an economy just 7 percent the size of the U.S. economy and one of the smallest militaries in the world, Mexico's power is relatively minor.[2] Exacerbating the asymmetry is the fact that Mexico has always been much more economically dependent on the United States than the other way around. This is no less true today than it was in the past. Upward of 80 percent of all Mexican exports are sold to the United States. Furthermore, the United States has long provided jobs and higher wages to millions of Mexicans who could not find them at home. The remittances from Mexican migrants living and working in the United States constitute one of the most important sources of external revenue for the Mexican economy. Finally, Mexico also benefits tremendously from the revenue generated by the transport to and sale of illegal drugs in the United States. If the pressure release valve of emigration were ever to close, or either of these two sources of income were to evaporate, the impact on Mexico's economy would be significant. The government would face substantially more pressure to provide resources and to create employment and educational opportunities for people who otherwise depend on migration or drugs to make a living.

Although the United States is not dependent on Mexico per se, what happens in Mexico often directly affects the United States. In the past, Mexican political and economic instability reduced U.S. export earnings and led to increased migration to the United States—with both good and bad consequences. Indeed, the sensitivity of the United States to what happens in Mexico is so acute that it led former U.S. ambassador to Mexico Jeffrey Davidow to say, "No nation in the world has a greater impact on the daily lives of average Americans than Mexico."[3] Mexico and the United States are clearly interdependent: events in one country are almost sure to have an impact on the other. Yet the power asymmetry mentioned above has often made it difficult for Mexico to gain the upper hand in negotiations, and the United States has often used its power to realize its own objectives on bilateral issues. As a result, Mexico often adopts a nationalist or contrarian stance toward the United States which (though sometimes counterproductive) serves to demonstrate some measure of independence. This dynamic, established from the earliest interactions between the two countries, has only recently begun to dissipate. In the following section we will discuss the evolution of the relationship between Mexico and the United States from the colonial period to the present.

Early Mexican-U.S. Relations

Mexico's relationship with the United States can be traced all the way back to the early nineteenth century when the *criollos* of New Spain sought to diversify their trading partnerships and gain access to foreign markets. The United States and especially Britain offered large markets for the colony's chief products: silver, animal hides, cotton, fibers, and sugar. Such raw materials were converted into finished products such as arms, books, candles, cloth, and soap. After Mexico's independence in 1821, trade with the United States increased, and U.S. actors began to influence events in Mexico. For example, the first U.S. diplomat to travel to Mexico, Joel Poinsett, sought to influence the outcome of the struggle between elite factions seeking to assume national leadership. On a broader scale, U.S. President James Monroe issued a statement in 1823 designed to discourage European powers from recolonizing the Western Hemisphere.

While the Monroe Doctrine did not stop European countries from intervening or even invading Mexico, it did set the tone for the future by making it clear that the United States considered all of Latin America to be within its sphere of influence, and that it would take the necessary measures to ensure its own regional position.[4] This pronouncement, combined with the firmly held conviction in manifest destiny—the idea that the United States had a historical and even moral obligation to control all of North America—committed the United States to playing an active role in the region and thereby began the history of U.S. intervention in Latin America.

In 1845, the United States annexed Texas, a breakaway republic that was settled by U.S. citizens and had seceded from Mexico in 1836. This action laid to rest any doubts about its commitment to dominating North American affairs. Mexico saw U.S. actions to incorporate the territory as a direct insult and broke off diplomatic relations with its northern neighbor. President James Polk's decision to send troops to the Texas border in 1846 is regarded by many to have been a direct provocation. Mexico responded by mobilizing its own troops. When Mexican soldiers clashed with U.S. troops in Matamoros, President Polk claimed that U.S. soil had been invaded and asked Congress to declare war. The result was the Mexican-American War, or as it is known in Mexico, the War of the North American Invasion. U.S. troops advanced west from Veracruz and captured Mexico City in September 1847 after defeating a group of young military cadets. The ensuing 1848 Treaty of Guadalupe Hidalgo ceded roughly half of Mexico's territory to the United States in exchange for $15 million in war indemnities. Mexico's territorial losses were compounded by the Gadsden Purchase of 1854 in which Mexico's leader, General Santa Anna, agreed to sell parts of southern Arizona and New Mexico to the United States for 10 million pesos (see figure 12.1).

For the United States, the outcome of its war with Mexico could hardly have been better. It nearly doubled its territory, acquiring the highly fertile and mineral-rich lands of what is now all or part of Texas, California, Arizona, New Mexico, Colorado, Nevada, and Utah. It also benefited from the addition of approximately 100,000 people to its population and workforce. For Mexico, the losses from the war were immeasurable—a fact that makes the War of the

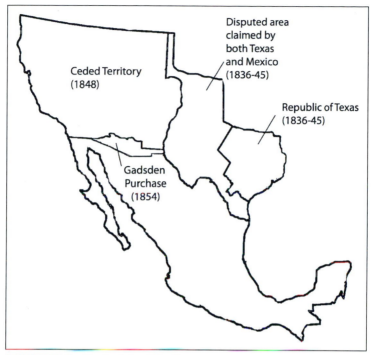

FIGURE 12.1 Mexico's Lost Territory

North American Invasion a painful and salient reminder of what many Mexicans, even today, perceived to be its northern neighbor's true intentions.

Mexico's relationship with the United States improved slightly during the period of liberal reform (1855–1867) when the U.S. government continued to recognize the republican government of Benito Juárez during the French occupation and reign of Emperor Maximilian, and reached new heights during the Porfiriato. After taking power in 1876, Porfirio Díaz renegotiated the country's foreign debt and invited foreign capital into Mexico. No one accepted the invitation more readily than U.S. investors. With a modernized banking system, few trade barriers, and foreign subsoil rights, American companies and individual entrepreneurs eagerly invested in all sectors of the Mexican economy, especially mining, oil, and agriculture. In 1897, U.S. investments in Mexico topped $200 million. By 1911 that figure had increased to $1 billion and represented more than all other domestic and foreign investment. Moreover, the United States consumed 74 percent of all Mexican exports.[5] U.S. economic interests became so firmly entrenched during the Porfiriato, that when the Díaz regime was ousted by Francisco Madero and other revolutionary forces, there was little doubt that the U.S. government would try to influence the outcome of the succession.

When Madero took office in 1911, the United States openly criticized him, demanded his resignation, and later supported Victoriano Huerta's counter-revolutionary coup. Once Madero was out of the picture, however, the United States turned against Huerta by selling arms to the revolutionary armies and applying military and economic pressure by occupying the port of Veracruz. This was but one U.S. effort at dollar diplomacy in Latin America: the use of military pressure and arms sales to protect its economic interests.[6] Later, when Obregón deposed Carranza, the United States was reluctant to recognize the new government because of concerns that Obregón was too radical and would act against U.S. oil interests.

U.S. fears stemmed from the addition of Article 27 of the 1917 constitution, which reversed the Porfirian provision allowing foreigners subsoil rights. Under the new constitution, the national government owned all subsoil, including oil deposits. However, the article was not retroactive and therefore posed no threat to U.S. or other foreign companies already operating in Mexico. Nevertheless, Obregón's reassurances failed to quell U.S. fears and in 1923 Mexico was pressured into signing the Bucareli Agreement. This agreement, signed in Mexican government offices on Bucareli Street in Mexico City, required Mexico to compensate the United States for property damage sustained during the revolution, and to guarantee in writing that Article 27 was not retroactive. In return, Mexico received some concessions on repayment of its external debt, which had skyrocketed as a result of the revolution, and official recognition of the Obregón administration.[7] As we saw in chapter 2, the Bucareli Agreement did not guarantee anything in the long term. In the late 1930s, Mexico scored its first victory in its battle of the wills with the United States when it nationalized the petroleum industry even in the face of U.S efforts to punish the action.

The subsequent loss to U.S. and especially British companies was in the hundreds of millions of dollars and, unsurprisingly, evoked demands for restitution or compensation. Some buyers implemented a boycott against Mexican petroleum, in an effort to "drown Mexico in its own oil." However, Mexico appeared able to withstand that pressure by selling to Germany and Italy, the emerging enemies of the United States and Britain. Moreover, U.S. banking interests began to raise concerns that Mexico might default on foreign debts if starved for oil revenue. Hence the United States ultimately accepted Mexico's terms—$29 million in compensation—and ensured itself access to Mexican oil amid the brewing of World War II.[8] Thus the nationalization of the petroleum industry marked two important turning points for Mexico. First, it was a huge domestic victory for the Cárdenas administration, which not only stood up to the United States and essentially won, but also secured Mexico's control over its most valuable natural and economic resource.[9] Second, the pro-Mexican resolution of the dispute, together with pledges of various types of U.S. economic assistance helped ensure Mexican and regional support of the United States and the Allied cause in World War II—an outcome that before 1939 was not a foregone conclusion.[10]

From the 1940s to the early 1980s, there were no major disputes between the United States and Mexico on par with events mentioned above. The Cold War created an "us" versus "them" environment that in many ways brought the two countries together and gave them an opportunity to realize their shared economic interests. For example, in 1942 the United States worked with Mexico to initiate the Bracero Program, an agreement that allowed almost half a million agricultural laborers a year to work legally, if temporarily, in the United States. Both sides benefited tremendously from this arrangement: Mexico did not have to create as many jobs and enjoyed the economic benefits of millions in remittances sent to families in the homeland, while U.S. agriculture benefited from less expensive labor. When the Bracero Program ended in 1964, Mexican laborers previously employed in the United States began to return home. In part to absorb these returning laborers into the Mexican economy, the Mexican government initiated a new program to promote economic development in the northern border region. That initiative was known as the Border Industrialization Program (BIP), and became the source of the vast *maquiladora* industry along the U.S.-Mexican border. This program allowed foreign-owned companies to set up labor-intensive assembly plants on the Mexican side of the border and import, duty free, parts used in the assembly of a broad range of manufactured goods (e.g., electronics, machinery, automobile components) that were then returned to the United States, duty free, for sale to consumers in the United States and other foreign markets. Again, this arrangement was mutually beneficial: Mexicans, particularly young women, had access to jobs and wage levels that were otherwise unavailable to them, while foreign companies (many U.S.-owned) increased their profit margins by paying wages substantially lower than what they would have paid American workers to do the same jobs. In other words, the *maquiladora* industry in Mexico was among the first large-scale outsourcing endeavors that would become so common by the turn of the century.

Finally, the relatively cordial bilateral relationship was facilitated by the fact that unlike some countries in the region, Mexico's adoption of an inward-oriented industrialization strategy did not drastically undercut the country's export sector; in fact, agricultural exports actually increased under ISI. Moreover, the Mexican version of ISI did not preclude U.S. firms from operating in Mexico: indeed, U.S. companies increased their holdings between 1940 and 1970 so that, for example, U.S. companies controlled 54 percent of Mexico's mining industry, 57 percent of the automotive sector, and 72 percent of the copper and aluminum industry.[11] Thus shared economic interests formed the basis of the bilateral relationship during the second half of the twentieth century.

Still, despite their growing interdependence, Mexico and the United States were not always of like minds during this period—in part because the asymmetry in the relationship persisted. Despite the mutually beneficial character of the arrangements mentioned above, the United States retained the upper hand as the wage setter and provider of capital. So, although the two countries often found ways to work together, they also had substantially different attitudes on a number of policy issues. In the words of one leading expert on U.S.-Mexican relations, Mexico adopted "a strategic or geopolitical view of the world which—without being diametrically opposed to Washington's—[was] nevertheless contradictory."[12]

On a number of occasions, Mexico steadfastly refused to support U.S. policies, and in some cases it sought to undermine them. This happened most frequently over the issue of communism in the region. Because of Mexico's position as a developing country and its history as the aggrieved neighbor of a great power, it was strongly committed to the principles of nonintervention in the affairs of another country and the right to self-determination. Therefore, when the United States adopted policies or engaged in activities designed to stop the spread of communism in Latin America, Mexico was quick to use anti-interventionist rhetoric and invoke the sanctity of national sovereignty.[13] Although many Latin Americans were highly critical of U.S. foreign policy in the region, it was relatively rare for countries to publicly rebuff the United States on these issues. Mexico stood out as an exception. Specifically, in 1960, Mexico refused to support U.S.-backed resolutions in the Organization of American States (OAS) condemning foreign intervention in the region and calling for economic and political sanctions on Cuba.[14] Even more infuriating for the U.S. government was Mexico's self-appointed leadership in the effort to condemn the Bay of Pigs invasion of 1961 intended to depose Fidel Castro. Moreover, unlike many countries in the region, Mexico never signed a military assistance treaty with the United States and it was the only country to maintain strong ties and uninterrupted diplomatic relations with Cuba after the Castro regime adopted socialism and became a close ally of the Soviet Union. Mexico was also among the most vocal supporters of Chilean President Salvador Allende, a proclaimed socialist who embarked on a far-reaching, highly controversial reform program to redistribute resources in that country.[15] That the United States tolerated Mexico's contrary stance is a bit of a surprise given the gravity of the issue during the Cold War. This was particularly true when Mexico championed the cause of leftist rebels in Central America during the 1980s (discussed below). Certainly the United States was never pleased with

Mexico's lack of solidarity, yet it tolerated it begrudgingly because the spread of communism to Mexico was never a real possibility: the postrevolutionary regime took pains to make sure that large-scale support for the ideology never materialized.[16] Moreover, the discovery of vast oil deposits in the late 1970s gave the United States a strong incentive not to push too hard on issues that were more symbolic and for domestic consumption than they were real challenges to the region's hegemon.

Most of the Mexican administrations that governed between 1960 and 1990 were genuinely committed to protecting the principles of national sovereignty and nonintervention, but their actions were often perceived as being anti-U.S. for the sake of being contrary. But if Mexico was simply trying to stick a thorn in the paw of the lion, what did it hope to gain? Some would argue that it was trying to extract concessions from the United States. If that was the case, the benefits were paltry indeed. The United States did grant some small concessions over the years, such as offers of financial aid in exchange for toning down the rhetoric, but these were relatively minor and arguably would have been forthcoming anyway given the importance of Mexican financial and political stability to the United States. Others would argue that Mexico's foreign policy stance vis-à-vis the United States provided important domestic political benefits for the PRI since the government's defense of national sovereignty and criticism of U.S. imperialism almost always played well among Mexican intellectuals and some within the political elite. But while Mexico may have gained something from publicly disagreeing with its northern neighbor, its foreign policy stance was firmly rooted in the belief that no state should use its power to influence or affect outcomes in another. Perhaps because Mexico knew all too well the meaning of power asymmetry, upholding the principle of nonintervention became the cornerstone of its foreign policy approach and an integral part of its national identity and sense of independence.

Ironically, Mexico's greatest leverage with the United States was its massive debt of over $80 billion. Like many countries, Mexico had borrowed heavily from international lenders in the 1960s and 1970s. In theory, Mexico was a good risk since its oil deposits virtually guaranteed its ability to repay the debt. However, when oil prices plunged in the early 1980s, it was only a matter of time before the bottom dropped out. As we saw in chapter 9, Mexico's announcement that it could no longer meet its debt obligation prompted other countries in similar situations to make the same claim and sent shockwaves through the financial world. This put the U.S. government in a difficult position because with all of the U.S. capital invested in the country and the outstanding loans extended by U.S. banks, default would have devastated both economies. Therefore, the Reagan administration had little choice but to put together a bailout package that included an advance of $1 billion on future oil purchases, a $1 billion credit on agricultural commodities, and a loan of $1.8 billion. The U.S. government then used its influence to compel private banks, which had almost $25 billion in outstanding loans in Mexico, to offer $9.5 billion in new loans and credit and reschedule debt payments. Without the help of the U.S. government, Mexico no doubt would have had a more difficult time obtaining such a deal from the private banks. Economic recovery was slow and painful for Mexico, but its efforts to stabilize its economy and meet its financial obligations created a more sound economy and paved the way for the reduction of trade barriers and the move toward economic integration with the United States and Canada.

The 1990s appeared to mark a new beginning for the relationship between the United States and all of Latin America. The end of the Cold War and a bipolar international environment allowed all countries to refocus their attention to issues of mutual interest, such as deepening democratic transitions and the emerging consensus regarding the need for neoliberal economic policies.[17] While the 1990s did not, as some predicted, reduce the power asymmetries between the United States and its Latin American neighbors, it was a time in which relations within the region were more balanced and mutually respectful than they had been in the past. In this spirit, Mexico and the United States began to work more cooperatively to solve what have historically been the most intractable bilateral problems: reducing trade barriers, addressing the myriad issues surrounding illegal Mexican migration to the United States, and combating drug trafficking. On all of these issues both Mexican and U.S. policy makers openly acknowledged that solutions required bilateral cooperation and pledged to work together. Making good on their promises, the Clinton and Zedillo administrations worked hard to emphasize the countries' similarities and common interests rather than stressing their differences. This effort paid off particularly well in the area of commerce with the implementation of the North American Free Trade Agreement (NAFTA) beginning in 1994.

Almost everyone expected that the gains made in the 1990s would be reinforced by the elections of Vicente Fox and George W. Bush in 2000. The two leaders professed their affection and respect for one another and pointed to their similar backgrounds as businessmen, ranchers, and straight talkers as reasons why they shared many of the same ideas and strategies for forging a strong and cooperative bilateral relationship. For his part, Fox announced upon taking office that changing the character of Mexican foreign policy was one of his goals. He and his foreign minister, Jorge Castañeda, planned to capitalize on Mexico's democratic bonus to advance their foreign policy objectives. Fox's election as the first non-PRI president and first to govern a democratic Mexico afforded the administration increased stature and credibility in the international arena, and increased the chances that it would be able to realize its foreign policy goals. Among his objectives, Fox counted deepening the partnership between Mexico and the United States as one of his top three priorities.[18] Fox's pledge coincided with Bush's promise to make the Western Hemisphere his administration's top foreign policy priority and to make good relations with Mexico a cornerstone of this commitment. He had publicly agreed with Fox on the need for immigration reform and the advantages of regulating migration with a guest worker program, and talked about the need to resolve outstanding trade disputes and work more closely to combat drug trafficking. By the early days of September 2001 the two countries seemed to be on track to make significant progress in achieving their goals. The two presidents met in a series of meetings to discuss long-standing issues and appeared to be committed to working together. Moreover, on September 9, 2001, the Bush White House feted Fox in its first state dinner, expressing appreciation for Fox's commitment to working with the United States.[19]

Any progress made by Fox and Bush appeared to vanish overnight in the wake of the September 11, 2001, terrorist attacks in the United States. While the Canadian and British leaders immediately offered condolences and public shows of support, Fox remained oddly silent. Meanwhile, the Mexican foreign minister, Jorge Castañeda, was under intense domestic pressure for first having said that Mexico would stand by the United States, and then, to calm critics who claimed that this amounted to a blank check of support, he announced that under no conditions would Mexico provide troops or military support to any U.S. effort at retaliation.[20] Mexico's actions were particularly hurtful to the United States, not only because they revealed a lack of understanding about the severity of the terrorist attacks, but also because they came in the wake of perhaps the most genuine display of cooperation and goodwill ever experienced between the two neighbors. From the American perspective, one of its closest friends had turned its back during the Americans' hour of greatest need. Although Fox and the government moved relatively quickly to mend the damage by publicly expressing solidarity, providing intelligence, and helping to secure the border, the incident marked the beginning of renewed bilateral tensions that would last for several years.

That the United States would focus all of its efforts on securing itself against further attacks and punishing the perpetrators of the September 11 attacks was both expected and understandable to everyone in Latin America. But Mexico and many other countries failed to understand how fundamentally 9/11 had altered U.S. foreign policy priorities. The war on terror was not to be a simple one- or even two-year change of focus: almost all other foreign policy objectives were put on hold indefinitely. Perhaps no country felt the cooling of relations more acutely than Mexico, which went from the front burner to the refrigerator. Fox had staked a significant amount of his presidency on his foreign policy objectives and especially on forging a bilateral immigration agreement with the United States and it soon became clear that progress on that front would not materialize. Mexican-U.S. relations further deteriorated in 2002 when Mexico withdrew from the largely symbolic Rio Pact, and more seriously in 2003 when it refused to support the use of force to remove Saddam Hussein from power.[21] As a member of the U.N. Security Council, Mexico would have had a vote on the U.N. Resolution 1441, the U.S.-backed initiative to gain authorization for the use of military force in Iraq.[22] Evidently the Bush administration assumed that Mexico would support the resolution. Yet when the United States withdrew the resolution due to a lack of support, Mexico added insult to injury by publicly stating that it would have voted against the resolution. While Mexico's position was in keeping with its historical record of opposing foreign military interventions, and perfectly in line with Mexican public opinion, it was a far cry from the promising spirit of solidarity and cooperation that abounded two years earlier. Furthermore, with Bush occupied by the wars in Afghanistan and Iraq, and later by his own reelection campaign, it was not until late in Fox's administration that the two leaders had the opportunity to renew their friendship and commitment to shared goals. In the end, this proved to be too little, too late. Fox became a lame duck once Mexico's 2006 presidential campaign began. By then, it was clear that what might have been a period of great collaboration and progress looked little different from past eras of suspicion and animosity. A great opportunity was lost to unfortunate circumstance and missteps on both sides.

Hopes are high that the Calderón administration will be able to cultivate positive and cooperative relationship with the United States. During his campaign for the presidency he distanced himself from Fox's position on immigration, stating publicly that Mexico had a responsibility to promote economic development and provide for its citizens. As president-elect, he met with President Bush and top cabinet officials in Washington, and hosted President Bush for a two-day visit shortly after taking office. Both visits yielded renewed commitment to collaboration on trade, development, immigration and security issues. More substantively, Calderón has demonstrated goodwill by extraditing several high-profile drug traffickers to the United States to stand trial, and the Bush administration continued to push for immigration, reform even after the Republican party made it clear that it was unlikely to support his initiatives. Thus there appears to be goodwill on both sides, but there is little doubt that the character of future relations between the two countries will depend on their ability to cooperate on what traditionally have been their most serious bilateral problems: trade disputes, migration, and drug trafficking. These issues are taken up in chapter 13.

Mexico on the World Stage

Although its relationship with the United States has always been Mexico's most important foreign policy priority, it has gradually cultivated a more global foreign policy agenda. Early in the twentieth century, while the government was preoccupied first with the revolution and later with national consolidation, Mexico's international role was relatively limited. This is not to say that Mexico was wholly absent from the world stage before that time. We've already seen that it played an active international role in World War II, declaring war on the Axis powers and providing labor and economic support to the Allied forces. Mexico also used international forums such as the Organization of American States (OAS) and the United Nations to express its opinion on international matters, which more often than not amounted to criticizing U.S. efforts to keep the hemisphere free of communist influence.[23] It was not until the 1970s under President Luis Echeverría that Mexico actively sought a higher profile in the international arena. This change in approach was the result of the confluence of several domestic and external factors, including greater self-confidence and loftier ambitions that came along with the discovery of massive new oil deposits. Also important was Mexico's desire to have greater weight in multilateral negotiations on various international economic issues. Mexico and other developing countries sought greater equality in the areas of trade, investment, foreign aid, and technology transfers.[24] The Echeverría administration, buoyed by the new clout bestowed on Mexico by huge oil reserves, reached out to form alliances with other developing countries with similar goals. Central to this effort was Mexico's active participation in the establishment of a New International Economic Order (NIEO), a multilateral agreement that sought the redistribution of global resources so as to promote greater equality among nations and create a new option for countries tired of operating within the constraints of the Cold War.[25] To the dismay of many, though very few in the industrialized world lamented its fate, the NIEO achieved very little. Ultimately the diversity of the signatories was too great to overcome and consensus on goals and strategies proved elusive. Yet Echeverría did position Mexico at the forefront of the movement and thereby broadened the country's international profile and aspirations.

Another aspect of Mexico's emerging international role was its willingness to publicly choose sides and later help to broker peace agreements in Central America's civil wars. In the 1970s and 1980s, both Nicaragua and El Salvador experienced intense civil wars that pitted pro-Marxist guerrilla forces against U.S.-backed, staunchly anticommunist authoritarian dictators accustomed to using repression to squelch opposition. Ironically, Mexico's decision to actively support the leftist rebels in Central America was an effort to uphold the sanctity of national sovereignty by countering U.S. intervention in the region. In 1979, President José López Portillo made it clear that Mexico would support leftist rebels in their efforts to challenge the status quo. In support of the Sandinistas in Nicaragua, he ordered his foreign minister to block a U.S. proposal in the OAS that would have paved the way for a cease-fire and a democratic transition, but that notably stopped short of ensuring that the Sandinistas would take power. The López Portillo administration then provided much diplomatic and economic aid to the Sandinistas in their war against the contras, an anticommunist paramilitary force aided by the Reagan administration. Although Mexico did not provide as much support to the Marxist Farabundo Martí Liberation Front (FMLN) in El Salvador, it openly showed its support by making a joint declaration with France that recognized the leftist rebels as a legitimate "representative political force" and called for negotiations with the military regime that enjoyed support from the United States.[26]

The 1982 inauguration of Miguel de la Madrid as Mexico's president ushered in a new foreign policy approach to Central America. The new administration drastically reduced aid to the Sandinistas and distanced itself from Cuba.[27] It also promoted the peace process as a member of the Contadora Group, a group comprised of the foreign ministers of Mexico, Venezuela, Colombia, and Panama, and, notably, excluded the United States. The resulting Contadora Initiative called for talks between warring parties and included "a comprehensive series of negotiating points, trade-offs, and mechanisms for verification and enforcement." It also stated that foreign intervention was forbidden and rejected the idea that the underlying causes for the problem were rooted in Soviet and Cuban subversion.[28] Initially, the final draft of the Treaty for Peace and Cooperation in Central America received broad support from key actors in the region, including El Salvador and Nicaragua. Thus, its prospects looked good when it was taken to the U.N. General Assembly for review. However, Contadora ultimately failed to bring about peace because the United States was displeased by the plan's failure to explicitly remove the Sandinistas from power in Nicaragua.[29] Despite the failure of Contadora, Mexico and the other countries were internationally praised for their efforts and rightly so, since the initiative served as the basis for a different plan drafted by Costa Rican President Oscar Arias in 1987 that succeeded in moving the Central American peace process forward.

The end of the Cold War made it possible for many countries to recast their foreign relationships and ushered in the era of neoliberal economics. Accordingly, during the 1990s, Mexico strengthened its economic ties to the United States and Canada and it also renewed its effort to broaden its trade relationships outside of North America.[30] Although the United States remains the country's most important trading partner, Mexico has diversified its trade

Table 12.1.
Mexico's Free Trade Agreements

Countries	Date
United States, Canada	1994
Colombia, Venezuela	1995
Bolivia	1995
Costa Rica	1995
Nicaragua	1999
Chile	1999
European Union	2000
Israel	2000
El Salvador, Guatemala	2001
Honduras	2001
EFTA (Iceland, Liechtenstein, Norway, Switzerland)	2001
Uruguay	2004
Japan	2005

partnerships and now has thirteen free trade agreements with forty countries, including most of Latin America, the European Union, and Japan (see table 12.1). In addition, Mexico has preferential trade agreements with a number of countries, including South Korea and the four countries that make up MER-COSUR (Argentina, Brazil, Paraguay, and Uruguay).

Although many assume that Mexico would naturally have strong economic ties with other Latin American countries, historically this was not always the case because of the geographic proximity and economic importance of the United States for Mexico. Indeed, many in South and Central America have long regarded Mexico as an extension of U.S. economic dominance rather than as a kindred spirit, much less an economic regional leader. These feelings were heightened with the implementation of NAFTA and led to the characterization of Mexico as "culturally Latin, financially NAFTA," and the widespread belief in the region that when push comes to shove, Mexico will inevitably side with the United States on economic issues.[31] Evidence of this truth is said to have emerged in 2003 during negotiations over the creation of a Free Trade Agreement of the Americas (FTAA) and in WTO meetings that same year. In these meetings, Brazil and Argentina insisted that both regional and global free trade agreements could not move forward until dominant economies like those of the United States and the European Union began to eliminate agricultural subsidies that protect their domestic producers at the expense of unsubsidized foreign competitors. While Mexico could benefit from more free trade in Latin America, it was understandably reluctant to support measures that would infringe on its privileged access to the U.S. market. This is particularly true when it comes to Brazil, Argentina, and to a lesser extent, Chile, its most serious regional competitors.

Mexico has long looked to Europe as its best option for diversifying its foreign economic relationships. In the 1970s and 1980s there were several halfhearted attempts to pursue this objective, with little success: European investment in Mexico was always very low compared to other countries in the region.[32] However, by the late 1990s, both sides had a clear interest in strengthening their ties to one another. Mexico dearly wanted access to the large European market to help boost its export earnings and reduce its dependence on the United States. The European Union wanted to enjoy Mexico's low production costs and ideal location as an exporter to the United States. Mutual benefit led to the ratification of a free trade agreement between Mexico and the European Union in 2000. After that, trade volume and earnings, as well as investment, increased in fits and starts. Between 1999 and 2001, trade increased more than 20 percent and European investment in Mexico more than tripled to $6.7 billion. Meanwhile Mexican foreign direct investment in Europe nearly doubled to $329 million.[33] In the economic downturn that followed September 11, 2001, trade and investment between the two sides followed global trends and declined, but still showed gains relative to the pre–free trade agreement era. With the subsequent rebound of Mexico's economy, most expect that Mexican-E.U. trade will increase significantly in the coming years. And while it is highly doubtful that the transatlantic relationship will ever seriously rival that of Mexico and the United States, it does represent a growing counterweight to U.S. economic dominance in the region (see table 12.2).

Mexico's economic ties with several countries in Asia have also grown significantly in recent years in terms of import. Japanese and South Korean firms have long had a presence in Mexico, with billions invested in the *maquiladora* industry along the U.S.-Mexican border.[34] Moreover, in 2006, Japan supplied 6 percent of Mexico's imports, while South Korea supplied slightly less at 4.1 percent. That year, Mexico and Japan also signed a free trade agreement that led to a 23 percent increase in trade between the two countries. Yet while Japanese and Korean firms were attracted to Mexico because of its competitive wages and close proximity to the U.S. market, this is not true of the newest Asian actor on the scene.

Table 12.2.
Mexico's Most Important Trade Partners, 2006

Exports (percent by destination)	Imports (percent by origin)
1. United States (84.9)	1. United States (51.5)
2. European Union (4.4)	2. European Union (11.4)
3. Canada (2.1)	3. China (9.5)
4. Colombia (0.9)	4. Japan (6.0)
5. Venezuela (0.7)	5. Korea (4.1)

Source: World Trade Organization

Many in Mexico see China as their most formidable international rival given the latter's ability to offer rock-bottom production costs. These fears are well founded: more than two-thirds of *maquiladoras* that closed by 2003 relocated to China, where the average daily wage per worker is $2–$6 less than the average wage in Mexico. Additionally, while foreign direct investment in Mexico has declined over the past few years, China receives the world's largest share of FDI.[35] China also gained trade share at Mexico's expense by keeping its currency undervalued—a strategy that makes Chinese products comparatively cheap on foreign markets, including Mexico's. In contrast, Mexico's past experience with financial crises led it to maintain large capital reserves, leading to an overvalued peso. The result is that Mexico's exports are more expensive and less attractive to consumers, especially relative to Chinese exports. Finally, China will soon make inroads in the Mexican automobile market, given current plans for Chinese firms to begin assembling small, affordable cars in Mexico.

There is little doubt that China and, to a lesser extent, other emerging economies like India, as well as lower-cost *maquiladoras* in Central America, challenge Mexico's ability to stay globally competitive. As we saw in chapter 9, this pressure has forced Mexico and other countries with midsize economies to recognize that in order to become more competitive, they must improve education, job training, and infrastructure if they are to maintain and attract new industries. Less attention has been paid to an equally important point: the Chinese and other emerging markets also offer important opportunities for those countries and industries that are poised to meet the growing demand for energy, natural resources, and investment. Therefore, it would benefit Mexico to focus at least as much attention on this aspect of the relationship as it does on lamenting the economic prowess of the country it considers to be among its most formidable rivals.

Mexico's most recent efforts to play a larger role on the world stage have been primarily focused on diversifying and strengthening its economic ties to countries other than the United States. The Fox administration was particularly active in pursuing this goal, drawing attention to Mexico's recent economic stability in order to generate greater trade and investment and forge new free trade agreements beyond NAFTA. Fox was also quick to capitalize on his country's successful transition to democracy—accepting an invitation for Mexico to join the Convening Group of the Community of Democracies, and making a strong commitment to strengthen democracy and human rights protections both at home and abroad.[36]

Whether President Calderón can build on the efforts of his predecessors remains an open question. Although his foreign policy approach differs in several respects from that of Fox, Calderón does share a commitment to some of the same priorities. For example, during his campaign he stated, "Instead of being mere observers, we must seek to participate actively in the construction of rules that will affect our country. The active participation of Mexico must allow us to . . . acquire a stronger influence in the geopolitical and geoeconomic arena."[37] Calderón's administration identifies among his foreign policy priorities the strengthening of Mexico's economic and cultural ties with Central and South America, and the intent to coordinate national efforts with those of European countries to combat environmental degradation, pandemics, and organized crime, and defend human rights.[38] Yet it remains unclear how Mexico will engage countries like China and India, and how it will position itself to remain globally competitive. Therefore, what the Calderón administration's longer-term foreign policy goals are and how much it will achieve in this area by 2012 is also uncertain.

Conclusion

Mexican foreign relations have changed substantially in the past several decades. It remains a very proud and independent-spirited country, but its governments are no longer prone to the fierce nationalism and overdefensiveness to U.S. words and actions that characterized the Cold War years. Disagreements and misunderstandings continue to occur, but in general, Mexican and U.S. leaders and diplomats tend to have a truer appreciation of one another's positions than they did, or perhaps cared to have, in the past. That the two sides are more likely to avoid inflammatory rhetoric and work harder at cooperation is due, in no small part, to changes in the international environment. The end of the Cold War and bipolarity created new opportunities for cooperation (e.g., NAFTA), that not so long ago would have been considered unthinkable. Furthermore, Mexican foreign policy reflects a more global outlook for the twenty-first century—one that envisions the country as much more than an inferior neighbor to the world's greatest power. Instead, Mexican leaders, business owners, and intellectuals talk realistically of regional leadership and strong economic ties to Europe and Asia. With strong economic relationships to a number of countries within and outside North America, membership in almost sixty major international organizations (e.g., WTO, OECD, IADB, OAS, and UN), and its pledge to promote democracy and human rights, Mexico is undeniably an important global economic actor.

Finally, Mexico's transition to democracy has also fundamentally altered the foreign policy process.[39] In the past, Mexican presidents, together with their foreign ministers, essentially dictated the country's foreign policy initiatives. Now the process is more dynamic, involving many political actors and interests. For example, once a rubber stamp, Congress now acts as a true check on the president's international agenda, debating, amending, and occasionally, rejecting foreign policy initiatives. Public opinion is also important, since unpopular policy decisions can now credibly lead to a party's defeat in the next elections. Other actors that play an important role in the foreign policy process include influential interest groups (e.g., business) and nongovernmental organizations (e.g., human rights groups), and subnational governments: it is now common for state governors to bypass the federal government and conduct their own negotiations with counterparts in the United States on trade, investment, tourism, and cultural exchange issues.[40]

The involvement of these actors in the foreign policy process has facilitated greater cooperation, particularly with actors in the United States, and to some degree, it has also potentially increased Mexico's leverage in bargaining situations by allowing the president to demand more or specific concessions from foreign actors, legitimately claiming that without them, he will be unable to convince relevant domestic interests to support and ratify the agreement. While these changes speak well of the development of Mexico's democracy and greater international clout, they also render the policy making process longer, more difficult, and less certain. Therefore, much like leaders in other democratic countries, the success of President Calderón's foreign policy agenda will face close public scrutiny and be determined not just by the actions of his foreign counterparts, but also by the behavior of a plethora of relevant domestic political actors.

Key Terms

1848 Treaty of Guadalupe Hidalgo
1854 Gadsden purchase
Article 27
Border Industrialization Program
  (BIP)
Bracero Program
Cold War
competition with China

Contadora Group
dollar diplomacy
maquiladora
Monroe Doctrine
New International Economic
  Order (NIEO)
Poinsett, Joel
UN Resolution 1441

Recommended Readings

Davidow, Jeffrey. *The Bear and the Porcupine: The US and Mexico.* Princeton, N.J.: Markus Wiener, 2007.

Grayson, George. *Oil and Mexican Foreign Policy.* Pittsburgh: University of Pittsburgh Press, 1988.

Katz, Frederich. *The Secret War in Mexico: Europe, the United States, and the Mexican Revolution.* Chicago: University of Chicago Press, 1981.

Pastor, Robert, and Jorge Castañeda. *Limits to Friendship: The United States and Mexico.* New York: Alfred A. Knopf, 1988.

Vázquez, Josefina Zoraida, and Lorenzo Meyer. *The United States and Mexico.* Chicago: University of Chicago Press, 1985.

Notes

1. For an excellent discussion of the European Game and U.S.-Latin American relations, see Peter Smith, *Talons of the Eagle: Dynamics of U.S.-Latin American Relations* (New York: Oxford University Press, 2000), chap. 1.

2. Mexico spends less than 2 percent of what the United States spends on its military and has just 15 percent the number of troops as the U.S. has on active duty. https://www.cia.gov/cia/publications/factbook/print/mx.html (accessed August 14, 2006).

3. He goes on to say, "What we produce in our factories and on our farms, the prices of many of our products, the wages we pay and receive, the language we teach in our classrooms and use in our schoolyards, the crime that afflicts us, the very demographic makeup of our country—who we are—and, in some locales, the air we breathe and the water we drink are all influenced by developments in Mexico." Jeffrey Davidow, *The U.S. and Mexico: The Bear and the Porcupine* (Princeton, N.J.: Markus Wiener, 2004), xiii.

4. Initially the Monroe Doctrine had no real effect. Latin America experienced direct intervention by European and North American armed forces at least sixteen times between 1823 and 1900. Mexico's experience was among the worst in the region: between 1823 and 1862, it was invaded at least once every six years. The most serious was the invasion and occupation by the French between 1862 and 1867. See Howard Molineu, *U.S. Policy toward Latin America: From Regionalism to Globalism*, 2nd ed. (Boulder: Westview, 1990).

5. James Cockcroft, *Mexico: Class Formation, Capital Accumulation, and the State* (New York: Monthly Review Press, 1990), 93.

6. Smith, *Talons of the Eagle*, 53–54.

7. Cockcroft, *Mexico*, 110, 117.

8. Thomas Skidmore and Peter Smith, *Modern Latin America* (New York: Oxford University Press, 2005), 271–72; Smith, *Talons of the Eagle*, 76–78.

9. Skidmore and Smith counter that Mexico's victory was a pyrrhic one because, for the next thirty years, the U.S. government and foreign oil companies continued to informally enforce the boycott on Mexican oil and prevent Mexico from obtaining equipment from foreign suppliers. This hindered the development of PEMEX, the state-owned oil monopoly. *Modern Latin America*, 273.

10. In the late 1930s, Germany made a concerted effort to develop strong trade and political relationships in Latin America and provided military training to most coun-

tries in the region. At one time, Brazil, Argentina, Chile, Colombia, Mexico, Peru, and Bolivia all had substantial partnerships of one kind or another with Hitler's government. Smith, *Talons of the Eagle*, 74–78, and table A2, p. 372.

11. This is but a small sample of the economic sectors of which U.S. companies owned a substantial share. See Cockcroft, *Mexico*, 158.

12. Jorge Castañeda, "Mexican Foreign Policy," in Robert Pastor and Jorge Castañeda, eds., *Limits to Friendship: The United States and Mexico* (New York: Knopf, 1988), 171.

13. The United States was either directly or indirectly involved in removing a number of Latin American leaders who introduced policies inspired by Marxist ideology, among them Jacobo Arbenz in Guatemala in 1954, Salvador Allende in Chile in 1973, and the Sandinistas in Nicaragua in the 1980s.

14. The OAS is a regional organization within the United Nations established in 1948 to promote cooperation, peace, and security in the Western Hemisphere. It currently has thirty-three members from the Americas and the Caribbean. See www.oas.org.

15. When Allende was removed from office by a military coup in 1973, the Echeverría administration immediately broke off diplomatic ties with his successor, the leader of the coup, Augusto Pinochet.

16. The regime outlawed the Communist party, coopted labor unions, and persecuted labor leaders who advocated more radical forms of leftist ideology.

17. Not everyone in Latin America supported neoliberal economic policies, but the fact that almost all of the region's major leftist parties tacitly accepted market-oriented strategies as the wave of the future contributed to the sense that neoliberalism was the only game in town.

18. His more specific goals included promoting the interests of Mexicans living in the United States and crafting a new plan to address Mexican migration to the United States. Additionally, Fox set out to broaden NAFTA to include countries in South America and to increase Mexico's role on the international stage. Andrés Rozental outlines and reviews the Fox administration's performance in achieving these and other goals in "Fox's Foreign Policy Agenda: Global and Regional Priorities," in *Mexico under Fox.* ed. Luis Rubio and Susan Kaufman Purcell (Boulder: Lynne Rienner, 2004), 87–114. See also Riordan Roett, "Mexico and the Western Hemisphere," in *Mexico's Democracy at Work: Political and Economic Dynamics*, ed. Russell Crandall, Guadalupe Paz, and Riordan Roett (Boulder: Lynne Rienner, 2005), 153–73.

19. The Fox administration took the unprecedented step of policing dangerous sections of its northern border in an effort to impede would-be migrants from crossing, and began to work more closely with U.S. authorities to apprehend narco-traffickers and publicly distanced itself from Fidel Castro's Cuba.

20. Davidow, *The U.S. and Mexico*, 4–10.

21. The Rio Pact was a collective security agreement signed in 1947 by most countries in the Americas, pledging to come to one another's aid in the event of foreign aggression. However, the terms of the agreement are vague with regard to the nature of the assistance; participation is not automatic and countries are not necessarily obliged to provide military support to one another. After the end of the Cold War, the pact was widely seen at outdated, and Mexico had planned to withdraw even before the terrorist attacks of 2001 occurred. After 9/11, Mexico postponed its withdrawal, toning

down the event to avoid any appearance that it was distancing itself from the United States. Molineu, *U.S. Policy toward Latin America*, 25–26.

22. In 2002 and 2003 Mexico held one of ten revolving seats on the U.N. Security Council. Its campaign for the seat was part of Fox's broader effort to increase Mexico's role in the global political arena.

23. From 1945 to the 1980s, Mexico's votes in the United Nations consistently opposed those of the United States. See Robert Pastor, "U.S. Foreign Policy," in *Limits to Friendship*, 165–66.

24. Jorge Castañeda, "Mexican Foreign Policy," in Pastor and Castañeda, *Limits to Friendship*, 176–77.

25. More specifically, the NIEO's goals included obtaining higher profits for Third World exports, greater access to international capital, lenient debt renegotiations, more foreign aid, the promotion of technology transfers, and a greater role in managing the international monetary system. Smith, *Talons of the Eagle*, 209.

26. Not coincidentally, it was during this same time period that the López Portillo administration renewed its ties with Cuba, inviting Castro to Mexico for his first visit to Mexico since 1956.

27. There are other reasons why Mexico's stance toward Central America changed after 1982. In particular, the debt crisis that began that year made it essential that the country maintain a cordial and cooperative relationship with the United States. Economic hardship also meant that Mexico had fewer resources available for foreign aid to its southern neighbors.

28. Jorge Castañeda, "Mexican Foreign Policy," in Pastor and Castañeda, *Limits to Friendship*, 182.

29. The Sandinistas and FMLN also lost faith in the initiative when convinced that it was insufficient for bringing out lasting peace—in large part because the United States was not on board.

30. During this time Mexico also joined or increased its role in a number of multilateral economic organizations. For example, it is now a member of the Inter-American Development Bank, the IMF, and the World Bank, and it was the first Latin American country to be admitted to the Organization for Economic Cooperation and Development (OECD).

31. Riordan Roett, "Mexico and the Western Hemisphere," in Crandall, Paz, and Roett, *Mexico's Democracy at Work*, 167.

32. Javier Santiso offers an analysis of why Mexico lagged behind South America in European trade and investment in "Mexico's Economic Ties with Europe: Business as Unusual?" in Crandall, Paz, and Roett, *Mexico's Democracy at Work*, 173–88.

33. Santiso, "Mexico's Economic Ties with Europe," 182.

34. Japanese firms employ approximately 7 percent of the workers in the *maquila* industry.

35. Russell Crandall, "Mexico's Domestic Economy: Policy Options and Choices," in Crandall, Paz, and Roett, *Mexico's Democracy at Work*, 78.

36. To this end, a new position, undersecretary for human rights and democracy affairs, was created within the Foreign Ministry. Mexico also signed a number of

international human rights agreements, most notably, an accord with the U.N. High Commissioner for Human Rights to evaluate the country's human rights record. See Rozental, "Fox's Foreign Policy Agenda," 92.

37. Excerpt from "Felipe Calderón's Foreign Policy" (presentation at the Mexican Council on Foreign Relations, March 2006).

38. Other goals include the establishment of a program to attract North American capital investment to migrant-sending regions in Mexico, the reduction of the costs associated with sending remittances, the resumption of trilateral talks to design a North American alliance for security and prosperity, and reform of the Mexican foreign service. See chapter 13 for further discussion of these issues.

39. These and other effects of democratization on Mexico's foreign policy process are discussed by Luis Carlos Ugalde in "U.S.-Mexican Relations: A View from Mexico," and Susan Kaufman Purcell, "The Changing Bilateral Relationship: A U.S. View," in Rubio and Purcell, *Mexico under Fox,* 115–41.

40. Ugalde, "U.S.-Mexican Relations," 119.

13

U.S.-Mexico Relations

The context of U.S.-Mexican relations has changed dramatically in recent years. Nearly a decade of increasing economic integration, demographic trends, and cultural influences tie the two nations more closely together than ever before. The immigration of millions of Mexicans, many with strong ties to their home communities, is rapidly expanding the Latino population of the United States, and U.S. consumers have become dependent on immigrant labor for a broad range of low-cost services. Similarly, U.S. influences in Mexico have increased significantly, especially with the two countries' increasing economic integration, which has brought innumerable and sometimes unexpected influences to Mexico: well-known U.S. franchises (McDonald's, Starbucks, Blockbuster), competition and instability in Mexico's agricultural sector, and large English-speaking retirement communities in places like San Miguel de Allende (Guanajuato) and Rosarito (Baja California). So significant is this blending of U.S. and Mexican culture and society that it has led people in both countries to ask whether such influences are positive or negative. Alongside these significant social and economic influences, there are also the violence and rule of law challenges posed by narco-trafficking from Mexico to the United States and the corresponding flow of illegal arms to Mexico from the United States.

Meanwhile, both countries experienced significant domestic political changes that influenced U.S.-Mexican relations. Mexico's democratization, for example, significantly altered the bilateral relationship in that its policy makers now benefit from greater political legitimacy in the eyes of the United States. These same Mexican policy makers must also operate in a political context where they are now limited by the checks and balances of the democratic process; this can slow or prevent the approval of policies and agreements that would have been easily instituted within a more authoritarian system, and which have implications for Mexico's relationship with the United States. At the same time, domestic po- litical pressures—notably, public fears of possible terrorism against the United States and conflicting calls for immigration reform—significantly influenced the foreign policy outlook of U.S. policy makers, especially with regard to deal- ing with Mexico and the U.S.-Mexican border.

In short, the increasingly interdependent bilateral relationship between the United States and Mexico brings with it important policy considerations. What is more, these challenging policy issues would be difficult if not impos- sible to address without significant binational cooperation: the two countries must inevitably work together to find constructive ways of dealing with them. To better understand these major challenges, in this chapter we look at the major bilateral policy issues affecting the bilateral U.S.-Mexican relationship: immigration, economic integration, and security. To tie together this analysis, we look at how each of these policy issues plays out in the U.S.-Mexican bor- der region, a place as complex, fascinating, and (often) poorly understood as the bilateral relationship itself.

Mexican-U.S. Migration

In the ten-year period from 1994 to 2004, the United States granted more visas for legal permanent residency to Mexicans than any other nationality, with an average of about 150,000 visas granted annually. Paradoxically, during this same period, Mexico was also the country that sent the largest number of undocumented immigrants to the United States. The estimated 9 million undocumented Mexican immigrants living in the United States represent al- most 10 percent of Mexico's population. Given the overwhelming number of Mexicans who have emigrated to the United States, it is not surprising that 80 percent of Mexicans have a family member, a close friend, or have themselves spent time living and working in the United States.[1] During a state visit by President Bush in March 2007, President Felipe Calderón, who comes from the prominent migrant-sending state of Michoacán, revealed that he had rela- tives living and working in the United States, some of whom may have lacked proper authorization.

The impact on the United States is significant, especially in those geographic locations (e.g., cities in California, Texas, Illinois) where Mexican-origin im- migrants make up nearly half of the total population. While the issue of immigration, and particularly illegal migration, has received a great deal of media and political attention in recent years, it is hardly a new phenomenon. Mexicans have crossed the border relatively steadily since the redrawing of national boundaries in 1848 and 1853. Yet it took roughly a hundred years for the common and mostly uncontroversial practice to take on greater economic and political weight, as the United States became dependent on Mexicans for a large supply of low-wage labor and Mexico became dependent on the United States to provide jobs and relatively high wages that were rarely found at home.

Causes of Migration

The availability of jobs with higher wages is probably the most important factor pulling Mexicans across the border into the United States. On average, a worker in the United States earns ten times more than another doing the same job in Mexico. Moreover, in the United States, jobs are readily available to anyone who is willing to accept low wages; for undocumented immigrants paid off the books, compensation may actually dip below the U.S. minimum wage. Meanwhile, U.S. employers in sectors such as agriculture, meatpacking, domestic services, and construction have come to rely on Mexican immigrants as a primary source of labor. Also, strong social networks create incentives for Mexicans to assume the risks of crossing the border, often illegally. Reunification with family members is a compelling reason to migrate, but social networks also have the effect of lowering the costs of migration by providing a ready-made community that can offer lodging, financial support, and a line on employment possibilities.

Yet if the demand for low-priced labor and social networks pull people across the border, there are also strong push factors emanating from Mexico. Political and especially economic crises that bring high levels of unemployment and low or stagnant wages serve as catalysts that force people to look for different economic survival strategies.[2] Migration to the United States is a strategy that has become embedded in the lives not just of individual Mexicans, but of entire communities, so that it is common for almost all able-bodied men in a Mexican village to live and work in the United States, supporting the family with remittances and returning only periodically.[3]

Today, people of Mexican origin make up the single largest immigrant group in the United States. In 2003, 33 million foreign-born people resided in the United States, 36 percent of them from Mexico.[4] A significant percentage of Mexicans residing in the United States do not have proper visas, and they account for nearly 57 percent of all undocumented residents living in the United States.[5] It is this very large illegal population that attracts the most attention, prompting heated debates about whether it contributes to or is a drain on U.S. society, and what measures the U.S. government should take to address the problem. Although almost everyone in the United States agrees that the country's immigration policies are in dire need of reform, they disagree about the nature and goals of reform. These differences transcend partisan affiliation and have long contributed to U.S. policies that at best lacked coherence, and at worst were counterproductive (see textbox 13.1). For its part, the Mexican government has rarely attempted to stop its citizens from leaving, prompting many to characterize its approach as a "policy of no policy." The following section provides a brief overview of each country's policies and discusses the most recent attempts by the U.S. government to implement immigration reform.

Migration Policy

Curiously, U.S. immigration policy has rarely been coherent or aimed at a clear goal. There have been a number of policy initiatives designed to strengthen border enforcement and punish employers who hire undocumented laborers. Yet there have also been large-scale efforts to attract Mexicans to the United States, first for jobs and later to reunite with their family members. That different aspects of U.S. immigration policy have long worked at cross purposes is partly due to the fact that powerful economic interests such as large agribusiness firms pressure lawmakers not to restrict their access to low-wage labor. At the same time, politicians feel pressure from constituents who, for a variety of reasons, demand restrictions on the number of immigrants, especially those without proper documentation, and increased border security.

Policy with specific regard to Mexico is similarly inconsistent, and even contradictory. Early in the twentieth century Mexican immigrants were given preferential treatment over their European counterparts because they were thought to be less likely to be members of unions agitating for labor reform. It was also easy to deport Mexicans in times of economic downturn (e.g., Great Depression). Mexican migrants benefited from the Bracero Program: a bilateral agreement that allowed Mexican agricultural laborers to work legally but temporarily in the United States. Originally designed to help the United States meet a wartime labor shortage in the 1940s, the Bracero Program lasted until 1964. However, privileged status came at a price. During wartime, the distinction between legal and illegal status was fuzzy since obtaining the documents necessary to legalize one's status was relatively easy and even facilitated by the U.S. Immigration and Naturalization Service (INS). But by the mid-1950s, public opinion turned against this practice and in language that both echoed the past and foreshadowed the future, undocumented migrants were deemed undesirable because they purportedly depressed wages, displaced U.S. workers, and posed a threat to national security. In response, the U.S.

Textbox 13.1. Mexican Migration to the United States: Good or Bad?

Those who oppose large-scale immigration (and particularly unauthorized immigration) and believe that U.S. immigration policy is not restrictive enough base their arguments on at least four different elements that are often combined into a single stance. First, they object to the fact that undocumented migrants flout and disrespect U.S. immigration laws and sovereignty and argue that "illegals" should be punished and deported. Further, they stress the necessity of sealing the border in order to ensure national security. Indeed the argument about respecting U.S. rule of law resonates with many, and in the post–September 11 era, the importance of national security can hardly be underestimated. Another point of contention is that large numbers of unauthorized migrants put a strain on resources that more appropriately belong to law-abiding, tax-paying citizens. A related argument is that low-wage labor depresses wages and takes jobs from U.S. citizens thereby contributing to unemployment and poverty. The effects of this dynamic are most acutely felt by members of the lower and working classes because they rely more heavily on government services and lack the education or job skills needed to broaden their economic opportunities. Finally, they claim that too much migration from a single country, particularly one that is culturally and linguistically distinct from our own, threatens to unalterably change the cultural makeup of the United States. Mexican-origin immigrants have been vulnerable to this charge because until very recently, they tended to concentrate in specific geographic areas (e.g., the Southwest) and therefore had a disproportionate effect on those locations.

Advocates of more liberal immigration laws tend to focus on the contributions that immigrants make to U.S. society. While few would claim that illegal entry into the United States is unequivocally acceptable, they tend to stress the fact that Mexicans migrate to the United States only because of the high demand for their labor and their desperate wish for a better life. From this perspective, Mexican emigration is an economic calculation that minimizes the importance of national boundaries and legal status. Furthermore, they stress the entrepreneurial spirit among immigrant populations and argue that the notion that immigrants take jobs from natives is folly because of the social stigma associated with doing many "immigrant" jobs (e.g., picking fruits and vegetables, working as domestics, cleaning and packing meat, etc.). Similarly, they dispute the claim that undocumented migrants do not pay into a public services system that they utilize since all residents, regardless of legal status contribute equally to flat taxes (e.g., sales tax), social security (even if they are using stolen cards), and indirect taxes (e.g., property tax figured into the price of rent). Immigration advocates also point to the experience of other immigrant groups to show that at one time almost all (Germans, Irish, Italians, Poles, Jews) were accused of resisting assimilation and adopting an "American" identity. Recent studies show that much like other immigrant groups, foreign-born and first-generation Mexican-origin immigrants acquire the English language slowly, while members of the second generation become well integrated (linguistically or otherwise) into U.S.

society. Finally, holders of a pro-immigrant stance acknowledge that there are economic costs associated with large immigrant populations in concentrated geographic areas, but counter by saying that they provide net gains to society by reducing the cost of many goods and services. The answer to whether Mexican immigration is good or bad for the United States probably lies somewhere between the two arguments.

government launched the effective (if offensively named) Operation Wetback that rounded up hundreds of thousands of Mexicans and sent them back to Mexico.[6] Despite such efforts, the guest worker program lasted another ten years and continued to facilitate the entry of migrants, both legal and unauthorized, into the United States.

The end of the Bracero Program in 1964 marked the first and last time that the United States and Mexico jointly managed the large-scale flow of migrants across their shared border, but it did not mean that U.S. immigration policy became more coherent. At the same time that the U.S. began to restrict immigration by abolishing the Bracero Program, introducing geographic quotas and a ceiling on the total number of immigrant visas, it did very little to dissuade or punish employers and it systematically underfunded the INS, the only agency charged with policing the border.[7] The next major reform, the Immigration Reform and Control Act (IRCA) of 1986, reinforced the dual nature of U.S. immigration policy. This is evident with a cursory review of IRCA's three main provisions. On the control side, it penalized those who knowingly employed undocumented migrants. This measure was obviously meant to reduce unauthorized migration by reducing demand for labor. But contradicting its spirit were the other two provisions—a pathway to legalization for those migrants who had U.S. residence before 1982 and sought to be reunitied with their families in the United States, and the creation of a temporary work program that facilitated legalization of some agricultural workers. On balance, the effects of employer sanctions were almost meaningless at producing real change because there were a number of loopholes that freed employers from responsibility and because the sanctions were rarely enforced. In the end, IRCA disappointed those who wanted more restrictive immigration laws but was immensely popular among immigrant advocates, including the Mexican government.

Over the long term, IRCA did little to reduce the number of undocumented migrants entering the United States. As a result, the issue of controlling immigration flows resurfaced periodically throughout the 1990s in ways that were openly hostile to Mexicans. For example, in the early 1990s, Texas and California, the two states that probably bear the greatest costs associated with undocumented migration, sought to get a hold on the problem by building border fences and beefing up border security for the express purpose of dissuading and apprehending illegal crossers. In 1994 California passed Proposition 187, a law that made undocumented immigrants ineligible for government-funded services such as public education and health care. Most provisions of the legislation were ultimately deemed unconstitutional, but the measure reflected growing disillusionment with federal immigration laws that would come to have national resonance ten years later.

For its part, Mexico has historically done little to stem the flow of its citizens across the border partly because of the benefits of emigration, which provided a pressure-release valve in difficult economic times. During PRI rule, Mexican politicians claimed that they lacked the resources to effectively police the northern border, and that attempting to prevent citizens from leaving the country would be an unconstitutional violation of their individual rights. Hence, while Mexican migration to the United States placed the issue at the top of the bilateral agenda, it is also an issue that, until recently, was a relatively low foreign policy priority in Mexico. Although the Mexican government talked publicly about the importance of defending the human and labor rights of its citizens living abroad, traditionally it was reluctant to discuss the broader phenomenon of migration with the United States. As Castañeda explains, "It has feared that such exchanges would inevitably open the door to suggestions and/or impositions of binational regulation of the flow of undocumented Mexican laborers."[8] Such a development has never been in the interest of Mexico, which in addition to gaining access to jobs, also benefits enormously from the more than $20 billion in remittances sent to Mexico annually. Rather than accept that Mexico's uneven rates of economic growth, poor job creation, low wages, and government inertia contributed to the high levels of emigration to the United States, many Mexicans and government officials instead focused on the difficult and dangerous conditions that characterize illegal crossings, the shoddy and exploitative treatment (both real and exaggerated) that many receive at the hands of Border Patrol agents, unscrupulous employers, and other U.S. actors and criticized the United States for its failure to protect the rights and lives of Mexican nationals. The Mexican media played a large role in shaping Mexicans' understanding of U.S. immigration policy, usually to ill effect. For example, California's Proposition 187 was widely portrayed as an anti-Mexican initiative motivated by racism and intolerance. While not entirely unfounded, this perception was overly narrow since it did not incorporate the very real truth that state and local governments in the United States often pay a disproportionate amount of the costs associated with undocumented migration.[9]

Mexico's policy of no policy on emigration issues started to change in the early 1990s, as the government began to participate in high-level talks with

Washington. Together with their American counterparts, Mexican officials helped draft a binational study of the problem in 1997. It also stepped up its efforts to improve human rights conditions along the border and promote awareness about labor rights.[10] Bilateral cooperation continued with the Fox administration, which placed a migration agreement between the two countries at the top of its foreign policy agenda. Shortly after taking office, Fox called for deepening regional integration to include the free flow of labor across national boundaries in a so-called NAFTA-plus relationship that more closely resembled the European Union. Fox was also interested in protecting Mexican migrants' human and labor rights, and regularizing the status of the estimated 10 million migrants in the United States without proper documentation. Also of great importance was Fox's pledge to increase domestic economic growth and employment opportunities so that Mexicans would have greater incentives to stay home. President Bush supported many of these ideas and pledged to work steadily toward an agreement. However, following September 11, 2001, the issue received almost no attention in the United States, and when Bush finally readdressed the issue in early 2004, Mexico was deeply disappointed at the narrowness of his proposal: a temporary worker program that matched willing workers and employers but offered no concrete provisions for protecting migrants' rights, facilitating the legalization process, increasing the number of visas available to Mexicans, reducing barriers to the flow of labor across the U.S.-Mexican border, or promoting economic development in Mexico.

In retrospect, it is clear that at least two factors held up progress on immigration reform in the United States. The first was that the events of September 11 made border security and enforcement one of the most important concerns in the United States. Wholesale reform that addressed the demand for labor, employer sanctions, and legalization was of little importance for the following three years. Second, despite President Bush's enthusiasm and apparent agreement with Fox on a number of points, the public and lawmakers in the United States are deeply divided about the issue. These divisions became starkly apparent when President Bush issued his temporary worker proposal in 2004 and was roundly criticized by many within his own party. After the failure of that proposal, the next attempt at immigration reform came in late 2005, when the House of Representatives passed the Border Protection, Antiterrorism, and Illegal Immigration Control Act of 2005 (HR 4437). This act would have significantly increased border surveillance and security, allowed for the construction of a 700-mile fence along the border, made unlawful presence a felony punishable with jail time, required local law enforcement agencies to enforce federal immigration laws, made it almost impossible for an undocumented migrant to gain legal status, and made it a felony for any individual or organization to aid undocumented migrants by providing them food, shelter, or aid of any kind.

This bill sparked enormous controversy both at home and in Mexico, and prompted the U.S. Senate to try to come up with an alternative. Lawmakers spent all of 2006 debating different proposals and holding regional hearings in an effort to draft a new, more comprehensive bill that could simultaneously address border security and the complexities of immigration reform.[11] Among the specific issues addressed by the various proposals were border security, temporary worker programs that authorized a limited number of Mexicans to work in specific sectors for a predefined period of time, employer sanctions to punish individuals and businesses that hired immigrants without valid legal documents, and legalization for immigrants already living and working in the United States. In the end, the U.S. Congress passed a bill calling for the construction of a 700-mile double-layered wall and beefed up border enforcement in the highest traffic areas of the border. Notably absent were provisions for a temporary worker program and reforms to current U.S. immigration laws. This legislation was narrowly focused on border security because many legislators were unwilling to cast votes on the more contentious issue of immigration reform during a midterm election year.

Not surprisingly, the plan to build a wall was roundly criticized in Mexico. Although many publicly acknowledged that it is Mexico's responsibility to give its citizens reasons to stay home, they also expressed dismay, calling the legislation a slap in the face. President-elect Calderón stated that a fence "is not and cannot be a solution to the problem." Even with increased surveillance, a fence is unlikely to seal the border and provide the security or immigration control that its proponents claim it will. Evidence from similar efforts in San Diego and El Paso has shown that fences and more border patrol agents simply push would-be migrants to more inhospitable desert territory where they risk death from dehydration or exposure and do very little, in the long term, to stem the flow of migrants across the border.

What the wall means for a future bilateral agreement is not entirely clear. Upon signing the fence bill into law, President Bush stated his intention to push for a temporary worker program before leaving office in 2008. Yet his attempts to do this in 2007 failed when the issue sparked bitter divisions within both political parties, and U.S. lawmakers were unable to agree on the form of any new legislation. One positive development has been President Calderón's willingness to publicly admit that Mexico bears some responsibility for the problem and that any solution must include job creation in Mexico. However, a solution to the problem will require more than platitudes: both countries will have to work together much more than they have in the past.

Bilateral Trade and Investment

The North American Free Trade Agreement (NAFTA) has come to dominate most discussions of trade between Mexico and the United States, but long before 1994, the two countries had well-established economic ties. After Mexico's independence, the United States cultivated commercial ties, and especially during the Porfiriato, the United States became Mexico's most important trade partner and source of foreign investment. While bilateral trade declined during the revolution and Great Depression, it took off again in the 1940s when the United States began to demand significantly more food and raw materials for the war efforts, first in Europe and Japan, and later in Korea. This demand helped double Mexico's exports during this period. Similarly, U.S. investment in Mexico increased dramatically, doubling in the 1950s, tripling in the 1960s, and quadrupling in the 1970s.[12] Again, bilateral trade dropped off during the recessions and economic crises of the 1970s and 1980s, but it was revived in the late 1980s after Mexico signed the General Agreement on Tariffs and Trade (GATT), an international agreement designed to liberalize trade by reducing tariffs and other trade barriers.

As discussed in chapter 9, liberalizing trade was one of the measures taken by the de la Madrid administration to bring Mexico out of the debt crisis and forge greater macroeconomic stability. Before Mexico's entry into GATT in 1986, it used tariffs to protect its domestic industries from foreign competition—this was an essential policy tool for the ISI model it adopted in the 1940s. While the use of protectionism helped insulate domestic producers, it also made trade with Mexico expensive. Not surprisingly, once Mexico began to lower its tariffs, trade volume increased substantially. Between 1982 and 1993 Mexican tariffs on U.S. goods were cut in half, from roughly 25 to 12 percent, and U.S. imports to Mexico increased significantly.[13] Below we consider how these increases continued under NAFTA as an outgrowth of Mexico's neoliberal economic opening.

NAFTA and Mexico's Economic Opening

NAFTA was an attempt to institutionalize freer trade and boost economic growth by increasing the flow of trade and investment in Mexico, the United States, and Canada. It was the most important example of economic integration in the 1990s, after the European Union. But why did three countries that already had extensive trade relations and relatively low tariffs feel it was necessary to sign an international treaty that committed them to reduce the protection of domestic industries in favor of free trade? The answer to that question is multifaceted.[14] One important component was certainly the pervasiveness of the Washington Consensus and its emphasis on free trade as a key to promoting economic growth and democracy. In the wake of recurring economic crises and balance of payment deficits, Mexico, like most Latin American countries, found itself under pressure from multilateral lending institutions to reduce domestic barriers to trade in the 1980s.[15] Technocrats within the PRI (e.g., de la Madrid, Salinas, and Zedillo) also advocated free trade and other neoliberal policy prescriptions to structurally alter the national economy and make it bigger and more stable. Salinas, in particular, aimed to bring Mexico into the first world by linking it to United States and Canada. Entry into NAFTA would not only give Mexico privileged access to one of the largest and most affluent markets in the world; it was also a way for Salinas to institutionalize neoliberalism in Mexico, since defenders of protectionism would have a difficult time overturning an international treaty.

The free trade agreement was also considered a way to ensure that Mexico would be insulated from any future movement within the United States to reinstate tariffs and other protectionist policies that could restrict Mexico's access to its market. Moreover, technocrats in Mexico saw NAFTA as part of the solid foundation necessary to attract more foreign investment from Europe and Japan, as well as the United States. Of course the free trade proposal was not meant to benefit only Mexico: the United States had its own motivations for entering into NAFTA. Perhaps highest on the minds of many U.S. politicians was finding a way to stay competitive with the European Union. Easy access to low-wage Mexican labor was seen as an integral part of its strategy. Also important were U.S. desires to secure access to Mexican oil and curtail Mexican emigration by creating new economic opportunities and incentives for Mexicans to stay in their homeland.

Thus NAFTA seemed like a winning proposal for both Mexican and U.S. interests, but not everyone was excited about the prospects of integrating the two economies (see textbox 13.2). Domestic groups within both countries raised strong objections to the initiative. In the United States, the most vocal opponents came from labor unions, which claimed that the agreement would lead to significant job loss and depressed wages. Environmental advocates were also concerned about the negative effects of industry and increased trade, especially in the border region. While neither of these groups was able to exert enough pressure to defeat the proposal, they were successful in convincing the Clinton administration to require side agreements that would ensure the protection of both labor standards and the environment. After a protracted and bitter congressional debate, both houses approved the agreement in 1993.

Textbox 13.2. NAFTA: What It Is . . . and Is Not

What It Is . . .

On January 1 1994, the North American Free Trade Agreement went into effect. The trilateral agreement signed by Canada, Mexico, and the United States had three main goals. First, it reduced barriers to trade among the signatories. All three countries pledged to reduce and eventually eliminate tariffs and other forms of protectionism on almost all manufactured and agricultural goods, financial and other services, transportation, and telecommunications within fifteen years, or by 2009. This allows all three countries' products to compete on a level playing field in all three markets. Second, it established an institutional framework to help the signatories coordinate their trade policies and resolve conflicts. The NAFTA Free Trade Commission strives to clarify rules and procedures and helps settle disputes when countries cannot resolve them on their own. Finally, it required Mexico to strengthen its laws protecting intellectual property rights (e.g., copyrights, patents) and reform other domestic laws in order to facilitate the flow of foreign investment into Mexico.

. . . and Is Not

While North America has the most extensive free trade area after the European Union, it stops short of promoting true regional integration. For example, NAFTA did not include the creation of any true governing institutions. All three countries retain complete sovereignty over their own affairs, including the freedom to decide whether to participate in conflict resolution mediated by the NAFTA Free Trade Commission, and whether to abide by the commission's rulings. Unlike the European Union, where the smaller and poorer economies were given significant financial assistance to offset the short- and medium-term dislocations caused by the transition to free trade, NAFTA did not provide aid to Mexico, the smallest and poorest of the three signatories. In spite of the scale and importance of Mexican migration to the United States, the agreement included no provisions to regulate or facilitate the flow of labor across national borders. Instead, the three governments signed a supplemental agreement that committed each country only to enforcing its own domestic labor laws. Nor did the accord incorporate a legal framework to protect the environment from the negative effects of international trade. Like labor, the environment was addressed only in a side agreement that calls for, but cannot enforce, environmental protection laws. More than ten years after NAFTA went into effect, many in Mexico are keen to renegotiate the agreement in order to address some of the negative effects that have occurred, at least in part, because so many issues were left out of the original accord.

In Mexico, many were concerned about the effects that a free trade agreement would have on the Mexican countryside where peasants might be forced off the land and find themselves without property or job prospects. There were also reservations about how long it would take Mexico to truly benefit from the agreement since it was the country with the highest tariffs and least competitive industries, and therefore the one that would experience the greatest economic dislocation.[16] Yet unlike their North American counterparts, opponents of NAFTA in Mexico were unable to exert enough pressure on the government to exact any concessions. In the words of Levy and Bruhn:

> Opponents to free trade within Mexico were ineffectively organized and politically marginalized. Salinas could count on a loyal legislature to approve the treaty without respect to its content. In fact, PRI legislators turned down opposition requests for regular updates on the progress of negotiations. In the end, the Mexican Congress approved the agreement essentially without debate.[17]

NAFTA went into effect on January 1, 1994, and since that time has had a significant effect on Mexico's economy and society. Mexico quickly rose to become the second most important source of U.S. imports, and increased trade with the United States has contributed to an increase in Mexico's GDP.[18] Thus many of those who predicted that NAFTA would bring economic benefits to Mexico were vindicated by economic figures that demonstrated a significant increase in the volume of trade with the United States: whereas trade between the two countries amounted to $88 billion in 1993, that figure increased to $157 billion by 1997, and $250 billion in 2002.[19] Currently, Mexican-U.S. trade is valued at over $330 billion. Proponents of NAFTA were also quick to point to the large increase in foreign direct investment in Mexico, from a pre-NAFTA average of $4 billion to $13 billion after the trade agreement went into effect. Furthermore, the Mexican government estimated that 1.7 million jobs were created as a result of NAFTA, while relatively few were lost in the United States—a big fear among U.S. detractors like organized labor.[20] Costs for consumers also dropped significantly thanks to NAFTA, as U.S. citizens and Mexicans can now purchase each other's goods without the extraordinarily high tariffs of the past. Other important benefits include the fact that Mexico now has a more diverse export-based economy, which means that it has somewhat reduced its dependence on oil exports for its income, and, thanks to stronger economic ties to the United States, improved ability to weather economic hardship (e.g., the peso crisis of 1994).

Yet for all of its positive effects, NAFTA has its drawbacks, such as Mexico's increased dependence on the U.S. economy. As the economic downturn after September 11 made clear, now more than ever, Mexico's economic fate is tied to that of the United States. NAFTA has also produced negative consequences for specific groups in Mexico because the gains of trade have not been equally distributed in society. Those individuals and regions with ties to investment and manufacturing have enjoyed growth in productivity, profits, and job creation. Meanwhile agriculture has suffered significant losses as Mexican farmers struggle and fail to compete with U.S. subsidized crops such as corn and sugar. Indeed, while Mexico now enjoys an overall trade surplus with the United States, its trade deficit in agricultural products has increased. The result is not only a loss of income as domestic agricultural prices become depressed, but the displacement of thousands of agricultural workers: between 1994 and 2004 the sector lost approximately 1.3 million jobs.[21] The majority of people who lost jobs have low levels of education, few job skills unrelated to agriculture, and virtually no safety net to facilitate a transition to another economic sector. While NAFTA has led to the creation of some new jobs, there are not nearly enough to absorb the nearly one million people entering the workforce every year. Nor has the agreement been able to offset job losses to countries in Central America and Asia, where labor and production costs are even lower than in Mexico. Thus it comes as no surprise that another negative effect of NAFTA is increased income inequality between the rich and poor: since 1994, "the top 10 percent of households have increased their share of national income, while the other 90 percent have lost income share or seen no change."[22] The effects of NAFTA are, therefore, mixed. The agreement brought Mexico important gains in the aggregate, but to those individuals and regions that experienced job and income losses, the effects of trade liberalization were devastating.

Moving Beyond NAFTA

After nearly fifteen years, Mexico has a better understanding of the benefits and limitations of NAFTA, but it must find a way to address the agreement's shortcomings if it is to more equitably distribute the gains from free trade and promote more broad-based economic growth and development. To this end, the Fox administration placed at the top of its bilateral policy agenda the resolution of outstanding problems with NAFTA's implementation and the pursuit of NAFTA-plus, an expanded version of the accord that included the free flow of labor among the three countries, common monetary policy, harmonized external tariffs, and compensatory funding—fiscal transfers from the United States and Canada to Mexico to offset the adjustment costs associated with liberalizing trade and investment.[23] As noted in chapter 12, Fox's strategy was to use Mexico's democratic bonus, or increased clout as a democracy, to help convince the other signatories that further economic integration would benefit all three countries as they sought to remain globally competitive. To their credit, presidents Fox and Bush resolved a number of ongoing trade disputes, including the U.S. refusal to comply with the terms of NAFTA that granted Mexican trucks to cross the border and make deliveries in the United States. However, the Mexican leader's more ambitious plan for NAFTA-plus was irreversibly derailed by the shift in U.S. foreign policy priorities after the events of September 11, 2001.[24]

Despite Fox's limited success, many within Mexico still believe that the solution to problems created by NAFTA lies in deepening, rather than reversing, regional integration. For example, Felipe Calderón stated during his campaign that one of Mexico's most important challenges is to consolidate integration with the rest of North America, and in his speech on his first hundred days in office, he made it clear that further integration is the key not only to spurring the country's economic development, but also to solving the problems associated with Mexican emigration. Among his administration's top priorities are several initiatives to promote greater communication and cooperation among NAFTA's three signatories, and a plan to channel new investment from Canada and the United States into migrant-sending areas in order to create new jobs and infrastructure that will encourage would-be migrants to stay home.

Also among Calderón's priorities is the reform of the North American Development Bank (NADBANK), an organization created by the NAFTA treaty and funded by all three countries to finance environmental protection projects. Currently NADBANK's mandate allows it to address only a narrow range of problems in the U.S.-Mexican border region. Building on a proposal introduced by the Fox administration, Calderón hopes to broaden the scope and reach of the institution, allowing it to finance a wider range of projects both in and outside the border region. If reformed, NADBANK funds might be used to offset some of the costs of job losses (e.g., education and retraining for displaced workers) and thus constitute a first and small step toward compensatory funding for Mexico.

Yet even if Calderón is able to secure domestic support for his proposals, any reform of NAFTA will require the assent of both Canada and the United States. Canada has long been wary of deeper trilateral integration, preferring to focus only on the promotion of free trade and sometimes making bilateral agreements with the United States rather than working within the framework of NAFTA.[25] Likewise, U.S. support for reforming NAFTA is anything but a foregone conclusion. The U.S. reluctance to seriously consider fundamental changes to the agreement stems from widespread public opposition to further economic integration, with Mexico or any other country. Myriad interest groups and lobbies including organized labor, farmers, manufacturers, and proponents of greater economic and political isolationism will strongly oppose efforts to tie U.S. economic policies closer to those of Mexico. Therefore, the success of Calderón's foreign policy agenda and the future of bilateral trade will depend on his ability to accomplish a Herculean task—convincing the United States to open its borders to Mexican labor and to invest more heavily in Mexico's economic development, while at the same time convincing skeptical Mexican citizens and legislators that deeper economic integration is in Mexico's best interests.

Binational Security Challenges

In January 2007, the Calderón administration extradited Osiel Cárdenas, the leader of the northeastern Gulf cartel, to the United States to face charges related to drug trafficking. Though the drug trafficker was imprisoned during the Fox administration, he allegedly continued to control his organization from behind bars. Indeed, while behind bars, Cárdenas was credited as the mastermind behind the creation of a highly skilled band of former Mexican military commandos, called the Zetas, who were employed by the Gulf cartel to ward off the forces of Joaquin "El Chapo" Guzman (a rival drug lord who himself escaped from prison during the early part of Fox's term). Though he was being held on charges for crimes committed in Mexico, Mexican authorities believed that extraditing Cárdenas was the best way to prevent his escape or continued involvement in drug-trafficking activities. Cárdenas's extradition was hailed in both the United States and Mexico as an illustration of effective bilateral cooperation, and a sign of goodwill and mutual trust on the part of authorities in both countries.

In recent decades, U.S.-Mexican collaboration on crime and security matters involves multiple challenges, including the proliferation of arms, narcotics and human smuggling, elevated levels of crime and violence, multiple forms of official corruption, and tensions over the appropriate goals and means for law enforcement. Yet binational cooperation to confront these challenges is essential, since many crime and security challenges in the U.S.-Mexican context are transborder in nature and impact. The Bush administration's early declarations that two major problems—narco-trafficking and immigration—stemmed from U.S. demand represented a long-overdue acknowledgment of a major shift in the U.S. perspective and paved the way for closer cooperation and new directions in policy formation. The announcement of significant blows against Mexican narco-trafficking organizations and proposals for major revisions to U.S. immigration policy provided a significant indication of this new promising and collaborative environment as presidents Bush and Fox met on September 8–9, 2001, in Washington, D.C. Both countries seemed poised to embrace changes that would bring about stronger networks for cooperation on key security issues.

Obstacles to Bilateral Cooperation on Security Issues

As noted earlier, the new security climate that developed in the United States after the devastating terrorist attacks of September 11, 2001, fundamentally altered the context for dealing with these binational policy issues. As U.S. priorities quickly became focused on seeking and destroying terrorist threats abroad, the foreign policy agenda shifted away from Mexico and turned elsewhere. For many U.S. policy makers and experts, Mexico appeared to be the weak link in the North American security chain. Domestic rule of law challenges—and the porous nature of the U.S.-Mexican border—led to considerable speculation that Mexico could become an entry point for terrorist attacks against the United States. The reorganization of the institutional apparatus for homeland security—the creation of the U.S. Department of Homeland Security in 2002—represented a dramatic shift in how these concerns would be addressed administratively.

Although tensions between the United States and Mexico heightened in the immediate aftermath of the 9/11 attacks, Mexican policy makers have necessarily placed security issues at the top of their domestic and foreign policy agendas, and have worked closely with their U.S. counterparts during the past few years. As discussed in chapter 11, in recent decades Mexico's serious rule of law challenges led a series of presidents—Zedillo (1994–2000), Fox (2000–2006), and Calderón (2006–2012)—to place significant emphasis on rule of law reform. Moreover, the U.S. and Mexico found important areas for collaboration in the post-9/11 security context, and have seen continued successes. Extradition of criminals, information exchange, police training, and the sharing of equipment and technology are important areas for cooperation in the U.S.-Mexican relationship in recent years.

Still, there are important obstacles to overcome. The key priorities in Mexico differ significantly from those identified in the United States. The U.S. vision of security remains significantly preoccupied with terrorism, and reducing illegal cross-border flows from Mexico. To the frequent frustration of U.S. officials, persistent problems in Mexican law enforcement—from lack of adequate resources to outright corruption—often set limits on binational cooperation to address these challenges. Meanwhile, Mexican officials are mainly focused on their own domestic rule of law challenges, as well as addressing southbound flows of illegal arms, dangers posed to northbound migrants, growing domestic drug use, and unlawful behavior by U.S. visitors to Mexico. To their frustration, U.S. unilateralism and reluctance to share intelligence too often subvert or undermine the domestic law enforcement efforts of Mexican officials.

Furthermore, because U.S.-Mexican security collaboration depends heavily on goodwill and ad hoc initiatives, rather than institutionalized mechanisms, there is an unfortunate lack of consistency and continuity. As García (2002) points out, binational cooperation typically tends to be more focused on "reducing cross-border interagency irritants and misunderstandings" rather than on coordinated operations, and while occasionally stronger at the local level interagency cooperation tends to vary "from place to place and time to time."[26] A number of high-profile setbacks seriously undermined collaboration on security matters in the 1980s and 1990s. One of the earliest and most notable breakdowns in U.S.-Mexican security collaboration occurred in the wake of the torture and murder of DEA agent Enrique "Kiki" Camarena in 1985. Camarena was conducting an undercover narco-trafficking investigation in Mexico, when his cover was blown by a corrupt Mexican official. U.S. frustration over this severe breach of the investigation and perceptions that Mexican authorities were doing too little to investigate Camarena's murder resulted in an eight-day partial shutdown of the U.S.-Mexican border in February 1985. In addition, five years later—in retaliation for Camarena's murder—under evident direction from DEA officials, U.S. bounty hunters abducted a Mexican doctor from Guadalajara who was accused of collaboration in Camarena's torture. This extra-territorial abduction was eventually challenged before the U.S. Supreme Court, in the case of *United States v. Alvarez-Machain* (1992), but its legality was ultimately upheld. Mexican authorities were outraged, just as U.S. officials would have been if Mexican law enforcement unilaterally authorized the abduction of a U.S. citizen for trial in Mexico.

By the mid-1990s, binational security relations appeared to improve gradually. Within the Binational Commission originally formed in 1977 to allow annual meetings of U.S. and Mexican cabinet officials, presidents Zedillo and Clinton authorized the formation of a High Level Contact Group in 1996 to specifically target narco-trafficking. However, bilateral efforts experienced another setback with the arrest of General Gutiérrez Rebollo, the head of the National Institute to Combat Drugs (Instituto Nacional de Combate a las Drogas, INCD), when it was discovered that he had ties to the Juárez drug cartel.

Such incidents of corruption have contributed to the evident distrust of U.S. law enforcement toward Mexican authorities, as well as responses that contribute to further irritations in the U.S.-Mexican relationship. For example, in an effort to avoid possible leaks from corrupt Mexican authorities, U.S. authorities opted to pursue an extraterritorial investigation of money-laundering activities in Mexico through Operation Casablanca. Operation Casablanca was the code name for a U.S. Customs investigation against operations of Colombia's Cali cartel on Mexican soil from 1995 to 1998. The operation resulted in significant successes (112 arrests and drug seizures of $103 million, 2 tons of cocaine, and 4 tons of marijuana), but also brought significant criticism from Mexican authorities that saw the unauthorized operation of U.S. law enforcement in Mexico as an excessive violation of national sovereignty.[27]

Cross-Border Collaboration

In recent years, however, U.S.-Mexican collaboration on security matters has shown significant signs of improvement, and relatively fewer major setbacks. One key area of collaboration between the United States and Mexico is the extradition of criminals and sharing of evidence for cross-border prosecutions. For most of the twentieth century, there was no formal agreement on the extradition process between Mexico and the United States, although some informal agreements existed (especially between local law enforcement agencies on either side of the border). In 1978, the United States and Mexico signed their current Extradition Treaty, which went into effect in 1980 with the provision that Mexico would refuse extradition in cases where defendants would be subject to the death penalty in the United States. In October 2001, the Mexican Supreme Court ruled that the extradition of criminals under charges that included life imprisonment represented a cruel and unusual punishment, and was therefore unconstitutional. This ruling frustrated U.S. prosecutors and law enforcement officials, who had to forgo both the death penalty and life imprisonment until a subsequent Mexican Supreme Court ruling in 2006 found that the domestic use of such sentences was not unconstitutional, thereby permitting similar sentences to be applied in international extradition cases.

Notwithstanding the temporary prohibition of life imprisonment, extraditions from Mexico to the United States grew at record levels between 2001 and 2006. Indeed, during the later part of the 1990s, the number of extraditions from Mexico to the United States averaged around eleven per year, yet this rate more than tripled by the end of the Fox administration (see figure 13.1). Thus the January 2007 announcement that Felipe Calderón's administration would extradite an impressive fifteen drug cartel members represented an important continuation of recent high levels of bilateral cooperation on extradition matters.

Yet another area of cross-border law enforcement collaboration in recent years can be found in cross-border evidence sharing and prosecutions. Mexico and the United States share a Mutual Legal Assistance Treaty (MLAT), which allows law enforcement to share evidence in courtrooms for criminal prosecutions. In addition, Article 4 of Mexico's Federal Penal Code also permits foreign law enforcement to present evidence in the domestic prosecution of Mexican nationals charged with committing crimes outside of Mexico.[28] In such cases, U.S. authorities can file briefs providing evidence that can be used against the accused in Mexican court. One caveat is that U.S. authorities cannot retry the individual upon return to the United States (because of the

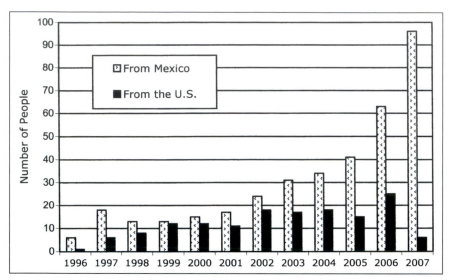

FIGURE 13.1   International Extraditions between Mexico and the United States, 1980–2006
Sources: Embassy of Mexico Fact Sheet, "Rounding Up Fugitives," May 12, 2004; "U.S. and Mexico Team Up to Arrest Mexican Fugitive from Justice (2004–2005); Matthew T. Hall, "Gonzales Lauds Mexico's Extradition of 15 to U.S.," The *San Diego Union Tribune,* January 21, 2007, and U.S. Embassy.

Fifth Amendment), even if the punishment is considered inadequate or the individual has evaded their complete sentence through bribery. Hence U.S. law enforcement authorities tend to pursue prosecution through the Article 4 procedure only to prosecute serious felonies, like murder or rape, when there is a strong indication that there will be adequate punishment.

Finally, this apparent trend toward greater bilateral U.S.-Mexican collaboration has been complemented by proposals for larger, regional security agreements involving Canada and Central America. After 9/11, some U.S. and Mexican authorities and security experts began to focus more on the big picture of North American security, with greater trilateral collaboration between Canada, Mexico, and the United States to address shared security threats. More specifically, some have called for a regional security perimeter that would extend beyond U.S. borders, with common security standards and greater information sharing in the North American context. In fact, such proposals have become a partial reality with initiatives such as the U.S.-Canadian and U.S.-Mexican smart border agreements, which articulated specific objectives and areas for collaboration in ensuring secure and efficient cross-border flows. In March 2005, Canada, Mexico, and the United States went one step further by trilateralizing security collaboration with the creation of the Security and Prosperity Partnership (SSP), an agreement to identify shared goals and coordinate security strategies between the three countries. More recently, during President Bush's 2007 goodwill tour of Latin America, conversations with Guatemalan President Oscar Berger and Felipe Calderón laid the groundwork for the development of a regional security plan. The initial framework for that agreement was announced in May 2007, with an emphasis on countermeasures to combat drug and arms trafficking, control immigration, and combat transnational gangs.[29] The plan was further developed by presidents Bush and Calderón in what became known as the Mérida Initiative (Plan Merida), an agreement for over one billion dollars in U.S. aid to help fund Mexican security initiatives.

The possible end result of such ambitious regional security agreements could be the development of a more comprehensive "NAFTA-plus" security regime. In the meantime, it is important to note that U.S.-Mexican collaboration on security matters has obtained a significant boost as a result of the so-called democratic bonus. That is, many U.S. authorities and law enforcement officials have evidenced a greater willingness to work with the governments of Vicente Fox and Felipe Calderón, who have been perceived as more legitimate and transparent than their PRI predecessors. Over the long term, a positive U.S. orientation toward Mexico's contemporary democratic leaders—as well as their genuine efforts to strengthen the rule of law as part of the process of democratic consolidation—may be the most important factor in improving the bilateral security relationship.

The U.S.-Mexican Border

Nowhere else are the contours of the U.S.-Mexican relationship—the opportunities and frustrations, the dynamism and inequities—more intensely illustrated than along their shared 2,000-mile border. Whether regarding the issue of immigration, bilateral trade, or transnational security threats, the border region factors heavily into national level policy debates and negotiations between the United States and Mexico. Still, most U.S. and Mexican citizens lack familiarity with the border region, and they often fail to appreciate the enormous interdependence of U.S. and Mexican border communities. In terms of binational policy, the border region is of tremendous importance, and in terms of daily life, the border is very much a part of the U.S. and Mexican reality. Thus the border is also worthy of interest and examination in its own right. In-depth study of the border reveals that it is extraordinarily dynamic and features great diversity, in terms of geography, ecology, demography, culture, industry, and economic development.

Table 13.1.
Significant U.S.-Mexican Border Cities (West to East)

• San Diego-Tijuana	• El Paso-Ciudad Juárez
• Calexico-Mexicali	• Presidio-Ojinaga
• San Luis-Yuma	• Del Rio-Ciudad Acuña
• San Luis-Río Colorado	• Eagle Pass-Piedras Negras
• Lukeville-Sonoita	• Laredo-Nuevo Laredo
• Nogales-Nogales	• McAllen-Hidalgo/Reynosa
• Douglas-Agua Prieta	• Brownsville-Matamoros
• Columbus-Las Palomas	

What is more, over the course of the twentieth century, more and more Mexicans and U.S. citizens found themselves living in the border region. During this period, Mexico's border population grew more than threefold and the U.S. border population more than doubled. By 1990, 65 million people lived in the ten U.S. and Mexican border states, and at least 14 million U.S. and Mexican residents live in near proximity to the border, mostly clustered in a few border twin city regions (see table 13.1). Today, numerous demographic groups live in the border region, including Anglos, Latinos, African Americans, Asians, and indigenous people. For all of these reasons, the border has been a major focus of binational policy concern, and a fascinating point of intersection for the two countries. Below, we consider the development of the border region and the way that the bilateral policy issues already discussed above play out along the U.S.-Mexican border.

The Development of the U.S.-Mexican Border Region

Defining any region is often challenging, since—by definition—a region does not always conform strictly to formal political, cultural, or economic boundaries. Defining a border region is especially difficult, as one observer noted, because "its defining boundary runs *through* it rather than around it."[30] We must take into consideration the multiple ways of conceptualizing the region. In strictly political terms, the border region can be thought of as the widely expansive area that includes the four U.S. and six Mexican border states, respectively, or as the more limited set of county and municipal governments immediately adjacent to the border region.

However, the border region is clearly more complex and fluid than a set of political lines. For example, expanding migration patterns and dissemination of cultural elements representative of the border region—like cowboy boots, *corridos,* and *burritos*—have spread to other regions of the United States and Mexico. There also exist significant subregional variations along the border, with major geographic, demographic, and cultural differences between twin city regions like El Paso–Ciudad Juárez and San Diego–Tijuana.

The nature of the U.S.-Mexican border has shifted over time. Initially an area of political and territorial conflict, by the 1880s, the U.S.-Mexican border relationship arguably advanced to become more cordial and coexistent, with both countries generally recognizing each other's sovereignty and territorial delimitations.[31] At the turn of the twentieth century, the two countries began to see growing transborder cultural, social, or economic interaction, and in the aftermath of the 1910 revolution, and especially since the mid-1950s, the U.S.-Mexican border relationship has become increasingly interdependent, with the two sides reflecting significantly greater mutual dependence, thanks to growing cross-border trade and economic activity, population flows, and cultural integration. Despite this progression, the U.S.-Mexican border relationship has not yet become fully integrated or characterized by shared and overlapping political authorities, such as are found in the European Union.

Whether the United States and Mexico will move toward greater shared governance remains to be seen. But for the time being, the border region is an important point of intersection for the two countries and embodies the much larger social, political, and economic dynamics of Mexico, the United States, and their bilateral relationship. We now consider how the major bilateral policy issues discussed in this chapter play out in the U.S.-Mexican border region.

Immigration and the Border

As noted earlier, much of the U.S. immigration debate has focused on the problem of undocumented immigration, and especially on unauthorized entry through the U.S.-Mexican border. Beginning in 1994, U.S. officials initiated a series of unilateral initiatives from Operation Hold the Line (also called the Blockade) in Texas to Operation Gatekeeper in San Diego. These efforts focused on enhancing border security primarily by establishing fencing, increasing the presence of border patrol personnel, and introducing lighting and high-tech surveillance equipment in major populated centers along the U.S.-Mexican border. The immediate impact of these initiatives was to accomplish a considerable degree of order in the areas where border enforcement measures were concentrated. However, ultimately the strategy did little to reduce undocumented migration to the United States.[32]

In focusing their immigration control strategies on the border, U.S. policies did little to deter undocumented migration and instead had other, sometimes unintended, effects. For example, rather than diminishing, undocumented migrant flows have been rerouted overland through dangerous desert and mountain areas, underground through sophisticated tunnel systems, and offshore along open U.S. coastal areas. Second, as undocumented migrants seek to avoid the perils of desert and mountain crossings, there has been a proliferation of people smuggling, document fraud, and visa overstays. Seeking to avoid detection at the border, undocumented persons increasingly rely on professional smugglers (*coyotes* or *polleros*) to transport them across the border.[33] Finally, as a result of the new dangers involved in land-based crossings, too many migrants crossing in the border's scorching deserts and formidable mountainous regions suffer a horrible fate, with thousands dying in the process over the past decade. At the October close of the Border Patrol's fiscal year for 2006, an estimated 4,045 migrants had died of extreme temperatures and other hazards at the border since 1995. A record 472 of those lives were lost in the 2005 fiscal year, while the number dipped approximately 5 percent in the 2006 fiscal year along with overall unauthorized flows during the same period. More dangerous and difficult border crossings have created incentives for undocumented individuals to stay in the United States for longer periods of time, rather than returning home, as many did in the past. Ironically, the implementation of tougher border controls unintentionally contributed a greater tendency toward long-term unauthorized residency.

The U.S.-Mexican Border Economy

The economy of the U.S.-Mexico border region began to develop during the Porfiriato, thanks in part to international investment capital from the United States, and the desire to tap into valuable minerals (e.g., gold, silver, lead, copper) of northern Mexico. Over the course of this early transformation of the border region, both sides of the border benefited from the expansion of infrastructure (railroads and irrigation) and the introduction of new technologies (gasoline engines and refrigeration) that allowed newcomers and entrepreneurs to penetrate the vast expanses and daunting climates of the border region.

The revolution seriously disrupted the border economy and the region did not experience an economic resurgence until the 1920s, when thousands of U.S. citizens began to go to Mexican border towns in search of the alcohol prohibited by the U.S. Volstead Act of 1919. This boom came to an end with the Great Depression, but beginning in the 1930s, the border region experienced the beginning of its third and most significant period of economic expansion, which extends into the present era. In part, this prolonged and significant period of economic growth was catalyzed by massive U.S. and Mexican government works projects—highways, dams, power plants, aqueducts, and irrigation projects—partly intended to jumpstart the countries' economies, bringing new manufacturing and agricultural activity to the border region. Additionally, the creation of the National Border Program (PRONAF) in 1961 and the 1965

Border Industrialization Program (BIP) in 1965 created the *maquiladora* sector and contributed to the development of new electronics and high-technology industries in states like Baja California and Chihuahua. Throughout the border region, the combined expansion of U.S. manufacturing and Mexican assembly plants—producing televisions, electric fans, and other consumer goods—enabled the border region to thrive as never before.

This in turn created a foundation for the increasing economic ties between the two countries—by expanding infrastructure, creating channels for foreign direct investment, and developing a highly skilled workforce—in the latter half of the twentieth century, which allowed the border region to benefit significantly from the expansion of U.S. and Mexican trade under NAFTA. By 2005, the U.S.-Mexican border processed roughly three times the amount of cross-border legal flows as the U.S.-Canadian border, with some 643,739 persons and 264,939 vehicles legally crossing the U.S.-Mexican border each day through 25 major corridors and 312 individual ports of entry.[34]

Today, thanks in large part to the booming import-export sector, the border region has experienced massive foreign investment from U.S., Japanese, Korean, and (more recently) Chinese companies. Manufacturing and assembly plants in northern Mexico take advantage of the region's low production costs and close proximity to U.S. consumers. As a result, significant numbers of administrators and businessmen reside in or regularly visit the U.S.-Mexican border region, often opting to work in Mexico while commuting from bedroom communities in the United States.

At the same time, significant gaps and notable social costs are associated with the border region's prodigious development over the last few decades. As prosperous as the region has been, both Mexican and U.S. communities along the border continue to reflect the enormous inequalities discussed in chapter 10, sometimes to a greater degree than other parts of Mexico. In the *maquiladoras*, for example, managers and engineers typically represent 15 percent of the company's workforce, while unskilled and uneducated workers represent the remaining 85 percent and have little hope of advancement.[35] In the U.S. Southwest, similar gaps have grown between high-tech and white-collar jobs and those employing low-skilled manual labor. The high cost of living in some urban areas on both sides of the border contributes to long commutes and the formation of squatter settlements, both of which have spillover consequences for the environment and the quality of life in the border region.

The region's economic development has had detrimental effects on the environment and public health, problems that often go unattended by the businesses responsible for them, and by the U.S. and Mexican governments that lack the resources, jurisdiction, or political inclination to address them (see textbox 13.3).

Textbox 13.3. The Natural Resources and Environment of the Border Region

Rapid urbanization and industrialization have brought significant economic growth to the border region, but also formidable environmental challenges. Although NAFTA legislation charged the Border Environmental Cooperative Commission (BECC), and the North American Development Bank (NAD-Bank) with addressing the environmental implications of NAFTA, these entities have had mixed results in dealing with the monumental environmental challenges of the border region. Because natural resource, ecological, and environmental issues frequently cross political boundaries, they have consistently been a point of bilateral concern in the border region. Yet for the same reason, such issues have not always received sufficient attention from policy makers on either side of the border. Some of the environmental areas that most require binational attention include reducing and treating air pollution, hazardous industrial waste, sewage runoff from squatter settlements, as well as increased demand for water and the disruption of wildlife corridors that span the border region. Although there are numerous governmental agencies and even more nongovernmental organizations attempting to address these issues, the broad scope of the problems makes environmental efforts appear disjointed in a manner that has the potential to impede comprehensive, sustainable environmental change. Recently, joint initiatives between the U.S. Environmental Protection Agency (EPA) and Mexico's Ministry of Environmental and Natural Resources (SEMARNAT) have contributed to encouraging progress. However, if binational environmental issues are not addressed in a comprehensive bilateral fashion, U.S. and Mexican communities along the border will likely continue to suffer the public health and long-term environmental consequences.

Border Law Enforcement and Security Challenges

No discussion of U.S.-Mexican relations would be complete without consideration of the transnational security challenges that are so significantly manifested at the border. Several years after 9/11, plans to develop a more open, freer flowing border remain on hold because the United States is still very concerned about the highly porous nature of its borders. To address this problem, it negotiated a smart border agreement with Mexico in order to improve border security and make it more difficult and time-consuming to enter the United States.

Although bigger budgets, new technologies, and increased manpower have created greater capacity for interdiction at the border, the elevated security has not necessarily curtailed illicit smuggling activities. Smugglers have simply become more creative in their efforts to move contraband into the lucrative U.S. black market. For example, some have modified SUVs with special armor and silicon-reinforced tires, and now brazenly crash these vehicles through port of entry facilities. Others have turned to subtler and more effective innovations, including sophisticated tunnel systems and maritime smuggling operations.

At the same time, the border region continues to confront other persistent law enforcement problems. Communities located near the border are generally more likely than others to experience certain forms of violent and property crime. For example, auto theft represents approximately 20 percent of all major property crime in San Diego. Proximity to the border is paramount here, since autos stolen in the United States are often smuggled to chop shops in Mexico or are used by smugglers to reenter the United States.

More problematic from Mexico's point of view is the trafficking of arms that are readily available in the United States—including high-caliber automatic weapons. Guns are illegal in Mexico, so the United States effectively serves as a gray market for arms traffickers, and—ironically—as a source of weapons for criminal organizations active in narco-trafficking and other cross-border crimes.[36] Law enforcement officials on both sides of the border have lobbied for stricter controls of arms flows from the United States. However, these measures have had little effect.

The smart border agreement framework, which also sets new terms of cooperation between Canada and the United States, may prove useful in moving toward a trilateral NAFTA-plus-security regime. Over the long term, the harmonization of North American security standards could help all three countries move toward a more effective regional policy coordination. What is clear is that, until a larger regional strategy develops, the border will likely remain at the center of U.S. and Mexican bilateral collaboration on security matters.

Conclusion

Over the past twenty-five years Mexico and the United States have become more interdependent. In every major arena—culture, economy, and security—the two countries are inextricably linked. Clearly, then, they cannot ignore each other. Nor can they revert to past practices of finger pointing and passing the buck when confronted with intractable problems like undocumented migration and drug trafficking. Instead, they must cooperate if they are to effectively address their shared challenges. Fortunately, despite the many obstacles to effective collaboration noted in this chapter, there appears to be a general willingness on the part of both U.S. and Mexican policy makers to work together. No doubt this sentiment stems from the mutual recognition that unilateral approaches to bilateral problems can never be fully successful. But most certainly the change in attitudes has also occurred as a result of Mexico's move away from authoritarianism. Electoral competition, power sharing, and increased voter sophistication have altered Mexican policy makers' perspectives and priorities. On the other side, the United States has shown greater willingness to trust and cooperate with Mexico's democratically elected leaders. Thus, improved bilateral relations appear to be yet another benefit of Mexico's embrace of democracy.

Key Terms

border region
Bracero Program
Camarena, Enrique "Kiki"
extradition
GATT
INS
IRCA
maquiladoras
migration
NAFTA-plus

NAFTA side agreements
Operation Gatekeeper
Operation Hold the Line
Operation Wetback
Proposition 187
protectionism
pull and push factors
remittances
smart border agreements
SSP

Recommended Readings

Andreas, Peter. *Border Games.* Ithaca, N.Y.: Cornell University Press, 2001.
Davidow, Jeffrey. *The Bear and the Porcupine: The US and Mexico.* Princeton, N.J.: Markus Wiener, 2004.
Ellingwood, Ken. *Hard Line: Life and Death on the U.S.-Mexico Border.* New York: Pantheon, 2004.
Kopinak, Katherine. *The Social Costs of Industrial and Urban Growth in Northern Mexico.* La Jolla, Calif.: Center for U.S.-Mexican Studies, 2004.
Lorey, David. *The U.S.-Mexican Border in the Twentieth Century.* Wilmington, Del.: Scholarly Resources, 1999.
Pastor, Robert. *Toward a North American Community: Lessons from the Old World for the New.* Washington, D.C.: Institute for International Economics, 2001.

Notes

1. Wayne A. Cornelius, "From Sojourners to Settlers: The Changing Profile of Mexican Migration to the United States," in *U.S.-Mexico Relations: Labor Market Interdependence,* ed. Jorge A. Bustamante, Clark W. Reynolds, and Raúl A. Hinojosa Ojeda (Stanford: Stanford University Press, 1992), 155–95.

2. It is not surprising that the largest waves of unregulated Mexican emigration to the United States occurred during the most tumultuous times in Mexico, the revolution (1910–1920), and the economic crises of the 1930s, 1970s, 1980s, and 1990s.

3. This phenomenon is especially common in the states of Michoacán and Zacatecas.

4. U.S. Census Bureau, *American Community Survey, 2003,* www.census.gov/population/www/socdemo/foreign/datatbls.html.

5. Michael Hefer, Nancy Rytina, and Christopher Campbell, *Estimates of Unauthorized Immigrant Population Residing in the United States: January 2006,* Department of Homeland Security Report, August 2007, www.dhs.gov/ximgtn/statistics/publications/index.shtm.

6. In 1982 the U.S. government used this tactic again in Operation Jobs, a mass deportation of undocumented Mexicans in response to rising unemployment and economic recession in the United States.

7. Kitty Calavita, "U.S. Immigration Policy and Responses: The Limits of Legislation," in *Controlling Immigration: A Global Perspective,* ed. Wayne A. Cornelius, Philip Martin, and James Hollifield (Stanford, CA: Stanford University Press, 1994), 61.

8. Jorge Castañeda, "The Fear of Americanization," in Robert Pastor and Jorge Castañeda, *Limits to Friendship: The United States and Mexico* (New York: Knopf, 1988), 316.

9. Unabashed criticism of the United States on migration issues is somewhat hypocritical, given that Mexico has long employed harsh measures to protect its southern borders with Guatemala and Belize from an influx of Central American immigrants.

10. For example, it created the Grupo Beta police force to rescue would-be migrants in danger and provide information on their human and labor rights. Marc Rosenblum, "Moving Beyond the Policy of No Policy: Emigration from Mexico and Central America," *Latin American Politics and Society* 4, no. 1 (2004).

11. U.S. interest groups also sought to influence the nature of reform. On the pro-immigrant side, public rallies in a number of major cities attracted hundreds of thousands of supporters. On the immigration control side, private citizens mobilized volunteers to monitor different points along the border and inform Border Patrol agents when they observed migrants making illegal border crossings.

12. James Cockcroft, *Mexico: Class Formation, Capital Accumulation, and the State* (New York: Monthly Review Press, 1990), 151.

13. Daniel C. Levy and Kathleen Bruhn. *Mexico: The Struggle for Democratic Development.* Berkeley: University of California Press, 2006.

14. Peter Smith discusses the motivations behind NAFTA in *Talons of the Eagle: Dynamics of U.S.-Latin American Relations* (New York: Oxford University Press, 2000) 260–62. See also Levy and Bruhn, *Mexico,* 247–50.

15. For its part, Canada had many of the same interests when it signed its first free trade agreement with the United States in 1989.

16. Unlike the European Union, NAFTA did not include resources or provisions to soften the blows to the smaller, weaker economies in the union.

17. Levy and Bruhn, *Mexico,* 248.

18. Other factors such as the decline in the value of the peso in the mid-1990s, and sustained growth in the U.S. economy during the same period, also contributed greatly to the flow of goods and services across the border. *The Effects of NAFTA on U.S.-Mexican Trade and GDP,* a study conducted by the U.S. Congressional Budget Office in 2003, www.cbo.gov/ftpdocs/42xx/doc4247/Report.pdf.

19. Gary Gereffi and Martha Martinez, "Mexico's Economic Transformation under NAFTA," in *Mexico's Democracy at Work: Political and Economic Dynamics,* ed. Russell Crandall, Guadalupe Paz, and Riordan Roett (Boulder: Lynne Rienner, 2005), 122. Trilateral trade also increased dramatically. In 1993 Mexico, Canada, and the United States traded $306 billion; by 2000, $621 billion. Jorge Castañeda, "NAFTA at 10: A Plus or a Minus?" *Current History,* February 2004, 51–55.

20. Many of the jobs created by NAFTA disappeared during subsequent economic downturns; roughly two-thirds of the 150,000 jobs lost in 2001 were in the *maquiladora* industry (Levy and Bruhn, *Mexico,* 252–53). Russell Crandall, "Mexico's Domestic Economy: Policy Options and Choices," in *Mexico's Democracy at Work,* ed. Russell Crandall, Guadalupe Paz, and Riordan Roett (Boulder: Lynne Rienner, 2005).

21. Castañeda, "NAFTA at 10," 52.

22. *NAFTA's Promise and Reality: Lessons from Mexico for the Hemisphere* (Carnegie Endowment for International Peace, 2004), 13.

23. Susan Kaufman Purcell, "The Changing Bilateral Relationship," in *Mexico under Fox,* ed. Luis Rubio and Susan Kaufman Purcell (Boulder: Lynne Rienner, 2004), 149.

24. Many have noted that given the domestic political climate of both the United States and Canada at the time, Fox probably would not have been able to achieve measurable success on any of these goals, even if the events of September 11 had not occurred.

25. Andrés Rozental, "Fox's Foreign Policy Agenda," in *Mexico under Fox,* 99–100.

26. J. Z. García, *Security Regimes on the U.S.-Mexican Border. Transnational Crime and Public Security: Challenges to Mexico and the United States,* ed. J. J. Bailey and J. Chabat (La Jolla, Calif.: Center for U.S.-Mexican Studies, 2002).

27. Davidow, *The U.S. and Mexico,* 2004.

28. This procedure may be used for the prosecution of non-Mexicans arrested and tried in Mexico for a crime committed outside of Mexico, if the case involves a Mexican victim.

29. "Frente multinacional contra narco, migración y ´maras´," *El Universal,* May 23, 2007.

30. David E. Lorey, *The U.S.-Mexican Border in the Twentieth Century* (Wilmington: Scholarly Resources, 1999), 6.

31. Martínez outlines these typologies in *Border People: Life and Society in the U.S.-Mexico Borderlands* (Tucson: University of Arizona Press, 1994), 28.

32. This was mainly due to the simultaneous relaxation of U.S. interior enforcement—workplace inspections and apprehensions of unauthorized residents.

33. A study by the National Foreign Intelligence Board reports that illegal migration is "facilitated increasingly by alien-smuggling syndicates and corrupt government officials." National Foreign Intelligence Board, "Growing Global Migration & Its Implications for the U.S.," March 3, 2001, www.cia.gov/nic/graphics/migration.pdf.

34. Bureau of Transportation Statistics (BTS), www.transtats.bts.gov.

35. Katherine Kopinak, ed., *The Social Costs of Industrial and Urban Growth in Northern Mexico* (La Jolla: Center for U.S.-Mexico Studies, 2004).

36. L. Lumpe, "The US Arms Both Sides of Mexico's Drug War," *Covert Action Quarterly* 61 (1997): 39–46.

Conclusion

Today, Mexico's political system has moved dramatically away from the entrenched authoritarian institutions and practices of the past. As the preceding chapters have shown, in the turbulent years from colonial times to the Porfiriato, Mexico struggled to realize the promise of liberal democratic governance. After the 1910 revolution gave rise to a prolonged period of single-party rule, a confluence of factors such as recurrent economic crises, institutional reform, civic awareness and activism, and the growth of the opposition eventually brought about the PRI's demise and the birth of a more plural and competitive political arena. Mexico now boasts many of democracy's essential elements, including impartial electoral institutions and competitive elections, a free press, and independent interest representation.

But Mexico's transition is not complete. The country still faces a number of important challenges if it is to consolidate its democracy. The question is whether the country will continue to move forward down this road. Felipe Calderón's razor-thin margin of victory in the 2006 presidential election, together with irregularities in the vote count and Andrés Manuel López Obrador's allegations of fraud, created concern that Mexico had taken a step back. Even after the Federal Electoral Institute's official ruling on the absence of fraud and validity of the result, many continued to believe that the election had been stolen from López Obrador, casting doubt on the impartiality of the electoral process. AMLO himself refused to stand down, instead establishing a parallel "legitimate" government, complete with cabinet and policy initiatives. Given his proven ability to mobilize thousands of supporters at a moment's notice, many expected him to use these methods to immobilize and sabotage the Calderón administration's efforts to move forward.

Now a few years into Calderón's *sexenio,* it appears that these expectations were unfounded. Although AMLO's government continues to regularly meet and issue statements criticizing the Calderón administration and offering alternative policy proposals, it has not substantially hindered the president's policy agenda. Indeed, Calderón's government successfully negotiated significant reforms to the pension system, the tax system, and the justice system, areas that are generally fraught with partisan disputes. What many feared would be the most immediate challenge to Mexico's new democracy—political gridlock and strife—has so far failed to materialize. Yet, since he took office, Calderón has also had to confront a number of challenges stemming from underlying political and socioeconomic problems that still threaten to undermine Mexico's democracy.

One issue that captured international headlines as the Fox administration prepared to transfer power to Calderón in late 2006 was the way that state and federal police handled protesters in the southern state of Oaxaca. The debacle began in the spring of 2006, when a teachers' strike in the state capital quickly grew into a large amalgamation of disenchanted groups intent on demonstrating their anger over the dire living conditions, and the dearth of education and employment opportunities present in the state of Oaxaca. Together these groups formed the Popular Assembly of Oaxacan People (APPO) and carried out blockades of important toll roads, sit-ins and vandalism of government offices, the takeover of local radio and TV stations, and violent clashes with the police. In response, Governor Ulíses Ruíz Ortiz ordered state police to forcibly remove the demonstrators from the central square. In this and subsequent violent clashes, hundreds of protesters were injured and arrested as the police used excessive force to subdue them. In October, another confrontation resulted in three deaths and prompted President Fox to send in the federal police. Even after the federal police arrived, the protests and violence continued, culminating in the bombing of two financial buildings in Mexico City in early November. Promising to use a firm hand against lawbreakers, incoming President Calderón immediately secured the arrest of the APPO's leader and the mass detention of its supporters. Although these moves initially took the wind out of the APPO's sails, the next summer the group was once again organizing demonstrations in Oaxaca.

Perhaps the highest-profile challenge Mexico faces today is the illicit drug trade. One of Calderón's first moves on taking office was to send military troops to several states to disrupt the drug trade and apprehend narco-traffickers. And while these efforts resulted in the capture of several high-profile cartel leaders, they have also led to human rights abuses and an escalation in violence that has claimed thousands of lives. While over 1,500 drug-related killings were reported in 2005, the number grew to over 2,200 in 2006, and over 2,300 in 2007. By fall 2008, the number reached nearly 3,000 drug killings, well above the previous year's. It is particularly disturbing that these figures include hundreds of Mexican public officials, including federal and local police, prosecutors, military personnel, and even elected officials. In 2006 and 2007, the largest number of drug-related killings were concentrated in three states: Michoacán, Guerrero, and Sinaloa. In mid-2007 there was a significant drop in drug violence, especially in the state of Michoacán. However, by late-2007 and into 2008, levels of violence spiked again, this time concentrated in the northern border states of Baja California and, especially, Chihuahua.

These grim developments have contributed to the overall sense of public insecurity in Mexico, and have been accompanied by a rash of kidnappings, organized crime, and other acts of random violence. For example, in July 2007, the Popular Revolutionary Army, a leftist guerrilla group, bombed four oil and gas pipelines in central Mexico, demanding the release of two of its members alleged to be illegally detained and "disappeared" by police in Oaxaca in 2006. Later, in August 2008, the abduction and brutal murder of Fernando Martí, the 14-year-old son of prominent Mexico City businessman Alejandro Martí, triggered a nationwide series of demonstrations involving hundreds of thousands of people. The Mexican public was particularly outraged upon discovery of the involvement of law enforcement—including federal police officers—in the kidnapping ring. The Martí family had paid an estimated sum of $2 million to the kidnappers to secure his return, but the boy was brutally murdered and his body discovered weeks later in the trunk of a car. While Martí's case received special attention due to his family's prominence, many ordinary people have been targeted for "express" kidnappings of short duration (usually as a means to gain access to their ATM accounts). As a result, the rate of kidnappings in Mexico has grown at an alarming rate in recent years, with an estimated three to four kidnappings daily, reportedly making Mexico's the worst rate in Latin America.

In the wake of the Martí murder, security measures were initiated by President Calderón and Mexico City mayor Marcelo Ebrard, including tougher sentences and special police units to prevent and investigate cases of kidnapping. Also, representatives from all three federal branches of government and state authorities met in a televised session to discuss a new 74-point security plan to be implemented over the next 100 days. While significant numbers of Mexicans supported these efforts, critics expressed skepticism since harsher sentences are not a significant deterrent without an effective criminal justice system. Meanwhile, Alejandro Martí, the father of the murdered kidnapping victim, urged authorities to do whatever they can to reduce crime: "If you can't, resign."[1]

Yet, Mexico's recent violence relates precisely to the fact that the Mexican government has adopted a more aggressive strategy toward organized crime in recent years. The arrest and extradition of high-profile cartel leaders and the deployment of federal troops to troubled states have destabilized major cartels. This led to a struggle for control between and among the cartels, with even higher levels of violence. Thus many are skeptical that use of the military and the increased violence will produce any long-term results. Targeting the leadership of the cartels has not necessarily made the fight against organized crime more manageable; indeed, it has possibly contributed to the proliferation of smaller, less organized crime groups and street-level drug crimes (narcomenudeo) that have more direct effects on Mexican society. Meanwhile, there is also a fear that the use of the military in domestic law enforcement—including the deployment of roughly 25,000 troops around the country in the first two years of the Calderón administration—has given the administration license to use a heavy hand in putting down other groups in society and look the other way if further human rights abuses occur.

As Mexico struggles to deal with these challenges, many Mexicans harbor feelings of resentment toward the United States over the war on drugs. The United States is the world's largest consumer of drugs, and is also the main source of weapons transported to Mexico (where most firearms are illegal). The fact that U.S. officials tend to be highly critical of Mexico's failure to control drug trafficking smacks of hypocrisy for many Mexicans. Many Mexicans also raise questions about the possible influence of drug cartel networks on U.S. public officials, pointing out that drug corruption and distribution cannot realistically stop at the U.S.-Mexico border. To address such concerns, President Bush and President Calderón negotiated an agreement at a 2007 bilateral meeting in Mérida, Yucatán, where the United States pledged over one billion dollars in financial assistance to support Mexico's counternarcotics efforts. This initiative—known in the United States as the Merida Initiative and in Mexico as Plan Mérida—would help pay for helicopters, equipment, surveillance, and training. Initially, the bilateral plan provoked a negative political response in both Mexico and the United States. U.S. legislators were reluctant to offer unrestricted assistance to Mexico, due to perceptions of widespread corruption and possible human rights abuses; Mexican legislators were reluctant to accept U.S. aid if it would be tied to conditions that might humiliate Mexico or reduce its sovereignty. Meanwhile, activist and human rights groups in both countries worried that ramping up the war on drugs in Mexico could lead to a downward spiral of violence similar to that experienced in Colombia, which had received billions of dollars of U.S. aid in recent years. Nevertheless, with minor modifications the Mérida Initiative was approved for implementation in the coming years.

Meanwhile, other tensions between the United States and Mexico remain to be resolved. In recent years, the U.S. government has continued to crack down on unauthorized immigration by beefing up border security and worksite enforcement. In August 2007, the Department of Homeland Security (DHS) announced that by the end of 2009 it would increase the security of the U.S.-Mexican border by nearly doubling the number of border agents, adding detention space to hold undocumented migrants, improving measures to identify and punish legal visitors who overstay their visas, and requiring passports of all travelers seeking to enter the United States. To complement the security effort, DHS also began working to make it more difficult for undocumented migrants to find jobs by punishing employers who hire them. To this end, DHS began to increase fines by 25 percent for employers who knowingly hire individuals with fraudulent documents. DHS also now requires employers to act on information from the Social Security Administration indicating that an employee's name does not match a legal social security number, and requires that government contractors use an electronic employment verification system. Other important elements of the strategy include streamlining existing guest worker programs and expanding assistance to state and local law enforcement to help them identify, apprehend, and deport migrants who enter the country illegally. In May 2008, in the largest raid to date for a U.S. worksite, 400 people were arrested at an Iowa meatpacking plant as the government stepped up its efforts to crack down on undocumented workers and employers.

All of these issues reveal a broad set of problems that Mexico—and the United States, to some degree—will need to address in the coming years. Failure to do so will limit Mexico's ability to maintain order and economic stability in the short term, and to consolidate democracy in the long term. As noted above, Mexico is in desperate need of greater overall public security and rule of law. As the Mexican government wrestles with severe public security challenges, several recent developments are worrisome. Militarization of the war on drugs and heavy-handed security tactics contribute to unlawful detention, excessive use of force, and other abuses that ultimately undermine the democratic rule of law in Mexico.

At the same time, the severity of poverty and economic inequality must be addressed, particularly in southern states where earning less than the minimum wage is the norm rather than the exception. Under such dire circumstances, violent protest, rather than peaceful negotiation or voting in elections, is too often seen as the only effective method of making one's demands heard. Moreover, in states where wages are inadequate, but people have sufficient means to seek out alternatives, the natural response has been to migrate to where there are jobs. Thus, if the United States wants to seriously address the issue of immigration, it would do well to assist in efforts to promote economic development in Mexico. Underdevelopment may well continue to be Mexico's most formidable challenge, and one that, if prolonged, will not bode well for democracy.

Note

1. "Unidades Antisecuestro de SSP inician operaciones," *Vanguardia*, August 11, 2008; "México, primer lugar en secuestros a nivel mundial: ONG," *El Universal*, August 14, 2008; "Con 200 agentes de PGJDF y 100 de la SSP crean Fuerza Antisecuestros," *La Crónica de Hoy*, August 20, 2008; "Pactan; les dan 100 días," *Reforma*, August 22, 2008.

Index

About the Authors

Emily Edmonds-Poli is associate professor of political science at the University of San Diego. She received her Ph.D. in political science at the University of California–San Diego in 2001. She was awarded a Fulbright-Garcia Robles fellowship in 1998–1999 and a Ford Foundation Fellowship in 1999–2000. During the 2000–2001 academic year she was a fellow at UCSD's Center for U.S.-Mexican Studies. Dr. Edmonds's research focuses on Mexican politics and decentralization and local democratic governance in Mexico. Her most recent article, "Decentralization under the Fox Administration: Progress or Stagnation?" was published in *Mexican Studies/Estudios Mexicanos*.

David A. Shirk is director of the Trans-Border Institute and assistant professor in the Political Science Department at the University of San Diego. He received his Ph.D. in political science at the University of California–San Diego and was fellow at the Center for U.S.-Mexican Studies in 1998–1999 and 2001–2003. He conducts research on Mexican politics, U.S.-Mexican relations, and law enforcement and security along the U.S.-Mexican border. Dr. Shirk is currently the principal investigator for Justice in Mexico (www.justiceinmexico.org), a binational research initiative on criminal justice and the rule of law in Mexico. Recent publications by Dr. Shirk include *Reforming the Administration of Justice in Mexico* (2007), coedited with Wayne Cornelius; *Evaluating Transparency and Accountability in Mexico: Local, National, and Comparative Perspectives* (2007) coedited with Alejandra Rios Cásares; "Law Enforcement Challenges and 'Smart Borders,'" in *Homeland Security: Protecting America's Targets* (2006); *Mexico's New Politics: The PAN and Democratic Change* (2005).